Happy Birthday
Craig

Happy reading
Andy.

Also by
BOB WOODWARD

The Last of the President's Men

The Price of Politics

Obama's Wars

The War Within:
A Secret White House History, 2006–2008

State of Denial

The Secret Man
(*with a Reporter's Assessment by Carl Bernstein*)

Plan of Attack

Bush at War

Maestro:
Greenspan's Fed and the American Boom

Shadow:
Five Presidents and the Legacy of Watergate

The Choice

The Agenda:
Inside the Clinton White House

The Commanders

Veil:
The Secret Wars of the CIA, 1981–1987

Wired:
The Short Life and Fast Times of John Belushi

The Brethren
(*with Scott Armstrong*)

The Final Days
(*with Carl Bernstein*)

All the President's Men
(*with Carl Bernstein*)

FEAR

Trump in the White House

Bob
Woodward

Simon & Schuster

New York   London   Toronto   Sydney   New Delhi

Simon & Schuster
1230 Avenue of the Americas
New York, NY 10020

First Simon & Schuster hardcover edition September 2018

SIMON & SCHUSTER and colophon are registered
trademarks of Simon & Schuster, Inc.

For information about special discounts for bulk purchases,
please contact Simon & Schuster Special Sales at 1-866-506-1949
or business@simonandschuster.com.

The Simon & Schuster Speakers Bureau can bring authors to
your live event. For more information or to book an event, contact
the Simon & Schuster Speakers Bureau at 1-866-248-3049 or
visit our website at www.simonspeakers.com.

Interior design by Lewelin Polanco

Manufactured in the United States of America

5   7   9   10   8   6

Library of Congress Cataloging-in-Publication Data is available.

ISBN 978-1-5011-7551-0
ISBN 978-1-5011-7553-4 (ebook)

To Elsa

Contents

AUTHOR'S PERSONAL NOTE   xi

NOTE TO READERS   xv

    ◆ *Prologue*   xvii

    ◆ *Chapters 1–42*   1

ACKNOWLEDGMENTS   359

SOURCE NOTES   363

PHOTOGRAPHY CREDITS   391

INDEX   393

Author's Personal Note

A heartfelt thanks to Evelyn M. Duffy, my assistant on five books that have covered four presidents. President Trump presents a particular hurdle because of the deep emotions and passions he brings out in supporters and critics. Evelyn immediately grasped that the challenge was to get new information, authenticate it and put it in context while reporting as deeply as possible inside the White House.

Evelyn knew this was history and we had to get as much as possible quickly while memories were fresh and documentation and notes still available. At times we researched, interviewed, transcribed and rewrote sections of the book in a day or two covering foreign policy from North Korea to Afghanistan and the Middle East; and on the full range of domestic issues from trade, immigration and taxes.

She made sure we built the story around specific scenes with specific dates, named participants and accounts of what happened. Evelyn maintains a remarkable work ethic and the deepest sense of fairness, curiosity and honesty. She provided me with thick packets of research, background, chronologies, clips, her insights, a list of major unanswered questions and additional interviews to pursue.

Evelyn brought her endless good sense and wisdom, serving as full collaborator and in the spirit—and with the level of effort—of a coauthor.

"Real power is—I don't even want to use the word—fear."

Presidential candidate Donald J. Trump in an interview with Bob Woodward and Robert Costa on March 31, 2016, at the Old Post Office Pavilion, Trump International Hotel, Washington, D.C.

Note to Readers

Interviews for this book were conducted under the journalist ground rule of "deep background." This means that all the information could be used but I would not say who provided it. The book is drawn from hundreds of hours of interviews with firsthand participants and witnesses to these events. Nearly all allowed me to tape-record our interviews so the story could be told with more precision. When I have attributed exact quotations, thoughts or conclusions to the participants, that information comes from the person, a colleague with direct knowledge, or from meeting notes, personal diaries, files and government or personal documents.

President Trump declined to be interviewed for this book.

In early September 2017, in the eighth month of the Trump presidency, Gary Cohn, the former president of Goldman Sachs
and the president's top economic adviser in the White House,
moved cautiously toward the Resolute Desk in the Oval Office.

In his 27 years at Goldman, Cohn—6-foot-3, bald, brash and full
of self-confidence—had made billions for his clients and hundreds
of millions for himself. He had granted himself walk-in privileges to
Trump's Oval Office, and the president had accepted that arrangement.

On the desk was a one-page draft letter from the president addressed to the president of South Korea, terminating the United
States–Korea Free Trade Agreement, known as KORUS.

Cohn was appalled. For months Trump had threatened to withdraw from the agreement, one of the foundations of an economic
relationship, a military alliance and, most important, top secret intelligence operations and capabilities.

Under a treaty dating back to the 1950s, the United States sta-
tioned 28,500 U.S. troops in the South and operated the most highly

classified and sensitive Special Access Programs (SAP), which provided sophisticated Top Secret, codeword intelligence and military capabilities. North Korean ICBM missiles now had the capability to carry a nuclear weapon, perhaps to the American homeland. A missile from North Korea would take 38 minutes to reach Los Angeles.

These programs enabled the United States to detect an ICBM launch in North Korea within seven seconds. The equivalent capability in Alaska took 15 minutes—an astonishing time differential.

The ability to detect a launch in seven seconds would give the United States military the time to shoot down a North Korean missile. It is perhaps the most important and most secret operation in the United States government. The American presence in South Korea represents the essence of national security.

Withdrawal from the KORUS trade agreement, which South Korea deemed essential to its economy, could lead to an unraveling of the entire relationship. Cohn could not believe that President Trump would risk losing vital intelligence assets crucial to U.S. national security.

This all stemmed from Trump's fury that the United States had an $18 billion annual trade deficit with South Korea and was spending $3.5 billion a year to keep U.S. troops there.

Despite almost daily reports of chaos and discord in the White House, the public did not know how bad the internal situation actually was. Trump was always shifting, rarely fixed, erratic. He would get in a bad mood, something large or small would infuriate him, and he would say about the KORUS trade agreement, "We're withdrawing today."

But now there was the letter, dated September 5, 2017, a potential trigger to a national security catastrophe. Cohn was worried Trump would sign the letter if he saw it.

Cohn removed the letter draft from the Resolute Desk. He placed it in a blue folder marked "KEEP."

"I stole it off his desk," he later told an associate. "I wouldn't let him see it. He's never going to see that document. Got to protect the country."

In the anarchy and disorder of the White House, and Trump's mind, the president never noticed the missing letter.

Ordinarily Rob Porter, the staff secretary and organizer of presidential paperwork, would have been responsible for producing letters like this to the South Korean president. But this time, alarmingly, the letter draft had come to Trump through an unknown channel. Staff secretary is one of the low-profile but critical roles in any White House. For months, Porter had been briefing Trump on decision memos and other presidential documents, including the most sensitive national security authorizations for military and covert CIA activities.

Porter, 6-foot-4, rail-thin, 40 years old and raised a Mormon, was one of the gray men: an organization man with little flash who had attended Harvard and Harvard Law School and been a Rhodes Scholar.

Porter later discovered there were multiple copies of the draft letter, and either Cohn or he made sure none remained on the president's desk.

Cohn and Porter worked together to derail what they believed were Trump's most impulsive and dangerous orders. That document and others like it just disappeared. When Trump had a draft on his desk to proofread, Cohn at times would just yank it, and the president would forget about it. But if it was on his desk, he'd sign it. "It's not what we did for the country," Cohn said privately. "It's what we saved him from doing."

It was no less than an administrative coup d'état, an undermining of the will of the president of the United States and his constitutional authority.

In addition to coordinating policy decisions and schedules and running the paperwork for the president, Porter told an associate, "A third of my job was trying to react to some of the really dangerous ideas that he had and try to give him reasons to believe that maybe they weren't such good ideas."

Another strategy was to delay, procrastinate, cite legal restrictions. Lawyer Porter said, "But slow-walking things or not taking things up to him, or telling him—rightly, not just as an excuse—but this needs to be vetted, or we need to do more process on this, or we don't have legal counsel clearance—that happened 10 times more frequently than taking papers from his desk. It felt like we were walking along the edge of the cliff perpetually."

There were days or weeks when the operation seemed under control and they were a couple of steps back from the edge. "Other times, we would fall over the edge, and an action would be taken. It was like you were always walking right there on the edge."

Although Trump never mentioned the missing September 5 letter, he did not forget what he wanted to do about the trade agreement. "There were several different iterations of that letter," Porter told an associate.

Later in an Oval Office meeting, the South Korean agreement was being heatedly debated. "I don't care," Trump said. "I'm tired of these arguments! I don't want to hear about it anymore. We're getting out of KORUS." He started to dictate a new letter he wanted to send.

Jared Kushner, the president's son-in-law, took Trump's words seriously. Jared, 36, was a senior White House adviser and had a self-possessed, almost aristocratic bearing. He had been married to Trump's daughter Ivanka since 2009.

Because he was sitting closest to the president, Jared started writing down what Trump was saying, taking dictation.

Finish the letter and get it to me so I can sign it, Trump ordered him.

Jared was in the process of turning the president's dictation into a new letter when Porter heard about it.

"Send me the draft," he told him. "If we're going to do this, we cannot do it on the back of a napkin. We have to write it up in a way that isn't going to embarrass us."

Kushner sent down a paper copy of his draft. It was not of much use. Porter and Cohn had something typed up to demonstrate they were doing what the president had asked. Trump was expecting an immediate response. They wouldn't walk in empty-handed. The draft was part of the subterfuge.

At a formal meeting, the opponents of leaving KORUS raised all kinds of arguments—the United States had never withdrawn from a free trade agreement before; there were legal issues, geopolitical issues, vital national security and intelligence issues; the letter wasn't ready. They smothered the president with facts and logic.

"Well, let's keep working on the letter," Trump said. "I want to see the next draft."

Cohn and Porter did not prepare a next draft. So there was nothing to show the president. The issue, for the moment, disappeared in the haze of presidential decision making. Trump got busy with other things.

But the KORUS issue would not go away. Cohn spoke to Secretary of Defense James Mattis, the retired Marine general who was perhaps the most influential voice among Trump's cabinet and staff. General Mattis, a combat veteran, had served 40 years in the Corps. At 5-foot-9 with ramrod-straight posture, he had a permanently world-weary demeanor.

"We're teetering on the edge," Cohn told the secretary. "We may need some backup this time."

Mattis tried to limit his visits to the White House and stick to military business as much as possible, but realizing the urgency he came to the Oval Office.

"Mr. President," he said, "Kim Jong Un poses the most immediate threat to our national security. We need South Korea as an ally. It may not seem like trade is related to all this, but it's central."

American military and intelligence assets in South Korea are the backbone of our ability to defend ourselves from North Korea. Please don't leave the deal.

Why is the U.S. paying $1 billion a year for an anti-ballistic missile system in South Korea? Trump asked. He was furious about the Terminal High Altitude Area Defense (THAAD) missile defense system, and had threatened to pull it out of South Korea and move it to Portland, Oregon.

"We're not doing this for South Korea," Mattis said. "We're helping South Korea because it helps us."

The president seemed to acquiesce, but only for the moment.

In 2016, candidate Trump gave Bob Costa and myself his definition of the job of president: "More than anything else, it's the security of our nation. . . . That's number one, two and three. . . . The military, being strong, not letting bad things happen to our country from the outside. And I certainly think that's always going to be my number-one part of that definition."

The reality was that the United States in 2017 was tethered to the words and actions of an emotionally overwrought, mercurial and unpredictable leader. Members of his staff had joined to purposefully block some of what they believed were the president's most dangerous impulses. It was a nervous breakdown of the executive power of the most powerful country in the world.

What follows is that story.

September 5, 2017

His Excellency Moon Jae-in
President of the Republic of Korea
The Blue House
Seoul
Republic of Korea

His Excellency Kim Hyun-chong
Minister for Trade
Ministry of Trade, Industry and Energy
402 Hannuri-daero
Sejong-si 30118
Republic of Korea

Dear Sirs:

The United States-Korea Free Trade Agreement (Agreement), in its current form, is not in the overall best interests of the United States economy. Thus, in accordance with Article 24.5 of the Agreement, the United States hereby provides notice that it wishes to terminate the Agreement. As prescribed by the terms of Article 24.5, the Agreement shall terminate 180 days after the date of this notice. During this period, the United States is prepared to negotiate with the Republic of Korea on economic issues of concern to both countries.

Respectfully,

Donald J. Trump
President of the United States

Robert E. Lighthizer
United States Trade Representative

KEEP

The September 5, 2017, draft letter to the South Korean president withdrawing from the trade agreement. Gary Cohn took it from President Trump's Oval Office desk so it wouldn't be signed and sent.

FEAR

I n August 2010, six years before taking over Donald Trump's winning presidential campaign, Steve Bannon, then 57 and a producer of right-wing political films, answered his phone.

"What are you doing tomorrow?" asked David Bossie, a longtime House Republican investigator and conservative activist who had chased Bill and Hillary Clinton scandals for almost two decades.

"Dude," Bannon replied, "I'm cutting these fucking films I'm making for you."

The 2010 midterm congressional elections were coming up. It was the height of the Tea Party movement and Republicans were showing momentum.

"Dave, we're literally dropping two more films. I'm editing. I'm working 20 hours a day" at Citizens United, the conservative political action committee Bossie headed, to churn out his anti-Clinton films.

"Can you come with me up to New York?"

"For what?"

"To see Donald Trump," Bossie said.

"What about?"

"He's thinking of running for president," Bossie said.

"Of what country?" Bannon asked.

No, seriously, Bossie insisted. He had been meeting and working with Trump for months. Trump had asked for a meeting.

"I don't have time to jerk off, dude," Bannon said. "Donald Trump's never running for president. Forget it. Against Obama? Forget it. I don't have time for fucking nonsense."

"Don't you want to meet him?"

"No, I have no interest in meeting him." Trump had once given Bannon a 30-minute interview for his Sunday-afternoon radio show, called *The Victory Sessions*, which Bannon had run out of Los Angeles and billed as "the thinking man's radio show."

"This guy's not serious," Bannon said.

"I think he is serious," Bossie said. Trump was a TV celebrity and had a famous show, *The Apprentice*, that was number one on NBC some weeks. "There's no downside for us to go and meet with him."

Bannon finally agreed to go to New York City to Trump Tower.

They rode up to the 26th floor conference room. Trump greeted them warmly, and Bossie said he had a detailed presentation. It was a tutorial.

The first part, he said, lays out how to run in a Republican primary and win. The second part explains how to run for president of the United States against Barack Obama. He described standard polling strategies and discussed process and issues. Bossie was a traditional, limited-government conservative and had been caught by surprise by the Tea Party movement.

It was an important moment in American politics, Bossie said, and Tea Party populism was sweeping the country. The little guy was getting his voice. Populism was a grassroots movement to disrupt the political status quo in favor of everyday people.

"I'm a business guy," Trump reminded them. "I'm not a professional ladder-climber in politics."

"If you're going to run for president," Bossie said, "you have to know lots of little things and lots of big things." The little things were filing deadlines, the state rules for primaries—minutiae. "You have to know the policy side, and how to win delegates." But first, he said, "you need to understand the conservative movement."

Trump nodded.

"You've got some problems on issues," Bossie said.

"I don't have any problems on issues," Trump said. "What are you talking about?"

"First off, there's never been a guy win a Republican primary that's not pro-life," Bossie said. "And unfortunately, you're very pro-choice."

"What does that mean?"

"You have a record of giving to the abortion guys, the pro-choice candidates. You've made statements. You've got to be pro-life, against abortion."

"I'm against abortion," Trump said. "I'm pro-life."

"Well, you've got a track record."

"That can be fixed," Trump said. "You just tell me how to fix that. I'm—what do you call it? Pro-life. I'm pro-life, I'm telling you."

Bannon was impressed with the showmanship, and increasingly so as Trump talked. Trump was engaged and quick. He was in great physical shape. His presence was bigger than the man, and took over the room, a command presence. He had something. He was also like a guy in a bar talking to the TV. Street-smart, from Queens. In Bannon's evaluation, Trump was Archie Bunker, but a really focused Archie Bunker.

"The second big thing," Bossie said, "is your voting record."

"What do you mean, my voting record?"

"About how often you vote."

"What are you talking about?"

"Well," Bossie said, "this is a Republican primary."

"I vote every time," Trump said confidently. "I've voted every time since I was 18, 20 years old."

"That's actually not correct. You know there's a public record of your vote." Bossie, the congressional investigator, had a stack of records.

"They don't know how I vote."

"No, no, no, not how you vote. How often you vote."

Bannon realized that Trump did not know the most rudimentary business of politics.

"I voted every time," Trump insisted.

"Actually you've never voted in a primary except once in your entire life," Bossie said, citing the record.

"That's a fucking lie," Trump said. "That's a total lie. Every time I get to vote, I voted."

"You only voted in one primary," Bossie said. "It was like in 1988 or something, in the Republican primary."

"You're right," Trump said, pivoting 180 degrees, not missing a beat. "That was for Rudy." Giuliani ran for mayor in a primary in 1989. "Is that in there?"

"Yes."

"I'll get over that," Trump said.

"Maybe none of these things matter," Bossie said, "but maybe they do. If you're going to move forward, you have to be methodical."

Bannon was up next. He turned to what was driving the Tea Party, which didn't like the elites. Populism was for the common man, knowing the system is rigged. It was against crony capitalism and insider deals which were bleeding the workers.

"I love that. That's what I am," Trump said, "a popularist." He mangled the word.

"No, no," Bannon said. "It's populist."

"Yeah, yeah," Trump insisted. "A popularist."

Bannon gave up. At first he thought Trump did not understand the word. But perhaps Trump meant it in his own way—being popular with the people. Bannon knew popularist was an earlier British form of the word "populist" for the nonintellectual general public.

An hour into the meeting, Bossie said, "We have another big issue."

"What's that?" Trump asked, seeming a little more wary.

"Well," he said, "80 percent of the donations that you've given have been to Democrats." To Bossie that was Trump's biggest political liability, though he didn't say so.

"That's bullshit!"

"There's public records," Bossie said.

"There's records of that!" Trump said in utter astonishment.

"Every donation you've ever given." Public disclosure of all political giving was standard.

"I'm always even," Trump said. He divided his donations to candidates from both parties, he said.

"You actually give quite a bit. But it's 80 percent Democratic. Chicago, Atlantic City . . ."

"I've got to do that," Trump said. "All these fucking Democrats run all the cities. You've got to build hotels. You've got to grease them. Those are people who came to me."

"Listen," Bannon said, "here's what Dave's trying to say. Running as a Tea Party guy, the problem is that's what they are complaining about. That it's guys like you that have inside deals."

"I'll get over that," Trump said. "It's all rigged. It's a rigged system. These guys have been shaking me down for years. I don't want to give. They all walk in. If you don't write a check . . ."

There was a pol in Queens, Trump said, "an old guy with a baseball bat. You go in there and you've got to give him something—normally in cash. If you don't give him anything, nothing gets done. Nothing gets built. But if you take it in there and you leave him an envelope, it happens. That's just the way it is. But I can fix that."

Bossie said he had a roadmap. "It's the conservative movement. Tea Party comes and goes. Populism comes and goes. The conservative movement has been a bedrock since Goldwater."

Second, he said, I would recommend you run as if you are running for governor in three states—Iowa, New Hampshire and South Carolina. They were the first three caucus or primary states. "Run and sound local, like you want to be their governor." A lot of candidates made the huge mistake of trying to run in 27 states. "Run three governor's races, and you'll have a really good shot. Focus on three. Do well in three. And the others will come."

"I can be the nominee," Trump said. "I can beat these guys. I don't care who they are. I got this. I can take care of these other things."

Each position could be revisited, renegotiated.

"I'm pro-life," Trump said. "I'm going to start."

"Here's what you're going to need to do," Bossie said. "You're going to need to write between $250,000 and $500,000 worth of individual checks to congressmen and senators. They'll all come up here. Look them in the eye, shake their hand. You're going to give them a check. Because we need some markers. You've got to do one-on-ones so these guys know. Because later on, that'll be at least an entry point that you're building relationships."

Bossie continued, "Saying, this check is for you. For $2,400"— the maximum amount. "It's got to be individual checks, hard money, to their campaign so they know it's coming from you personally. Republicans now know that you're going to be serious about this."

All the money, Bossie said, was central to the art of presidential politics. "Later that's going to pay huge dividends." Give to Republican candidates in a handful of battleground states like Ohio, Pennsylvania, Virginia and Florida.

In addition, Bossie said, "You're going to have to do a policy book. You ought to do a book about what you think about America and these policies."

Bannon gave an extended brief on China and its successful efforts to take jobs and money from the United States. He was obsessed with the threat.

"What do you think?" Bossie later asked Bannon.

"I'm pretty impressed with the guy," Bannon said. As for running for president, "Zero chance. First off, those two action items. The fucker will not write one check. He's not a guy who writes checks. He signs the back of checks" when they come in as payments to him. "It was good you said that because he'll never write a check."

"What about the policy book?"

"He'll never do a policy book. Give me a fucking break. First off, nobody will buy it. It was a waste of time except for the fact that it was insanely entertaining."

Bossie said he was trying to prepare Trump if he ever did decide to run. Trump had a unique asset: He was totally removed from the political process.

As they walked on, Bossie found himself going through a mental exercise, one that six years later most Americans would go through. He'll never run. He'll never file. He'll never announce. He'll never file his financial disclosure statement. Right? He'll never do any of those things. He'll never win.

"You think he's going to run?" Bossie finally asked Bannon.

"Not a chance. Zero chance," Bannon repeated. "Less than zero. Look at the fucking life he's got, dude. Come on. He's not going to do this. Get his face ripped off."

———— ◆ ❖ ◆ ————

Six Years Later

I t is almost certain that if events had not unfolded in the following unlikely, haphazard, careless way, the world would be
vastly different today. Donald Trump accepted the Republican
nomination on July 21, 2016, and his quest for the presidency took
a significant turn early the morning of Saturday, August 13, 2016.

Steve Bannon, now the chief of the right-wing Breitbart News operation, sat on a bench in Bryant Park in New York City and huddled
with his newspapers, his Saturday ritual. He first thumbed through
the *Financial Times* and then moved to *The New York Times*.

"The Failing Inside Mission to Tame Trump's Tongue," read the
headline on the *Times* front page. The presidential election was three
months away.

"Oh, my God," Bannon thought.

The first act of the Bannon drama is his appearance—the old
military field jacket over multiple tennis polo shirts. The second act
is his demeanor—aggressive, certain and loud.

The reporters of the *Times* story said they had 20 Republican
unnamed sources close to Trump or in communication with his campaign. The article painted Trump as bewildered, exhausted, sullen,

gaffe-prone and in trouble with donors. He was in precarious condition in Florida, Ohio, Pennsylvania and North Carolina, battleground states that would decide the election. It was an ugly portrait, and Bannon knew it was all true. He calculated that Trump could lose to Democratic nominee Hillary Clinton by perhaps as many as 20 points, certainly double digits.

Trump was a media spectacle for sure, but he still had no operation beyond what the Republican National Committee had supplied. Bannon knew the Trump campaign was a few people in a room—a speechwriter, and an advance team of about six people that scheduled rallies in the cheapest venues, often old, washed-out sports or hockey arenas around the country.

Despite that, Trump had won the Republican nomination over 16 others and was a big, profane, subversive presence, out front seizing the nation's attention.

Bannon, now 63 years old and a Harvard Business School graduate with fervently nationalistic, America-first views, called Rebekah Mercer.

Mercer and her family were one of the biggest and most controversial sources of campaign money in the Republican Party and money was the engine of American politics, especially in the Republican Party. The Mercers were a bit on the fringe but their money bought them a place at the table. They also had an ownership stake in Breitbart.

"This is bad because we're going to get blamed for this," Bannon told Mercer. Breitbart had stood by Trump in his darker hours. "This is going to be the end of Breitbart."

"Why don't you step in?" Rebekah said.

"I've never run a campaign in my life," Bannon replied. Not even close. The idea was preposterous.

"This guy Manafort's a disaster," she said, referring to the Trump campaign manager, Paul Manafort. "Nobody's running the campaign now. Trump listens to you. He's always looking for adult supervision."

"Look," Bannon said, "I'll do it in a second. But why would he do that?"

"He's been an outsider the entire time," she said, and mentioned the *New York Times* article. "This thing's in panic mode." In short, Trump might hire Bannon because he was desperate.

The Mercers contacted Trump, who was going to be at the East Hampton, Long Island, home of Woody Johnson, the New York Jets owner, for a fundraiser. Normally the Mercers wrote the checks and said they didn't even need to see the candidate. This time they wanted 10 minutes with Trump.

In a small sunroom, Rebekah, a tall redhead, let loose. Her father, Bob Mercer, a high-IQ mathematician, barely talked. He was one of the brains behind a fabulously successful hedge fund, Renaissance Technologies, that managed $50 billion.

"Manafort has got to go," she told Trump. She said it was chaos.

"What do you recommend?" Trump asked.

"Steve Bannon will come in," she said.

"He'll never do it."

He "definitely" would, she answered.

Bannon reached Trump that night.

"This thing is embarrassing in the paper," Bannon said, referring to the *New York Times* piece. "You're better than this. We can win this. We should be winning this. It's Hillary Clinton, for God's sake."

Trump went off on Manafort. "He's a stiff," he said. He can't do TV effectively.

"Let's meet tomorrow and put this thing together. We can do this," Bannon gushed. "But let's keep it totally quiet."

Trump agreed to meet the next morning, Sunday.

Another worried political figure that day was Reince Priebus, the 44-year-old chairman of the Republican National Committee, and a Wisconsin lawyer. Priebus had been Mr. Outreach and Mr. Networker in his five years as chairman. His cheery demeanor masked an empire builder. Priebus made the party's finance decisions, hired the field staff of 6,500 paid workers, appeared on TV regularly and had his own communications operation. He was in an awkward position.

Privately, Priebus viewed the month of August as a catastrophe. "A constant heat lamp that wouldn't go away." And the person responsible was candidate Trump.

Priebus had tried to navigate the campaign from the beginning. When Trump called Mexicans "rapists" in the speech announcing his candidacy on June 16, 2015, Priebus called him and said, "You can't talk like that. We've been working really hard to win over Hispanics."

Trump would not tone it down, and he attacked anyone who attacked him. No national party chairman had ever dealt with a headache quite like Trump.

Senator Mitch McConnell, the wily Republican majority leader, had called Priebus confidentially. His message: Forget Trump, divert Republican money to us, the Senate candidates, and shut off the money faucet to Donald Trump.

But Priebus wanted to preserve a relationship with Trump, and he decided to plant himself firmly in the middle between Trump and McConnell. It was tactically sound, he thought. Survival for the party and him. He had told Trump, "I'm with you 100 percent. I love you. I'm going to keep working for you. But I have to protect the party. I have a responsibility that's different than just you."

Priebus had agreed to come out and campaign with Trump and introduce him at rallies. He saw it as extending a hand to a drowning man.

The *Times* article about the failure to tame Trump was a jolt. "Holy shit!" Priebus thought. This is really bad stuff." The campaign was falling apart. "It wasn't a campaign," he had concluded. "They were a joke."

There was so much talking in the *Times* article that Priebus realized the 20 sources were either trying to sabotage the campaign or, as usual, make themselves look good.

Perilous times, maybe the worst, for Trump and the party, Priebus thought. There was only one path forward: escalation on all fronts. Maximize aggression to conceal vital weakness.

That Sunday morning, Steve Bannon arrived at Trump Tower in Manhattan and told security he had a meeting with Mr. Trump.

"That's terrific," the security guard said. "He's never here on weekends."

Bannon phoned Trump.

"Hey," the candidate explained, "I'm in Bedminster"—where Trump National Golf Club was located. "Since you're not here, I'll go play golf. Come out here, we're having lunch. Be here, like, one o'clock."

He proceeded to give detailed instructions for the drive 40 miles west of New York City.

"I'll find it," Bannon said.

No, turn right on Rattlesnake Bridge Road, then take a right for about a mile.

"I'll find it. It's your Trump National."

No, Trump persisted, you've got to understand. Trump provided full driving instructions with more detail than Bannon had ever heard him give on anything.

Bannon had a driver take him to Bedminster to arrive at noon to make sure he was on time. Inside the clubhouse, he was shown to a table set for five.

You're early, said someone from the staff. The others won't be here until 1 p.m.

The others? Bannon asked.

Roger Ailes, Governor Chris Christie and "the Mayor"—Rudy Giuliani—also were attending.

Bannon was pissed. He was not there to audition in front of anyone. He and Trump had agreed, made a deal which should not be reviewable.

Ailes, the founder and head of Fox News and longtime Republican political operative, going back to Richard Nixon, came in first. He had been a mentor to Bannon.

"What the fuck?" Ailes said, and launched into a criticism of the campaign.

"How bad are the numbers?" Bannon asked.

"This is going to be a blowout."

"I talked to Trump last night," Bannon said. "The Mercers talked to him. I'm supposed to be coming in and taking over the campaign, but don't tell the other two guys that."

"What the fuck?" Ailes said again. "You don't know anything about campaigns." It was out of the question.

"I know, but anybody could get more organized than this thing is."

Though Bannon had known Ailes for years, he would not appear on Ailes's Fox News network.

Bannon once said, "I've never been on Fox because I didn't want to be beholden to him. . . . Never be beholden to Roger or he fucking owns you."

This contrasted sharply with his relationship to Trump, who, in his view, was a supplicant. Trump had appeared on a series of *Breitbart News Daily* radio interviews with Bannon on SiriusXM between November 2015 and June 2016.

Ailes said they were there for their weekly debate prep. The first presidential debate against Hillary Clinton was a month and a half away, on September 26.

"Debate prep?" Bannon said. "You, Christie and Rudy?"

"This is the second one."

"He's actually prepping for the debates?" Bannon said, suddenly impressed.

"No, he comes and plays golf and we just talk about the campaign and stuff like that. But we're trying to get him in the habit."

Campaign manager Paul Manafort walked in.

Bannon, who regularly called himself "a fire-breathing populist," was disgusted. Manafort was dressed in what could pass for yachting attire, with a kerchief. Live from Southampton!

Trump arrived and sat down. Hot dogs and hamburgers were laid out. The fantasy diet of an 11-year-old kid, Bannon thought, as Trump wolfed down two hot dogs.

Citing the *New York Times* story about the failure to tame his tongue, Trump asked Manafort how such an article could appear. It was one of Trump's paradoxes: He attacked the mainstream media with relish, especially the *Times*—but despite the full-takedown language, he considered the *Times* the paper of record and largely believed its stories.

"Paul, am I a baby?" Trump asked Manafort. "Is that what you are saying, I'm a baby? You're terrible on TV. You've got no energy. You don't represent the campaign. I've told you nicely. You're never going on TV again."

"Donald . . .," Manafort tried to respond.

Bannon suspected this familiar, first-name, peer-to-peer talk irked Trump.

"One thing you've got to understand, Mr. Trump," Bannon said, "the story had a lot of these unnamed sources, we don't know the veracity."

"No, I can tell," Trump replied, directing his fire at Manafort. "They're leakers." He knew the quotes were true.

"A lot of this is not for attribution," Bannon said. No one by name, all hiding. "*The New York Times* is, it's all fucking lies. Come on, this is all bullshit," Bannon continued his full-body, opposition-party pitch, though he knew the story was true.

Trump wasn't buying it. The story was gospel, and the campaign was full of leakers. The assassination of Manafort continued for a while. Trump turned to a few war stories for half an hour. Manafort left.

"Stick around," Trump told Bannon. "This thing's so terrible. It's so out of control. This guy's such a loser. He's really not running the campaign. I only brought him in to get me through the convention."

"Don't worry about any of these numbers," Bannon said. "Don't worry about the 12 to 16 points, whatever the poll is. Don't worry about the battleground states. It's very simple." Two thirds of the country thinks we're on the wrong track, and 75 percent of the country thinks we're in decline, he argued. That set the stage for a change agent. Hillary was the past. It was that clear.

In a way, Bannon had been waiting all his adult life for this moment. "Here's the difference," he explained. "We're just going to compare and contrast Clinton. Here's the thing you've got to remember," he said, and recited one of his mantras: "The elites in the country are comfortable with managing the decline. Right?"

Trump nodded agreement.

"And the working people in the country are not. They do want to make America great again. We're going to simplify this campaign. She is the tribune of a corrupt and incompetent status quo of elites who are comfortable managing the decline. You're the tribune of the forgotten man who wants to make America great again. And we're just going to do it in a couple of themes.

"Number one," Bannon went on, "we're going to stop mass illegal immigration and start to limit legal immigration to get our sovereignty back. Number two, you are going to bring manufacturing jobs back to the country. And number three, we're going to get out of these pointless foreign wars."

These weren't new ideas for Trump. In an August 8 speech to the Detroit Economic Club a week before, he had sounded all these notes and hammered Clinton. "She is the candidate of the past. Ours is the campaign of the future."

"Those are the three big themes that she can't defend against," Bannon said. "She's part of the thing that opened the borders, she's part of the thing that cut the bad trade deals and let the jobs go to China, and she's the neocon. Right?"

Trump seemed to agree that Hillary was a neoconservative.

"She's supported every war out there," Bannon said. "We're just going to hammer. That's it. Just stick to that."

Bannon added that Trump had another advantage. He spoke in a voice that did not sound political. This was what Barack Obama had in 2008 in the primary contest against Clinton, who spoke like the trained politician she was. Her tempo was overly practiced. Even when telling the truth, she sounded like she was lying to you.

Politicians like Hillary can't talk naturally, Bannon said. It was a mechanical way of speaking, right out of the polling and focus groups, answering the questions in political speak. It was soothing, not jarring, not from the heart or from deep conviction, but from some highly paid consultant's talking points—*not angry.*

Trump said okay, you become the Chief Executive Officer of the campaign.

"I don't want some big brouhaha story about palace intrigue," Bannon said. "Let's keep Manafort in as chairman. He'll have no authority. Let me manage that."

They agreed that Kellyanne Conway—a feisty, outspoken Republican pollster who was already helping the campaign—would be designated campaign manager.

"We're going to put her on television every day as the female-friendly face on the thing," Bannon proposed. "Because Kellyanne is a warrior. And she'll just take incoming. But people like her. And that's what we need is likability."

In a moment of self-awareness, he added, "I'll never be on TV."

Conway had never run a campaign either. That made three of them—the shiny neophyte candidate, the campaign CEO and the campaign manager.

Kellyanne Conway was supervising the filming of some campaign ads that month.

"Am I paying for these people?" Trump asked her.

He complained about the camera setup. The equipment seemed old and he didn't like the lighting. The shoot wasn't high-definition (HD). He groused about the camera crew. "Tell them I'm not going to pay." It was a standard line.

Later he said, "I want everyone to leave except Kellyanne."

"Everybody tells me that I'm a much better candidate than Hillary Clinton," he said, half-asking for her evaluation.

"Well, yes, sir. No poll necessary." But they could do some things different. "You're running against the most joyless candidate in presidential history. And it's starting to feel like we are that way as well."

"No we're not."

"It just feels that way. I used to watch you during the primaries, and you seemed much happier."

"I miss the days when it was just a few of us flying around doing the rallies, meeting the voters," Trump said.

"Those days are gone," she acknowledged. "But in fairness to you, we should be able to replicate them to a general election strategy and process that allows you to maximize those skills and the enjoyment."

She took a stab at candor. "You know you're losing? But you don't have to. I've looked at the polls." CNN that day had him down five to 10 points. "There's a path back."

"What is it?"

She believed that he had done something without realizing it. "This fiction of electability that was sucking the lifeblood out of the Republican Party," that somehow he could not win and was not electable.

The voters were disillusioned with Republican presidential nominees. These arguments went, "You have to get behind Mitt Romney. He's the only one who can win. You have to support John McCain. He can win. Jeb can win. Marco can win. This one," Trump, you, "can't win. The people decided. I will not be fooled again," and he had won the Republican nomination.

"You get these massive crowds where you have not erected a traditional political campaign. You have built a movement. And people feel like they're part of it. They paid no admission. I can tell you what I see in the polling. We have two major impediments." She said they should never do national polling, ever. "That is the foolishness of the media," which did national polls. Winning obviously was all about the electoral college—getting the 270 electoral votes. They needed to target the right states, the roughly eight battleground states.

"People want specifics," Conway said. It had been great when Trump released his 10-point Veterans Administration reform plan in July, or a planned five-point tax reform plan. "People want those kinds of specifics, but they need them repeated again and again.

"The second vulnerability I see is people want to make sure you can actually make good on your promises. Because if you can't deliver, if the *businessman* can't execute and deliver, you're just another politician. And that's who you're not."

It was a sales pitch, a path forward that Trump seemed to embrace.

"Do you think you can run this thing?" he asked.

"What is 'this thing'?" she asked. "I'm running this photo shoot."

"The campaign," Trump said. "The whole thing. Are you willing to not see your kids for a few months?"

She accepted on the spot. "Sir, I can do that for you. You can win this race. I do not consider myself your peer. I will never address you by your first name."

That Sunday night, Bannon headed to work—Trump Tower in New York City. The campaign headquarters. It was his first visit, and 85 days until the presidential election.

He rode up to the fourteenth floor. The sun was still out on this August night. He expected to walk in and have a thousand or so people ask, What's Bannon doing here? He would need a cover story.

He walked into the war room, the rapid response center, with all the TV sets.

There was one person there. To Bannon's eyes, he was a kid.

"Who are you?" Bannon asked.

"Andy Surabian."

"Where the fuck is everybody?"

"I don't know," Surabian replied. "This is like it is on every Sunday."

"This is the campaign headquarters?"

"Yeah."

"I mean like the place where the whole thing's run out of?"

Yeah. Surabian pointed out Jason Miller's office—the senior communications director—and Hope Hicks's—the young former model who had become the campaign's main press person and perhaps the staff member closest to Trump. Surabian was the war room director.

"Do you guys work weekends?"

Surabian said yeah again. Some worked in D.C., some guys phoned in.

Bannon tried once more. "On weekends, does this place have people in it?"

"This is about average."

"Where the fuck is Jared? I've got to talk to Jared and Ivanka." Bannon had heard that Jared Kushner, Trump's son-in-law, was the mastermind and genius here.

Jared and Ivanka were on entertainment mogul and Democratic donor David Geffen's $300 million yacht—one of the largest in the world—off the coast of Croatia, on vacation with Wendi Deng, a businesswoman and former wife of Rupert Murdoch.

Manafort called Bannon. He wanted to meet.

"Why don't you come up?" Manafort said.

Where?

"The Tower."

Bannon had to go back to the lobby to get the elevator to the residences. On the ride up, he wondered if this was the deal that Trump cut with his campaign chief. "If he's going to toss me some penthouse in the Trump Tower, why not?" It would be better than his small place on Bryant Park.

It turned out that Manafort owned the place.

Bannon felt sorry for Manafort. The campaign manager had been astonished at the success and power of Trump's Twitter account, and had started one of his own. But the New York *Daily News* had run this item in April: "Make America kinky again," noting that Manafort—perhaps unaware that Twitter was a public forum—had followed a Midtown bondage and swingers' club called Decadence.

"Manafort was following the swanky spank spot—which bills itself as the city's 'most intimate swing club.'"

Manafort's place was beautiful. Kathleen Manafort, his wife, an attorney who was in her 60s but looked to Bannon like she was in her 40s, was wearing white and lounging like Joan Collins, the actress from the show *Dynasty*.

"I really want to thank you for trying to step in," Manafort said. "That's just Donald. This is the way he acts all the time."

"I thought he took some real cheap shots at you," Bannon said.

Manafort waved him off. "Listen, everybody tells me you really know media," he said.

"I run a right-wing website. I know advocacy."

"I need you to look at something for me," Manafort said, handing him a copy of a draft story coming in from *The New York Times* headlined: "Secret Ledger in Ukraine Lists Cash for Donald Trump's Campaign Chief."

Bannon read, "Handwritten ledgers show $12.7 million in undisclosed cash payments designated for Mr. Manafort" from the pro-Russian political party.

"Twelve million fucking dollars in cash out of the Ukraine!" Bannon virtually shouted.

"What?" Mrs. Manafort said, bolting upright.

"Nothing, honey," Manafort said. "Nothing."

"When is this coming out?" Bannon asked.

"It may go up tonight."

"Does Trump know anything about this?"

Manafort said no.

"How long have you known about this?"

Two months, Manafort said, when the *Times* started investigating.

Bannon read about 10 paragraphs in. It was a kill shot. It was over for Manafort.

"My lawyer told me not to cooperate," Manafort said. "It was just a hit piece."

"You should fire your lawyer."

"I'm thinking about it."

"You've got to call Trump . . . go see him face-to-face. If this comes out in the paper, and he doesn't know about it, it's lights out for you. How do you even take $12.7 million in cash?"

"It's all lies," Manafort said. "I had expenses."

"What do you mean?"

"I'm just a general consultant," he explained. "I've got guys." Many others had worked for him in Ukraine. "It all was paid to the guys. I didn't take $500,000 out of there."

"That's all lost. It's not laid out in the article. It's 'you got $12.7 million in cash,' okay?"

Bannon called Jared.

"You've got to get back here," he said.

The *Times* article on Manafort ran online that night and in the paper the next morning. As Bannon predicted, Trump was apoplectic. He'd had no heads-up.

Trump called Reince Priebus to tell him that Steve Bannon was coming in as CEO. Priebus marveled that Trump would again bring in someone with little experience running anything, but he didn't say much. He'd come around on Bannon's Breitbart operation. After getting killed for about two years by Breitbart as part of the Republican elite, he'd developed a new strategy: It was a lot easier to work with Breitbart, and get less killed.

Polls showed only 70 percent of Republicans were for Trump. They needed 90 percent. That meant getting the party apparatus on Trump's side.

"Look, you don't know me," Bannon said. He had met Priebus briefly years before. "I need to have you here this afternoon. And this girl Katie Walsh, who I just hear is a superstar." Priebus and

Walsh, the RNC chief of staff, had the Republican database on every likely voter in the country.

Bannon wanted to be sure that the RNC was not going to leave Trump. There were rumors about donors fleeing and how everyone in the party was trying to figure a way out of the Trump mess.

That's not the case, Priebus assured him. We are not going anywhere.

"We've got to work as a team," Bannon said.

"You think you can do it?"

"Look, Trump doesn't care about details," Bannon said. It was up to them.

As Bannon later remarked with his trademark profanity, "I reached out and sucked Reince Priebus' dick on August 15 and told the establishment, we can't win without you."

Even if Trump and his campaign didn't know it, Priebus knew Trump needed the RNC to stick with him. Trump had almost no field operations out where the voters were, and didn't know some of the most fundamental things—Politics 101.

Priebus had spent the last years overseeing a massive effort to rebuild the RNC into a data-driven operation. Borrowing from Obama's winning campaign strategy, the RNC started pouring vast sums—eventually more than $175 million—into analytics and big data, tracking individual primary voters, and using that information in areas divided into neighborhood "turfs" staffed with armies of volunteers.

All along, the expectation had been that once the Republican nominee was selected, the RNC would hitch this massive shiny new wagon to an already fairly robust and large campaign apparatus. For all the abuse the RNC had taken during the primaries—at one point Trump had called the RNC a "disgrace" and "a scam" and said that Priebus "should be ashamed of himself"—the RNC was effectively the Trump campaign staff.

The first step was for field staff to get an absentee or early voting ballot to those they deemed pro-Trump because they scored a 90 or above on a scale of 0 to 100 in the national database. In Ohio, out of perhaps 6 million voters, approximately 1 million would score 90 or above. Those 1 million would be targeted for early voting ballots, and the field staff and volunteers would hound each one until the ballot was sent in.

Next the field staff would move to persuade those who scored 60 or 70, trying to convince them to vote for Trump. The system was designed to reduce the randomness of voter contact, to make sure the volunteers and field staff concentrated their efforts on those most likely to vote for Trump.

The campaign announced the leadership changes on August 17. *The New York Times* reported, "Trump's decision to make Stephen K. Bannon, chairman of the Breitbart News website, his campaign's chief executive was a defiant rejection of efforts by longtime Republican hands to wean him from the bombast and racially charged speech that helped propel him to the nomination but now threaten his candidacy. . . . For Mr. Trump, though, bringing in Mr. Bannon was the political equivalent of ordering comfort food."

Bannon tried to sit down with Trump and walk him through refinements of the strategy and how to focus on particular states. The candidate had no interest in talking about it.

Bannon assured Trump, I have "metaphysical certitude you will win here if you stick to this script and compare and contrast" with Hillary Clinton. "Every underlying number is with us."

"I realized," Bannon said later, "I'm the director, he's the actor."

Kellyanne Conway had gone to the four-day Democratic convention in Philadelphia in July. She had listened to the speeches, talked to delegates, appeared on television. Her observations shaped her current strategy. "Their message is Donald Trump is bad, and we're not Donald Trump. The rest of the message was race, gender, LGBT."

Conway coined the phrase "the hidden Trump voter." These were the people who found themselves perplexed by the vote ahead of them, saying, "God, my daddy, my granddaddy and I are all in the union. I'm going to vote for Donald Trump?" Putting a question mark at the end. "I'm going to vote for a billionaire Republican?" Another question mark.

"And you'd have these women who'd say, you know, I'm pro-choice . . . but I don't think *Roe v. Wade* is going to change. But I don't understand why we can't afford everyday life anymore, so I'm voting on that."

Much of the media did not buy "the hidden Trump voter" line. But Priebus and Walsh's database gave the RNC and the campaign insight into almost everything about every likely voter—what beer they drank, the make and color of the car they drove, the age and school of their kids, their mortgage status, the cigarettes they smoked. Did they get a hunting license every year? Did they subscribe to gun magazines, or liberal magazines like *The New Republic*?

And Conway said, "There's not a single hidden Hillary voter in the entire country. They're all out and about."

About Clinton, she said, "She doesn't seem to have a message. Now if I'm her, I'm going to find a message. I'm going to buy a message. And it's going to be very positive and uplifting and optimistic. All I can see from her so far is not optimism."

Clinton had not cracked 50 percent in eight key states that Obama had won twice with over 50 percent. Conway agreed with Bannon that if the Trump campaign could make the race about Hillary, not Trump, they would win with those hidden Trump voters. If the race stayed about Trump, "we'll probably lose."

Repeating the impression he'd formed six years earlier when he first met Trump in 2010, Bannon said, "Literally, I've got Archie Bunker. . . . He's Tiberius Gracchus"—the second-century BC Roman populist who advocated transfer of the land from the wealthy patrician landowners to the poor.

Bannon looked at the schedule—Education Week coming up,

then Women's Empowerment Week. The third week was Small Business Week. It was as if the first George Bush were running in the 1980s. Classic country-club Republican. "Throw this shit out," he said.

Bannon suggested a new plan to Jared Kushner. Trump was down double digits in every battleground state. There would be three stages:

First, the next six weeks, mid-August to September 26, when the first debate with Hillary was scheduled. "If we can get within five to seven points, that can build a bridge to win."

Second was the three weeks of debates. This was the period of extreme danger. "He's so unprepared for the debates," Bannon said. "She'll kill him because she's the best" at debating and policy. Bannon said the way to handle debates was spontaneity. Trump had no problem being unpredictable. "We're going to call nothing but audibles in these debates. That's the only thing we've got . . . where he can walk around and connect." Still he was pessimistic. "Look, we're going to get crushed. . . . We're going to lose ground here."

Third was the final three weeks to election day, from the final debate to November 8. Bannon saw the fundraising by Steve Mnuchin, a Goldman Sachs alumnus and national finance chairman for the campaign, as an inadequate joke. They were going to have to turn to Trump himself. A candidate could spend unlimited amounts of his or her own money.

Bannon said he had seen data suggesting that Ohio and Iowa could be winnable. Also they had to win Florida and North Carolina. Then Pennsylvania, Michigan, Wisconsin and Minnesota could come back to the Republicans. It all seemed like a giant fantasy.

"This is Götterdämmerung," the final battle, he said.

Manafort's departure was announced on August 19.

On August 22, *Time* magazine ran a cover illustration of Trump's dissolving face headlined: "Meltdown."

CHAPTER

4

Signs of Russian "reconnoitering," or digital intrusions as the National Security Agency called them, first appeared in local and state electoral boards' computerized voter registration rolls—lists of voters' names and addresses—in the summer of 2015. The first showed up in Illinois, then spread across the country to include 21 states.

As the NSA and FBI picked up more information on these cyber intrusions, Director of National Intelligence James Clapper worried that Russia might use the data to change or manipulate votes in some way. Is this just Russia, he wondered. The Russians were always trying to make trouble.

Clapper made sure the initial information was included in Obama's President's Daily Brief (PDB), the highest-level top security briefing. Obama read it each day on a preprogrammed iPad, which he returned. Similar iPads were distributed by designated PDB briefers to the secretary of state, the secretary of defense, the national security adviser and the CIA director, although in these cases the briefers remained in the room while the principals read the PDB and then reclaimed the iPads.

In July of 2016, WikiLeaks and DC Leaks, another site known for releasing hacked government and military materials, began publishing emails taken from a Democratic National Committee server by groups of Russian hackers identified as "Cozy Bear" and "Fancy Bear."

Intelligence about Russian meddling caused deep concern in Obama's National Security Council. Over time, the intel got better and more convincing.

Should President Obama go on prime-time national television and announce these findings? Would it look like he was attacking Trump, linking the Republican nominee with Russia? Could it backfire and look like he was meddling in the U.S. election, trying to tip the scales?

To remain silent had its perils: Oh my God, we know about this Russian meddling and we're not acting, we're not telling the public? There could be a backlash directed at Obama and his national security team after the election.

In the very unlikely, almost inconceivable chance that Trump won, and the intelligence became public, the questions would come: What did they know? When did they know it? And what did they do?

John O. Brennan, director of the CIA, argued vehemently against showing their hand. Brennan was protective of the agency's human sources. "Now you see the dilemma," he said, for him personally and the CIA institutionally. The mantra always was PROTECT THE SOURCES. Yet, he wanted to do something.

Brennan needed to speak to his counterpart, Russian FSB intelligence chief Alexander Bortnikov, about Syria and harassment of U.S. diplomats. He asked Obama if he could raise the election meddling issue with Bortnikov.

Obama approved the under-the-radar approach.

On August 4, Brennan told Bortnikov, You're meddling in our election. We know it. We have it cold.

Bortnikov flatly denied it.

The next day, August 5, Mike Morell, who had been deputy CIA director from 2010 to 2013 and twice acting director, published an op-ed in *The New York Times*. The headline: "I Ran the CIA. Now I'm Endorsing Hillary Clinton." Morell accused Trump of being "an unwitting agent of the Russian Federation."

Clapper was chosen to brief the so-called Gang of Eight in Congress—four Republican and Democratic leaders in both the Senate and House plus the four chairmen and vice chairmen of the Senate and House intelligence committees.

Clapper was stunned by how partisan the leaders were. Republicans disliked everything about the briefing. The Democrats loved every morsel, peppering him with questions about the details and sourcing. He left the briefing dismayed that intelligence was increasingly another political football to kick around.

By fall, the intelligence reports showed that Moscow—like almost everyone else—believed that Clinton was likely to win. Russian president Vladimir Putin's influence campaign shifted strategy to focus on undermining her coming presidency.

Clapper and Secretary of Homeland Security Jeh Johnson were the most anxious to alert the public to the Russian interference. At 3 p.m. on Friday, October 7, they released a joint statement officially accusing Russia of trying to interfere in the U.S. election, although they didn't name Putin in the public release.

"The U.S. intelligence community is confident the Russian government directed the recent compromise of emails from U.S. persons and institutions. These thefts and disclosures are intended to interfere with the U.S. election process. Russia's senior-most officials are the only ones who could have authorized the activities."

Clapper, Johnson and the Clinton campaign expected this to be the big news of the weekend, as did the reporters who began working on the story.

But one hour later, at 4:05 p.m., David Fahrenthold at *The Washington Post* released a story headlined, "Trump Recorded Having Extremely Lewd Conversation About Women in 2005."

The *Post* released an audio outtake recording from the NBC show

Access Hollywood of Trump bragging crudely about his sexual prowess. He said he could grope and kiss women at will. "When you're a star, they let you do it," Trump said. "You can do anything. Grab them by the pussy."

The *Access Hollywood* tape was a political earthquake. The Russia story essentially disappeared.

"I expected it to be something that would have a lot of currency over the following days," Jeh Johnson later said. "And that it would be a continuing conversation with more questions from the press." But the press went "off to the other end of the pasture 'cause of greed and sex and groping."

Trump issued a brief statement to the *Post*: "This was locker-room banter, a private conversation that took place many years ago. Bill Clinton has said far worse to me on the golf course—not even close. I apologize if anyone was offended."

Less than a half hour later, at 4:30 p.m., WikiLeaks capped the day's news by dumping thousands of emails hacked from Clinton campaign chairman John Podesta's personal account online. They revealed excerpts of Hillary Clinton's paid speeches to Wall Street financiers, which she had refused to release, Podesta's emails with campaign staff and correspondence between the Clinton campaign and DNC chair Donna Brazile regarding questions and topics to be raised at upcoming debates and events.

After midnight—and hours of outraged responses to the *Access Hollywood* tape spreading across the political spectrum—Trump released a videotaped apology: "I've never said I'm a perfect person . . . these words don't reflect who I am. I said it, I was wrong and I apologize. . . . I pledge to be a better man tomorrow, and will never, ever let you down. Let's be honest. We're living in the real world. This is nothing more than a distraction. . . . Bill Clinton has actually abused women and Hillary has bullied, attacked, shamed and intimidated his victims. . . . See you at the debate on Sunday."

The Trump high command assembled the next morning, Saturday, October 8, in the penthouse of Trump Tower.

Priebus told Bannon, "The donors are all out. Everybody's dropped. Paul Ryan's going to drop this afternoon." The loss of the money people and the Republican house speaker signaled the end. "It's over," Priebus said.

"What do you mean it's over?" Bannon said.

"Everybody's pulling their endorsements. I don't even know if Pence is going to be on this thing." The fastidiously loyal Mike Pence, Trump's running mate, was doubting.

"Are you fucking kidding me?" Bannon replied. "It's a tape, dude."

"You don't understand," said Priebus. "It's over."

The team gathered in Trump's residence. Trump sat in his big gold chair.

"What's the percentages?" he asked. "Okay, let's go around. I really want to know, what's your recommendation? What's your advice?"

"You have two choices," Priebus began. "You either drop out right now or you're going to lose in the biggest landslide in American history and be humiliated for life. I'm getting crushed. I've got every leader, every congressman, every senator, everyone I care about on the Republican National Committee—they're going crazy. And they're telling me you're either going to lose big, in a massive way, or you need to drop out of the race. I can't make it any better."

"Well," Trump said, "I'm glad we're starting off on a positive note."

"Cut the bullshit," Bannon said to Priebus. "That's bullshit."

"If you want to do it now," Priebus continued, "Pence is prepared to step up, and Condi Rice will come in as his VP." Rice had been national security adviser and secretary of state under George W. Bush.

"That's never going to happen," Bannon said loudly. "That's ridiculous. Fucking absurd." In less than two months as campaign CEO they had cut the polling gap in half with endless rallies. Trump was a rock star now.

New Jersey governor Chris Christie was sitting in sweatpants and ball cap.

"This is not about the campaign," Christie said with a note of finality. "That's over. This is about your brand. You've worked your entire life. These kids—" He pointed to Trump's son Don Jr. and Jared Kushner. "You need to save the brand for them or the brand's finished."

Rudy Giuliani said that Trump now had less than a 50 percent chance of winning. "Basically you've got 40 percent."

"Do we call *60 Minutes*?" Kellyanne Conway asked. She proposed a public confessional. "You can't do it Sunday because the debate's on Sunday. . . . Or you call ABC or NBC and have him on the sofa with Ivanka on one side and Melania on the other, basically crying, saying I apologize."

Melania Trump had come down and wandered behind the sofa where Conway was proposing they sit. It was clear she was seething.

"Not doing that," Melania said in her Slovenian accent, dismissively waving her hand. "No way. No, no, no."

Bannon believed she had the most influence with Trump of anyone, that she could discern who was sucking up and who was telling the truth. "Behind the scenes she's a hammer."

"What do you think?" Trump asked Bannon.

"One hundred percent," Bannon said.

"One hundred percent, what?" asked Trump.

"One hundred percent, metaphysical certitude you're going to win." He often declared certainty with 100 percent.

"Cut the shit," Trump yelled. "I'm tired of the 100 percent. I need to know what you really think!"

Priebus didn't believe the 100 percent, and thought no one in the room did. He saw that Trump was upset with himself.

"It's 100 percent," Bannon repeated. Trump's words were "locker-room talk." Your supporters will still be with you. "They are worried about saving their country." The comparison with Bill Clinton was handy. "We're going to compare your talk with his action." Bill

Clinton was as much Trump's opposition as Hillary, perhaps now more than ever.

"How are we going to do that?" Trump asked.

"Jared and I reserved the Hilton Hotel ballroom for 8 tonight. We're going to put it on Facebook and get 1,000 hammerheads"—one of Bannon's terms for diehard Trump supporters—"in red ball caps. And you're going to fucking do a rally and attack the media. We're going to double down. Fuck 'em! Right?"

Trump seemed delighted.

The others were opposed. There was a huge fight, but a compromise emerged.

Conway would call ABC and arrange for David Muir, the ABC anchor, to helicopter in. Giuliani and Christie would write an introduction for Trump and Muir could do a 10-minute interview.

Political suicide, thought Bannon. This would make the campaign over for sure, and Trump would lose by 20 points.

He said they had to let the Hilton know about the rally because they would have to put up cash.

Priebus said again that Trump just had to drop out. "You guys don't know what you're doing. You're going to go down."

Prominent Republicans began to call for Trump to step aside for Mike Pence, who had been making campaign appearances in Ohio. He had gone to ground when the news broke about the *Access Hollywood* tape.

Just before 1 p.m., Pence released a statement saying, "As a husband and a father, I was offended by the words and actions described by Donald Trump in the 11-year-old video released yesterday. I do not condone his remarks and cannot defend them. I am grateful that he has expressed remorse and apologized to the American people. We pray for his family and look forward to the opportunity he has to show what is in his heart when he goes before the nation tomorrow night."

Stories circulated that Pence had given Bannon a sealed letter urging Trump to drop off the ticket.

Two hours later, Melania Trump released a statement: "The words my husband used are unacceptable and offensive to me. This does not represent the man that I know. He has the heart and mind of a leader. I hope people will accept his apology, as I have, and focus on the important issues facing our nation and the world."

At 3:40 p.m., Trump tweeted, "The media and establishment want me out of the race so badly—I WILL NEVER DROP OUT OF THE RACE, WILL NEVER LET MY SUPPORTERS DOWN! #MAGA"

Trump took a seat. Preparations for the ABC interview were in motion—it was likely to be a record-breaker. Giuliani and Christie handed a sheet of their suggestions to Trump.

Trump read: "My language was inappropriate, not acceptable for a president." It was political speak—not Trump, all Giuliani and Christie. Trump was surly.

"I can't do this," he said. "This is bullshit. This is weak. You guys are weak."

Bannon realized he had this one. He just had to keep his mouth shut.

"Donald, you don't understand," Christie said.

"Donald, Donald, Donald," Giuliani said. "You've got to do this." Think about the suburban moms.

The clock was ticking.

Bannon turned to Conway. "What do you do to kill this?"

"You can't kill it," she replied. "They're already here"—ABC and David Muir.

"What do you do to kill it?" Bannon repeated.

"All my credibility is on the line. You can't kill this thing. It's in motion. It's going to happen," Conway said.

"It's not going to happen," Bannon said. "He ain't going to do it. If he does do an introduction," Bannon continued, "you can't have him do a live interview. He'll fucking get cut to pieces." The apology road was not Trump, and if he was questioned afterward he would backtrack and contradict himself.

They tried to reword it.

Trump went through two lines.

"I'm not doing this."

The glass in Trump Tower was thick, but they could hear the roaring crowd of Trump supporters in the street—a riot of "deplorables," who had adopted Hillary Clinton's derisive term as their own.

"My people!" Trump declared. "I'm going to go down. Don't worry about the rally. I'm going to do it right here."

"You're not going down there," a Secret Service agent insisted. "You're not going outside."

"I'm going downstairs," Trump said. He headed out. "This is great."

Conway tried to intervene. "You just can't cancel" on ABC.

"I don't care. I'm never doing this. It was a dumb idea. I never wanted to do it."

Bannon was about to follow Trump into the elevator when Christie said, "Hang on for a second."

He stayed back as Trump went downstairs with Conway, Don Jr. and the Secret Service.

"You're the fucking problem," Christie said to Bannon. "You've been the problem since the beginning."

"What are you talking about?"

"You're the enabler. You play to every one of his worst instincts. This thing's over, and you're going to be blamed. Every time he's got terrible instincts for these things, and all you do is get him all worked up. This is going to be humiliating."

Christie was in Bannon's face, looming large. Bannon half-wanted to say, You fat fuck, let's throw down right here.

"Governor," he replied instead, "the plane leaves tomorrow." They were heading to St. Louis for the second presidential debate. "If you're on the plane, you're on the team."

Downstairs, the Secret Service relented. Trump could go out on the street, but only briefly. There could be weapons all over the place. It was a baying mob of supporters and protesters.

At 4:30 p.m. Trump stepped out, giving high fives and shaking hands for a few minutes, flanked by the Secret Service and New York police.

Will you stay in the race? a reporter asked.

"One hundred percent," Trump said.

Everyone on the Trump campaign refused to appear on the Sunday-morning talk shows except Rudy Giuliani. Priebus, Christie, even the reliable, thick-armored, never-say-no Conway had been scheduled. All canceled.

Giuliani appeared on all five, completing what is called a full Ginsburg—a term in honor of William H. Ginsburg, the attorney for Monica Lewinsky, who appeared on all five network Sunday programs on February 1, 1998.

Giuliani gave, or tried to give, the same spiel on each show: Trump's words had been "reprehensible and terrible and awful," and he had apologized. Trump was not the same man now that he had been when captured on tape in 2005. The "transformational" presidential campaign had made him a changed man. And besides, Hillary Clinton's speeches to Goldman Sachs, which had come out in WikiLeaks's release of John Podesta's emails, revealed a private coziness with Wall Street that clashed with her liberal public positions. The country would view that much more harshly.

Bannon, not a regular viewer of Sunday talk shows, tuned in. The morning was a brutal slog. When CNN's Jake Tapper said Trump's words had been a depiction of sexual assault that was "really offensive on just a basic human level," Giuliani had to acknowledge, "Yes, it is."

Giuliani was exhausted, practically bled out, but he had proved his devotion and friendship. He had pulled out every stop, leaning frequently and heavily on his Catholicism: "You confess your sins and you make a firm resolution not to commit that sin again. And then, the priest gives you absolution and then, hopefully you're a changed person. I mean, we believe the people in this country can change."

Giuliani, seeming punch-drunk, made it to the plane for the departure to the St. Louis debate. He took a seat next to Trump, who was at his table in his reading glasses. He peered over at the former mayor.

"Rudy, you're a baby!" Trump said loudly. "I've never seen a worse defense of me in my life. They took your diaper off right there. You're like a little baby that needed to be changed. When are you going to be a man?"

Trump turned to the others, particularly Bannon.

"Why did you put him on? He can't defend me. I need somebody to defend me. Where are my people?"

"What are you talking about?" Bannon asked. "This guy's the only guy that went on."

"I don't want to hear it," Trump replied. "It was a mistake. He shouldn't have gone on. He's weak. You're weak, Rudy. You've lost it."

Giuliani just looked up, his face blank.

Shortly after the planned departure, Chris Christie had not appeared. "Fuck this guy," Bannon said, and the plane took off.

Giuliani had said twice, on CNN and NBC, that he did not anticipate Trump going after Bill Clinton or Hillary's private life in the debate that evening. But Bannon had arranged what he thought would be a well-timed kill shot.

Four of the women who claimed Clinton had attacked them or who Hillary had tried to undermine would be at the debate, Bannon explained to Trump. They were Paula Jones, who said Clinton had exposed himself to her, and with whom Clinton had settled a sexual harassment suit, paying her $850,000; Juanita Broaddrick, who claimed Clinton had raped her; Kathleen Willey, who alleged that Clinton sexually assaulted her in the White House; and Kathy Shelton, who, when she was 12, alleged that Hillary had smeared her while defending her client, who allegedly had raped Shelton.

It was an Oscar list from Clinton's past, triggering memories of his steamy Arkansas and White House years.

Prior to the debate, Bannon said, they would sit the four women at a table with Trump and invite in reporters.

"That fucking media, they think they're going to come in for the end of debate prep. And we're going to let them in the room and the women will be there. And we'll just go live. Boom!"

Scorched-earth, just the way Bannon liked it.

Trump had been tweeting links to Breitbart stories about the Clinton accusers throughout the day.

"I like it," Trump said, standing and looking imperial. "I like it!"

Just before 7:30 p.m., reporters entered the room at the St. Louis Four Seasons where Trump and the women were waiting. Bannon and Kushner stood in the back of the room, grinning.

At 7:26, Trump tweeted, "Join me on #FacebookLive as I conclude my final #debate preparations"—effectively live broadcasting events as CNN picked up his feed.

The women breathed fire into the microphones.

"Actions speak louder than words," Juanita Broaddrick said. "Mr. Trump may have said some bad words, but Bill Clinton raped me, and Hillary Clinton threatened me."

The debate organizers barred the Clinton accusers from sitting in the VIP family box right in front of the stage as Bannon had planned, so they walked in last and sat in the front row of the audience.

Early on, CNN's Anderson Cooper, the debate co-host, raised the *Access Hollywood* tape, saying, "That is sexual assault. You bragged that you have sexually assaulted women. Do you understand that?"

Trump parried. "When we have a world where you have ISIS chopping off heads . . . where you have wars and horrible, horrible sights all over and you have so many bad things happening . . . yes, I am very embarrassed by it and I hate it, but it's locker-room talk and it's one of those things. I will knock the hell out of ISIS."

A short time later, Trump said, "If you look at Bill Clinton, far worse. Mine are words and his was action. . . . There's never been anybody in the history of politics in this nation who's been so abusive to women."

Then Trump announced that Kathy Shelton and Paula Jones were in the audience and said, "When Hillary . . . talks about words that I said 11 years ago, I think it's disgraceful and I think she should be ashamed of herself."

ABC's Martha Raddatz, the co-moderator, had to step in to ask the audience to hold their applause so that Hillary Clinton could speak.

Bossie, now Bannon's deputy campaign manager, was involved in the day-to-day management and hundreds of daily decisions and quickly learned who had the real authority. He would be in a meeting with Bannon, Conway and Kushner, where a decision would be made: for example, on the next three TV spots.

Bossie would pass the decision to the person running digital ads, but then see that they didn't run. "What the hell!" he said. "I came in here. I told you what to do. We had a meeting, we decided."

"Oh, no, no," he would be told. "Jared came in after you and said, 'Don't do that.'"

This was a "very important light bulb moment." If Kushner didn't fully buy in, things wouldn't get done. So after decision meetings, Bossie approached Kushner to make sure he understood what Jared wanted. Kushner, without the title, was running the campaign, especially on money matters. He knew that his father-in-law considered it all his money and Jared had to sign off on everything.

Kushner scoffed at Bannon's suggestion that Trump put $50 million of his own money into his presidential campaign. "He will never write a $50 million check," Kushner told Bannon in August.

"Dude," Bannon said, "we're going to have this thing in a dead heat." They would soon be tied with Hillary. "We need to finally go up on TV with something." They needed to contribute to the ground game. "We're going to need at least $50 million. He's going to have to write it."

Under election rules and law, the candidate can make unlimited personal contributions to his or her own campaign.

"He'll never do it," Kushner insisted.

"It's about being president of the United States!"

"Steve, unless you can show him he's a dead lock"—a certain

winner—"I mean a dead lock, up three to five points, he'll never write that size check."

"Well, you're right," Bannon agreed.

"Maybe we can get $25 million out of him," said Kushner, adding a caveat: "He doesn't have a lot of cash."

After the final presidential debate in Las Vegas on October 19, Trump returned to New York. It was now the three-week sprint to election day.

Bannon, Kushner and Mnuchin, the former Goldman Sachs executive, presented Trump with a plan for him to give $25 million to the campaign.

"No way," Trump said. "Fuck that. I'm not doing it." Where were the famous Republican high-donor guys? "Where the fuck's the money? Where's all this money from these guys? Jared, you're supposed to be raising all this money. Not going to do it."

The next day they came up with a new proposal for $10 million and presented it to Trump on his plane. This wouldn't even be a loan, but an advance against the cash donations coming in from supporters. These were the "grundoons" or "hobbits" as Bannon playfully and derisively called them. And he had a deadline: They had to have the $10 million that day.

The supporters' donations "will keep coming in, win, lose or draw," Bannon said. "But I say you're going to win."

"You don't know that," Trump snapped. "We're three points down."

It showed how little confidence Trump had in victory, Bannon thought.

After two days of pushing for the $10 million, Trump finally told them, "Okay, fine, get off my back. We'll do $10 million."

Steve Mnuchin handed Trump two documents to sign. The first was a terms sheet outlining how he would be paid back as money came into the campaign.

"What's this?" Trump asked about the second document.

"Wiring instructions." Mnuchin knew that every Trump decision was tentative and open to relitigation. Nothing was ever over.

"What the fuck," said Trump. The wire order should be sent to someone in the Trump Organization.

Mnuchin said no, it needed to be done right then.

Trump signed both documents.

Money questions ignited Trump. When he learned that Christie, who would be the head of his transition team, was raising money for the operation, he summoned him and Bannon to Trump Tower.

"Where the fuck is the money?" Trump asked Christie. "I need money for my campaign. I'm putting money in my campaign, and you're fucking stealing from me." He saw it all as his.

Christie defended his efforts. This was for the required transition organization in case Trump won.

Trump said that Mitt Romney had spent too much time on transition meetings as the nominee in 2012, and not enough time on campaign events. "That's why he lost. You're jinxing me," he told Christie. "I don't want a transition. I'm shutting down the transition. I told you from day one it was just an honorary title. You're jinxing me. I'm not going to spend a second on it."

"Whoa," Bannon interjected. A transition might make sense.

"It's jinxing me," Trump said. "I can't have one."

"Okay, let's do this," Bannon said. "I'll shut the whole thing down. What do you think *Morning Joe*'s going to say tomorrow? You've got a lot of confidence you're going to be president, right?"

Trump agreed, finally and reluctantly, to a slimmed-down, skeletal version of the transition. Christie would cease fundraising.

"He can have his transition," Trump said, "but I don't want anything to do with it."

Two weeks before the election, October 25, 2016, I was in Fort Worth, Texas, giving a speech to about 400 executives from a firm called KEY2ACT that provides construction and field service management software. My topic was "The Age of the American Presidency. What Will 2016 Bring?" The group was mostly white and was from all over the country.

I asked for a show of hands. How many expected to vote for Hillary? As best I could tell there were only about 10. How many expected to vote for Trump? Half the room raised their hands—approximately 200. Wow, I thought, that seemed like a lot of Trump voters.

After the speech, the CEO of the firm approached. "I need to sit down," he said, taking a chair near where I was standing. He was breathing heavily. "I'm flabbergasted. I have worked with these people every day for more than a year. I know them. I know their families. If you had told me that 200 plan to vote for Trump, I would have told you that is impossible." He said he would have expected more or less an even split. But 200, he was astonished. He offered no explanation, and I certainly did not have one.

Ten days before the election, Trump flew to North Carolina, a must-win state. He was down several points in most national polls. The NBC/*Wall Street Journal* poll had him down six points.

Bannon spoke with Congressman Mark Meadows, who represented the 11th District. Meadows was a Tea Party favorite and the chairman of the powerful Freedom Caucus of about 30 conservative and libertarian Republicans. He was a big Trump supporter. Over the summer he had led rally attendees in their favorite anti-Clinton chant, "Lock her up."

Of all the battleground states, Bannon told Meadows, "This is the one that worries me the most." The campaign seemed not to be clicking.

Meadows disagreed. "The evangelicals are out. They're ringing doorbells. I'm telling you, you do not need to come back to North Carolina. We've got this." Meadows's wife and other conservative women had chartered a bus after the *Access Hollywood* tape and traveled across the state urging women to vote for Trump. Everything was holding and getting better, Meadows said.

Meadows had big plans to oust Speaker Paul Ryan. He handed Bannon a folder. "Read this," he said. "Some 24 hours after Trump wins, we call the question on Ryan and he's finished. We take over the House of Representatives. And then we have a real revolution."

Bannon was still worried, though he saw some positives in the Trump-Pence strategy. They were using Pence well, Bannon believed, running him essentially on a circuit of states—at least 23 appearances in Pennsylvania; 25 in Ohio; 22 in North Carolina; 15 in Iowa; 13 in Florida; eight in Michigan; seven in Wisconsin. The theme was for Pence to campaign as if he were running for governor of those states, focusing on local issues and what a President Trump in Washington could do for the state. "And every now and then we'd pull him [Pence] out to Jesus-land," Bannon said.

Trump, he said, was essentially running as county supervisor in 41 large population centers.

Bannon was amazed that the Clinton campaign did not use President Obama strategically. Obama had won Iowa in 2008 and 2012 by six to 10 points. "He never goes." Clinton never went to Wisconsin in the general election. She didn't talk enough about the economy.

"When I saw her go to Arizona, I said, they've lost their fucking minds," Bannon said. "What are they doing?"

Historians will write books in the coming years trying to answer that question and related 2016 campaign matters. I was planning on writing a book on the first year or two of the next president. It seemed likely that would be Hillary Clinton, but Fort Worth gave me pause.

Two days before the election, November 6, I appeared on *Fox News Sunday* with Chris Wallace. The discussion turned to the possibility that Trump could win.

According to the transcript, I said on the show, "If Trump does win, how is that possible? What's been missed? And I think I find in travels around the country talking to groups from Texas to Florida to New York, people don't trust the polls. And they look at voting as much more personal. They don't like the idea, oh, I'm in a demographic group, so I'm going to go this way. They want to decide themselves."

Wallace asked if I thought that meant people were lying to the pollsters.

"I think that's quite possible," I said. But I didn't see any signal or have any inside information. I was far from understanding what was going on.

The day before election day, Trump made a five-state swing, including North Carolina. He was exhausted.

"If we don't win," he said at a rally in Raleigh, "I will consider this the single greatest waste . . . of time, energy and money. . . . If we don't win, all of us—honestly? We've all wasted our time."

It was an odd thing to say, seemingly a downer, but the crowd appeared to love it and took it as motivational.

One of Clinton's last rallies was at Philadelphia's Independence Hall, where tens of thousands gathered on November 7. President Obama was there. According to Clinton's book, he hugged her and whispered to her, "You've got this. I'm so proud."

About 5 p.m. on election day Trump received the latest exit polls. They were brutal. Tied in Ohio and Iowa, down nine in Pennsylvania, down seven in North Carolina.

"There's nothing else we could have done," Trump told Bannon. "We left it all on the field."

On election night, it was remarkable to watch the needle on the live forecast dial on the *New York Times* website, which started out giving Clinton an 85 percent chance of winning. But the dial began to swing swiftly toward Trump. A good sign for Trump was North Carolina. African American and Latino turnout was down. The state was called for Trump at 11:11 p.m. It was announced he had won Ohio at 10:36 p.m., Florida at 10:50 p.m. and Iowa at 12:02 a.m.

President Obama sent a message to Hillary Clinton that he was concerned that another uncertain election outcome, as had happened in the 2000 presidential election, would be bad for the country. If she was going to lose, she should concede quickly and with grace.

The AP called Wisconsin for Trump at 2:29 a.m. and declared him the winner.

"Donald, it's Hillary," Clinton began her concession phone call shortly afterward.

Trump went to speak to the crowd at the New York Hilton in Midtown Manhattan, a few blocks from Trump Tower.

"Now it's time for Americans to bind the wounds of division," he said in remarks right out of a good-government playbook. "I pledge to every citizen of our land that I will be president for all Americans.

"As I've said from the beginning, ours was not a campaign, but rather an incredible and great movement . . . comprised of Americans from all races, religions, backgrounds and beliefs.

"We must reclaim our country's destiny and dream big and bold and daring.

"We will seek common ground, not hostility; partnership, not conflict."

He thanked his family, Conway, Bannon, Alabama Republican senator Jeff Sessions ("great man"), who had given Trump an early endorsement, and General Michael Flynn, a retired Army general and national security adviser to the campaign. Flynn had forged an extraordinarily close relationship with Trump.

The president-elect dwelled on Priebus. "Reince is a superstar. But I said, 'They can't call you a superstar, Reince, unless you win.' Reince come up here." He located Priebus in the audience and summoned him to the stage.

Priebus stumbled up from the crowd.

"Say a few words," Trump said. "No, come on, say something."

"Ladies and gentlemen," Priebus said, "the next president of the United States, Donald Trump."

"Amazing guy," Trump said, and as if he fully understood what the RNC had done for him—all the money, the workers, the volunteers, the canvassing—added, "Our partnership with the RNC was so important to the success and what we've done."

He closed by saying, "It's been an amazing two-year period. And I love this country."

Bannon was convinced that Trump himself was stunned. "He has no earthly idea he's going to win," Bannon said later. "And he had done no preparation. He never thought he would lose, but he didn't think he would win. There's a difference. And you've got to remember, no preparation, no transition team."

Putin called from Russia with congratulations, as did President Xi Jinping from China. Many other world leaders called. "It's finally dawning on him," Bannon recalled, "that this is the real deal. This is a guy totally unprepared. Hillary Clinton spent her entire adult life getting ready for this moment. Trump hasn't spent a second getting ready for this moment."

After a few hours of sleep, Bannon started flipping through the transition documents. Garbage supreme, he thought. For secretary of defense they listed some big campaign donor from New Hampshire. Unbelievable. Now there were 4,000 jobs to fill. He realized they would have to at least temporarily embrace the establishment. Perhaps a better word would be fleece—pluck off some people who knew something.

"Give me the executive director of this thing," Bannon ordered, seeking some connection with whatever transition apparatus existed. "Get him in my office immediately." He didn't remember his name.

Bannon reached the director's office. Can he come in? he asked.

"It's going to be tough."

Why?

"He's in the Bahamas."

"This is the Island of Misfit Toys," Bannon said. "How the fuck are we going to put together a government? We relieve the watch in 10 weeks at noon. We've got to be up and running."

Priebus and Bannon were now going to share top staff power. They worked out an unusual arrangement. Bannon would be "chief strategist"—a new title and idea. Priebus would be White House chief of staff. The press release listed Bannon first, which Priebus agreed to in order to keep Bannon from being chief of staff, traditionally listed at the top.

CHAPTER

6

Aweek after the election President-elect Trump invited retired four-star Army General Jack Keane to Trump Tower
for an interview to become secretary of defense.

"You're my number-one guy," Trump said.

Keane, 73, a regular on Fox News and a close adviser to former
vice president Dick Cheney, declined. Financial debts from taking
care of his wife who had recently died made accepting impossible.
In an hour-long meeting, he gave Trump a tour of the world and
offered some advice.

Mr. President-elect, he said, Congress, public opinion and your
cabinet will be involved with your domestic agenda. "In national
security and foreign policy, this is really your lane. The world's problems have a way of coming to 1600 Pennsylvania Avenue whether
you want them or not.

"Mistakes on the domestic side have a correcting mechanism.
You can get a do-over. There are no do-overs" in national security.
"When we make mistakes, it has huge consequences."

He thought President Obama had been too timid in a dangerous
world.

"By our actions or lack of actions, we can actually destabilize part of the world and cause enormous problems," Keane warned.

Trump asked who he would recommend as secretary of defense.

For practical purposes, Keane said, Jim Mattis. He was the retired four-star Marine general whom Obama had sacked as central commander in the Middle East. Obama had relieved Mattis in 2013 because he was thought to be hawkish and too eager to confront Iran militarily.

"He's a good man, Mattis. Isn't he?" Trump said. He had heard of the general, whose nicknames were "Mad Dog" and "Chaos."

"Yes, sir," Keane said. "He's a good man." There are advantages to Mattis, he added. "He's very current. So if we have major problems on our hands, you've got a guy that can roll up his sleeves on day one and get after these problems. That's number one.

"Number two, he's very experienced, particularly in the most volatile neighborhood in the world, in the Middle East. And he's a very experienced combat veteran" in both Afghanistan and Iraq. "And highly regarded inside the military but also highly regarded outside.

"What's not obvious is how thoughtful he is," Keane said. "And how deliberate he is."

"What do you mean?" Trump asked.

"He thinks things through. He spends time thinking through the problem." Mattis had not married and he read books all the time. He had 7,000 books in his library. Also known as the "Warrior Monk," he had been totally devoted to the military with more than four decades of service. He was single-minded but calm. "I have a lot of respect for him," Keane said. "He's a man of courage and a man of integrity."

Back in his car, Keane punched in Mattis's number. He explained that Trump had asked him first, and he had said no. Mattis seemed to want assurances.

"You can't do this, Jack?" Mattis said.

"No, I can't," Keane said. "Jim, you can do it, can't you?"

"Yeah, Jack," Mattis replied.

"They seem to have their minds set on a military person to do it because of the challenges they're facing."

Later in November, Trump invited Mattis, 66, to Bedminster. Mattis's quiet presence was imposing.

We have to take care of ISIS, Trump emphasized. The Islamic State had grown out of the remains of al Qaeda in Iraq and expanded brutally into Syria with the ambition of establishing and ruling as a caliphate. Trump had promised to defeat ISIS in the campaign, and the threat was growing.

Mattis looked directly at Trump. "We need to change what we are doing," he said. "It can't be a war of attrition. It must be a war of annihilation."

Trump loved the concept. Perfect. He offered Mattis the job, though they agreed not to announce it right away.

Bannon considered Mattis too liberal on social policies and a globalist at heart, but the connection Trump and Mattis had made was central. Mattis was both a warrior and comforter. Bannon soon was calling him "the Secretary of Assurance" and "the moral center of gravity of the administration."

At Bedminster, Bannon arranged to make the photo shoots of candidates being interviewed look like 10 Downing Street as Trump and visitors walked through the large door.

"It'll be perfect," he told Trump. "We'll put the media across the street. And you'll meet and greet like a British prime minister."

The photograph that ran in many newspapers was Trump and Mattis in front of the door—Trump's fingers joined in the air, Mattis with his perfect Marine posture, erect, the quiet general.

As a colonel, Mattis had taken the Marines into Afghanistan after the 9/11 terrorist attacks. Navy captain, and SEAL for 17 years, Bob Harward had led the SEALs in.

"Hey, want to go together?" Mattis had asked Harward in 2001. In the dozen years that followed, Harward had major assignments under Mattis.

In the summer of 2013, now a vice admiral, Harward was sent to MacDill Air Force Base in Florida to become deputy central commander to Mattis. He checked into the BOQ, Bachelor Officer Quarters, worked a day, and went back to his room. All his belongings had been moved out. He was told everything had been moved to General Mattis's house.

Harward went over to the house. He walked into the kitchen and found General Mattis there, folding Harward's underwear.

"Sir," Harward said, "what the fuck are you doing?"

"I did my laundry," Mattis said. "I figured I'd do yours too."

Harward found Mattis the most gracious, humble officer he had ever served under. Rather than introduce Harward as "my deputy," Mattis said, "I want you to meet my co-commander."

When Harward retired and moved to the Middle East as the chief executive of Lockheed Martin in the United Arab Emirates, he kept in touch with Mattis.

Mattis worried about the effects of the Obama administration's failure to deter Iran.

But "if you know Jim Mattis," Harward said, "he's not a fan of going to war."

In Marine lore, Iran had inflicted a wound on the Corps that had never healed and had not been answered. Iran had been behind the terrorist bombing of the Marine Barracks in Beirut in 1983. The attack killed 220 Marines, one of the largest single-day death tolls in the history of the Corps. Another 21 U.S. servicemen died, bringing the toll to 241—the largest terrorist attack against the U.S. before 9/11. Mattis had been a Marine Corps officer for 11 years and was a major.

As CentCom commander from 2010 to 2013, according to one senior aide, Mattis believed that Iran "remained the greatest threat to the United States interests in the Middle East." He was concerned that the Israelis were going to strike the Iranian nuclear facilities and pull the United States into the conflict.

Mattis also believed the United States did not have enough military force in the region and did not have robust rules of engagement. He wrote a memo to President Obama through Secretary of Defense Leon Panetta seeking more authority to respond to Iranian provocations. He was worried that the Iranians might mine international waters and create an incident at sea that could escalate.

Tom Donilon, the national security adviser, answered Mattis. A memo, soon referred to as "the Donilon memo," directed that under no circumstances would Mattis take any action against Iran for mining international waters unless the mine was effectively dropped in the path of a U.S. warship and presented an imminent danger to the ship. The Donilon memo would be one of the first orders Mattis rescinded when he became secretary of defense.

Mattis continued to beat the drum on Iran. He found the war plan for Iran insufficient. It was all aviation dependent; all air power. It did not have a broad joint-force plan. The plan had five strike options—first against small Iranian boats, another against ballistic missiles, another against other weapons systems and another for an invasion.

"Strike Option Five" was the plan for destroying the Iranian nuclear program.

Mattis wrote a scathing memo to the chief of naval operations saying your Navy is completely unprepared for conflict in the Persian Gulf.

Panetta told Mattis his stance on Iran put him in real trouble with the Obama White House. Give me something to counter that perception, he asked.

"I get paid to give my best military advice," Mattis replied. "They make the policy decisions. I'm not going to change what I think to placate them. If I don't have their confidence, then I go."

And go he did. Mattis was relieved five months early, and when he left in March 2013, he shredded what he called "a big smartbook," almost a foot thick, containing all his key memos, documents, notes, issue summaries, and memory joggers. For someone who reveled in history, he didn't choose to keep any of it for others.

As part of his end-of-tour report Mattis attached a 15-page strategy for Iran because he didn't believe the Obama administration had one. Though he noted that Obama had made several statements on Iran, Mattis remarked, "Presidential speeches are not a policy."

His draft strategy focused on confronting and not tolerating Iran's destabilizing actions through Hezbollah, the Quds Force operations, and their actions in Iraq to undermine the U.S. It was designed to reestablish U.S. military credibility. The second part was a long-term engagement plan to shape Iranian public opinion.

With Mattis out the door, no one cared about his views on Iran. When he was nominated as secretary, there was a sudden run on the plan and copies could not be made fast enough. The question was, did Mattis's appointment as secretary of defense in a hawkish Trump presidency mean a likely military conflict with Iran?

At the suggestion of former secretary of state James A. Baker III and former defense secretary Robert Gates, Trump met with Rex Tillerson, 64, the CEO of Exxon for the past decade.

Trump was impressed with the native Texan's confidence. He had a big presence. Tillerson had spent 40 years at Exxon and was untainted by government experience. Here was a man who saw the world through the lens of deal making and globe-trotting, a businessman who had negotiated oil contracts worldwide, including billions with Russia. Putin had awarded Tillerson the Russian Order of Friendship in 2013.

In December, Trump thumbed his nose at the Washington political world but embraced the business establishment and named Tillerson as his secretary of state, the top cabinet post. Trump told aides that Tillerson looked the part he would play on the world stage. "A very Trumpian-inspired pick," Kellyanne Conway said on television, promising "big impact."

CHAPTER

7

J ared Kushner invited Gary Cohn, the president of Goldman Sachs, to come talk to his father-in-law on November 30 about the economy. A meeting was arranged for Cohn at Trump Tower. Cohn was a legendary risk taker at the premier investment banking firm. He had an ego and sureness to match Trump's. He was advised that Trump routinely kept meetings to 10 minutes.

In Trump's office were Bannon, Priebus, Kushner and Steve Mnuchin, also a former Goldman banker and hedge fund manager who had been Trump's chief fundraiser during the last six months of the campaign. Mnuchin had been rewarded with the cabinet post of treasury secretary though the appointment had not yet been announced.

The American economy overall is in okay shape, Cohn told Trump, but it was ready to experience a growth explosion if certain actions were taken. To achieve this, the economy needed tax reform and the removal of the shackles of overregulation.

Cohn knew this was what Trump wanted to hear. Then the New York City Democrat told the president-elect something he did not want to hear. We're a trade-based economy, he said. Free, fair and open trade was essential. Trump had campaigned against international trade deals.

Second, the United States is an immigration center to the world. "We've got to continue to have open borders," Cohn said. The employment picture was so favorable that the United States would run out of workers soon. So immigration had to continue. "We have many jobs in this country that Americans won't do."

Next, Cohn repeated what everyone was saying: Interest rates were going to go up over the foreseeable future.

I agree, Trump said. "We should just go borrow a lot of money right now, hold it, and then sell it and make money."

Cohn was astounded at Trump's lack of basic understanding. He tried to explain. If you as the federal government borrow money through issuing bonds, you are increasing the U.S. deficit.

What do you mean? Trump asked. Just run the presses—print money.

You don't get to do it that way, Cohn said. We have huge deficits and they matter. The government doesn't keep a balance sheet like that. "If you want to do something that would be smart—and you actually do control this—I would add a 50-year and a 100-year bond from the U.S. Treasury."

With interest rates going down in recent years, Treasury had brought the duration of bonds down to 10 years as much as possible. That was the right thing to do, Cohn said. With rates increasing, the insurance companies and the pensions will lend the government money for 50 years or 100 years. And you could probably do it at 3¾ percent. That would be really cheap money over the next 50 to 100 years.

"Wow!" Trump said. "That's a great idea." He turned to Mnuchin. "Can we do that?"

"Oh, sure," the designated treasury secretary said. "We can absolutely do that."

"Do you agree with him?" Trump asked.

"Yeah, I agree with him," Mnuchin said.

"You've been working for me six months," Trump said. "Why the hell have you never talked to me about this? Why's he the first person to ever tell me that?"

There was nothing in the world that was then yielding 3¾ percent risk-free, Cohn said. There would be a run on these bonds and plenty of buyers. The 50-year corporate bond was selling all over the place. Investors wanted high, risk-free yield.

Turning to the Federal Reserve, Cohn noted that the U.S. had had an effective zero interest rate for years. There was only one way to go, interest rates would go up, for two reasons. The economy was getting much stronger and higher rates would tamp down inflation.

"So if I'm running the Fed, I'm going to raise rates," he said.

Trump knew that presidents liked low rates to help the economy. He said, "Well, I'm not going to choose you to run the Fed ever."

"That's fine," Cohn said. "It's the worst job in America."

Turning to taxes, Cohn said, "The 35 percent corporate tax rate has been great for my business for the last decade. We've been inverting companies to 10 percent tax jurisdictions and they pay us enormous fees." He was speaking as a Goldman president. An inversion refers to relocating a corporation's legal home to a low-tax country such as Ireland or Bermuda in the form of a new parent company while retaining operations and management as a subsidiary in the higher-tax country.

Goldman had facilitated dozens of companies' moves abroad. The company's leaders and boards had a responsibility to shareholders to maximize profits and moving, inverting, dramatically raised earnings. Nearly all the drugmakers and insurance companies had moved.

Cohn bragged, "Where else can I take a company doing X in business that does X tomorrow and has 20 percent more earnings just by changing their corporate headquarters?"

Arguing against Goldman's self-interest, Cohn added, "We can't allow that to happen. We've got to get our corporate tax in line with the average, which is about 21, 22 percent."

Though there had been some restrictions imposed by Congress, there were ways to skirt the new laws. "We can't allow companies to just keep inverting out of the United States. It's just bad. It's wrong for business. It's wrong for jobs. I'm talking against my business. We made a ton of money."

Trump returned to printing money. "We'll just borrow," he said, enamored with the idea of heading the federal government, which had the best credit rating in the world, so they could borrow at the lowest interest rate.

Cohn didn't mention a report that had come out during the campaign which said the Trump Organization's business credit score was a 19 out of 100, below the national average by 30 points, and that it could have difficulty borrowing money.

You just can't print money, Cohn said.

"Why not? Why not?"

Congress had a debt ceiling which set a cap on how much money the federal government could borrow, and it was legally binding. It was clear that Trump did not understand the way the U.S. government debt cycle balance sheet worked.

Inflation would probably be steady. Automation was coming, Cohn said—artificial intelligence, machine learning, robotics. We'll manage the labor supply more efficiently now than we ever did in the history of mankind. So look, you're in the most precarious time in terms of job losses. We now can create labor with machines.

"If you're here eight years, you're going to deal with the automation of the automobile and truck. About 25 percent of the U.S. population makes a living driving something. Think about that."

"What are you talking about?" Trump asked.

With the self-driving, autonomous vehicle, millions of people are going to have to reenter the workforce in different jobs. That would be a big change and possible large disruption.

"I want you to come to work for me," Trump said.

"Doing what?"

Trump mentioned deputy secretary of defense.

"First of all, I don't want to be deputy secretary of anything," Cohn said.

How about director of national intelligence?

Cohn indicated no. He was not sure what the job did. He later learned it entailed overseeing the CIA and all the other intelligence agencies.

"You trade commodities," Trump said. "Why don't you think about being secretary of energy?"

No interest.

Trump tried to convince Cohn to become director of the Office of Management and Budget.

No. Cohn knew it was a horrible job.

"You know what?" Trump said at the end of what had become an hour-long meeting. "I hired the wrong guy for treasury secretary. You should be treasury secretary. You would be the best treasury secretary."

Mnuchin, right there, didn't say a thing or show any reaction.

"Come back and tell me what you want," Trump said. "You'd be great to have on the team. It'd be fantastic."

Five minutes later while Cohn was still in the building, he saw a television flash breaking news: President-elect Trump has selected Steve Mnuchin as treasury secretary.

"That's crazy," Jared said. "Mnuchin just put that out. You freaked him out so badly in the meeting."

Cohn did some homework, and spoke with other former Goldman executives who had worked in government. Robert Rubin, who had been head of the White House National Economic Council (NEC) for Clinton and later secretary of the treasury, said that if Cohn could get the director of the National Economic Council job with a pledge he would be the chief economic czar, then he should take it. Being there in the West Wing was an enormous advantage if he had an agreement with the president.

Cohn's wife, Lisa, said he should do it because he owed the country a great deal. "You're too slow, you're too fat and too old to serve your country any other way."

Cohn returned to see Trump and expressed his interest in the NEC job, as long as any economic business ran through him. It was the equivalent portfolio in economic matters to the national security adviser in foreign policy.

"Of course," Trump said, "it'll be however you want it to run. We're going to do such great things."

Priebus, who was in the meeting, worried about the on-the-spot hires. He later said to Trump, "We're going to hire the guy, a Democrat who voted for Hillary Clinton, to run our economic council? Why? Shouldn't we talk about this? I'm sure he's really smart. Shouldn't we have a conversation before we offer a job like this?"

"Oh," Trump said, "we don't need to talk about it." Besides, the job had been offered and accepted. "He's going to be great."

The day after Christmas 2016 I reached Michael Flynn, Trump's newly designated national security adviser, by telephone. He was on vacation in Florida visiting his grandchildren. Flynn, a controversial retired three-star general and intelligence specialist, had been by Trump's side during the campaign as foreign policy adviser. At the Republican National Convention, he enthusiastically led the crowds in "Lock Her Up" chants about Hillary Clinton. He later apologized.

Obama had removed Flynn from head of the Defense Intelligence Agency in 2014 for management failures. And after the campaign Trump had ignored advice from Obama not to take Flynn as his national security adviser.

I called Flynn to get his take on Russia. Several intelligence and Pentagon officials had told me that Russia had moved in recent years to modernize and improve their nuclear capability with a new Submarine Launched Ballistic Missile and two new ICBMs.

"Yes, exactly," Flynn said on the record. Under Putin's direction in the last seven or eight years, he said, Russia had not "outmatched the United States but had outsmarted us."

He said he had begun talking to Trump about the Russian buildup 18 months before in 2015 when they had first met. He said that they agreed that the United States had given up too much of its capability, training, readiness and modernization.

Putin, he said, had "in a systematic way" upgraded not only his nuclear forces but his tactical, conventional and Special Forces. "If Russia became an adversary and we went toe-to-toe with them, we'd face the reality of Putin using innovation, technology and sheer effort."

Flynn then spoke openly about the possibility the United States might have to begin testing nuclear weapons. The last U.S. test had been in 1992. "We are going to have to decide if we test again," he said. The computer tests might not be sufficient and it was important to see if the weapons worked.

"My counsel to the boss, I said we are going to have to devote time, energy and resources to this." He said Trump's plan was to talk and act tough—send "a shot across the bow" of Putin. He added, "We will be leaning on the Reagan playbook." Be aggressive and then negotiate. "We have to make it clear at the same time that we'll deal with Russia. You can't just have one view of Russia."

Flynn was being widely criticized for going to Russia to speak for $33,750 from the Russian state–owned television network in 2015. He said it was an opportunity and he got to meet Putin. "Anyone would go," he said.

Flynn did a question-and-answer session in Moscow. He made a standard plea for better U.S. relations to defeat ISIS, the importance of defining the enemy, and not trying just to contain ISIS as Obama had done. Overall on foreign policy Flynn told me, "The president-elect is taking on this plate of shit throughout the world. The world is a mess. There's lots of cleaning up to do."

After the election, President Obama directed his intelligence chiefs to produce a definitive, highly classified report on Russian election interference, with all the sources and details. It would be briefed to the Gang of Eight in Congress and to President-elect Trump.

An unclassified, scaled-back version with the same conclusions, but without identifying the sources, would be made public before Obama left office on January 20.

Director of National Intelligence James Clapper, CIA Director John Brennan, FBI Director James Comey and National Security Agency Director Mike Rogers met to work on talking points for the briefing to Trump. They knew he would see the report as challenging his win, casting doubt on the legitimacy of his election. They agreed they would have to speak with one voice.

"This is our story and we're sticking to it," Clapper said, encouraging solidarity. Clapper would be the main briefer. It was essential they speak with confidence. Clearly the briefing was going to stir the beast.

Earlier, in December, Brennan had called Clapper. He had received a copy of a 35-page dossier, a series of reports from former British MI6 senior officer Christopher Steele that detailed alleged efforts by Russia to interfere with and influence the presidential election—to cause chaos, damage Hillary Clinton and help Trump. The dossier also contained salacious claims about Trump, Russian prostitutes and "golden showers."

"You should read this," Brennan told Clapper. The FBI already had a top secret counterintelligence investigation under way to see if there was any collusion between the Trump campaign and Russia. "This will add substantiation to what we are doing." It was not proof, but it seemed to be on the same trail.

Clapper consulted with the FBI. How should we handle it with Trump?

The FBI was familiar with the document. Steele had shared portions of the dossier with them, and on December 9 Senator John McCain had shared a copy with FBI director Comey.

Andrew McCabe, the FBI deputy, was concerned. He thought if they failed to tell President-elect Trump about the dossier when they briefed him about the intelligence community report on Russia, it would make the FBI look as if they were back in the old days of J. Edgar Hoover—as if to say, we have dirt on people, and we're keeping it to ourselves. Comey agreed. The Hoover legacy still cast a shadow over the bureau.

Clapper wanted to make sure they developed a consistent trade-craft model as they merged their intelligence into one report. The FBI and CIA have different standards.

The FBI conducts criminal investigations in addition to gathering intelligence. The bureau tends to be more rigorous in their sourcing and verification. What began as a pure counterintelligence investigation might morph into a criminal investigation, with intelligence becoming evidence that must stand up in court.

The CIA's mission is to gather intelligence and disseminate it to the White House and the rest of the federal government. It does not have to be as solid because normally it would not be used in a criminal trial.

Just as the FBI was haunted by Hoover, the CIA had its own ghost. In the run-up to the 2003 invasion of Iraq, the CIA made a huge mistake. In part as a result of lies told by a key source—amazingly code-named "Curveball"—who claimed he had worked in a mobile chemical weapons lab in Iraq, the CIA had concluded that Iraq had weapons of mass destruction (WMD). The case had been a "slam dunk," according to a presentation CIA director George Tenet made to President George W. Bush. The alleged presence of WMD was the key justification for the Iraq invasion. No WMD were found, an acute embarrassment for the president and the CIA.

Clapper knew that mistake hung over much of what the CIA did and analyzed. One agency procedure was to polygraph sources as often as possible. While passing a lie detector test would never be considered complete proof, passing was a good barometer of truthfulness.

The sources that Steele used for his dossier had not been polygraphed, which made their information uncorroborated, and potentially suspect. But Brennan said the information was in line with their own sources, in which he had great confidence.

The dossier was in circulation among journalists, and Steele had given confidential off-the-record interviews to reporters. It had not yet been published.

On the second page it said: "According to Source D, where s/he had been present, TRUMP's (perverted) conduct in Moscow included hiring the presidential suite of the Ritz Carlton Hotel, where he knew President and Mrs OBAMA (whom he hated) had stayed on one of their official trips to Russia, and defiling the bed where they had slept by employing a number of prostitutes to perform a 'golden showers' (urination) show in front of him. The hotel was known to be under FSB control with microphones and concealed cameras in all the main rooms to record anything they wanted to."

This was designed to obtain "'kompromat' (compromising material) on him," according to the dossier.

It was a spectacular allegation. There was no available indication who Source D might be.

Since the FBI had the dossier, Comey said, he ought to present it to Trump after their core presentation of the intelligence community assessment. It would be an annex, virtually a footnote.

The 35 pages were reduced to a one-and-three-quarter-page summary that focused on the allegation of coordination between the Russians and the campaign.

Trump's response to the growing chorus of news reports saying that the intelligence services had concluded Russia had interfered with the election was belligerence.

On December 9, Trump said those sounding alarm in the intelligence community were "the same people that said Saddam Hussein had weapons of mass destruction." He later told Fox News, "They have no idea if it's Russia or China or somebody sitting in a bed some place." He tweeted, "Unless you catch 'hackers' in the act, it is very hard to determine who was doing the hacking. Why wasn't this brought up before the election?"

On January 5, the Senate Armed Services Committee held a hearing on Russian hacking. Clapper, who was to brief Trump the next day, testified. Angry at the criticism Trump was leveling at the intelligence community, he stated, "There's a difference between skepticism and disparagement. Public trust and confidence in the intelligence community is crucial. And I've received many expressions of concern from foreign counterparts about . . . the disparagement of the U.S. intelligence community."

The next day, Kellyanne Conway said on CBS This Morning, "Why would Russia want Donald Trump to win the presidency here? Donald Trump has promised to modernize our nuclear capability."

In a telephone interview with The New York Times, Trump said, "This is a political witch hunt."

Hope Hicks, 28, the public relations specialist who had been Trump's press secretary during the campaign, was situated in a small 14th floor conference room in Trump Tower during the transition in early January 2017. She had two qualities important to Trump—loyalty and good looks. She had modeled as a teenager and now, with perfectly made-up eyes and long brown hair swept back on one side, she had the polished and glamorous look Trump liked. She also had genuine public relations skills.

Trump had asked her what job she wanted in the White House. Anxious to avoid the daily hand-to-hand combat with the press, she had picked strategic communications director so she could manage his media opportunities, which were, of course, now endless. She'd been the gatekeeper to his interviews. Everyone wanted Trump and she felt that he had lost some of his leverage with the media by being overexposed during the campaign. Exploiting those opportunities would now require careful calibration. As well as anyone, she knew that might be impossible with the president-elect.

Hicks was convinced the media had "oppositional defiance syndrome," which is a term from clinical psychology most often applied to rebellious children. "Oppositional defiance syndrome" is characterized by excessive anger against authority, vindictiveness and temper tantrums. As far as she was concerned, that described the press.

Hicks was already working on a response to the reports of Russian meddling in the election. The excessive news reporting on what she called the "alleged hacking by Russia" only made the United States look weak and Russia more influential than she thought possible.

On January 6, the intelligence chiefs came to Trump Tower. Comey met Trump for the first time. In his book, Comey offers a description, perhaps to demonstrate his keen eye: "His suit jacket was open and his tie too long, as usual. His face appeared slightly orange, with bright white half-moons under his eyes where I assumed he placed small tanning goggles, and impressively coiffed, bright blond hair, which upon close inspection looked to be all his. I remember wondering how long it must have taken him in the morning to get that done. As he extended his hand, I made a mental note to check its size. It was smaller than mine, but did not seem unusually so."

In the Trump Tower briefing, Clapper summarized the Key Judgments, the heart of any intelligence assessment:

- Russia has had a long-standing desire "to undermine the US-led liberal democratic order" but in the 2016 presidential election there was "a significant escalation in directness, level of activity and scope of effort."
- Putin "ordered an influence campaign in 2016 aimed at the US presidential election . . . to undermine public faith in the US democratic process, denigrate Secretary Clinton and harm her electability and potential presidency. We further assess Putin and the Russian Government developed a clear preference for President-elect Trump."
- "When it appeared to Moscow that Secretary Clinton was likely to win the election, the Russian influence campaign began to focus more on undermining her future presidency."

It was a mild formulation. Trump was a "clear preference" and the effort was aimed very much at "discrediting" and "undermining" Clinton. There was no suggestion that Trump or his associates had colluded or coordinated with the Russian effort.

All the sources fit together and told a consistent story from different vantages in the Kremlin, Clapper said. These human sources had been so-called "legacy sources"—they had been right in their intelligence and assessments over the years, and at least one source had provided reliable information going back a generation.

What has not been previously reported: One source was in such jeopardy that the CIA wanted to exfiltrate that person from Russia to safety abroad or in the United States. The source refused to leave, apparently out of fear of repercussions against the person's family if the source suddenly left Russia or disappeared.

Clapper did not give the sources' names to Trump, though he could have asked for them.

"I don't believe in human sources," Trump replied. "These are people who have sold their souls and sold out their country." He wasn't buying. "I don't trust human intelligence and these spies."

This remark caused Brennan, whose CIA relied almost entirely on human sources, later to remark, "I guess I won't tell the employees about that."

This has also not been previously reported: The CIA believed they had at least six human sources supporting this finding. One person with access to the full top secret report later told me he believed that only two were solid.

Trump asked if there was anything more.

"Well, yes, there is some additional sensitive material," Clapper said.

Do you want us to stay or do this alone? Priebus asked Trump.

Comey suggested, "I was thinking the two of us."

"Just the two of us," Trump agreed.

Though he could play the tough G-man, Comey somewhat soft-pedaled the summary he had. He explained that there was a dossier with allegations. He was passing it on. It was out there; he didn't want the president-elect to be blindsided because it was in wide circulation, and certainly it, or parts of it, would surface in the media.

The dossier alleged that Trump had been with prostitutes in a Moscow hotel in 2013 and the Russians had filmed it. Comey did not mention the allegation in the dossier that Trump had prostitutes urinate on each other on the bed President Obama and Michelle Obama had once used.

Comey later wrote, "I figured that single detail was not necessary to put him on notice about the material. This whole thing was weird enough. As I spoke, I felt a strange out-of-body experience, as if I were watching myself speak to the new president about prostitutes in Russia."

Trump denied the allegations. Did he seem like a guy who needed prostitutes?

In *A Higher Loyalty*, Comey wrote, "The FBI was not currently investigating him. This was literally true. We did not have a counterintelligence case file open on him. We really didn't care if he had cavorted with hookers in Moscow, so long as the Russians weren't trying to coerce him in some way."

This is what Comey wrote about how he conveyed this message to Trump at the end of their private meeting: "As he began to grow more defensive and the conversation teetered toward disaster, on instinct, I pulled the tool from my bag: 'We are not investigating you, sir.' That seemed to quiet him."

The private meeting lasted five minutes.

Trump later told his attorney that he felt shaken down by Comey with the presentation about the alleged prostitutes in Moscow. "I've got enough problems with Melania and girlfriends and all that. I don't need any more. I can't have Melania hearing about that."

After the briefing Trump released a statement calling the briefing "constructive," but he was clearly unswayed by the impact. Attempts by "Russia, China, other countries" to interfere had had "absolutely no effect on the outcome of the election including the fact that there was no tampering whatsoever with voting machines."

Four days later, January 10, BuzzFeed published the 35-page dossier online.

This was when I read the document. On page 27, it said, "Two knowledgeable St. Petersburg sources claim Republican candidate TRUMP has paid bribes and engaged in sexual activities there but key witnesses silenced and evidence hard to obtain."

It added, "all direct witnesses to this recently had been 'silenced' i.e. bribed or coerced to disappear."

It made clear there was apparently no path to seek verification.

I was surprised, not at the allegations, which might be true, but that the intelligence chiefs, particularly the FBI director, would present any of this to Trump.

The core of their presentation on January 6 had been the intelligence community's assessment on Russian election interference. It was a report they felt was one of the most important, well-documented, convincing assessments by the intelligence community in recent times. In *Facts and Fears*, Clapper called it "a landmark product—among the most important ever produced by U.S. intelligence." The CIA, NSA, FBI and the other intelligence agencies had invested heavily in the intelligence gathering. They had also taken a risk by putting so much sensitive information in one report that could leak or be described.

And then, almost as an afterthought, Comey had introduced the dossier as if to say, by the way, here is this scurrilous, unverified, unsupported footnote with some of the ugliest allegations against you.

They wanted the formal assessment to be believed by the president-elect. Why pollute it with the dossier summary? They knew enough about Trump to know it would rile him up. It likely would have riled anyone up. Why would they accompany some of their most serious work with this unverified dossier?

The material in the dossier is the sort of stuff that a reporter or the FBI might more than reasonably follow up on, try to track down its origins, even locate some of the sources and see if any confirmation can be found. Clearly, the FBI had an obligation to make this effort—as they later would.

But including it, even in scaled-down form, in one of the most important briefings the intelligence chiefs might ever present to a president-elect made little sense to me. It would be as if I had reported and written one of the most serious, complex stories for *The Washington Post* that I had ever done—and then provided an appendix of unverified allegations. Oh, by the way, here is a to-do list for further reporting and we're publishing it.

In *A Higher Loyalty*, published a year later, Comey writes at length about his misgivings about how he was going to handle the dossier before he met with Trump.

"I was staying on as FBI director," he wrote. "We knew the information, and the man had to be told. It made complete sense for me to do it. The plan was sensible, if the word applies in the context of talking with a new president about prostitutes in Moscow."

Perhaps it may turn out to all be true, but imagine being told that by the FBI director.

As Comey continued, "Still, the plan left me deeply uncomfortable. . . . There was a real chance that Donald Trump, politician and hardball deal-maker, would assume I was dangling the prostitute thing over him to jam him, to gain leverage. He might well assume I was pulling a J. Edgar Hoover, because that's what Hoover would do in my shoes. An eyebrow raise didn't quite do this situation justice; it was really going to suck."

On January 15, five days before the inauguration, I appeared on *Fox News Sunday*. I said, "I've lived in this world for 45 years where you get things and people make allegations. That is a garbage document. It never should have been presented as part of an intelligence briefing. Trump's right to be upset about that." The intelligence officials, "who are terrific and have done great work, made a mistake here, and when people make mistakes they should apologize." I said the normal route for such information, as in past administrations, was passing it to the incoming White House counsel. Let the new president's lawyer handle the hot potato.

Later that afternoon Trump tweeted: "Thank you to Bob Woodward who said, 'That is a garbage document . . . it never should have been presented . . . Trump's right to be upset (angry) . . .'"

I was not delighted to appear to have taken sides, but I felt strongly that such a document, even in an abbreviated form, really was "garbage" and should have been handled differently.

The episode played a big role in launching Trump's war with the intelligence world, especially the FBI and Comey.

Five days after taking the oath of office, January 25, President Trump invited his top advisers and his national security team to the White House for dinner. Mattis, the new secretary of defense, presented Trump with plans for a SEAL Team Six operation against a senior al Qaeda collaborator in Yemen.

He described how several dozen commandos would attack, hoping to capture intelligence, cell phones and laptop computers, and kill the collaborator, one of the few al Qaeda leaders still alive.

It would be the first operation in Yemen in two years. It had been considered and delayed by President Obama. The military wanted a moonless night for the attacks, and one was coming up.

Bannon had questions about the larger problems in Yemen. The former Navy lieutenant commander wondered why the arms to the rebel Houthis could not be cut off and stopped by sea. Iran was their only ally.

"You control the air," Bannon said. "You've got the U.S. Navy, and you control the sea. How tough is it?"

"It's a big coastline," Mattis replied.

"Steve," Trump said impatiently, "these guys, this is what they do. Let them do it." In other words, shut up.

Trump signed the order the next day and the raid was carried out before dawn on Sunday, January 29. A lot went wrong. During a 50-minute firefight one SEAL was killed, three wounded. Civilians, including children, were killed. A $75 million Marine MV-22 Osprey made a hard landing, disabling the plane. It had to be destroyed to keep it from falling into the hands of the enemy.

Chief Special Warfare Operator William "Ryan" Owens, 36, from Peoria, Illinois, was the first combat casualty in Trump's presidency. Trump decided to go to Dover, Delaware, to observe the ceremony for the arrival of his body. Ivanka accompanied him.

When they arrived at Dover, the commander pulled the president aside. According to what Trump told his senior staff later, the commander said: I want to prepare you for this, Mr. President. When you walk in, the family is going to come up to you. It will be an experience like no other. You're the commander in chief. The respect they show to you, and their grieving, will be incredible. You'll be there to comfort them. When the plane rolls up, when the flag-draped casket comes down, some of the family are going to lose it and they will lose it very badly. On the other hand, be prepared to have some people say something inappropriate, even harsh.

No one said anything harsh, but there was a definite coldness that the president remembered.

"That's a hard one," he said afterward. He was clearly rattled. He let it be known he would make no more trips to Dover.

Owens's father, Bill Owens, was at Dover but he and his wife did not want to meet with Trump.

"I'm sorry," Owens told the chaplain. I don't want to meet the president. I don't want to make a scene about it, but my conscience won't let me talk to him.

He later also said, "For two years prior, there were no boots on the ground in Yemen—everything was missiles and drones—because there was not a target worth one American life. Now, all of a sudden we had to make this grand display."

Instead of striking out as Trump had done against the Khans, the Gold Star parents who had appeared at the Democratic convention in 2016, Trump expressed sympathy for Owens's father.

"I can understand people saying that," Trump said later. "I'd feel—you know, what's worse? There's nothing worse."

Several former Obama administration officials said the operation had been planned months earlier but they distanced Obama from it, saying he had never approved it.

In an interview on Fox the morning of his first joint address to Congress, Trump said the Yemen raid was something his "very respected" generals "were looking at for a long time doing."

"And they lost Ryan," he said.

Trump invited Carryn Owens, Ryan's widow and mother of three young children, to sit in the balcony at the joint address to Congress on February 28. She sat next to Ivanka.

To the congressional audience and 47 million television viewers, the president said, "We are blessed to be joined tonight by Carryn Owens. Ryan died as he lived, a warrior and a hero—battling against terrorism and securing our nation."

Because the operation was being criticized, Trump added, "I just spoke to General Mattis, who reconfirmed that, and I quote, 'Ryan was a part of a highly successful raid that generated large amounts of vital intelligence that will lead to many more victories in the future against our enemies.' Ryan's legacy is etched into eternity."

The president turned to Owens's widow in the balcony and said "Thank you."

Thunderous applause broke out.

At first Carryn Owens fought back tears, exhaled and mouthed, "I love you, baby." The applause continued and tears began to stream down her face. She stood, joined her hands in apparent prayer, looked up and mouthed, "I love you."

Trump said, "For as the Bible teaches us, there is no greater act of love than to lay down one's life for one's friends. Ryan laid down his life for his friends, for his country, and for our freedom—we will never forget him."

The applause and standing ovation from the Congress and the audience lasted nearly two minutes.

"Ryan is looking down right now," Trump said. "You know that. And he is very happy because I think he just broke a record."

Carryn Owens smiled and clapped. The president greeted and embraced her in the hallway following the speech.

Afterward, when Trump had phone calls with the families of others from the military who had been killed, the White House staff noticed how hard and tough it seemed for him.

"He's not that guy," Bannon said. "He's never really been around the military. He's never been around military family. Never been around death." The deaths of "parents of small kids" struck him particularly hard. "That had a big impact on him, and it's seen throughout everything."

A staffer who sat in on several calls that Trump made to Gold Star families was struck with how much time and emotional energy Trump devoted to them. He had a copy of material from the deceased service member's personnel file.

"I'm looking at his picture—such a beautiful boy," Trump said in one call to family members. Where did he grow up? Where did he go to school? Why did he join the service?

"I've got the record here," Trump said. "There are reports here that say how much he was loved. He was a great leader."

Some in the Oval Office had copies of the service records. None of what Trump cited was there. He was just making it up. He knew what the families wanted to hear.

Whether the international order would have a footing in the new
Trump administration was tested in the first month.

During the campaign, Trump disparaged the North Atlantic
Treaty Organization (NATO), the 68-year-old alliance with Europe.
NATO is often considered the most successful effort to counter the
Soviet Union during the Cold War, and a foundation of Western
unity. The members pledged collective defense, meaning an attack
on one would be considered an attack against all.

Trump had argued that NATO might be obsolete. Much of his
criticism had to do with money. NATO's goal was for each member
nation eventually to spend 2 percent of its GDP on defense. The
United States spent 3.5 percent of its GDP, while Germany spent
only 1.2 percent.

Secretary of Defense Mattis had a speech coming up in Munich,
Germany, in mid-February, and the administration's NATO policy
needed to be settled by then. Was Trump in or out?

As a private citizen Mattis had blasted Trump's anti-NATO ideas
as "kooky." Much of the foreign policy establishment as well as European allies had been unnerved by Trump's comments.

Priebus arranged a 6:30 p.m. dinner for Wednesday, February 8,
in the Red Room of the residence so Trump could hear arguments
from Mattis, Chairman of the Joint Chiefs General Joseph Dunford
and several others. He also invited a pillar of the Washington Republican establishment, C. Boyden Gray. Gray, 73, had most recently
been the U.S. ambassador to the European Union for two years in
the administration of President George W. Bush. He had been legal
consigliere to George H. W. Bush during the eight years Bush had
been vice president and four years as president.

As they sat down to dinner, Trump wanted to gossip about the
news of the day. Senator John McCain, displaying his maverick credentials, had publicly criticized the U.S. military raid in Yemen.

Trump lashed out, suggesting that McCain had taken the coward's way out of Vietnam as a prisoner of war. He said that as a Navy pilot during the Vietnam War McCain, whose father was Admiral John McCain, the Pacific commander, had been offered and taken early release, leaving other POWs behind.

"No, Mr. President," Mattis said quickly, "I think you've got it reversed." McCain had turned down early release and been brutally tortured and held five years in the Hanoi Hilton.

"Oh, okay," Trump said.

Gray, who had served five years in the Marine Corps, was struck that the secretary corrected the president directly, and that Trump, known to bristle when challenged, would be so accepting.

It was not until the dessert course that Priebus finally said, "We've really got to deal with the NATO issue."

Retired Lieutenant General Keith Kellogg, the National Security Council chief of staff, was representing the NSC. A combat veteran of Vietnam with Silver and Bronze Stars and the first Gulf War, Kellogg launched into a critique. Echoing some of Trump's negative language, he said NATO was "obsolete" and set up after World War II when the United States was richer and facing an aggressive Soviet Union. Now, the cost to the United States was unfair and out of proportion with European allies. The United States was being used.

"Those wouldn't be my views, Mr. President," said General Joseph Dunford.

"Oh, really?" Trump interjected. "What would your views be?"

Dunford, the top military man, offered a spirited defense. It's an alliance that shouldn't be disbanded, and it would be hard to put it back together, he said. With Eastern European nations such as Poland feeling threatened by Putin's invasions in Crimea and eastern Ukraine, it was important to maintain solidarity and unity. "It's terribly important to keep Europe united politically, strategically and economically." He agreed that the member nations should meet their commitment to 2 percent of their annual GDP.

I think the Germans will make good on their commitment to pay 2 percent of GDP, and they are the most important, Mattis added.

Jared Kushner jumped in. "As a percentage of our own defense budget the shortfall is really small," he said. "Pennies on the dollar."

Priebus cautioned that the 2 percent was not an obligation but a recent agreement that all the NATO countries would strive to get there by 2024. This was not a payment to NATO but a commitment to defense spending.

"But it is a political problem when your allies don't pay their fair share," Trump said. He would make his case on fairness, and he kept returning to that theme. Why should the United States pay for the European defense?

Priebus realized that the president didn't care that it was a goal, not an obligation. Trump cared that he could sell it and try to win over public opinion.

"I don't care if it's a goal or not," Trump finally said. "It's what they should do."

Boyden Gray pointed out that Europe had lots of economic problems. "Not that we don't, but theirs are worse." The countries need to grow their economies more. "Part of the reason they don't pay is because they're not growing fast enough."

"Are you saying they can't pay?" Trump asked.

"No," Gray said. But the United States should help Europe with their anemic economic growth rate. European business culture largely avoided taking risks.

"Which is going to be the next country to drop out?" Trump asked. Under the Brexit referendum, approved by British voters, Great Britain had to leave the European Union.

"I don't think there will be another country to drop out," Gray replied.

Trump said he agreed.

"If you didn't have NATO, you would have to invent it," Mattis said. "There's no way Russia could win a war if they took on NATO."

By the end of the dinner, Trump seemed to be persuaded. "You can have your NATO," he told Mattis. The administration would support the alliance, "but you become the rent collector."

Mattis laughed. And then he nodded.

In his speech in Munich on February 15, Secretary Mattis found middle ground. "America will meet its responsibilities," he said, but would "moderate" its commitment if the other NATO countries did not meet theirs. Nonetheless he said the alliance was a "fundamental bedrock" of U.S. policy.

At a news conference with the NATO secretary general two months later, Trump said, "I said it was obsolete. It is no longer obsolete."

When Trump met the European leaders in May in Brussels, he castigated NATO countries for "chronic underpayments." He said that "23 of the 28 member nations are still not paying what they should be paying and what they're supposed to be paying for their defense."

He made it clear that he was addressing the United States domestic audience. "This is not fair to the people and taxpayers of the United States."

CHAPTER

10

W hat the hell! Priebus thought as he scanned a February 9 story in *The Washington Post* reporting that National Security Adviser Michael Flynn had discussed sanctions against Russia with the Russian ambassador before Trump was in office.

In one of his last acts as president, Obama had imposed sanctions on Russia on December 29 in retaliation for Russian meddling in the election. He expelled 35 suspected Russian spies and ordered the closure of two Russian-owned compounds in Maryland and New York believed to be involved in espionage.

Priebus had asked Flynn many times about any discussions. Flynn had firmly denied discussing the sanctions with Ambassador Sergey Kislyak, the convivial man-about-town.

Two weeks earlier, on January 26, Deputy Attorney General Sally Yates had come to the White House. She told White House Counsel Donald McGahn that intercepts showed that Flynn had not been truthful about contacts with Russians and was worried that Flynn could be a blackmail target.

Flynn had denied discussing the sanctions at least 10 times, Priebus calculated.

The *Post* story, carrying the bylines of three of the paper's experienced intelligence and national security reporters, stated "Nine current and former officials" were sources for their categorical assertion. Flynn had been interviewed by the reporters and had denied the allegations with a categorical "no" twice before backing away with a more fuzzy response. His spokesman was quoted: Flynn "couldn't be certain that the topic never came up."

Priebus tracked down White House Counsel McGahn, 48, who was an expert on campaign finance law and had served five years as a Republican-appointed member of the Federal Election Commission. Priebus asked him if they could get the transcripts of the conversations that Flynn had with the Russian ambassador.

Yes, McGahn said, of course. Soon he had the highly classified transcripts of three communications between Flynn and Kislyak that the FBI had intercepted during the routine monitoring of the Russian ambassador.

McGahn and Priebus were joined by Vice President Pence in the Situation Room to review the transcripts. Pence had backed Flynn's denial publicly. According to a six-page internal White House Counsel's Office memo, Flynn said if he and Kislyak discussed sanctions, "It was only because Kislyak brought it up. From the transcripts, Flynn had brought up the issue. McGahn and Priebus agree that Flynn has to be let go."

In all three transcripts, Flynn and the ambassador discussed the sanctions. In the last call, initiated by Kislyak, the ambassador thanked Flynn for his advice on the sanctions, and said the Russians would follow it.

That nailed the story and it explained Putin's curiously passive response to the sanctions. Normally the Russian president would be expected to retaliate, expelling some Americans from Russia. But the day after Obama announced the sanctions, Putin announced he would not.

President-elect Trump praised Putin, tweeting, "Great move on delay (by V. Putin)-I always knew he was very smart!"

The sequence suggested that Trump might have known of Flynn's role. But it was unclear what Flynn had said to the president about his conversations with Kislyak.

Priebus told the president he would have to let Flynn go. Flynn's security clearance might be pulled. The embarrassment would be significant.

Flynn's resignation was announced on February 13. The chief reason offered publicly was that Flynn had lied to Vice President Pence. Trump told others in his administration that he let Flynn go because Flynn was not up to the job.

The next nine months were difficult for Flynn. He later pled guilty to one count of lying to the FBI.

Flynn told associates that he didn't think he lied to the FBI when he was interviewed four days into the administration. The FBI agents had come to talk to him about matters other than Russia and he had not believed it was a formal interview.

Why did Flynn plead guilty? A range of possible offenses were being investigated, including his failure to report income from Turkey, report overseas contacts and to register as a lobbyist prior to joining the Trump administration.

Flynn told associates that his legal bills were astronomical, as were his son's, who was also being investigated. A one-count guilty plea for lying seemed the only way out. His statement said, "I accept full responsibility for my actions," and said he now had an "agreement to cooperate." He denied that he had committed "treason," an apparent denial that he had colluded with the Russians.

On Saturday, February 25, after five weeks in office, Mattis called a noon meeting at the secretary of defense's residence at the Old Naval Observatory near the State Department. Attending were some foreign policy graybeards, retired General Anthony Zinni, several former ambassadors and some Mattis staff. Mattis had almost no furniture. They all sat around what looked like a government-issue dining room table. Mattis said he had showed up with four suitcases.

"You should see the SCIF I have," he said. The Sensitive Compartmented Information Facility for securely discussing the most sensitive, Top Secret and Special Access Programs was upstairs. "I never have to leave. I can do all the work from here."

President Trump is a good listener, Mattis said, as long as you don't hit one of his third rails—immigration and the press are the two big ones. If you hit one, he is liable to go off on a tangent and not come back for a long time. "Secretaries of Defense don't always get to choose the president they work for."

Everyone laughed.

The subject of the meeting was the counter-ISIS plan that Trump wanted immediately. Fundamentally, Mattis said, we are doing things backwards. We are trying to devise a counter-ISIS strategy without any larger, broader Middle East strategy. Ideally we'd have the Middle East strategy and the ISIS piece would plug in underneath and support it. But the president's tasking required ISIS first.

In the end the Combat ISIS strategy was a continuation of the strategy under Obama but with bombing and other authorities granted to the local commanders.

Mattis was worried about Iranian expansion. At one point he later referred to "those idiot raghead mullahs."

Early one morning in February, a team of senior intelligence officials came to Priebus's West Wing office to brief him on how to be alert to those who might seek to influence him improperly. It is a standard warning for those with the highest security clearances.

"Before we leave," said Deputy FBI director Andrew McCabe, raising his hand, "I need five minutes with you alone in your office."

What the hell is this? thought Priebus. He only recalled McCabe because he had met him several weeks earlier in the Situation Room.

Trump had raised hell about McCabe's wife, Jill, a Democrat, during the campaign. She had received $675,288 for an unsuccessful 2015 campaign for the Virginia Senate from Governor Terry McAuliffe's political action committee and the Virginia Democratic Party. McAuliffe was one of Bill and Hillary Clinton's closest personal and political friends. He had been the top fundraiser for Bill Clinton's reelection in 1996.

Trump had described the money as donations from Hillary. He had not let go of the issue, talking and tweeting about it later.

After the security briefing and everyone cleared out, McCabe shut the door to Priebus's office. This is very weird, thought Priebus, who was standing by his desk.

"You know this story in *The New York Times*?" Priebus knew it all too well. McCabe was referring to a recent *Times* story of February 14 that stated, "Phone records and intercepted calls show that members of Donald J. Trump's 2016 presidential campaign and other Trump associates had repeated contacts with senior Russian intelligence officials in the year before the elections, according to four current and former American officials."

The story was one of the first bombs to go off about alleged Trump-Russian connections after Flynn's resignation.

"It's total bullshit," McCabe said. "It's not true, and we want you to know that. It's grossly overstated."

Oh my God, thought Priebus.

"Andrew," he said to the FBI deputy, "I'm getting killed."

The story about Russia and election meddling seemed to be running 24/7 on cable news, driving Trump bananas and therefore driving Priebus bananas.

"This is crazy," Trump had told Priebus. "We've got to stop it. We need to end the story."

McCabe had just walked in with a big gift, a Valentine's Day present. I'm going to be the hero of this entire West Wing, Priebus thought.

"Can you help me?" Priebus asked. "Could this knockdown of the story be made public?"

"Call me in a couple of hours," McCabe said. "I will ask around and I'll let you know. I'll see what I can do."

Priebus practically ran to report to Trump the good news that the FBI would soon be shooting down the *Times* story.

Two hours passed and no call from McCabe. Priebus called him.

"I'm sorry, I can't," McCabe said. "There's nothing I can do about it. I tried, but if we start issuing comments on individual stories, we'll be doing statements every three days." The FBI could not become a clearinghouse for the accuracy of news stories. If the FBI tried to debunk certain stories, a failure to comment could be seen as a confirmation.

"Andrew, you're the one that came to my office to tell me this is a BS story, and now you're telling me there's nothing you can do?"

McCabe said that was his position.

"This is insanity," Priebus said. "What am I supposed to do? Just suffer, bleed out?"

"Give me a couple more hours."

Nothing happened. No call from the FBI. Priebus tried to explain to Trump, who was waiting for a recanting. It was another reason for Trump to distrust and hate the FBI, a pernicious tease that left them dangling.

About a week later on February 24 CNN reported an exclusive: "FBI Refused White House Request to Knock Down Recent Trump-Russia Story." Priebus was cast as trying to manipulate the FBI for political purposes.

The White House tried and failed to correct the story and show that McCabe had initiated the matter.

Four months later on June 8, Comey testified under oath publicly that the original *New York Times* story on the Trump campaign aides' contacts with senior Russian intelligence officials "in the main was not true."

T rump needed a new national security adviser, and he wanted to act fast. He said he was getting killed in the media and was convinced a new person would erase the Flynn debacle.

Another general, perhaps? Bannon believed the media was Trump's main concern. Everything was through the eyes of, "Does he look the part?" Everything was movies. Dunford and Mattis struck him as Marines because they were men of few words. They got to the point.

High on the list was Army Lieutenant General H. R. McMaster—5-foot-9, bald, green-eyed, barrel-chested, ramrod-straight posture—who was the rare combination of war hero and scholar. He had written *Dereliction of Duty: Lyndon Johnson, Robert McNamara, the Joint Chiefs of Staff, and the Lies That Led to Vietnam*. It was a groundbreaking work that indicted military leaders for failing to confront their civilian leaders. McMaster was considered a renegade and an outsider in the Army club, but no one doubted his bona fides.

General McMaster was going to get two hours with Trump. Bannon met with him at Mar-a-Lago and offered his usual advice: Don't lecture Trump. He doesn't like professors. He doesn't like intellectu-als. Trump was a guy who "never went to class. Never got the sylla-bus. Never took a note. Never went to a lecture. The night before the final, he comes in at midnight from the fraternity house, puts on a pot of coffee, takes your notes, memorizes as much as he can, walks in at 8 in the morning and gets a C. And that's good enough. He's going to be a billionaire."

Final advice: "Show up in your uniform."

McMaster wore a suit.

"Told you to show up in your uniform," Bannon said.

"I called around," McMaster replied, "and they said it wouldn't be appropriate because I've got my retirement papers in." If he was selected, he would retire and serve as national security adviser as a civilian.

"I got you up here because you're an active duty general," Bannon reminded him.

The meeting with Trump did not go well. McMaster talked too much and the interview was short.

Bannon, who sat in on it, later reported, "McMaster ran his fucking mouth for all of 20 minutes giving his theories of the world. A fucking Petraeus book guy." In 2007, McMaster had been part of a "Baghdad brains trust" advising General David Petraeus on the Iraq War.

After McMaster left, Trump asked, "Who was that guy? He wrote a book didn't he? It said bad things about people. I thought you told me he was in the Army."

"He is in the Army."

"He's dressed like a beer salesman," the president said.

Bannon, noted for his terrible wardrobe, agreed. He thought Mc-Master's suit looked like it cost only $200, or maybe only $100.

Next to be interviewed was John Bolton, a far-right former U.N. ambassador. He was a summa cum laude graduate from Yale who sup-ported the Iraq War and promoted regime change in Iran and North Korea. He was a regular on Fox News—he reported an income of

$567,000 in 2017, just from Fox. His answers were fine, but Trump did not like his big, bushy mustache. He didn't look the part.

Lieutenant General Robert Caslen, the superintendent of West Point, was next up.

Before he entered, Trump turned to General Kellogg, the NSC chief of staff, who was sitting in on the interviews.

"General, what do you think of this guy?"

"Bobby Caslen's the best gunfighter in the Army," Kellogg said.

Caslen, who had big ears and wore medals on his uniform up to the top of his shoulder, gave short answers, mostly "Yes, sir" or "No, sir." He was like Clint Eastwood. Trump started pitching him, telling him stories from the campaign.

Bannon thought Trump was selling this guy. He thought Caslen was in.

That night Kushner said that all the media loved McMaster—combat veteran, thinker, author.

"But Trump's got no chemistry with this guy," Bannon reminded him. The chemistry had been there with Caslen, but he was a field general with no Washington experience except a short tour on the Joint Staff in a junior position. "We'll get lit up," Bannon noted.

They agreed that McMaster and Bolton should have another round the next day, and to invite Caslen to the White House later for a one-on-one lunch.

The next day Bolton came in. He was fine, the same, but still had the mustache.

McMaster arrived in his uniform. He looked better—high and tight. There was better chemistry, though not great.

Bannon and Kushner told Bolton and McMaster to wait; there would be a decision in the next couple of days. McMaster hung around Mar-a-Lago.

"You know, we're getting killed with bad stories on the Flynn thing," Trump said. "Let's just make a decision."

"I don't think we can just make a decision," Bannon said. "Caslen and McMaster are two serving Army officers. I don't think they've run the traps on this." They had to inform their Army superiors. The Army chief of staff, General Mark Milley, said that Caslen would be the best possible pick. "They've got jobs. So there's a process."

"No, no, no," Trump said. "We're getting killed. Bad stories."

"The media loves McMaster," Jared said.

"Because he's a fucking liberal," Bannon said. "No offense, he has not been that impressive in this thing. You guys don't have great chemistry."

"Yeah, but you know," the president said. "Get him over here."

Bannon retrieved McMaster. "The president wants to talk to you. Come on over."

What do you think is going to happen? McMaster asked.

"I think the president may offer you the job."

"I've got to tell some people. I can't tell the president that I can take it. I've got to tell the Army."

"Just play it by ear," Bannon said. "We'll figure it out." That was the Trump way. Playing by ear, acting on impulse. Pure Trump.

"Do you want this job?" the president asked McMaster.

"Yes, sir."

"You got it," Trump said and shook McMaster's hand. "Get the media. Get the cameras in here." He wanted a picture with his latest general who looked out of Central Casting.

McMaster sat awkwardly on a gold brocade sofa beside the president. A large gold vase holding roses was on the table behind them.

"I just wanted to announce, we've been working all weekend very diligently, that General H. R. McMaster will become the national security adviser," Trump told reporters. "He's a man of tremendous talent and tremendous experience."

"I'm grateful to you for that opportunity," McMaster said. "I

look forward to joining the national security team and doing everything that I can to advance and protect the interests of the American
people."

McMaster's shell shock was plain on camera as he shook Trump's
hand.

"I've got to call the Army chief of staff," McMaster said to Bannon.

"Do it," Bannon said. "But you've already taken the job."

Trump's choice played well. The media saw McMaster was an
adult. There would be no more crazies. The president basked in the
positive stories.

CHAPTER

12

McMaster knew the biggest national security challenge would be North Korea. It had been on the most difficult list for years.

Six months earlier, on September 9, 2016, President Obama had received unsettling news as he entered the final months of his eight years. North Korea had detonated a nuclear weapon in an underground test, the fifth in a decade, and the largest.

Seismic monitors had instantly revealed that the vibrations recorded were not caused by an earthquake. The 5.3 magnitude tremor had been instantaneous and had originated less than a mile within the earth, measured precisely at the Punggye-ri test site of the four previous nuclear detonations. The estimated yield was equivalent to 10 kilotons of TNT—approaching the 15 kilotons of the 1945 Hiroshima bomb.

Dispelling any doubt, North Korea's 73-year-old female version of Walter Cronkite, Ri Chun-hee, appeared on state-controlled television to announce the test. She almost always appeared for the big moments. Wearing pink, and speaking in a gleeful, soaring voice, she told viewers that the regime had built a better, bigger and more versatile bomb.

The North's nuclear weapons center said the new nuclear bomb could be mounted on a ballistic missile, a disturbing claim, although seriously doubted by U.S. intelligence.

To compound the potential North Korean threat, four days earlier the North had launched three medium-range ballistic missiles that had flown 1,000 kilometers before dropping in the Sea of Japan, making South Korea and Japan reachable targets. These tests matched an earlier single 1,000-kilometer launch the month before. Three was not a fluke.

Even with his intense desire to avoid a war, Obama decided the time had come to consider whether the North Korean nuclear threat could be eliminated in a surgical military strike. As he prepared to hand over the presidency, he knew he needed to address the North Korea mess head-on.

That successor, of course, would almost certainly be Hillary Clinton. He assured his aides in so many words that the American people would do the right thing and elect her.

From the outset President Obama had authorized several Special Access Programs (SAP), the most classified and compartmented operations conducted by the military and intelligence, to deter North Korean missiles. One program pinpointed cyber attacks on the command, control, telemetry and guidance systems before or during a North Korean missile test launch. These high-risk cyber attacks had begun in his first year as president. Their success rate was mixed.

Another highly secret operation focused on obtaining North Korean missiles. And a third enabled the United States to detect a North Korean missile launch in seven seconds. Officials have asked that I not describe the details in order to protect national security operations deemed vital to the interests to the United States.

The North Korean threat had not been diminished, and in September 2016 Obama posed a sensitive question to his National Security Council: Was it possible to launch a preemptive military strike, supported by cyber attacks, on North Korea to take out their nuclear and missile programs?

This unfinished business was particularly gnawing for Obama. His predecessors, Bill Clinton and George W. Bush, had addressed but not solved problems that had been mounting for decades. And now the United States had run out of road. The Hermit Kingdom was creating a force that could extend an arc of potential devastating nuclear destruction to the homeland.

James Clapper, Obama's director of national intelligence, had begun his career commanding a signals intelligence listening post in Thailand during the Vietnam War. Now 75 years old, bald and bearded with a wide, expressive face, he was the granddaddy of American intelligence—gruff, direct, outspoken, seasoned.

Clapper rang the bell loud and clear with Obama: The reporting showed that the new North Korean weapon systems would work in some form. But what threat did they pose? To South Korea? Japan? The United States? How immediate? Was the North just looking for a bargaining chip?

The intelligence assessment showed an increasing level of effort, strongly suggesting that Kim Jong Un was building a fighting force of nuclear weapons, or at least he wanted to make it appear that way.

Despite the public cartoon that cast him as an unstable madman, sensitive intelligence reporting showed that Kim, now age 34, was a much more effective leader of the North's nuclear weapons and missiles programs than his father, Kim Jong Il, who had ruled for 17 years from 1994 to 2011.

The elder Kim had dealt with weapons test failures by ordering the death of the responsible scientists and officials. They were shot. The younger Kim accepted failures in tests, apparently absorbing the practical lesson: Failure is inevitable on the road to success. Under Kim Jong Un, the scientists lived to learn from their mistakes, and the weapons programs improved.

Obama tasked the Pentagon and intelligence agencies with examining whether it would be possible to take out all of North Korea's nuclear weapons and related facilities. Could they effectively target all of this? They would need to update the satellite, signals and human intelligence. So much was not known or certain.

Pakistan, which had nuclear weapons since 1998, had miniaturized their nukes and put them in mines and artillery shells. Did North Korea have that capability? Current intelligence assessments could not answer definitively.

The intelligence assessment also showed that a U.S. attack could not wipe out everything the North had. There would be lost targets because they did not know about them, and partial destruction of other targets.

The greater Seoul megalopolis was home to approximately 10 million people and went right up to the 2.5-mile-wide Demilitarized Zone (DMZ) dividing North and South Korea. North Korea had thousands of artillery pieces near the DMZ in caves. In exercises the North Koreans wheeled the artillery out, practiced shooting and went back into the caves. This was called "shoot and scoot." Could a U.S. attack deal with so many weapons?

After a month of study, U.S. intelligence and the Pentagon formally reported to Obama that perhaps 85 percent of all known nuclear weapons and nuclear weapons facilities could be attacked and destroyed and that was only the identified ones. Clapper believed the projected success rate would have to be perfect. A single North Korean nuclear weapon detonated in response could mean tens of thousands of casualties in South Korea.

Any U.S. attack could also trigger the North's potentially devastating artillery, other conventional weapons and a ground army of at least 200,000 and many more volunteers.

The Pentagon reported that the only way "to locate and destroy—with complete certainty—all components of North Korea's nuclear program" was through a ground invasion. A ground invasion would trigger a North Korean response, likely with a nuclear weapon.

That was unthinkable to Obama. In his Nobel Peace Prize acceptance speech in 2009 he said, "War promises human tragedy," and "War at some level is an expression of human folly."

Frustrated and exasperated, he rejected a preemptive strike. It was folly.

Informal, backchannel diplomacy between the United States and North Korea continued. Former U.S. government officials met with current North Korean officials to keep a dialogue open. These were most often called Track 1.5 meetings. Government-to-government meetings were called Track 1. If both sides were nongovernment or former officials these meetings were called Track 2.

"We're has-beens, but they're not," in the words of one former U.S. official deeply involved in the Track 1.5 meetings. One meeting had been held recently in Kuala Lumpur, Malaysia, with the vice foreign minister of North Korea. Former U.S. negotiator Robert Gallucci said the North Koreans warned him at this meeting, "they will always be a nuclear weapons state."

A second Track 1.5 meeting with the head of North Korea's American affairs division followed the 2016 election and took place in Geneva. "The North Koreans don't take it seriously," said one former U.S. official, because they know the U.S. representatives can't propose anything new. "But they're probably better than not having" the meetings.

Trump had a history of public statements about North Korea, dating back to an October 1999 *Meet the Press* appearance. "I would negotiate like crazy," Trump said. In a 2016 campaign speech, he said, "President Obama watches helplessly as North Korea increases its aggression and expands even further with its nuclear reach." In May of 2016, he told Reuters, "I would have no problem speaking to" Kim Jong Un. As president, in 2017, he called Kim a "smart cookie."

Without a tenable military option, DNI Clapper thought the U.S. needed to be more realistic. In November 2014, he had gone to North Korea to retrieve two U.S. citizens who had been taken prisoner. From his discussions with North Korean officials he was convinced that North Korea would not give up their nuclear weapons. Why would they? In exchange for what? North Korea had effectively bought a deterrent. It was real and powerful in its ambiguity. U.S. intelligence was not certain of the capability. He had argued to Obama and the NSC that for the United States to say that denuclearization was a condition for negotiations was not working, and would not work.

Also, Clapper said, he understood the North Korean desire for a peace treaty to end the Korean War, which had been formally resolved with an armistice in 1953—a truce between the commanders of the militaries involved, not the nations at war.

The United States needed to understand how North Korea looked at the situation: The U.S. and South Korea seemed permanently poised, dramatically at times, to attack and to do away with the Kim regime.

There was a single argument he made, Clapper said, that the North Koreans had not pushed back on during his 2014 visit. The United States, he had argued, has no permanent enemies. Look, he said, we had a war with Japan and Germany but now are friends with both. We had a war with Vietnam but now we are friends. Clapper had recently visited Vietnam. Even after a full-scale war, peaceful coexistence was possible.

Clapper wanted the U.S. to set up an interest section in Pyongyang. This would be an informal channel in which another government with an embassy in the North Korean capital would act as intermediary. It would be less than full diplomatic relations, but it would give the U.S. a base, a place in the capital where they could obtain information and also get information into North Korea.

Clapper was a voice in the wilderness. No one agreed. Obama was hard-line: North Korea would have to agree to give up its nuclear weapons. Obama, a determined advocate for reducing nuclear weapons worldwide, wanted to turn the clock back. He condemned the North's September 9 nuclear test in a long public statement, repeating U.S. policy: "To be clear the United States does not, and never will accept North Korea as a nuclear state."

The overriding fact, Clapper argued, was that no one really understood what drove Kim Jong Un. "No one knows his ignition point," he said. That was the assessment they needed and didn't have. Instead the analysts debated whether Kim Jung Un was a brilliant, strategic genius manipulating other countries, including the U.S., or an inexperienced, impulsive fool.

As the Obama administration fanned through possible options, the discussion turned to the possibility of increasing the cyber attacks on North Korea. Some viewed cyber as the below-the-radar magic wand that might mitigate the North Korean threat.

To launch broader cyber attacks effectively, the National Security Agency would have to go through servers that North Korea had in China. The Chinese would detect such an attack and could conclude it was directed at them, potentially unleashing a cataclysmic cyber war.

"I can't promise you that we can absorb a cyber counterattack," one senior Obama cabinet member told Obama. And that was a big problem. The use of cyber could trigger escalation and set off a round of attacks and counterattacks that could cripple the Internet, financial systems like banking and credit cards, power grids, news and other communications systems, potentially bringing the American or even the world economy to its knees.

The administration lawyers who had the top security clearances and were involved in the discussion objected strenuously. It was too risky. Little new happened.

North Korea's cyber capability had been demonstrated powerfully in a 2014 attack on Sony Pictures Entertainment designed to stop the release of a satirical movie about Kim Jong Un. The movie, a comedy called *The Interview*, depicted two journalists going to North Korea to assassinate the youthful dictator.

Investigators later discovered that North Korean hackers had lurked inside Sony's networks for three months waiting to attack. On November 24, North Korea took over Sony's computer screens. To maximize shock value, the screens displayed a menacing red skeleton coming at the viewer and the text "Hacked by #GOP," short for "Guardians of Peace," stating, "We've already warned you, and this is just a beginning." North Korean hackers destroyed 70 percent or more of Sony's computers, including laptops.

Employing thousands of hackers, the North was now regularly using cyber programs to steal hundreds of millions of dollars from banks and others on a global scale.

Two days after the election, Obama and Trump met at the White House. The meeting was intended to last for 20 minutes, but it continued for over an hour. Korea is going to be the biggest, most important thing you've got going, Obama told the president-elect. It's my biggest headache. Trump told staff later that Obama warned him that North Korea will be your biggest nightmare.

One intelligence analyst with vast experience and who also had served in South Korea said, "I'm shocked that the Obama administration closed their eyes and acted like the deaf, mute and blind monkey on this issue. And now I understand why the Obama team said to Trump that the major problem you have is North Korean nukes. They've been hiding the problem."

I n February, General Dunford stopped by the office of Senator
Lindsey Graham, the South Carolina Republican, for a private
talk.

Probably few in the Senate worked harder on military matters
than Graham. A bachelor and colonel in the Air Force reserve, he
seemed always on duty. He had built a vast bipartisan network in
Washington. Former vice president Joe Biden, who had served 36
years in the Senate, said that Graham had the "best instincts" of
anyone in the upper chamber. Graham, 61, a senior member of the
Senate Armed Services Committee, was best friend and virtual permanent sidekick to the committee's chairman, the outspoken Senator John McCain.

When Dunford arrived at Graham's office, Graham could see
that the chairman was shaken. Trump was asking for a new war plan
for a preemptive military strike on North Korea, Dunford confided.

The intelligence on North Korea was not good enough, Dunford
said. "We need better intelligence before I give the president a plan."

A Marine and combat veteran and former commandant of the

Marine Corps, Dunford had served as commander of the 5th Marine Regiment during the 2003 invasion of Iraq. His nickname was "Fighting Joe" and he had served under then Major General James Mattis. He was clearly rattled by Trump's impulsive decision-making style. Graham sensed that Dunford was stalling Trump's request given the risk.

Graham had a contentious relationship with Trump during the primaries. One of 16 besides Trump running for the Republican nomination, Graham had not made it past the second tier. He'd called Trump a "jackass," and in retaliation Trump gave out his cell phone number at a campaign rally in South Carolina, flooding his phone with so many calls that Graham destroyed it in a comic video. He endorsed Jeb Bush, contrasting him to Trump: Bush "hasn't tried to get ahead in a contested primary by throwing dangerous rhetoric around."

Priebus urged Graham to build a relationship with Trump. One of the selling points, he told Graham: "You're a lot of fun. He needs fun people around him."

Graham was pounding Trump pretty hard, especially on the first executive order, on the Muslim ban. "Some third grader wrote it on the back of an envelope," he said.

Graham and McCain had released a joint statement: "We fear this executive order will become a self-inflicted wound in the fight against terrorism. This executive order sends a signal, intended or not, that America does not want Muslims coming into our country. That is why we fear this executive order may do more to help terrorist recruitment than improve our security."

Graham was now willing to put the past behind.

Several weeks later, on March 7, Trump invited Graham to lunch at the White House. Graham had prepared a little speech.

When he walked into the Oval Office, Trump was sitting behind the Resolute Desk. He jumped up, moved swiftly toward Graham, and gave him a big hug. "We've got to be friends," Trump said. "You're going to be my friend."

"Yes, sir," Graham replied. "I want to be your friend."

Trump said he shouldn't have publicly given out Graham's cell phone number.

"That was the highlight of my campaign," Graham joked.

"What's your new number?" Trump asked. He wrote it down, laughed and asked how their rift had occurred.

"It was a contest," Graham said. "You know I never got any traction. I couldn't get on the big stage. Now you won. I'm humbled by being beat, and I accept your victory." He knew this was what Trump wanted to hear. "Do you want me to help you?"

Trump said he did.

"Before we go into lunch," Graham said, "I want to apologize to you for a very fucked-up Republican majority. Congress is going to fuck up your presidency. We have no idea what we're doing. We have no plan for health care. We're on different planets when it comes to cutting taxes. And you're the biggest loser in this." Tax reform and a replacement for Obamacare should have been done years ago. "Now you're the one who can do it. You're a deal maker. These leaders in Congress don't know how to do something as simple as buying a house. If there was ever a time for a deal maker, this is it. There are a lot of good people, but most of them never made a deal in the private sector. There are not five people on Capitol Hill I'd let buy me a car. I'd let you buy me a car. And here's what I want to convince you of: that you'd let me buy you a car."

They went into the adjoining dining room. The large TV screen was tuned to the Fox cable channel with the sound off. McMaster and Priebus joined them.

"What's on your mind?" Trump asked.

"Short term, North Korea," Graham said. "There'll come a day when somebody's going to come in and say, 'Mr. President, they're on the verge of getting a missile. They've miniaturized a nuclear weapon to put on it. They can hit the homeland. What do you want us to do?'"

Suddenly everyone's attention was drawn to four North Korean missiles shooting across the giant TV screen. Just days before, on March 5, North Korea had fired four missiles into the Sea of Japan.

Trump's eyes were as big as silver dollars.

"That's old footage, old footage," Graham said, trying to calm everyone. He had seen it before.

"I've got to do something about this," Trump said, pointing to the screen.

"That day is coming," Graham said. "What are you going to do about it?"

"What do you think I should do about it?" he asked.

"You can accept they've got a missile and tell them and China that if you ever use it, that's the end of North Korea," Graham said. "And have a missile defense system that has a high percentage of knocking it down. That's scenario one. Scenario two is that you tell China that we're not going to let them get such a missile to hit our homeland. And if you don't take care of it, I will."

"What would you do?" the president asked.

It had to be the second option, Graham said. You can't let them have that capability. Number one is too risky.

The president leaned toward McMaster. "What do you think?"

"I think he's right," the national security adviser said.

"If it gets to be a mature threat," Graham said, "don't let us [Congress] just sit on the sidelines and bitch and moan. If you had the evidence, the day that they come in and tell you that, you call the congressional leadership up and say, I may have to use force here. Let me tell you why I want your backing for authorization to use force against North Korea. If we had a vote that was decisive and you had that authority in your back pocket, it may prevent you from having to use it."

"That'd be very provocative," Priebus said.

"It's meant to be provocative," Graham replied. "You only do that as a last resort."

"That will get everyone worried and excited," Priebus said.

"I don't give a shit who I make nervous," Trump said.

"You don't want it on your résumé that North Korea, a nuclear power, got a missile that could reach the United States on your watch," Graham said.

Trump said he had been thinking about that.

"If they have a breakout," Graham said, "and have a missile that will reach the United States, you've got to whack them. If you get congressional authorization, you've got something in your back pocket." It would be an intermediate step and would give Trump leverage.

"They think if they get a missile with a nuclear weapon on top, they're home free. You've got to convince them if they try to get a missile with a weapon on top, that's the end of them."

McMaster said that the intelligence on North Korea was incomplete.

"Call me before you shoot," Graham told them.

Graham urged as much bipartisanship as possible. Bring in the Democrats. He wanted to provide a roadmap to Trump for dealing with Congress. "Mr. President, you've got to buy some Democrats," Graham said. "The good news is they come cheap." He said that Trump needed to get to know key Republicans and Democrats. "Use your deal-making past and skills. You've got to put something on the table for these people. Look, I've been doing this with Republicans and Democrats for 10 years."

Would there be disagreements? Yes, he said. Good friends disagree all the time. "Washington is always about the next thing. After something doesn't work out, you've got to move on."

The president had to knock off the tweeting. The week prior, on March 4, he had sent out four tweets accusing Obama of wiretapping Trump Tower.

"You got an upper cut to the jaw, delivered by you," Graham said of the widespread negative reaction to the tweets. "They're out to get you. Don't help them."

"Tweeting," the president said, "that's the way I operate."

"It's okay to tweet to your advantage, Mr. President. Don't tweet to your disadvantage. They're always trying to drag you into their swamp. You've got to have the discipline not to take the bait."

Trump phoned Graham the next day to thank him for the discussion.

"Invite John McCain and his wife, Cindy, to dinner," Graham said. "John is a good guy. You guys need to get along, and he can help you on lots of things."

In 2015, Trump had made one of his most cruel and thoughtless comments about McCain. "He's not a war hero. He's a war hero because he was captured. I like people who weren't captured."

Graham knew McCain hated Trump. He knew that in Washington, you had to deal with people who hated you. But he did not impart that particular piece of advice to the president.

"My chief job is to keep John McCain calm," Graham remarked. Senate majority leader Mitch McConnell was "scared to death of John McCain. Because John knows no boundaries. He'll pop our leadership as much as he'll pop their leadership. And I will, at times, but mine's more calculated. John's just purely John. He's just the world's nicest man. And a media whore like me. Anyway, he's a much nicer guy than I am."

The dinner with McCain and Cindy was arranged for April. Graham also attended. Cindy McCain had dedicated her life to fighting human trafficking, and Graham suggested that Trump make her his ambassador for that cause.

At the dinner in the Blue Room, Trump pulled out a letter. He read it to Cindy McCain line-by-line, drawing it out.

I would very much like you to be my ambassador at large for

human trafficking, he read, noting that she had devoted her life to human rights causes.

"I'd be honored," she said, and teared up.

McCain was visibly touched. As chairman of the Armed Services Committee, he also thanked the president for promising to rebuild the military.

What do you want us to do to help you? McCain asked.

"I just want to get to know you," Trump said, laying it on very thick. "I admire you. You're a very tough man. You're a good man."

It was as close as he might get to, I'm sorry.

McCain again seemed touched. "It's a tough world out there," he said. "We want to help you."

What about North Korea? Trump asked.

"Everybody screwed this up," McCain said. Democrats, Republicans—the last three presidents over 24 years, George W. Bush, Barack Obama and Bill Clinton.

"Here's the decision, Mr. President," Graham said, repeating what he'd already told Trump. A containment strategy—let North Korea get the advanced missile with a nuclear weapon, betting you could shoot it down, or that they would be deterred and never shoot—or telling China that the United States would stop North Korea from getting the capability.

What do you think? Trump asked McCain.

"Very complicated," he said. "They can kill a million people in Seoul with conventional artillery. That's what makes it so hard."

Graham offered a hawkish view: "If a million people are going to die, they're going to die over there, not here."

"That's pretty cold," Trump interjected. He said he believed that China loved him. He seemed to say it almost 10 times, and that it gave him great leverage.

During a spring meeting in the Oval Office, discussion turned to the controversy in South Korea about the deployment of the Terminal

High Altitude Area Defense (THAAD) missile defense system, which had become an issue in the South Korean presidential race. The system would help protect South Korea from a North Korea missile attack. More crucially, it could be used to help protect the United States.

"Have they already paid for it?" Trump asked.

"They didn't pay for it," McMaster said. "We paid for it."

"That can't be right," Trump said. He wanted an explanation so McMaster set out to get some answers from the Pentagon.

"It's actually a very good deal for us," McMaster said when he returned in the afternoon. "They gave us the land in a 99-year lease for free. But we pay for the system, the installation and the operations."

Trump went wild. "I want to see where it is going," he said. Finally some maps came in that showed the location. Some of the land included a former golf course.

"This is a piece of shit land," said the former golf course and real estate developer. "This is a terrible deal. Who negotiated this deal? What genius? Take it out. I don't want the land."

The major missile defense system might cost $10 billion over 10 years, and it wasn't even physically in the United States, Trump said. "Fuck it, pull it back and put it in Portland!"

Trump was still outraged by the $18 billion trade deficit with South Korea and wanted to pull out of what he called the "horrible" KORUS trade deal.

Rising tensions around THAAD were bad enough. South Korea was a crucial ally and trade partner. Trump met with McMaster and Mattis. Both said that given the crisis with North Korea, it was not the time to bring up the trade deal.

"That's exactly when you bring it up," Trump said. "If they want protection, this is when we get to renegotiate the deal. We have leverage."

Trump later told Reuters that the initial cost for THAAD was an estimated $1 billion. "I informed South Korea it would be appropriate if they paid," he said. "It's a billion-dollar system. It's phenomenal, shoots missiles right out of the sky."

On April 30, McMaster called the South Korean national security chief. He told Chris Wallace on Fox News, "What I told our South Korean counterpart is until any renegotiation, that the deals in place, we'll adhere to our word."

As a first step, the South Korean trade ministry later agreed to start to renegotiate the KORUS trade deal.

CHAPTER

14

In February, Derek Harvey, a former Army colonel—one of the premier fact-driven intelligence analysts in the U.S. government—was appointed director for the Middle East on the National Security Council staff. It was a plum position in a region that was on fire.

Harvey, a soft-spoken, driven legend, approached intelligence like a homicide detective—sifting through thousands of pages of interrogation reports, communications intercepts, battle reports, enemy documents, raw intelligence data and nontraditional sources such as tribal leaders.

The result was at times unorthodox thinking. In some circles he was referred to as "The Grenade" because of his ability and willingness to explode conventional wisdom.

Before the 9/11 terrorist attacks Harvey had written a paper concluding that Osama bin Laden and his al Qaeda network posed a strategic threat to the United States. He was almost alone in forecasting the persistence and power of the insurgencies in Iraq and Afghanistan after the U.S. invaded. His argument was often that certain aggressive, ambitious ideas were "doable but not sellable," meaning the political system would not provide or sustain them, such as maintaining tens of thousands of U.S. troops in Afghanistan for years.

Harvey went to see Jared Kushner, who had a small office adjacent to the Oval Office.

Kushner sat back, crossed his legs and listened to Harvey's case.

Harvey's number-one worry in the Middle East was Hezbollah, the Iranian-supported terrorist organization. The sensitive intelligence showed that Hezbollah had more than 48,000 full-time military in Lebanon, where they presented an existential threat to the Jewish state. They had 8,000 expeditionary forces in Syria, Yemen and region-wide commando units. In addition, they had people worldwide—30 to 50 each in Colombia, Venezuela, South Africa, Mozambique and Kenya.

Hezbollah had a stunning 150,000 rockets. In the 2006 war with Israel they'd had only 4,500.

Iranian Revolutionary Guard commanders were integrated into the Hezbollah structure. Iran was paying Hezbollah's bills—at a staggering $1 billion a year. That did not include what Hezbollah made from money laundering, human trafficking, the cocaine and opium trades, and selling ivory tusks from Mozambique.

Hezbollah dominated in Lebanon, a state within a state, with a willingness to use violence. Nothing of import happened in Lebanon without Hezbollah's acquiescence. It was committed to destroy Israel.

Hezbollah was a perfect proxy for Iran to use to pressure and attack Israel, whose air bases could be pummeled with rockets. Israel's defenses of Iron Dome, David's Sling and Arrow missiles would be inadequate.

Harvey argued there was potential for a catastrophic war, with immense humanitarian, economic and strategic consequences. An Iranian-Israeli conflict would draw in the United States and unhinge efforts to bring regional stability.

Trump was given a *Reader's Digest* version of the Hezbollah briefing. DNI Dan Coats and CIA Director Mike Pompeo supported the case in morning Oval Office PDB briefings. Mattis, McMaster and Secretary of State Rex Tillerson supported it in a matter-of-fact way.

Harvey felt the others did not appreciate the degree to which the fundamental balance of power had shifted. Another Arab-Israeli war would come home to Israel as no attack ever had. A full-scale assault could impact their ability to actually fight.

Harvey underscored this to Kushner strongly: The new Trump administration was unprepared for what could happen. He pushed to follow up on Trump and Israeli prime minister Benjamin Netanyahu's agreements from their meeting in February—the importance of a strategic dialogue to take a fresh look and confront the new realities on the ground. He wanted to enhance the relationship that he believed had deteriorated over eight years under the Obama administration.

In the summer, the Israeli ambassador to Washington and its national security adviser wanted Harvey to come to Israel.

McMaster said Harvey couldn't go, though he gave no reason.

In early July, Harvey arranged to meet with senior intelligence officials from Mossad, military intelligence, and representatives from the Israeli Air Force and Army. McMaster, angry with Harvey, would not let him move forward.

The big question: Had Harvey uncovered the next ticking time bomb—Hezbollah—in the array of foreign policy problems facing the United States and Trump?

Soon Harvey was back to see Kushner.

"What do you think about the president going to Riyadh as our first presidential trip?" Kushner asked.

"It fits perfectly with what we're trying to do," Harvey said, "to reaffirm our support for the Saudis, our strategic objectives in the region. Our position has deteriorated so much during the Obama years."

Harvey believed that Obama had spent too much time on mollifying Iran with the nuclear deal and neglecting, even scorning, relations with the Saudis and Israel. Making Saudi Arabia the first presidential trip could go a long way to signaling that the Trump administration had new priorities. It was also very attractive to Harvey that the president's first trip might be to his region because all the other senior NSC staffers would be clamoring to have the first trip in theirs.

A summit in Saudi Arabia would also benefit Israel. The Saudis and Israelis, both longtime foes of Iran, had both open and important backchannel relations.

Harvey knew to focus rigorously on such a suggestion from Kushner, who was obviously not just another senior presidential adviser. The son-in-law was speaking with at least the president's knowledge if not his encouragement.

Harvey was as well connected as any intelligence officer to Israeli intelligence and knew that Kushner had established his own connections there. Netanyahu was a longtime Kushner family friend.

Kushner told Harvey he had important and reliable intelligence that the key to Saudi Arabia was the deputy crown prince, the charismatic 31-year-old Mohammed bin Salman, known as MBS. The son of the Saudi king, MBS was also the defense minister, a key position and launching pad for influence in the Kingdom. MBS had vision, energy. He was charming and spoke of bold, modernizing reforms.

When McMaster learned of Kushner's Saudi summit idea, he asked Harvey nervously, "Who's pushing this? Where's it coming from?"

Harvey was not sure what role the president might or might not have.

McMaster clearly disliked the out-of-channel approach but there was not much he could do about it.

Harvey held a series of meetings with the intelligence agencies including the CIA. The message from them was that Kushner better be careful. The real solid guy was the current crown prince, Mohammed bin Nayef, 57, who was known as MBN. He was the king's nephew credited with dismantling al Qaeda in the Kingdom as head of the Interior Ministry. Showing favoritism to the younger MBS would cause friction in the royal family.

From decades of intelligence contacts in the Middle East, Harvey believed that Kushner was right—MBS was the future. MBS saw that transformative change in Saudi Arabia was the only path to survival for the Kingdom. With Kushner as his patron, Harvey had unusual authority to begin planning. Harvey reached out to Defense, Treasury and the White House National Economic Council. The risks, Harvey believed, were substantial, but he saw high, high upsides.

In March, McMaster chaired a principals meeting on the possibility of a Saudi summit.

"From my experience at Exxon," said Secretary of State Tillerson, waving his hand dismissively, "the Saudis always talk a big game. You go through the dance with them on the negotiations. When it comes time to putting the signature on the page, you can't get there." Engagement with MBS should be taken with a grain of salt. The U.S. could work hard on a summit, and in the end have nothing.

"It's a bridge too far," Mattis said. Arranging arms sales and other projects beneficial to the United States economy, the necessary deliverables for such a summit, would take a long time. "We're better off waiting until next year. A new administration should be more careful and prudent."

Secretary of Energy Rick Perry said there was too much to do in too short a time.

No one supported the idea of a summit in two months as Kushner was now proposing.

Kushner sat at the opposite end of the table from McMaster.

"I understand this is very ambitious," the president's son-in-law said. He stood. "I understand the concerns. But I think we have a real opportunity here. We have to recognize it. I understand we have to be careful. We need to work this diligently, as if it's going to happen. And if it looks like we can't get there, we'll have plenty of time to shift gears. But this is an opportunity that is there for the seizing."

No one said no. Harvey knew they really couldn't, and he continued to plan as if it were going to happen. He set some thresholds, deciding that they would have to have over $100 billion in military contracts agreed on beforehand.

Execution fell to Harvey. MBS sent a team of 30 to Washington and Harvey arranged multiple conference rooms in the Eisenhower Office Building. Working groups of Americans and Saudis were set up on terrorism, terrorism financing, violent extremism and information campaigns. The Pentagon held meetings on contracts and security partnerships.

Harvey did not want to ask too much of the Saudis, who he knew did not have as deep pocketbooks as generally thought. Oil prices had dropped, cutting into Saudi revenue.

McMaster was still not enthusiastic. Because Kushner wants it, he told Harvey, we need to keep working it. But there's not a lot of support for it. We'll go through the motions, and then we'll kill it at some point.

Kushner said that if the United States was going to stay engaged in the region, they needed to help the Saudis and Israelis succeed. The president was not going to continue paying the bills for U.S. defense in the Middle East when the primary beneficiaries were the countries in the region, according to Kushner.

His worry was increased Iranian influence and subversive operations in the region, especially Hezbollah, which threatened Israel.

Get the Saudis to buy more, Kushner said. If they bought weapons systems, it would help the U.S. economy and job creation. They would buy large stockpiles of munitions, 10-year maintenance and support contracts.

The Saudi team came back to Washington for a second visit. For at least four days straight they all had meetings that went to 1 a.m.

Kushner held daily interagency meetings of the key U.S. players in his office where a dozen people crowded in.

At times the Saudis were not delivering enough on contracts or arms purchases.

"I'll make a phone call," Kushner said to Harvey. He phoned MBS directly and the Saudis increased their arms purchases.

When it looked like they were close, Kushner invited MBS to the United States and brought him to the White House where he had lunch March 14 in the State Dining Room with Trump. Attending were Pence, Priebus, Bannon, McMaster and Kushner. This violated protocol, unsettling officials at State and the CIA. Lunch at the White House with the president for a middle-rank deputy crown prince was just not supposed to be done.

Tillerson and Mattis continued to express their doubts. This is too hard, too much work to do, too many questions about the contracts.

Trump finally gave the go-ahead and the trip to both Saudi Arabia and Israel was announced on Thursday, May 4.

Trump went to Saudi Arabia from May 20 to 21 and was lavishly welcomed. He announced $110 billion in Saudi-funded defense purchases and a grab bag of several hundred billion in other contracts—certainly an exaggerated number.

Harvey believed the summit had reset the relationships in a dramatic way, a home run—sending a strategic message to Iran, the principal adversary. The Saudis, the Gulf Cooperation Council countries (Bahrain, Kuwait, Oman, Qatar, the United Arab Emirates and Saudi Arabia) and Israel were united. The Obama approach of straddling was over.

The next month Saudi king Salman at age 81 appointed MBS, age 31, the new crown prince and next in line to lead the Kingdom perhaps for decades to come.

CHAPTER

15

Trump was one of the most outspoken foes of the 16-year-old Afghanistan War, now the longest in American history. To the extent Trump had a bedrock principle, it was opposition, even ridicule, of the war. Beginning in 2011, four years before his formal entry into the presidential race, he launched a drumbeat of Twitter attacks.

In March 2012, he tweeted, "Afghanistan is a total disaster. We don't know what we are doing. They are, in addition to everything else, robbing us blind."

In 2013, the tweets picked up. In January, it was, "Let's get out of Afghanistan. Our troops are being killed by the Afghanis we train and we waste billions there. Nonsense! Rebuild the USA." In March, "We should leave Afghanistan immediately. No more wasted lives. If we have to go back in, we go in hard & quick. Rebuild the US first." In April, "Our gov't is so pathetic that some of the billions being wasted in Afghanistan are ending up with terrorists." And in November, "Do not allow our very stupid leaders to sign a deal that keeps us in Afghanistan through 2024-with all costs by U.S.A. MAKE AMERICA GREAT!"

And in December 2015, Trump tweeted, "A suicide bomber has just killed U.S. troops in Afghanistan. When will our leaders get tough and smart. We are being led to slaughter!"

Like all presidents, Trump was living with the unfinished business of his predecessors. In the 21st-century presidency, nothing illustrated this more clearly than Afghanistan. The war, begun after the 9/11 terrorist attacks when Afghanistan had been the sanctuary for Osama bin Laden and al Qaeda, was a thicket of high expectations, setbacks, misunderstandings and massive commitments of money, troops and lives.

Under Presidents Bush and Obama, debates and discussions of troop numbers had dominated internal NSC and public discussion and generated expectations of progress or resolution. Media coverage focused on the troop number and timetable story lines. The number of U.S. troops engaged in the war had become a proxy for progress.

During the Obama presidency, troop numbers were a roller coaster, peaking at 100,000 and dropping to 8,400 with heady expectations, later abandoned, that the combat mission against the insurgent Taliban could end. But internally the experts knew it was futile.

White House coordinator Lieutenant General Douglas Lute labeled the war "a house of cards" in a 2010 meeting soon after Obama added another 30,000 troops.

Dr. Peter Lavoy, Obama's deputy assistant secretary of defense for Asian and Pacific security affairs, later in charge of South Asia for the Obama NSC staff, was a soft-spoken authority on South Asia— Pakistan and Afghanistan. Lavoy was largely unknown to the public but critical to the functioning of the defense and intelligence world. He was both academic and practitioner. He believed the obsession with U.S. troop numbers had been the Achilles' heel of the Obama administration policy in Afghanistan.

"There are literally thousands of sub-tribes in Afghanistan," Lavoy said. "Each has a grievance. If the Taliban ceased to exist you would still have an insurgency in Afghanistan." Victory was far-fetched. Winning had not been defined.

H. R. McMaster saw he would have a major confrontation with President Trump on the Afghanistan War. He knew Afghanistan. From 2010 to 2012 he had served as the deputy to the commander for planning (J5) at the Afghanistan war commander's headquarters in Kabul.

During the Gulf War in 1991 in Operation Desert Storm, just seven years out of West Point as an Army captain, McMaster led nine tanks in a battle that destroyed 28 Iraqi Republican Guard tanks. Captain McMaster suffered no losses and the battle lasted 23 minutes. He was awarded a Silver Star for valor.

In the Iraq War as a colonel he led 5,300 soldiers of the 3rd Armored Cavalry Regiment, successfully using protect-the-population counterinsurgency tactics to reclaim the city of Tal Afar in 2005. President Bush had publicly cited it as a model operation to give "reason for hope for a free Iraq."

In McMaster's 1997 book *Dereliction of Duty*, he called the Joint Chiefs who oversaw the Vietnam War "five silent men" who had failed to establish the essential personal rapport with civilian leaders so they could speak their minds. *Dereliction of Duty* was a field manual for avoiding another Vietnam.

The irony was that Trump was now saying that Afghanistan was Vietnam, a quagmire with no clear national security purpose, the latest example of the incoherence of American policy. McMaster's job was to align the military's recommendations for Afghanistan with the president's goals, but this president's only goal was to get out.

Staff work at the NSC ground on. On March 1 and 10, 2017, Army Ranger Lieutenant Colonel Fernando Lujan, the National Security Council staffer for Afghanistan, chaired the first middle-level meetings of the interagency in the Trump administration. It included representatives from the State Department, Pentagon and the intelligence agencies.

Lujan, a holdover from the Obama administration, knew the Afghanistan policy under Obama had been simple in practice: Avoid catastrophe. There was lots of uncertainty, and the possibilities of calamity were immense. He gave the Afghan police, for example, key to long-term stability, a D minus or F.

At the first meeting, a State Department official teed up the discussion with a series of fundamental questions: Why do we think we need a counterterrorist base in Afghanistan to prevent another attack? What's the justification for it? What do we think the terrorist threat emanating from Afghanistan really is? Why do we think thousands of U.S. troops and intelligence specialists are needed to combat that when we have drones and everything else? Our enduring presence, he noted, can cause further instability from not only insurgents but also regional players, such as Pakistan.

The State official said the United States maintained it did not want to establish a permanent presence when it invaded Afghanistan in 2001. So how do we square that now, after 16 years?

No, no, no, said the military representative. The U.S. presence was not to be permanent.

This led to the question, When might it all end? Was a political settlement possible? Would a political settlement be the ends or the means? How could a political settlement be possible if the insurgent Taliban did not want the United States to have any kind of a presence in Afghanistan? Could a possible political settlement be a way to sell continued engagement?

If a political settlement became a top priority, that would require compromise. Was President Trump willing to do so?

Was all of this a fig leaf so the United States could continue doing what it wanted to do? Was a democratic or stable government needed in Afghanistan? How invested was the U.S. in a real political settlement?

Another State Department representative noted that the central government lacked legitimacy in the eyes of the Afghan public, the lowest in 10 years, according to polling done in the country. He observed that the illicit economy, opium and illegal mining, was the size of the regular economy, and a significant portion was under control of Taliban insurgents.

After 9/11, the CIA and military had paid off the Afghan war-lords to go after the Taliban. Some of that money had been used to target political opposition. Now the U.S. was spending about $50 billion a year in Afghanistan. Was the government, which was deeply corrupt, just taking money from the U.S. and the allies to fund themselves? Was the large level of assistance taking away the Afghan government's incentive to develop real reforms and the political will to take on opium and profits from mining? American money was one of the poisons in the Afghan system.

A larger question loomed: Should the United States be playing to win in Afghanistan, or merely not to lose?

After one meeting they took whiteboards and broke into three groups to attempt to define the problem and state vital strategic objectives. Common to all three was the goal of preventing further attacks on the homeland.

They raised additional questions: What kind of government did Afghanistan need? And what kind of stability did the U.S. need to achieve the goal of preventing further terrorist attacks?

Initially, in meetings with representatives from the Pentagon, State Department and the intelligence agencies, McMaster laid out his four frames or goals: 1. Achieve political stability that will include a political settlement with the insurgent Taliban. 2. Push for institutional actions by the Afghan government to counter the Taliban. 3. Increase pressure on neighboring Pakistan, which was playing a double game—nominally allied with the United States, but also supporting terrorists and the Taliban. 4. Maintain international support from the 39 countries allied with the United States in a coalition.

Casting about for a middle ground on more troops, McMaster considered a proposal for adding thousands more, perhaps 3,000 to 5,000, to prevent another terrorist attack. One staff proposal called for thinking about eventually adding tens of thousands.

At a Principals Committee meeting—so-called because unlike a NSC meeting, the principals meet without the president—Attorney

General Sessions erupted at everyone, including McMaster, over the idea of more troops.

You're basically walking the president into exactly what he doesn't believe in, to a place he doesn't want to go, Sessions said. We're losing too many lives in Afghanistan. I don't understand what you guys don't get. This is not where the president's at.

Priebus said, You have not spent the time working with the president on what his basic philosophy and foreign policy positions are, and why. With the president, he said, "why" is the most important part. Why are we here? Why are we doing this? What do you want to happen? And what exactly are we trying to accomplish?

This was precisely the question that Peter Lavoy had been asking in the Obama administration. Neither Priebus nor Lavoy received a satisfactory answer.

The principals' consensus settled on adding up to 4,000 troops.

"Has anyone told the president," Priebus asked, "that the option you're choosing basically says we're going to be in Afghanistan for decades? If you explain it to him, he's going to go crazy. Who's talking to him about these details?"

Silence.

Afterward, Priebus called a meeting of the key players.

"Look," he said, "we've got a problem. We are not connecting with the president over the more basic issues. Why do you want to be there? What is the purpose? What is the fundamental value to the United States for risking American lives? You have to come to a fundamental understanding and agreement on those basic issues before you start talking about how many troops are we going to have in Afghanistan. You guys are like 10 steps ahead of yourselves."

It was not enough for McMaster to declare the objective was to prevent another terrorist attack. The question was simple: How would several thousand more troops help to achieve that?

There were four missions in Afghanistan: train and advise the Afghan Army and police; logistical support; counterterrorism; and the intelligence mission. McMaster had to craft a strategy that avoided escalation, or the appearance of escalation. It could not directly or brazenly challenge Trump's stated desire to get out, but had to softly market a new approach that soon would be called "stay the course."

On March 28, McMaster proposed what became known to the NSC staff as the R4s: reinforce, realign, reconcile and regionalize. These were the components of the Afghanistan strategy he was proposing, and they fit neatly within his concept of four frames. Reinforcing meant more equipment and training; realigning meant targeting funding for areas under control of the Afghan government, rather than contested areas held by the Taliban; reconciling meant trying to get the Afghan government to be inclusive, hold elections and work with power brokers; and regionalizing meant the U.S. working with regional actors such as India.

By May, the proposed plan had settled on the middle ground of adding 3,000 to 5,000 more troops. Some would come in "off the books," meaning they would not be counted in official public numbers.

The plan would be counterterrorism-centric. An aviation battalion would be available to help the Afghan Army when they were in a serious fight with the Taliban. The rules of engagement were being altered—previously, U.S. forces could only use force if they were threatened; now they could be used when the Afghan Army was threatened.

Around the same time, Senator Lindsey Graham was pushing Trump for more troops. Graham and Trump had three conversations about Afghanistan in May.

"Do you want on your résumé that you allowed Afghanistan to go back into the darkness and the second 9/11 came from the very place the first 9/11 did?" Graham asked. It mirrored his argument to Trump about North Korea.

"Well," Trump asked, "how does this end?"

"It never ends," Graham said. "It's good versus evil. Good versus evil never ends. It's just like the Nazis. It's now radical Islam. It will be something else one day. So our goal is to make sure the home-land never gets attacked from Afghanistan. Look at the thousands of extra troops as an insurance policy against another 9/11. Listen to your generals." Graham landed on a metaphor that he knew Trump would love. "General Obama was terrible. General Biden was terri-ble. General Susan Rice was awful. General Valerie Jarrett . . ." But "General Trump is going to be no better. General Graham is not better. Listen to your generals or fire them."

At one point, Vice President Pence called Graham to say, "You've got to tell him how this ends." It would never end, Graham repeated.

Graham was aware of the internal warfare in the White House. General Kellogg, NSC chief of staff, was siding with Bannon, argu-ing to get out. That meant Kellogg was at war with McMaster, his own boss.

Graham saw the stories Bannon or someone else was leaking to the press, calling this "McMaster's War." He called Trump at once.

"This is Trump's war, my friend," Graham told the president. "Nobody in history is going to remember McMaster or Bannon. They're going to remember you."

In Bannon's eyes, the old order would do what it always did—stay the course or retreat in disgrace. He wanted to find a way to mitigate the downside risk, providing cover for Trump.

In a May 31 op-ed in *The Wall Street Journal*, Erik Prince, the founder of the controversial defense contractor Blackwater, declared "Afghanistan is an expensive disaster for America." He proposed the creation of a "viceroy" to lead all military efforts in Afghanistan and the replacement of all but a small special operations command of the U.S. military with "cheaper private solutions," contractors who would make multiyear commitments to train the Afghan security forces. "The U.S. should adjust course from the past 15-plus years of nation building and focus on pounding the Taliban and other terrorists so hard that they plead for negotiation. Until they feel real pressure and know the U.S. has staying power, they will win."

This did not get very far because it meant private contractors like Prince, a brother of Education Secretary Betsy DeVos, would make lots of money.

Bannon asked CIA Director Mike Pompeo if he could find a middle solution. Pompeo agreed to go to Afghanistan in the first week of August.

For years the CIA had run a 3,000-man top secret covert army in Afghanistan. The CTPT, short for Counterterrorism Pursuit Teams, were Afghans paid, trained and controlled by the CIA. They were the best Afghan fighters, the cream of the crop. They killed or captured Taliban insurgents and often went into tribal areas to eliminate them. They conducted dangerous and highly controversial cross-border operations into neighboring Pakistan. Could this CIA paramilitary force be expanded, making a troop increase unnecessary? Could the CIA paramilitary force and several thousand Army Special Forces do the job so the big regular ground force of the U.S. Army could get out?

Mattis called Senator Graham. A proposal was forthcoming, he explained. The military would coordinate with the CIA. "The CIA has got some high-value targets that they want to hit." There were four operations: "Two on either side of the Afghanistan-Pakistan border."

When McMaster tried to sell a slimmed-down version of concepts like "frames" or the R4s, Trump was cruelly dismissive. He had one question: "What the fuck are we doing there?" But he had an idea for Secretary Mattis and Bannon. "I want to get some enlisted guys, some real fighters, over here who are not officers." He wanted their on-the-ground views of Afghanistan.

Mattis rolled his eyes.

Bannon, always looking to history to serve his purposes, was reminded of President Lincoln's almost mystical devotion to hearing from soldiers as commander in chief.

On July 18, Trump had lunch at the White House with three soldiers and an airman who had served in Afghanistan. Trump, Pence

and McMaster sat on one side of the wide, gleaming table in the Roosevelt Room; on the other side sat the four young men in their dress
uniforms, looking uncomfortable as cameras documented their visit.

The president said, "I want to find out why we've been there 17
years, how it's going and what we should do in terms of additional
ideas. We have plenty of ideas from a lot of people but I want to hear
it from people on the ground."

Afterward, Trump summed up their views for Bannon: "Unani-
mous. We've got to figure out how to get the fuck out of there. Totally corrupt. The people are not worth fighting for . . . NATO does
nothing. They're a hindrance. Don't let anybody tell you how great
they are. It's all bullshit."

The National Security Council gathered in the Situation Room at
10:00 the next morning, July 19, to brief Trump on the Afghanistan
and Pakistan strategy.

McMaster spent the initial part of the meeting identifying objectives and framing issues for discussion. Trump looked bored and
seemed disengaged. After about five minutes, he interrupted. "I've
been hearing about this nonsense about Afghanistan for 17 years
with no success," he said before McMaster had finished laying out
the issues. We've got a bunch of inconsistent, short-term strategies.
We can't continue with the same old strategy.

He brought up his meeting with the troops the previous day. The
best information I've gotten was from a couple of those line soldiers,
not the generals, he said. "I don't care about you guys," he told Mattis, Dunford and McMaster.

We're losing big in Afghanistan. It's a disaster. Our allies aren't
helping. Ghost soldiers—those paid but not serving—are ripping
us off.

NATO is a disaster and a waste, he said. The soldiers had told
him that NATO staff were totally dysfunctional.

"Pakistan isn't helping us. They're not really a friend," despite the

$1.3 billion a year in aid the U.S. gave them. He said he refused to send any additional aid.

The Afghan leaders were corrupt and making money off of the United States, he insisted. The poppy fields, largely in Taliban territory, are out of control.

"The soldiers on the ground could run things much better than you," the president told his generals and advisers. "They could do a much better job. I don't know what the hell we're doing."

It was a 25-minute dressing-down of the generals and senior officials.

"Look, you can't think of Afghanistan in isolation," Tillerson said. "You've got to think about it in a regional context. We've never before taken this sort of multilateral approach to Afghanistan and the region."

"But how many more deaths?" Trump asked. "How many more lost limbs? How much longer are we going to be there?" His antiwar argument, practically ripped from a Bob Dylan song lyric, reflected the desires of his political base whose families were overrepresented in the military forces.

"The quickest way out is to lose," Mattis said.

Trump pivoted. Prime Minister Modi of India is a friend of mine, he said. I like him very much. He told me the U.S. has gotten nothing out of Afghanistan. Nothing. Afghanistan has massive mineral wealth. We don't take it like others—like China. The U.S. needed to get some of Afghanistan's valuable minerals in exchange for any support. "I'm not making a deal on anything until we get minerals." And the U.S. "must stop payments to Pakistan until they cooperate."

Mattis described their strategic framework and goals for nuclear nonproliferation. We need a bridge strategy until we're able to empower the Afghans, he said.

"Why can't we pay mercenaries to do the work for us?" Trump asked.

"We need to know if the commander in chief is fully with us or not," Mattis said. "We can't fight a half-assed war anymore." In order for the military to succeed, Mattis needed Trump to be all-in on the strategy.

"I'm tired of hearing that we have to do this or that to protect our homeland or to ensure our national security," Trump said.

The official full written NSC record of the meeting said simply that Trump "endorsed" the use of a "mix of tools" to pressure Pakistan to abandon its covert support of the Taliban. Contrary to his words, the document stated the U.S. would continue to engage Pakistan where there were mutual interests, and civil assistance to Pakistan would continue, while military assistance would be conditioned on better behavior. Rhetorically and operationally it would be a new, get tough strategy.

Later in the day those who had been in the meeting huddled in Priebus's office to discuss Afghanistan and South Asia strategy. McMaster worked to frame things in a way that showed he had heard the president's views and was trying to execute on the general orientation of them in as responsible a manner as possible. He tried to be upbeat. But it was clear that he, Mattis and Tillerson were close to their wits' ends.

That evening, Priebus hosted a dinner strategy meeting. Bannon seemed to be driving the agenda. Priebus, Bannon and Stephen Miller, a young, hard-line policy adviser and speechwriter who had previously been Jeff Sessions's communications director, complained about the NSC process. McMaster didn't seem to want to implement the president's viewpoints, but was trying to convince Trump of his own. Bannon wanted to replace McMaster with Kellogg, the NSC chief of staff, whose worldview aligned more closely with the president's and his own.

Graham told Trump that Ashraf Ghani, the president of Afghanistan, would allow him to have as many counterterrorism troops as he could want, plus CIA bases wherever he wanted. It was the best listening post and platform to attack international terrorism in the world. "They would take 100,000 troops," Graham said, exaggerating. "You should jump for joy that you have a counterterrorism partner in Afghanistan which will prevent the next 9/11."

"That's not nation building," Trump said.

"We're not going over there to try to sell Jeffersonian democracy," Graham agreed. His worry was the increasing, endless tension between Pakistan and India. "Pakistan is spending a lot of money to build more nuclear weapons. It's getting really out of control."

Graham had recently visited Afghanistan and left depressed. "We don't have a game plan in Afghanistan on the diplomatic side." There was no special representative, the role that had been filled by Richard Holbrooke in the first part of the Obama administration. "We don't even have an ambassador." For all he could tell, there was only one person at the State Department on the South Asia desk.

"We're going to fail on the political," he said. A peace settlement with the Taliban was the only way out. "The Pakistanis are going to double deal until they see the Taliban losing."

Trump had a solution. Did Graham want to be the ambassador to Pakistan?

"No, I don't want to be ambassador to Pakistan," Graham said.

They left it at that.

At the White House, Trump began repeating a line he had heard at a meeting: "The way we're going to win is to run an insurgency against the insurgency of the Taliban."

Trump loved the idea of a renegade operation, a campaign that the establishment was sure no one could win. The president said, "These guys in the 1980s against the Russians on horses." Perfect.

Bannon added fuel to the renegade fire by criticizing the weak Afghan Army. "We spent a trillion dollars to take the world's best fighters," Bannon said, "and turn them into the world's worst army."

Trump loved that also. Bannon had pushed about as far as he thought he could. They were trying to make policy on a string of one-sentence clichés.

Graham had one more warning for Trump.

"Pull them all out, because 8,600 [troops] ain't going to work, and accept the consequences," he warned Trump, referring to the number currently in Afghanistan. "And here are the consequences: It becomes Iraq on steroids. There are more international terrorists in Afghanistan than there ever were in Iraq. The deterioration will be quick and the projection of terrorism coming from Afghanistan will exponentially grow. And the next 9/11 is coming from where the first 9/11 was. And you own it. The question is, are you going to go down the Obama road, which is to end the war and put us all at risk, or are you going to go down the road of stabilizing Afghanistan?"

Y ou've got to be kidding me," Priebus had told Secretary of
State Tillerson in a phone call in early March. The controversial Iran deal negotiated by Obama had to be reviewed
every 90 days. They now had two days to renew or reject, Tillerson
said. In February, Trump had called it "One of the worst deals I've
ever seen." As a candidate in 2016, he had said, "My number one
priority is to dismantle the disastrous deal with Iran."

Tillerson wanted to renew as a matter of both practicality and
principle. Central was the fact Iran was in compliance with the deal
as Obama had negotiated it. He came up with some language for
renewal.

"The president's not going to go for it," Priebus said. "You need
to come up with a better statement. Mild, matter-of-fact won't cut
it. We need language that's going to actually make the case for President Trump's position. He's not going to like it. Secondly, if he reads
this, he's going to really blow up."

When Priebus briefed Trump on Tillerson's proposal, the president retorted, "You aren't going to jam this down my throat!"

Priebus ran shuttle diplomacy between the president and the secretary of state.

"They're not in violation," Tillerson said. The intelligence community and the allies who were signatories to the deal agreed that Iran was not in violation.

"Those arguments would not fly" with the president, Priebus said. Tillerson held his ground. "We've got a problem then," Priebus said. He felt he had to remind Tillerson. "The president is the decision maker here." He took himself off the hook. "I'm not trying to give you a hard time."

Tillerson went to see the president. "This is one of my core principles," Trump said. "I'm not in favor of this deal. This is the worst deal that we have ever made, and here we are renewing this deal." Since it was only for 90 days, he would go along. "This is the last time. Don't come back to me and try to renew this thing again. There's going to be no more renewals. It's a shitty deal."

Mattis found a diplomatic, quieter way to agree with Tillerson. "Well, Mr. President," Mattis said, "I think they are probably in technical compliance."

Priebus watched in admiration. Mattis was not meek but he sure knew how to handle Trump.

Tillerson had to send a letter to Speaker Paul Ryan by April 18. Trump didn't like the first draft. He directed that the short letter include that Iran was "a leading state sponsor of terror" and that the NSC would review whether to continue the suspension of economic sanctions that were part of the deal.

When the letter was first released, television commentators pounded Trump. Watching this made him more upset. He ordered Tillerson to hold a press conference to denounce both the deal, which had just been renewed, and Iran. It was extraordinary to unleash an attack within hours of renewing a landmark diplomatic agreement.

In a five-minute presentation, Tillerson read a prepared list of all the grievances against Iran: ballistic missile testing, "the world's leading sponsor of terrorism," threats to Israel, human rights violations, cyber attacks, arbitrary detention of foreigners including U.S. citizens, harassing U.S. Navy ships, jailing or executing political opponents, "reaching the agonizing low point of executing juveniles," and support to the "brutal Assad regime in Syria."

The Iran deal, Tillerson said, "fails to achieve the objective of a non-nuclear Iran. It only delays their goal of becoming a nuclear state."

Obama had defined the deal as a "non-binding agreement" rather than a treaty which requires Senate ratification. "Perhaps," Priebus said to Trump, "we can declare this a document that needs to be sent to the Senate for approval. Just take it out of our hands. Give it to the Senate and say, you pass it with two thirds and declare it a treaty."

Trump seemed intrigued but soon understood he would be giving up authority by sending it to the Senate. He agreed that for the moment they were stuck with it. Only for the moment.

Priebus and Tillerson and McMaster made sure they were "calendaring"—as they say in the White House—when the next 90-day renewal would come up.

"They're in violation," Trump said in a meeting before the July 17 deadline, "and you need to figure out how the argument is going to be made to declare that."

One day Tillerson came to the dining room next to the Oval Office to see Trump and Priebus and explain to the president again that there was no violation.

"They are in violation," Trump insisted, "and you should make the case that this agreement is done and finished." He suggested they might consider reopening the terms of the deal. "And that maybe we'd be willing to renegotiate."

"Mr. President," Tillerson said in exasperation, "you have the authority. You're the president. You just tell me what you want me to do. You call the shots. I'll do what you say."

He was getting dangerously close to violating the protocols of dealing with a president.

CIA Director Pompeo did not disagree with Tillerson's arguments on Iran and the reality of the Iran deal, but he, like Mattis, handled it more softly with the president. "Well, Mr. President this is how I understand it works technically."

Mattis still saw Iran as the key destabilizing influence in the region. In private, he could be pretty hard-line, but he had mellowed. Push them back, screw with them, drive a wedge between the Russians and Iranians, but no war.

Russia had privately warned Mattis that if there was a war in the Baltics, Russia would not hesitate to use tactical nuclear weapons against NATO. Mattis, with agreement from Dunford, began saying that Russia was an existential threat to the United States.

Mattis had formed a close relationship with Tillerson. They tried to have lunch most weeks. Mattis's house was near the State Department and several times Mattis told his staff, "I'll walk down and say hello to him."

McMaster considered Mattis and Tillerson "the team of two" and found himself outside their orbit, which was exactly the way they wanted it.

To complicate things, Tillerson was having rows with the White House over personnel for the State Department. Priebus called a meeting with Tillerson and half a dozen White House staffers on the patio outside the chief of staff's corner office. At one point Tillerson had adamantly opposed the person suggested by the White House for a senior post and he had hired his own person.

Johnny DeStefano, the director of personnel for the White House, objected. Tillerson erupted. "No one's going to tell me who to hire and not to hire. When I got this job I was told I got to hire my people."

"You get to hire your people," Priebus said, intervening. "But the problem we've got here is that it's going so slowly. Number one, we're bogged down not having personnel where they need to be. Number two, it's making us look like fools. You need to either hire these people by the end of July, or I'm going to have to start picking people."

Tillerson soon engaged in another fight, this time in the Oval Office and in front of the president. He belittled policy adviser Stephen Miller, a Trump favorite, charging he didn't know what he was talking about. "What did you ever really run?" he asked Miller condescendingly.

White House Press Secretary Sean Spicer, who was a commander in the Naval Reserves, tried several times to persuade Mattis to appear on Sunday talk shows on behalf of the administration. The answer was always no.

"Sean," Mattis finally said, "I've killed people for a living. If you call me again, I'm going to fucking send you to Afghanistan. Are we clear?"

"I'm never signing one of these recertifications again," Trump said. "I can't believe I'm signing this one. There's no way you're going to get me to sign another one."

McMaster later signed and put out a 27-page methodical Iran strategy with two prongs. The first was engagement, which was really a subversion campaign to influence Iran's population. The second was confrontation for their malign actions.

CHAPTER

17

During the campaign, Trump had pounded almost as hard on U.S. trade agreements as he had on Hillary Clinton. As far as he was concerned, the current U.S. trade agreements allowed cheaper foreign goods to flood into the United States, which took away jobs from American workers.

At a rally in June 2016 at a Pennsylvania scrap metal facility, he said the loss of industrial jobs was a "politician-made disaster" and "the consequence of a leadership class that worships globalism over Americanism." The result was that "Our politicians took away from the people their means of making a living and supporting their families . . . moving our jobs, our wealth and our factories to Mexico and overseas." He blasted Clinton "and her friends in global finance [who] want to scare America into thinking small."

Nearly all economists disagreed with Trump, but he found an academic economist who hated free trade as much as he did. He brought him to the White House as both director of trade and industrial policy and director of the National Trade Council. Peter Navarro was a 67-year-old Harvard PhD in economics. "This is the president's vision," Navarro publicly said. "My function really as an economist is to try to provide the underlying analytics that confirm his intuition. And his intuition is always right in these matters."

Gary Cohn was convinced that trade deficits were irrelevant and could be a good thing, allowing Americans to buy cheaper goods. Goods from Mexico, Canada and China were flooding into the United States because they were competitively priced. Americans who spent less money on those imported goods had more money to spend on other products, services and savings. This was the efficiency of global markets.

Cohn and Navarro clashed. At one meeting in the Oval Office with Trump and Navarro, Cohn said that 99.9999 percent of the world's economists agreed with him. It was basically true. Navarro stood virtually alone.

Navarro took Cohn on, calling him a Wall Street establishment idiot.

The core of Navarro's argument was that U.S. trade deficits were driven by high tariffs imposed by foreign countries like China, currency manipulation, intellectual property theft, sweatshop labor and lax environmental controls.

The North American Free Trade Agreement (NAFTA) had sucked the manufacturing lifeblood out of the U.S. just as Trump predicted, Navarro said, turning Mexico into a manufacturing powerhouse, while driving U.S. workers to the poorhouse. U.S. steelworkers were being laid off and steel prices were dropping. Trump should impose tariffs on imported steel.

Trump said he agreed.

"If you just shut the fuck up and listen," Cohn said to both Trump and Navarro, dropping deference for the moment, "you might learn something."

Goldman Sachs, to Cohn, had always been about research, data and fact. Anytime you went into a meeting, you should have more hard, documented information than anyone else in the room.

"The problem," Cohn said, "is that Peter comes in here and says

all this stuff and doesn't have any facts to back it up. I have the facts."
He had sent Trump a heavily researched paper on the service econ-
omy. He knew Trump had never read it and probably never would.
Trump hated homework.

Mr. President, Cohn said, trying to summarize, "You have a Nor-
man Rockwell view of America." The U.S. economy today is not
that economy. Today, "80 plus percent of our GDP is in the service
sector." Cohn knew it was about 84 percent but he did not want to
be called out for rounding numbers up. The Goldman way was to
carefully round down.

"Think about it, sir, when you walk down a street in Manhattan
today versus when you walked down a street in Manhattan 20 or 30
years ago." He chose a familiar intersection from memory. Twenty
years before, the four corners had been occupied by a Gap, a Banana
Republic, J.P. Morgan and a local retailer.

"Banana Republic and Gap don't really exist anymore, or they
exist in the shadow of themselves. The local retailer doesn't exist.
J.P. Morgan still exists.

"Now it's Starbucks, a nail salon and J.P. Morgan. They're all
service businesses.

"So when you walk down Madison Avenue today or you walk
down Third Avenue or you walk Second Avenue, it's dry cleaners, it's
food, it's restaurants, it's Starbucks and it's nail salons. We no longer
have Ma and Pa hardware stores. We don't have Ma and Pa clothing
stores. Think of who you rent space to in Trump Tower."

"I do have the largest Chinese bank as one of my major tenants,"
Trump said.

"Who's your one retailer in the Trump Tower?"

"Starbucks," Trump replied. "And a restaurant in the basement.
Oh, and two more restaurants in the basement."

"Exactly," Cohn said. "So your retail space today is services. It's
not people selling shoes, or hard goods, or white goods. This is what
America is today. So if we're 80-plus percent services, if we spend
less and less money on goods, we have more disposable income to
spend on services or do something miraculous called savings."

Cohn found he almost had to shout to be heard. "Look," he said, "the only time that our trade deficit goes down" were times like the financial crisis in 2008. "Our trade deficit goes down because our economy's contracting. If you want our trade deficit to go down, we can make that happen. Let's just blow up the economy!"

On the other hand, Cohn said, if they did it his way—no tariffs, no quotas, no protectionism, no trade wars—"if we do things right, our trade deficit's going to get bigger."

And when the trade deficit got bigger each month, Cohn went to Trump, who grew more and more agitated.

"Sir, I told you this was going to happen," Cohn said. "This is a good sign. It's not a bad sign."

"I went to parts of Pennsylvania," the president said, "that used to be big steel towns and now they're desolate towns and no one had a job and no one has work there."

"That may be true, sir," Cohn said. "But remember there were towns 100 years ago that made horse carriages and buggy whips. No one had a job either. They had to reinvent themselves. You go to states like Colorado, you've got 2.6 unemployment rate because they keep reinventing themselves."

Trump did not like, or buy, any of the arguments. "It has nothing to do with it," Trump said.

Cohn brought in Lawrence B. Lindsey, a Harvard economist who had held Cohn's job under President George W. Bush. Lindsey bluntly asked, Why are you spending any time thinking about our trade deficit? You should be thinking about the economy as a whole. If we can buy cheap products abroad and we can excel in other areas—service and high-tech products—that should be the focus. The global marketplace provided immense benefits to Americans.

"Why don't we manufacture things at home?" Lindsey asked. "We're a manufacturing country."

Of course the United States manufactured things, but reality did not match the vision in Trump's mind. The president clung to an outdated view of America—locomotives, factories with huge smoke-stacks, workers busy on assembly lines.

Cohn assembled every piece of economic data available to show that American workers did not aspire to work in assembly factories.

Each month Cohn brought Trump the latest Job Openings and Labor Turnover Survey, called JOLTS, conducted by the Bureau of Labor Statistics. He realized he was being an asshole by rubbing it in because each month was basically the same, but he didn't care.

"Mr. President, can I show this to you?" Cohn fanned out the pages of data in front of the president. "See, the biggest leavers of jobs—people leaving voluntarily—was from manufacturing."

"I don't get it," Trump said.

Cohn tried to explain: "I can sit in a nice office with air conditioning and a desk, or stand on my feet eight hours a day. Which one would you do for the same pay?"

Cohn added, "People don't want to stand in front of a 2,000 degree blast furnace. People don't want to go into coal mines and get black lung. For the same dollars or equal dollars, they're going to choose something else."

Trump wasn't buying it.

Several times Cohn just asked the president, "Why do you have these views?"

"I just do," Trump replied. "I've had these views for 30 years."

"That doesn't mean they're right," Cohn said. "I had the view for 15 years I could play professional football. It doesn't mean I was right."

Staff secretary Rob Porter had been hired by Priebus. He came into the job with five-star recommendations from people who had served as staff secretaries to Republican presidents. Priebus had required Porter almost to sign a blood oath of loyalty to him. "It's great you went to Harvard, Oxford; you're smart and everybody vouches for you. But what really matters to me is that you're going to be loyal to me."

Porter had overlapped at Harvard with Jared Kushner, who had taken a class there taught by Porter's father, Roger Porter, who had served on the staffs of Presidents Ford, the first Bush and Reagan.

Jared and Porter met during the transition for about two hours. The first hour also seemed like a loyalty test.

Trump had great instincts and was a political genius, Kushner said, but he was going to take some getting used to. "You're going to have to learn how to handle him. How to relate to him."

Though he had not been a Trump supporter during the 2016 campaign, Porter had accepted the job. By Inauguration Day he had not yet met Trump. During the speech Porter sat behind the podium and winced when Trump invoked "American carnage." He left two thirds of the way through the speech so he could begin his duties and meet the new president.

"I'm Rob Porter, Mr. President. I'm your staff secretary." It was clear Trump had no clue what that was or who Porter was. Jared told Trump that Porter was going to structure and order Trump's life.

Trump looked at the two of them as if to say, What are you talking about? You're not doing anything like that. No one's going to do that. The president walked away without saying anything to find a TV screen.

The first official piece of paper for Trump to sign was the legislation granting retired Marine General James Mattis a waiver to become secretary of defense. Mattis had retired from the military less than the legally mandated seven years before being permitted to serve as secretary of defense.

Another matter was withdrawing the United States from the Trans-Pacific Partnership, or TPP, a regional free trade deal negotiated under Obama that lowered tariffs and provided a forum to resolve intellectual property and labor disputes between the U.S. and 11 other nations, including Japan, Canada and numerous countries in Southeast Asia.

During the transition several people had told Trump that he didn't have to do it on day one. It was a little more complicated. It ought to be discussed.

"No way, no how," Trump said. "This was on the campaign. We're not backing off this. We're signing it. Draw it up."

He signed the papers to formally withdraw on January 23, the first full weekday of his presidency.

"The Trump trade agenda does indeed remain severely hobbled by political forces within the West Wing," Peter Navarro, the White House assistant heading the National Trade Council, wrote in an Eyes Only two-page memo to the president and Chief of Staff Priebus on March 27, 2017.

Navarro, who agreed with Trump's view that trade deficits mattered a great deal, was furious. He had been unable to get traction in the first two months of the Trump presidency. "It is impossible to get a trade action to your desk for consideration in a timely manner," Navarro wrote.

He unleashed at Rob Porter, the staff secretary. "Any proposed executive action on trade that moves through the Staff Secretary process is highly vulnerable to dilution, delay or derailment."

Cohn "has amassed a large power base in the West Wing and his two top aides on trade . . . are skilled political operatives fundamentally opposed to the Trump trade agenda.

"Not reported in the press is that Treasury Secretary Mnuchin is part of Cohn's 'Wall Street Wing,' which has effectively blocked or delayed every proposed action on trade."

Navarro identified those fighting against "the Cohn headwinds" as Bannon, Stephen Miller, Commerce Secretary Wilbur Ross and himself.

"Mr. President, are you aware that under pressure from the Cohn faction, I was demoted on Day One from Assistant to Deputy, given zero staff on trade, went almost three weeks without an office and have had no direct access to the Oval Office?"

Using an analogy sure to be understood by Trump, he said, "In golf terminology, I have been given only a five iron and a putter and ordered to shoot par on trade—an impossible task." He proposed that he and the National Trade Council be given more power, staff and access. He included some news articles critical of Cohn and re-porting on his increased power.

Navarro handed the memo to Porter to be forwarded to Trump and Priebus. Porter was trying to present himself as the honest bro-ker but he had taught economics at Oxford and was convinced that Navarro's views were outdated and unsupportable. As far as Porter was concerned Navarro was a member of the Flat Earth Society on trade deficits, like the president himself.

Porter and Cohn had formed an alliance. The staff secretary was squarely a member of the "Wall Street Wing."

At the same time Porter saw clearly that Navarro represented the president's heart on trade. If he forwarded the memo it could inten-sify the trade policy struggle and mushroom into a major fight.

Porter showed the memo to Priebus.

"This is a terrible idea," Porter said. "I'm not going to give it [out]. I'm going to keep it on my desk, keep it in my files. Not going anywhere."

Priebus didn't disagree.

Porter again spoke with Priebus about trade. "We've got to do something about this," he said. "An absolute and complete mess"—the Cohn-Mnuchin faction versus the Navarro-Ross faction. "It's just a free-for-all, a melee, a sort of every-man-for-himself state of nature."

"Well," Priebus said, "what do you think we ought to do?"

"Somebody needs to coordinate trade."

"Who should it be?" Priebus asked.

"In a normal administration, it would be the National Economic Council and Gary Cohn," Porter said. That was the job—gather all the points of view, the data, integrate them if possible and present the president with some options, get a decision and develop an im-plementation plan.

Priebus knew the theory.

"Gary Cohn can't do it," Porter said, "because he's a self-identi-fied globalist. Peter Navarro and Wilbur Ross would never let him be an honest broker coordinator of anything, and would never respect it." And "He doesn't want to do it anyway."

"Well," Priebus said, adopting Trump's management habit of picking the person in the room, the closest at hand, "why don't you do it?"

So Porter, the 39-year-old staff secretary with no previous experience in the executive branch, became the coordinator for trade policy and took charge of one of the major pillars and promises of the Trump presidency.

Porter began chairing 9:30 a.m. trade meetings every Tuesday in the Roosevelt Room. He invited all interested parties. Priebus gave it his blessing but did not announce anything. It just happened. Soon half a dozen cabinet secretaries and more senior staffers were showing up.

Trump later found out about the Tuesday meetings because he was talking to Porter so much on trade. Porter had developed a close enough relationship with the president, and had spent enough time with him, that all the others apparently thought his authority to chair trade coordination had come from the president.

In the meantime, Robert Lighthizer, a Washington lawyer and former deputy in Reagan's trade office, was confirmed on May 11 as the U.S. trade representative. He was the person who was supposed to be in charge of trade issues.

On July 17, Lighthizer and Navarro brought a large poster to show Trump in the Oval Office, a brightly colored collection of boxes and arrows titled "The Trade Agenda Timeline." It was a vision of a protectionist Trump trade agenda with 15 projected dates to start renegotiations or take action on the South Korea KORUS trade deal, NAFTA, and to launch investigations and actions regarding aluminum, steel and automobile parts. It proposed imposing steel tariffs in less than two months, after Labor Day.

Navarro and Lighthizer began the presentation. Trump seemed very interested.

Porter arrived several minutes after and soon began objecting strenuously, calling Lighthizer and Navarro out on their process foul. Since March 22, when he had spelled out the rules in a three-page memo, Priebus had required formal paperwork for presidential meetings and decisions. The memo said in bold, "**Decisions are not final—and therefore may not be implemented—until the staff secretary files a vetted decision memorandum signed by the President.**" Knowing how the Trump White House worked, the memo also said in bold, "**On-the-fly decisions are strictly provisional.**"

Porter said that several of the actions on the poster required congressional authorization. "You don't have authority," he told the president.

There had been no attempt to coordinate the arguments. "Peter and Bob represent one viewpoint," Porter said. "You need to get the viewpoint of Commerce [Wilbur Ross]. You need to get the viewpoint of Treasury [Mnuchin]. You need to get the viewpoint of the National Economic Council [Cohn]. We need to vet and have a process."

For the moment, but only for that moment, the trade issues gave way to process. Nothing moved forward.

By spring, Bannon saw that the constant disorder at the White House wasn't helping him or anyone. "You're in charge," Bannon told Priebus. "I'm going through you. No more of me doing my own thing." A chief of staff who was not in charge had become too disruptive even for certified disrupter and loner Steve Bannon.

It was a major concession that Jared and Ivanka would not make. They were their own silo in Priebus's view. He could not get them into some orderly program. The whole arrangement was hurting everyone. It was hurting him. Hurting them.

"You don't think they should be here?" Trump asked several times.

No, they shouldn't, Priebus answered each time. But nothing happened. He believed he could go no further to try to oust Trump's daughter and son-in-law from the West Wing. No one could fire the family. That was not going to happen.

The president would go as far as to say a number of times, "Jared and Ivanka are moderate Democrats from New York." It was more description than complaint.

Bannon was convinced that Jared had leaked a recent story to

Britain's *Daily Mail* about Trump blowing up at him and Priebus and blocking them from traveling on Air Force One to Florida. It wasn't true they had been kicked off the trip. Both had declined to travel that day. "You fucking set me up," he said to Kushner. "You trashed Reince in this story. And I know you did it."

Kushner vehemently denied it, and seemed offended at the accusation. For his part, he was convinced that Bannon had leaked a story to *The New York Times* about his December 2016 meeting with the Russian ambassador, adding fuel to the allegations that the Trump campaign had colluded with Russia.

During a meeting in Priebus's corner office Bannon and Ivanka got into an altercation.

"You're a goddamn staffer!" Bannon finally screamed at Ivanka. "You're nothing but a fucking staffer!" She had to work through the chief of staff like everyone else, he said. There needed to be some order. "You walk around this place and act like you're in charge, and you're not. You're on staff!"

"I'm not a staffer!" she shouted. "I'll never be a staffer. I'm the first daughter"—she really used the title—"and I'm never going to be a staffer!"

The rift widened.

Bossie, Trump's deputy campaign manager, still kept in close touch with Bannon even though he had not received a White House appointment. Bannon was running a full-frontal assault against Kushner in the White House, and Bossie offered some advice.

"Steve," Bossie said, "one of you is the father of his grandchildren and the other is not. If you put yourself in the president's shoes, which one of you guys is he siding with?"

Priebus had his troubles with Bannon but Bannon had fallen in line and was 10 times the unifier that Jared and Ivanka were.

Priebus was still having trouble getting McMaster to click with Trump. When the national security adviser came to the Oval Office for scheduled meetings, the president would often say, "You again?

I just saw you." McMaster's briefing style was all wrong for Trump. It was really the opposite of Trump in almost every way. McMaster was order and discipline, hierarchy and linear thinking. Trump would go from A to G to L to Z. Or double back into D or S. McMaster was incapable of going from A to C without hitting B.

Priebus found that McMaster was also a bit of a hothead. The prime minster of India, Narendra Modi, who had been courted assiduously by Obama, was coming for a visit to the United States in June to see Trump. India was the counterweight to Pakistan, which was giving the new administration as much trouble as it had given previous ones by hedging maddeningly on terrorism. Modi wanted to go to Camp David and have dinner, bond with Trump.

It's not in the cards, Priebus told McMaster. "We're just going to do dinner here. It's what the president wants."

"What the fuck?" McMaster blew up. "It's India, man. It's fucking India." He understood the strategic importance of India, a sworn enemy of Pakistan. Outreach and strong relations were essential.

The later event for Modi was a "no-frills" cocktail reception. The working dinner was at the White House.

Donald Trump, full of emotion, phoned his secretary of defense James Mattis at the Pentagon on the morning of Tuesday, April 4. It was the third month of his presidency. Pictures and videos of a sarin gas attack on Syrian rebels were flooding into the White House.

It was a gruesome, brutal attack, killing dozens. Among the dead were women and children—babies, beautiful babies. Choking, mouths foaming, parents stricken with grief and despair. This was the work of the Syrian dictator Bashar al-Assad on his own people.

"Let's fucking kill him!" the president said. "Let's go in. Let's kill the fucking lot of them."

The military had the capability to launch a covert top secret leadership air strike in Syria.

Trump sounded personally attacked. Syria had promised not to use chemical weapons—an apparent reference to Syrian president Assad's agreement to destroy all his chemical weapons.

Yes, Mattis said. He would get right on it.

He hung up the phone.

"We're not going to do any of that," he told a senior aide. "We're going to be much more measured."

They would develop small, medium and large options for a conventional air strike, the standard three tiers.

Mattis saw that the administration had been presented with a rare golden opportunity to do something without doing too much, but certainly more than Obama.

In 2012, Obama had announced that chemical weapons use by Assad would be a red line. The next year, Assad killed 1,400 civilians with chemical weapons. Obama had the military prepare a strike plan, but he equivocated. He wanted to avoid another armed conflict and quagmire.

It was Vladimir Putin, of all people, who came to Obama's rescue. The Russian leader brokered an agreement under which Assad would agree to destroy all his chemical weapons. An astonishing 1,300 tons of chemical weapons were removed from Syria.

Obama basked in the success. In 2014 he said, "We mark an important achievement in our ongoing effort to counter the spread of weapons of mass destruction by eliminating Syria's declared chemical weapons stockpile." Secretary of State John Kerry went further. "We got 100 percent of the chemical weapons out."

Classified intelligence reports dispute this. In 2016, DNI Clapper said publicly, "Syria has not declared all the elements of its chemical weapons program."

As the Syrian civil war ground on, Obama was tagged with a strategic failure. The war had left more than 400,000 killed and millions of refugees.

After the chemical attack, McMaster and his NSC Mideast chief Derek Harvey went into action at the White House to develop options.

Bannon got word of what was in progress. It was impossible to miss. When Trump was on fire, everyone in his orbit could feel the heat. Bannon confronted Harvey in a West Wing hallway.

"What the fuck are you doing?" he asked.

"Developing options for the president," Harvey replied. "He asked for options, and this is how the process works."

The process was precisely what Bannon hated. He saw it as tilted toward military action, toughness, with a momentum and concept of its own: America as the world's policeman. Do something, became the mantra; fix it. They hadn't even answered Trump's question about exactly what the United States was doing with its large presence in the Middle East.

Bannon saw Ivanka's hand at work. She knew how to work her father better than anyone. She took pictures of the suffering or dead babies to him in the residence. The gas attack was a true horror, Bannon understood, but a military response was exactly what Trump should not want.

In sharp contrast, Derek Harvey was tired of being involved in managing national security policy to inconclusive results. Syria was a classic case study of words and half measures almost designed not to solve the problem. This was a chance to maximize a military response.

The middle option called for a strike of about 60 Tomahawks at one airfield.

"We have an opportunity here to do more," Harvey argued to McMaster, "and we have to think in terms of hitting multiple airfields." They could strike with real impact. "Take out their air power because that's a force multiplier for the regime. We're trying to shape the endgame and put more pressure on the regime to engage politically."

Harvey said they should "take out his air force—not 15 or 20 percent, let's take out 80 percent of it." That would mean using 200 Tomahawks, more than triple the 60 from the middle option.

"Derek, I know," McMaster said, "but we've got to deal with the reality of Mattis" who "is berating me for the direction we are heading here."

Mattis wanted to be careful. Action in any form was risky. Russians were working at the Syrian airfields; kill Russians, and they would have a whole new ball game, a confrontation or a catastrophe.

A National Security Council meeting was scheduled to discuss options. Bannon availed himself of his walk-in privileges and went to see Trump alone in the Oval Office. He told the president that part of avoiding unnecessary wars and overseas commitments was not responding with missiles the way his advisers were proposing.

Jump in and make sure you are vocal, Trump said.

In a public statement on April 4, Trump attacked both Assad and Obama. "These heinous actions by the Bashar al-Assad regime are a consequence of the past administration's weakness and irresolution. President Obama said in 2012 that he would establish a 'red line' against the use of chemical weapons and then did nothing."

At the NSC meeting, the three options were presented: hot, medium and cold. The largest option was a 200-missile attack on all the major Syrian airfields; the medium option was 60 missiles; and the smallest was almost none, or none at all.

The potential target list was large. In 2013 when Obama had threatened a missile attack, he had approved a target list including a government compound housing the chemical weapons program. It didn't make the current target list because Mattis and the Pentagon wanted to keep the attack as narrow as possible.

Mattis had scoped it down just to the one airfield in the 60-missile strike. A housing complex at the airfield was also taken off the target list because of the likelihood that family members would be there.

"If that's the standard," Bannon argued, "let me go get some pictures of sub-Saharan Africa. Okay? Let me get some of what's happening down in Guatemala and Nicaragua. If this is the standard for a fucking missile strike, let's go everywhere. Let's do everything." He thought he had the president on his side.

"This will be another pinprick," Bannon continued. If they were going to strike, do something dramatic, he added sarcastically. "This is very Clinton-esque," he said, deploying the biggest insult. "You're going to drop a couple of cruise missiles onto a runway that will be fully back up and operational in a day or two."

But then the middle option advocates worked the president. Bannon thought it was insidious. Their argument was that this was not designed to start a war. It was really a messaging operation, designed to avoid one.

On Friday, Trump flew to Mar-a-Lago and in the evening convened an NSC meeting in a SCIF. Fourteen people were there—Tillerson, Priebus, McMaster, Kushner, Bannon, Cohn and Deputy National Security Adviser for Strategy Dina Powell. Mattis was on the video screen. The middle option of 60 sea-launched missiles was on the table. The targets were Syrian aircraft on the ground, hardened aircraft shelters, storage facilities for petroleum and other material, ammunition supply bunkers, air defense systems and radar.

Trump had stepped back from his initial desire to kill Assad. He was unusually focused on the details. He had a series of questions about risk. What happens if a missile or missiles go off course? What happens if we hit a school? If we hit a hospital? Or a target we did not intend to hit? What was the possibility of killing civilians?

Mattis provided assurances. These were the best ships and men.

Trump asked to talk on a secure line with the captains of the two ships, the USS *Porter* and the USS *Ross*, both guided missile destroyers. He told the skippers: I'm going ahead with this strike tonight. Are your guys the best at programming the missiles?

Both captains gave assurances. Trump then went around the room and asked each for an opinion. What do you think? If anyone here has a second opinion, I want to hear it here, not later.

There was agreement, even strong support.

Intelligence showed convincingly that the Russians would be in just one compound at the airfield. The timing of the strike—4:40 a.m. in Syria—virtually ensured they would not be working around the aircraft. About 15 minutes before the Tomahawks would hit, a warning was sent to the Russians at the airfield. When the call was made, the Russian who picked up the phone at the airfield sounded intoxicated.

Trump gave the go-ahead for his first significant military action. Fifty-nine Tomahawks hit their targets; one fell into the Mediterranean after launch.

Trump went to dinner with Chinese president Xi Jinping, who was visiting Mar-a-Lago as part of a two-day summit to discuss trade and North Korea. As dessert was being served Trump said to Xi, "We're in the process of bombing Syria because of its gas attack."

"Say that again," Xi said through the interpreter. Trump repeated it.

"How many missiles?" Xi asked.

Trump said 59.

"59?" Xi asked.

Trump confirmed 59.

"Okay," Xi said, "I understand. Good, he deserved it."

And that was the end of the dinner.

Afterward, Bannon called Harvey a "warmonger. You and H.R. are trying to start a war."

About midnight, Trump called Senator Lindsey Graham.

"Did I wake you up?" Trump asked.

"Yeah," Graham said.

"Sorry."

"No, I'm glad to hear from you, Mr. President."

"I bet you are the happiest guy in town."

"Happy is not the right word. I'm proud of my president." Graham could hear a pin drop. "You did something that should have been done a long time ago."

"A hundred countries have called," Trump said.

Graham thought, probably, maybe, 10.

"They're all calling me, patting me on the back. You know what the Chinese president told me? When I told him during dessert, we just shot 59 Tomahawks at Assad? Good, he deserved it!"

A blow to the Bannon model! Graham thought.

"Obama," Trump said, "he's a weak dick. He would've never done that."

"And his failure to do that has cost about 400,000 people their lives," Graham said, pointing to the number who had died in the entire Syrian war.

Trump kept talking about the kids—burnt, peeling skin, horrifying deaths and injuries.

"Mr. President," Graham said, "I can show you pictures like that from all over the Mideast." He didn't seem to know he was echoing Bannon about the worldwide human rights atrocities. "You did the right thing not because of how he killed these kids. He was just so brazen, telling everybody in the world, fuck you. And you said, no, fuck you!"

Graham knew Trump-speak, meeting a "fuck you" with a much bigger "fuck you." "That's what you are saying to him: Fuck you. Here's what you've got to watch for. What are you going to do if they repair the damage to that very base and start flying sorties out of it again and drop a barrel bomb on kids? You need to get ready for that. Because that's poking you in the eye."

The problem was not so much just the chemical weapons, Graham said, it was the bombing of civilians. That shouldn't be permitted with any weapon.

"If you don't say that," Graham pressed, "then all the things you've gained are going to be lost, because he's just saying fuck you, okay, I'll kill them another way. That's what Assad will be saying to you. This is a test. One and done is not the right answer here. You let that fucker know that if he takes off from that air base and he bombs a bunch of kids with barrel bombs, you'll shoot him down."

Whenever a commander in chief starts shooting, even with only 59 Tomahawks, political and public opinion tend to actively rally around him. This was no exception. Trump was almost universally praised for a quick and decisive response.

The next morning, Senator John McCain appeared on *Morning Joe*. "The signal that was sent last night, as you said, was a very, very important one."

Host Joe Scarborough said it was important not only to Russia and Assad, but to China and North Korea. "And our friends," McCain added. "A lot of the Arab countries are willing to be partners with us as long as they think they can rely on us."

Scarborough observed that Sunni Arabs had felt that under Obama the U.S. hadn't "had their back. Does last night change that?"

"It begins to," *Washington Post* columnist David Ignatius, who was among the panel discussing the strike, said. "They want to see more."

McCain praised Trump's national security team, and praised the president for listening to them: "That's what's most encouraging to me, is that he respects Mattis. He respects McMaster."

Some of the highest praise came from surprising foreign policy experts. Anne-Marie Slaughter, who had been director of the powerful Policy Planning staff in the State Department during Hillary Clinton's first two years as secretary of state in the Obama years, tweeted, "Donald Trump has done the right thing on Syria. Finally!! After years of useless handwringing in the face of hideous atrocities."

In the days and weeks afterward, Trump often told aides in the West Wing that he did not think the strike on the air base was sufficient. Shouldn't the U.S. do more? He toyed with the idea of ordering a covert leadership strike on Assad.

He had been briefed or read some papers on what nerve gas did to the human body. "Do you realize what it's like?" he asked at one point. He had a visual image which he described. The lungs fill up. Breathing stifles, and there is foaming at the mouth. Drooling, blindness, paralysis. Uncontrollable vomiting, urination and defecation. Excruciating pain all over, especially abdominal cramps. Seizures. The organs of the body become disconnected from the brain. After this, 10 minutes of torture, death. Children. Babies.

He wanted options. They were plentiful. The United States military had all the imaginable lethal capabilities. What could he do? He wanted to know.

Secretary Mattis was alarmed that Trump might order a second strike and worked to tamp down and discourage another military action in Syria.

After weeks Trump's outrage subsided and he turned, but not quickly, to other matters.

McMaster complained to Jared about his lack of authority to move decisions forward. Like most secretaries of state and defense, Tillerson and Mattis did not want a strong national security adviser.

On one occasion after the Syrian strike, the president wanted some information about recent Russian and Iranian provocations in Syria. The U.S. had killed some Iranian-sponsored Hezbollah troops on the road east of Palmyra and shot down a threatening Iranian armed drone. Trump had some questions for McMaster. What happens if Americans get killed? What are we going to do? What are the options?

McMaster phoned both Tillerson and Mattis. No response. He summoned Harvey and lit into him. The F-words flew. This is your job, get your counterparts over there.

Nine hours passed, and still no response from either Tillerson or Mattis.

The Joint Staff from the Pentagon arrived at the White House to brief Harvey. The Defense Department had some strike options but nothing about what would happen if Americans got killed in the Syrian border town of Tanf where U.S. forces were operating. Or if a U.S. ship was hit by a mine.

It was incredible to both McMaster and Harvey. No answers were forthcoming. But Trump soon forgot his questions.

I want an executive order withdrawing the United States from NAFTA"—the North American Free Trade Agreement—"and I want it on my desk by Friday," President Trump ordered.

Gathered with him in the Oval Office on Tuesday, April 25, were Vice President Pence, Commerce Secretary Ross, Kushner, Porter and Navarro. The president wanted to be able to announce it on his 100th day in office.

When no one pushed back or offered any objections, Porter, who had been chairing the Tuesday-morning trade meetings, noted that it could not be an executive order but would have to be a 180-termination notice as required by the trade agreement.

"There's a huge timing problem with this," he told Trump and the others, "because no matter how quickly you end up renegotiating NAFTA under the Trade Promotion Authority rules, it's going to take time." A renegotiated agreement would have to be passed by Congress and that would take more than the 180 days.

Porter was the youngest and most junior person in the room. "We don't want a gap," he continued, "and a period where we don't have any deal. We've got a timing problem. We can't just start the 180-day clock willy-nilly."

The others were silent and only seemed to be encouraging Trump. Porter was appalled that the president was even considering a preemptive withdrawal from NAFTA. The trade agreement had been the foundation of economic and national security in North America for more than two decades. The agreement lifted tariffs between the U.S., Canada and Mexico. Annual trade among the three was more than $1 trillion. U.S. trade each with Canada and Mexico was almost as great as U.S. trade with China, the largest trading partner.

"We need to have a process to make sure that we do this in proper order, that we've thought through these things." Porter gestured toward Pence, Ross, Kushner and Navarro. "It's great that these people are here, but Gary Cohn's not here. Steve Mnuchin's not here. I understand you want to move fast," but we have to slow it down.

"I don't care about any of this stuff," Trump said. "I want it on my desk on Friday."

Porter went to see McMaster to enlist his support. McMaster had not been very involved in the trade discussion but said he agreed that withdrawal from NAFTA would be a national security nightmare, and an unnecessary one. It would rattle the allies. I'm on board, he promised.

An emergency meeting was called with the relevant cabinet secretaries and senior advisers in the Roosevelt Room the next day. The fuse was lit. It looked like they had only a day or two before Trump would sign.

As Navarro pushed for withdrawal, Homeland Security Secretary John Kelly and others said a perceived threat that the United States might terminate was good leverage, but actually doing it would be catastrophic. The United States would be shooting itself in the foot. The ripple effects would be huge. It would roil the financial markets and lead to instant retaliation. Trading partners around the world would wonder if they were next.

After the meeting broke up, on his way to the Oval Office to go over the documents that Trump wanted prepared, Porter stopped Agriculture Secretary Sonny Perdue, who had just assumed office. Perdue was a former Republican governor of Georgia, the first from his party since Reconstruction.

"Sonny," Porter said, "why don't you come in?" Wilbur Ross joined them in the Oval Office.

"NAFTA has been a huge boon for American ag interests," Perdue told Trump. "We export $39 billion a year to Mexico and Canada. We wouldn't have markets for these products otherwise. The people who stand to lose the most if we withdraw from NAFTA are your base, the Trump supporters."

Perdue showed Trump a map of the United States that indicated the states and counties where agriculture and manufacturing losses would be hit hardest. Many were places that had voted for Trump.

"It's not just your base," Perdue said. "It's your base in states that are important presidential swing states. So you just can't do this."

"Yeah," Trump said, "but they're screwing us, and we've got to do something."

The president finally decided they should amp up the public rhetoric and threat, but not actually send a 180-day notice.

Jared passed word to Porter. "The president's agreed not to withdraw for now."

Porter knew that everything with Trump was provisional, but he was surprised how close they had come to the edge. And it was not over.

Peter Navarro slipped into the Oval Office for an ad hoc, unscheduled meeting with the president.

"The only thing we've done is withdraw from TPP," the president said, referring to the Trans-Pacific Partnership. "Why haven't we done anything else on trade?"

"The staff secretary process is holding all this stuff up," Navarro said.

"Madeleine," Trump called to his assistant, Madeleine Westerhout. "Get Rob up here right now."

Porter ran up the stairs to the Oval Office.

"What the fuck are you stalling for?" Trump said to Porter. "Why aren't we getting this done? Do your job. It's tap, tap, tap. You're just tapping me along. I want to do this."

The president was serious again. Porter drafted a 180-day notification letter to be signed by Trump that the United States would withdraw from NAFTA.

Porter was more and more convinced that it could trigger an economic and foreign relations crisis with Canada and Mexico. He went to see Cohn.

"I can stop this," Cohn said to Porter. "I'll just take the paper off his desk before I leave." And he later took it. "If he's going to sign it, he's going to need another piece of paper."

"We'll slow-walk that one too," Porter promised.

Cohn knew, of course, that the president could easily order another copy, but if the paper was not sitting in front of him, he'd likely forget it. If it was out of sight, it was out of mind.

Porter agreed. Trump's memory needed a trigger—something on his desk or something he read in the newspaper or saw on television. Or Peter Navarro sneaking into the Oval Office again. Without something or someone activating him, it might be hours or days or even weeks before he would think, Wait, we're going to withdraw from that, why didn't we do that? Without a trigger, it conceivably might never happen.

Sonny Perdue gave a presentation in the Situation Room on May 4 on the role of agriculture in trade. Sensitive intelligence showed that if the United States imposed new tariffs on China, the Chinese would retaliate with their own tariffs.

The Chinese knew exactly how to inflict economic and political pain. The United States was in kindergarten compared to China's PhD. The Chinese knew which congressional districts produced what products, such as soybeans. They knew which swing districts were going to be important to maintain control of the House. They could target tariffs at products from those districts, or at a state level. The Chinese would target bourbon from McConnell's Kentucky and dairy products from Paul Ryan's Wisconsin.

Several days later Wilbur Ross laid out the reasoning on the importance of trade deficits. Echoing the president, Ross said trade deficits are the lodestar and were a mark of our economic instability and weakness. The president was focused on trade deficits, he reminded everyone, and they ought to be focused on them.

Porter took off his honest-broker cap. "Trade deficits don't matter," he said, "at least with individual countries. That's an absurd way of thinking." His tone was probably the most disrespect that Porter had ever shown to a cabinet officer. "Trade policy, especially the trade deals that we negotiate, isn't a primary driver of our trade deficit." That deficit depends on economic conditions, which country can produce various goods most efficiently and cheaply, the savings rate and the value of the currencies. All protectionist policies are not in our economic interest.

"Well," Ross shot back, "I've made billions of dollars and I've worked on Wall Street. I know how these markets work. You don't understand supply and demand." If the U.S. puts tariffs on China and they retaliate, we will be able to buy products from other countries.

In the spring of 2017, Ross negotiated a deal with China for the U.S. to import Chinese chicken and export beef. He called it "a herculean accomplishment." But there was some serious criticism of the deal. A *New York Times* headline read, "China Surrenders Little to U.S. in First Round of Trade Talks."

In a meeting at the White House, the president tore into Ross. "I can't believe you made this deal. Why didn't you tell anybody? You didn't tell me about this. You just went off and did it on your own. And it's a terrible deal. We got screwed. Wilbur, maybe you used to have it." As an investment banker representing casino bondholders angry at Trump in 1990, Ross had struck a deal with Trump that acknowledged the value of his famous name and allowed him to avoid bankruptcy.

"I thought you were a killer," Trump said to the 79-year-old Ross. "When you were on Wall Street, you made some of these deals. But you're past your prime. You're not a good negotiator anymore. I don't know what it is, but you've lost it. I don't trust you. I don't want you doing any more negotiations." Bob Lighthizer would handle NAFTA and other trade agreements.

Ross tried to defend the deal—the U.S. would be exporting more beef—but Trump had tuned out.

The president held a meeting on steel tariffs—one of his obsessions—in the Oval Office on June 8. Gary Cohn, Wilbur Ross, Porter and Secretary of Defense Mattis crowded in seats around the Resolute Desk.

"We're ready to go," Ross said. "I want to submit this report." He was recommending tariff rate quotas especially on China. A high prohibitive tariff would be imposed if China increased its current rate of steel exports to the United States.

Porter cited a number of legal problems. The Commerce Department hadn't consulted with the Defense Department, as required by law, to determine whether the imports posed a threat to national security.

"Yes, we have," Ross said. "We've done that."

"I've never been consulted on anything related to any of this," Mattis said.

"That's all right," Ross replied. He had talked to the assistant secretary of defense who dealt with these issues. He had some emails documenting this.

"Well," Mattis said, "you never talked to me."

Porter jumped in to point out that the law said that the defense secretary had to be consulted, not just someone in the department.

These were the legal bureaucratic niceties that drove Trump crazy. "Wilbur, talk to Jim! Get this sorted out," he said. "I'm sick and tired of dealing with this. And get it done quickly, because I want to do this."

Porter saw the issue as an exquisite way to kick the can down the road for several more weeks, if not more. Mattis was helpful in drawing it out, later telling Ross he needed an analysis before he could give his opinion.

Later analysis by the Defense Department for Mattis, however, showed that "U.S military steel usage represents less than one-half percent of the total U.S steel demand" and Defense would be able "to acquire the steel necessary to meet national defense requirements."

Trump said he wished he had fired Comey at the beginning of the administration but now he wanted Comey out.

Bannon disagreed and offered this argument to Trump alone in the Oval Office: "Seventy-five percent of the agents do hate Comey. No doubt. The moment you fire him he's J. fucking Edgar Hoover. The day you fire him, he's the greatest martyr in American history. A weapon to come and get you. They're going to name a special fucking counsel. You can fire Comey. You can't fire the FBI. The minute you fire him, the FBI as an institution, they have to destroy you and they will destroy you."

Bannon thought Trump did not understand the power of the permanent institutions—the FBI, CIA, the Pentagon and the broader military establishment. He also did not understand the sweeping powers of a special counsel who could be appointed to investigate everything a president touched.

"Don't try to talk me out of it," Trump told McGahn and Priebus, "because I've made my decision, so don't even try." Comey is a grandstander and out of control.

By early May, Trump felt that Comey was vulnerable because of his recent testimony in the convoluted investigation of Clinton's private emails. He dictated a letter listing the reasons to fire Comey.

McGahn told him that the deputy attorney general, Rod Rosenstein, was coming in for a meeting. One thing Rosenstein wanted to discuss was Comey, and apparently Rosenstein also wanted to get rid of Comey, McGahn said.

McGahn explained that there was a process here—the deputy attorney general was the person who oversaw the FBI. Let's hear Rosenstein out. This was a stall tactic that the White House staff was using more and more. Let's cool this off, let's talk to Rod and we'll get back to you with a plan.

Rosenstein told Trump that he thought Comey should be fired. He had no problem writing a memo outlining his reasoning. He brought a three-page memo to the White House. The subject: RESTORING PUBLIC CONFIDENCE IN THE FBI. It stated that on July 5, Comey "announced his own conclusions about the nation's most sensitive criminal investigation," which was Hillary Clinton's emails, preempting the decision of the prosecutor and offering "derogatory information" by calling Clinton's conduct "extremely careless." Then, 11 days before the election, he announced he was reopening the Clinton investigation because he believed it was a question of "speak" or "conceal." This misstated the issue, Rosenstein said. He quoted five former attorneys general or deputy attorneys general agreeing that Comey had violated the rules.

Done, said the president. He could not have said it better himself. He sent a brief letter to Comey informing him that he was "terminated and removed from office, effective immediately."

The plan to stall the firing had backfired. It had sped up the process. The Rosenstein memo had nothing to do with the decision, Priebus knew. The president already had made up his mind.

Bannon believed, "100 percent," that the reason for firing Comey was because the FBI was seeking financial records from Jared. It was pure speculation. Ivanka had complained to her father about the FBI.

As the months ground on, Priebus saw that if Trump was planning to or said he was going to fire someone, it did not mean it would happen. One of his favorite sayings became, "Nothing is dead until it's buried around here."

It appeared, for the moment, that Comey was at least dead, but he and his story were not buried.

Trump was watching lots of cable news coverage of his May 9 firing of FBI Director Comey. It was not going well. He had muddied the waters and contradicted himself on May 11 when he told NBC's Lester Holt that he was going to fire Comey no matter what recommendations he had received from Deputy Attorney General Rosenstein and Attorney General Sessions. In a long rambling response to Holt, Trump stated, apparently giving some of his reasoning, "I said to myself, you know, this Russia thing with Trump and Russia is a made-up story."

This answer seemed very much at odds with his letter to Comey saying he was being fired because of Rosenstein's memo severely criticizing Comey for his handling of the Hillary Clinton email investigation.

The evening of Tuesday, May 16, Michael Schmidt of *The New York Times* published a blockbuster story. Comey had written contemporaneous memos of his conversations with Trump. In an Oval Office meeting February 14, while Comey was still FBI director, he wrote that the president had asked him about the investigation of Flynn and said: "I hope you can see your way clear to letting this go, to letting Flynn go. He is a good guy. I hope you can let this go."

Trump hovered around the TV, glued to coverage. On CNN that evening, David Gergen, a voice of experience and reason who had served as a White House adviser to Presidents Richard Nixon and Bill Clinton during their impeachment investigations, sounded an alarm.

"I think we're in impeachment territory," Gergen said. "What we see is a presidency that's starting to come apart."

Porter could see that Trump was about to lose it at the mention of impeachment. The president voiced outrage that Comey seemed to have turned the tables on him.

The next day, Wednesday, May 17, Trump was in the Oval Office when he learned that Rosenstein had appointed Robert Mueller, who had run the FBI for 12 years, of all people, as special counsel to look into Russian election meddling and any connection to the Trump presidential campaign.

Trump's mood deteriorated overnight and the next day, May 18, was the worst. The president erupted into uncontrollable anger, visibly agitated to a degree that no one in his inner circle had witnessed before. It was a harrowing experience. "We barely got by," Porter said to an associate.

Normally Trump sat behind the Resolute Desk or in his private dining room. But this day he mostly stayed on his feet as he stormed between the two rooms.

The president turned to his lifeline—cable news. He watched a two-hour block of Fox News, and then most of the two-hour-long blocks of MSNBC and CNN that he had TiVo'd.

He raged at the coverage as top aides came in and out—Priebus, Bannon, Kushner, McGahn, Cohn, Hicks and Porter. Why was Mueller picked? Trump asked. "He was just in here and I didn't hire him for the FBI," Trump raged. "Of course he's got an axe to grind with me."

"Everybody's trying to get me," the president said. "It's unfair. Now everybody's saying I'm going to be impeached." What are the powers of a special counsel? he asked.

A special counsel had virtually unlimited power to investigate any possible crime, Porter said. It was Watergate, Iran-contra and Clinton's Monica Lewinsky scandal.

"Now I have this person," Trump said bitterly, "who has no accountability who can look into anything, however unrelated it is? They're going to spend years digging through my whole life and finances."

Trump could not focus on much of anything else. Meetings were canceled and parts of the day eventually scrapped.

Porter had never seen Trump so visibly disturbed. He knew Trump was a narcissist who saw everything in terms of its impact on him. But the hours of raging reminded Porter of what he had read about Nixon's final days in office—praying, pounding the carpet, talking to the pictures of past presidents on the walls. Trump's behavior was now in the paranoid territory.

"They're out to get me," Trump said. "This is an injustice. This is unfair. How could this have happened? It's all Jeff Sessions' fault. This is all politically motivated. Rod Rosenstein doesn't know what the hell he is doing. He's a Democrat. He's from Maryland."

As he paced the floor, Trump said, "Rosenstein was one of the people who said to fire Comey and wrote me this letter. How could he possibly be supervising this investigation?"

Bob Mueller had all these conflicts that ought to bar him from being special counsel investigating him. "He was a member of one of my golf courses"—Trump National Golf Club in Sterling, Virginia— and there was a dispute over fees and Mueller resigned. Mueller's law firm had previously represented Trump's son-in-law.

"I'm getting punched," Trump said. "I have to punch back. In order for it to be a fair fight, I have to be fighting."

Back and forth most of the day, the president rotated to watch TV in the dining room and then come out to the Oval Office in a frenzy, asking questions and voicing his anger that he had lost control of the investigation.

"I am the president," Trump said. "I can fire anybody that I want. They can't be investigating me for firing Comey. And Comey deserved to be fired! Everybody hated him. He was awful."

Marc Kasowitz, the seasoned, gray-haired litigator who had represented Trump for decades in divorces and bankruptcies, asked John Dowd, 76, one of the most experienced attorneys in white-collar criminal defense, to his office in New York at 4:00 p.m. on May 25, 2017.

"We need you in Washington to represent the president," to defend Trump in the Russia investigation being launched by special counsel Robert Mueller, Kasowitz said. Several high-profile attorneys had already turned down the job, citing conflicts or the difficulty in managing Trump. But Dowd, a former prosecutor with a long list of prominent clients, jumped at the chance to round out a 47-year legal career with the highest-profile case in the country.

"Oh my God," he replied. "That's incredible. I'd be happy to represent the president."

"It's no day at the beach."

"I think I've figured that out," Dowd said.

Dowd was both good-old-boy figure and hard-nosed investigator. He had been a Marine Corps lawyer in the 1960s and a mob prosecutor as chief of the Justice Department Organized Crime Strike Force in the 1970s. In the 1980s, he was special counsel to the commissioner of baseball. He ran several investigations, the most prominent leading to the banning of Pete Rose of the Cincinnati Reds for betting on baseball games. After that, as a defense attorney, Dowd represented Wall Street and political figures, including Senator John McCain in the Keating Five ethics investigation. He had been a partner in the prominent law firm Akin Gump and was now retired.

Dowd had a conference call with Trump and Kasowitz, and then several conversations with the president. The Mueller investigation, Trump told him, was consuming him and his presidency. He had done nothing wrong. "John, this thing is an enormous burden. It interferes particularly with foreign affairs. It's embarrassing to be in the middle of a deal and the guy, the premier or the prime minister on the other side says, 'Hey Donald, are you going to be around?' It's like a kick in the nuts."

Dowd said he would not charge by the hour. He would set a fee. They agreed on $100,000 a month, which was about half his normal rate. Trump instructed him to send the invoice to his office in New York and he would be paid the next day. (He was.)

The president was outraged by the Mueller investigation. He listed his complaints to Dowd.

First, he had been blindsided by Attorney General Sessions's March 2 decision recusing himself from any investigation of Russian election meddling. He had expected political protection from his attorney general and was now left unprotected.

Second, Trump related how he learned on May 17 that Mueller had been appointed special counsel by Rod Rosenstein, the deputy attorney general. It was absolutely outrageous. He had been in the Oval Office with Sessions when one of the White House lawyers brought the news. Sessions said, "I didn't know about this." He had turned to Sessions, "Well, doesn't he work for you?" Sessions's recusal left Rosenstein in charge of any Russia inquiry.

Worse, Trump said, he had interviewed Mueller just the day before to come back as FBI director and he had turned him down.

Now Mueller was suddenly in charge. "So two times I'm fucking bushwhacked by the Department of Justice."

Third, Trump said that after he fired Comey, the former FBI director had gone on a testifying and leaking crusade to state that Trump asked him to drop the Flynn investigation. "I didn't do anything," Trump told Dowd. "It's all bullshit. Comey's a fucking liar."

Kasowitz concurred that he and one of his partners had investigated to see if there was anything that connected Trump to the Russian meddling. After a full month their initial conclusion was there was nothing.

The way Trump rattled off the denials suggested to Dowd that his outrage was genuine. Of course, that did not mean he was innocent. In addition to blaming Comey, Trump said he did it to himself by not having strong people and lawyers.

Dowd examined the one-page Rosenstein order appointing Mueller May 17. Not only did it authorize a Russian investigation but it directed Mueller to investigate "any matters that arose or may arise directly from the [Russian] investigation." Dowd had never seen anyone in Justice with such broad authority.

The president expressed his distrust. A lot of Democrats were on Mueller's team of prosecutors.

Dowd agreed there might be a political motive. "This is a royal fuck job by a bunch of losers," he told Trump.

Dowd's theory of defending a client is to be his advocate, and also to be a friend. Trump began calling him at all hours, all days. Despite Trump's outgoing, in-your-face style, Dowd could see the president was very lonely.

Dowd discussed the known facts with Trump's legal advisers and reviewed the material for possible vulnerabilities. Based on a preliminary review of the known evidence, he did not see anything to support a charge of collusion with the Russians or obstruction of justice.

Perhaps the most troubling pieces of evidence were former FBI director James Comey's memo and testimony that Trump had appealed to him to go easy on General Flynn after Flynn's firing. According to Comey, Trump had said, "I hope you can see your way clear to letting this go, to letting Flynn go. He is a good guy. I hope you can let this go." Comey said he believed Trump was asking him to drop the investigation.

Trump denied he had said that or anything like it.

What did you say? Dowd asked the president.

"Well, I didn't say that." Trump said Comey had raised the prospect of Trump coming to FBI headquarters to talk to the agents. "And so I was asking him when he wanted me to do that. And he said he would get back to me. But I never commented on Flynn. I mean, as far as I was concerned, Flynn was over."

Dowd continued his own inquiry, being briefed on the testimony of all known witnesses and reviewing documents.

He wanted to establish a relationship with Mueller, whom he knew. Years ago at a Marine Corps parade, Dowd had run into Mueller when he was FBI director.

"What are you up to?" Mueller asked.

"I'm representing Congressman Don Young."

"That crook?" Mueller replied. "How could you do that?"

"That's our system," answered Dowd, who was offended that the FBI director would speak that way. Young was never charged, though the House Ethics Committee later rebuked him. Young soon became the longest-serving member of Congress.

While Mueller had not yet made a specific request for documents, one would likely be coming soon. White House Counsel Don McGahn did not want to turn over much of anything. He wanted the president to assert privileges, such as executive privilege.

Dowd disagreed with McGahn. If there was nothing to hide, Trump's cooperation could help the prosecutor perhaps see it his way. He recommended to Trump that "we'd get a hell of a lot more with honey than we would with vinegar."

"I have friends who tell me we ought to tell them to go fuck themselves," the president said in one call. "I don't trust these guys."

Dowd argued that cooperation would speed up the resolution and Trump eventually approved the honey-over-vinegar approach.

Dowd recommended hiring Ty Cobb, an experienced Washington lawyer known for his white handlebar mustache (Dowd called him "Colonel Sanders" after the Kentucky Fried Chicken icon) as special counsel on the White House staff. Cobb would be in charge of the delivery of documents to Mueller and his team. Dowd couldn't do this because he was Trump's personal lawyer, and the documents were White House documents. Cobb was really brought in to override McGahn's advice to fight document requests.

Dowd emphasized to the president, "I want to build a relationship where we engage [Mueller] and then there are no secrets. And that can be done."

Dowd went to his first meeting with Mueller and his chief deputy, James "Jim" Quarles, a veteran of the Watergate special prosecutor's office 40 years earlier, at the special counsel's office on June 16 at 1 p.m.

"We're not waiving objections to your appointment," Dowd said, "and how the hell you got here." Rosenstein's order was too broad and no one in the Justice Department had the authority to investigate any matter they stumbled on. "That order will not stand. But we are not going to throw rocks."

Mueller did not respond. He was a master of silence.

"The president has authorized me to tell you he will cooperate," Dowd said. His words to me were, "Tell Bob I respect him. I'll cooperate."

Mueller seemed relieved.

"What do you need?" Dowd asked him. "We'll get it to you. But let's get this investigation done." The president's position is that he has nothing to hide. He is not happy with the investigation to say the least but we want to avoid a protracted battle. "But we'd like you to reciprocate. And that is, engage."

"John," Mueller said as he stood, "the best cases are ones where we can fully engage."

"The reason we're cooperating is to get this damn thing over with," Dowd said. "We're not going to assert any privileges. This is over the objection of Don McGahn, but the president wants to do it. He wants you to see everything, talk to everyone."

Ty Cobb had come up with a way to maintain, but get around, an executive privilege claim on testimony or documents. He had told Mueller, "Bob, we're going to give it to you. We're not waiving the privilege. After you see it, and at the end if you feel like you've got to use it, let us know and we'll get you the waiver. As to the balance that's in your archives, you've got to return them with the privilege."

Mueller seemed thrilled that he would see all the documents. Let's just do that verbally, said Mueller and Quarles. We don't want to create a lot of paper.

Dowd said that was fine. No written record.

"John," Mueller said, "you know me. I don't let any grass grow under me." Dowd, a veteran of special investigations, knew they could go on endlessly. The length of these investigations often became the abuse. Mueller said, "Jim will be the lead for me, he'll be the deputy, but you guys can call me anytime and I'll see you."

"Great," said Dowd, "same here. You guys need something, call me. And we'll get it for you or we'll answer whatever question or help get witnesses."

The case that was being built, as reported in *The New York Times* and *The Washington Post*, had to be examined seriously. On alleged collusion the questions included Trump's 2013 trip to Moscow, what he might have known about efforts by his former campaign manager Paul Manafort and his longtime attorney Michael Cohen to do business in Russia during the campaign, and what Trump might have known about other aides, such as Roger Stone's alleged role in Hillary Clinton's hacked emails.

In a celebrated July 27 news conference during the 2016 campaign, Trump had invited Russia to publish the emails that Clinton's lawyer had deleted because he had determined they were not relevant to the FBI investigation.

"Russia, if you're listening," candidate Trump said, "I hope you're able to find the 30,000 emails that are missing. I think you will probably be rewarded mightily by our press."

He later tweeted, "If Russia or any other country or person has Hillary Clinton's 30,000 illegally deleted emails, perhaps they should share them with the FBI!" The next day he said, "Of course I'm being sarcastic."

Dowd thought that the declaration and request to Russia, sarcastic or not, hardly suggested hidden subterfuge to work with Russia that seemed to be the focus of the Mueller investigation.

The major problem might be allegations of obstructing justice by urging Comey to drop the Flynn investigation, and then firing Comey. But Dowd believed that the president's Article II constitutional authority clearly encompassed firing an FBI director.

How Mueller might look at this would turn on the evidence of Trump's conduct. The key would be fathoming Trump's intent. Was there a "corrupt" motive, as required by the statute, in his actions to impede justice?

In most cases that is a high bar and generally prosecutors need evidence such as urging others to lie to investigators, destroying documents or ordering the payment of money for illegal actions, such as buying the silence of witnesses as Nixon had in Watergate.

The thousands of hours of secret Nixon tape recordings provided an unusual clarity about the obstruction of justice or cover-up in Watergate.

Dowd had found no Trump tapes or witnesses unfavorable to Trump other than Comey.

At the same time, he had been a prosecutor. He knew the culture. Prosecutors like to make cases, especially high-profile ones.

Inside the White House, it was obvious Mueller's Russian investigation was getting to Trump. Those who spent the most time in the West Wing and Oval Office found it was consuming too much of his emotional energy. It was a real distraction. Trump had a hard time compartmentalizing. Entire days were consumed by his frustration with Mueller, Jeff Sessions and Rod Rosenstein.

Even during meetings on policy issues that were Trump obsessions, like Chinese tariffs, he would bring up the Mueller investigation. Often it was about what he had seen on TV. "How is this playing?" he asked. "What do you think I should do to push back?"

The staff in the meetings who were not on the legal team did not want to offer ideas.

Trump rarely missed a chance to declare that it was unfair and a "witch hunt."

It was driving him crazy, Porter saw. It would ebb and flow, but there were times when Trump became consumed by it, and would become distracted from the job and the business of being president. He felt it was unfair, and he had done nothing wrong. There were people investigating him who seemed to have unlimited powers.

Trump was worried about wiretaps that might have been authorized by the Foreign Intelligence Surveillance Act. Porter told others Trump was "very bothered by the possibility of FISA wiretaps in the campaign . . . a sense of sort of feeling violated. But that there was someone that had some power over him where he wasn't the top dog."

Trump had another objection to Mueller. "I can't be president," he said. "It's like I have my hands tied behind my back because I can't do anything that looks like it's favorable to Russia or to Putin because of Mueller."

West Wingers and those who traveled regularly with Trump noticed that he and Melania seemed to have some sincere affection for each other despite media speculation. But she operated independently. They ate dinner together at times, spent some time together; but they never really seemed to merge their lives.

Melania's primary concern was their son, Barron. "She's obsessed with Barron," one person said. "That is her focus 100 percent."

Trump gave some private advice to a friend who had acknowledged some bad behavior toward women. Real power is fear. It's all about strength. Never show weakness. You've always got to be strong. Don't be bullied. There is no choice.

"You've got to deny, deny, deny and push back on these women," he said. "If you admit to anything and any culpability, then you're dead. That was a big mistake you made. You didn't come out guns blazing and just challenge them. You showed weakness. You've got to be strong. You've got to be aggressive. You've got to push back hard. You've got to deny anything that's said about you. Never admit."

Trump debated tariffs for months. He wanted to impose a 25 percent tariff on auto imports. "I want an executive order," he said.

He did not have the legal authority to do that, Porter said.

"Fine, we'll challenge it in court. But I don't care. Let's just do it!"

Another time the president told Porter, "Go down to your office right now. Get it all written up. Bring me my tariffs!"

One day in the Oval Office, Cohn brought in the latest job numbers to Trump and Pence.

"I have the most perfect job numbers you're ever going to see," Cohn said.

"It's all because of my tariffs," Trump said. "They're working."

Trump had yet to impose any tariffs, but he believed they were a good idea and knew Cohn disagreed with him.

"You're a fucking asshole," Cohn said, half-joking and smacking Trump gently on the arm.

Cohn turned to a Secret Service agent. "I just hit the president. If you want to shoot me, go ahead."

Cohn wrote a joke for Trump to use at the Gridiron Dinner: "We've made enormous progress on the wall. All the drawings are done. All the excavating's done. All the engineering is done. The only thing we've been stumbling with is we haven't been able to figure out how to stretch the word 'Trump' over 1,200 miles."

Trump wouldn't use it.

Porter observed that anytime anybody challenged Trump—in a policy debate, in court, in the public square—his natural instinct seemed to be that if he was not exerting strength, he was failing.

He stopped counting the times that Trump vented about Sessions. His anger never went away. Sessions's recusal was a wound that remained open.

Jeff Sessions, Trump said in one of many versions, was an abject failure. He was not loyal. If he had any balls, if he had been a strong guy, he would've just said, I'm not going to recuse. I'm the attorney general. I can do whatever I want.

Within the intelligence and military world there exist what President Obama once told me are "our deep secrets." These are matters so sensitive, involving sources and methods, that only a handful of people including the president and key military and intelligence officials know about them.

After the 9/11 terrorist attacks the American espionage establishment ballooned, making secret surveillance a way of life.

Near the end of May 2017, I learned of one such "deep secret." North Korea was accelerating both its missile and nuclear weapons programs at an astonishing rate, and would "well within a year" have a ballistic missile with a nuclear weapon that perhaps could reach the United States mainland. Previously the intelligence showed North Korea would not have that capability for at least two years if not longer. This new intelligence was a rare earthquake in the intelligence world, but it did not travel far. It was to be protected at almost any cost.

In response, a preliminary Top Secret Pentagon war plan called for the United States to send escalation signals to put the country on a war footing: reinforce the Korean Peninsula with two or three aircraft carriers; keep more U.S. Navy attack submarines in the region (capable of firing barrages of Tomahawk missiles); add another squadron of F-22s and more B-2 stealth bombers. Perhaps even withdraw U.S. dependents, family members of the 28,500 U.S. military in South Korea. Add more ground forces, thicken the theater missile defense systems, disperse troops to make them less vulnerable, harden infrastructure to help withstand artillery attacks.

I began checking around about whether North Korea was "well within a year" of a new ICBM nuclear weapon capability. At the top levels of the Pentagon, I was told "There is nothing like that," providing an absolute knockdown of my information.

At the top levels of the intelligence community, I was told "there was nothing new" and "no significant change" in the two-year-plus assessment. There was nothing to be alarmed about.

I talked with a person with the broadest, most authoritative access to such current intelligence. The absolute denials were repeated emphatically, categorically. Then something happened that had never occurred in 46 years of reporting. This person said, "If I am wrong I will apologize to you."

That was definitely a first. But the meaning was unclear. I have had officials lie outright about something very sensitive. Asked later, they have said they felt it was better to dissemble. Why agree to talk or meet? Silence could be interpreted as confirmation, they usually replied. That is the real world of reporting on sensitive intelligence matters. The offer to apologize if wrong had never happened before to me.

I decided not to seek out the person to get the apology, but I was soon entitled to one.

Just over a month later, on July 3, North Korea successfully tested its first ICBM, a Hwasong-14. The missile only traveled 930 kilometers and was in the air only 37 minutes, but the intelligence showed that with a flatter trajectory, it could possibly have reached the United States mainland. This was what my source had warned about two months earlier.

Trump was briefed that night. The next day, July 4, he hosted an Independence Day celebration at the White House. That afternoon, McMaster chaired an emergency principals meeting in the Situation Room. Trump was not present.

CIA Director Pompeo said there was confirmation of an ICBM. It had been fired via an eight-axle mobile vehicle that had been imported from China. So much for the hope that China would be a restraining influence on North Korea.

Tillerson said he had been unable to contact the Chinese, but had called for an emergency meeting in the U.N. Security Council. "We need to work with Russia to get their support and focus on countries that are not abiding by the existing sanctions," he said. "This ought to be a topic of discussion at the G20, especially with Japan and the Republic of Korea."

Tillerson raised the concern that the administration was targeting China with steel tariffs at a time when they needed its help to corral North Korea. He was also worried about allies' reactions to Trump's threatened steel tariffs, like Japan, South Korea and the European Union.

Ambassador to the United Nations Nikki Haley said, "China has been avoiding us, but eventually they agreed to a U.N. Security Council meeting tomorrow." The U.S. needed to identify more companies who did business with North Korea for additional sanctions.

"We need a persuasive press statement to gain allies on this," Mattis said. "We don't want to show any daylight between us and the Republic of Korea." He walked through military contingency plans, including possible strikes in North Korea—the full range, from limited pinpoints to an all-out attack, and even a leadership strike. The U.S. didn't have all of the ships and other assets it might need in the region. They were not ready for every contingency, and it would take time to get everything in line.

"Our first choice ought to be U.N.-led sanctions," Mnuchin said. "Otherwise we can have another dozen primary sanctions available."

Mike Rogers, NSA director, outlined the United States' defensive posture on cyber security. He did not address offensive cyber attack capabilities.

"There really ought to be a question of how much technical data we share with China and Russia," cautioned DNI Dan Coats, "in terms of what we picked up about the ICBM and other things." U.S. intelligence had a pretty full picture, and it had to be protected.

"We're going to find out pretty soon here whether China is with us as promised," said Tillerson. If the United States was ready to impose a ban on American citizens traveling to North Korea, we ought to get other countries to do the same.

"The big challenge is going to be the loss of human intelligence," Pompeo said, alluding to a possible impact on sensitive CIA sources.

"I hope we go slow on this," said Mattis. He knew the details of the Special Access Programs. "That loss of human intelligence would be a big thing."

"Continued travel poses the risk of hostage taking," Tillerson said, but he did not disagree with Pompeo and Mattis about the importance of the human sources.

The consensus was that without taking bold action, the U.S. risked being seen as tepid and lacking in the new normal of an ICBM-equipped North Korea.

North Korea's missile launch was a full-scale crisis: Kim Jong Un now had mobile ICBM capability and missiles that could potentially reach the homeland. U.S. intelligence had incontrovertible evidence that the Chinese had supplied the eight-axle vehicle that was a key component of these complex missile systems. The CIA risked losing sensitive sources if the U.S. tightened travel restrictions. And if the president decided to order some sort of significant military response, the assets would not be immediately available.

I later learned that the person I had spoken to in May believed the information to be so sensitive, it had been decided that it was better to lie.

Less than two months later, September 3, North Korea conducted an underground test of its most powerful nuclear weapon, its sixth. This was at least 17 times more powerful than the bomb that destroyed Hiroshima in 1945.

During the campaign, on February 10, 2016, Trump said on *CBS This Morning* he would get China to make Kim "disappear in one form or another very quickly." He called Kim "a bad dude—and don't underestimate him."

An executive order signed in 1981 by President Reagan stated, "No person employed by or acting on behalf of the U.S. government shall engage in, or conspire to engage in, assassination." But government lawyers had concluded that a military strike on a leader's command-and-control headquarters during hostilities would not violate the assassination ban.

One of the early applications of leader-command-and-control targeting occurred near the end of the Clinton presidency. The military strike is little remembered because it came in the midst of the congressional debate on the impeachment of the president. In December 1998, Clinton ordered a military strike in Iraq.

The Desert Fox operation included 650 bomber or missile sorties against fewer than 100 targets over three days. It was billed as a large bombing attack to punish Iraq for failing to allow United Nations weapons inspectors to search for weapons of mass destruction.

Desert Fox was not explicitly designed to kill Iraqi leader Saddam Hussein, but fully half the targets were his palaces or other locations he might use that were protected by special intelligence and Republican Guard units. Saddam was not hit, though many in the administration, particularly Secretary of Defense William Cohen, had hoped it would be the end of him.

In the run-up to the 2003 invasion of Iraq, President George W. Bush and his National Security officials again pondered whether it was possible to kill Saddam through covert action.

CIA officers in the demoralized Iraqi Operations Group—often referred to within the agency and among themselves as "The House of Broken Toys"—gave a dramatic no. It would be too hard; Saddam was too well protected. The security and intelligence organizations existed to keep him alive and in power. The Operations Group posed a military invasion as the only way to remove the dictator.

On the eve of the U.S. invasion of Iraq, CIA human sources, code-named ROCKSTARS, reported with increasing certainty that Saddam was at Dora Farm, a complex southeast of Baghdad on the banks of the Tigris River. Told that Saddam was holed up in a bunker, Bush ordered a strike with bunker-busting bombs. Hours later, CIA director George Tenet called the Situation Room. "Tell the president we got the son of a bitch." They had not.

Days later, the CIA base chief in northern Iraq visited Dora Farm, which looked like the ruins of a flea market. He found no bunker, just a subterranean pantry for food storage. One thing was clear: Saddam had escaped, or he had never been there. He was captured nine months later when U.S. forces found him hiding in a spider hole under a small shack.

The CIA engaged in some high-level introspection over the next several years. Officials asked the crucial after-action question: Suppose Saddam had been killed by covert action or military strike? Would that have made the invasion and long war unnecessary? The cost in lives included more than 100,000 Iraqis by conservative count and 4,530 Americans. The U.S. cost was at least $800 billion and probably $1 trillion. How much Middle East instability did the war cause and enable Iran? The Middle East and world history seemed to pivot around the Iraq War for years.

This self-examination peaked years later during the time John Brennan was CIA director, 2013 to early 2017. An agency man to the core with a smooth, confident and austere manner, he had vast CIA experience and a track record for being right. On television he rarely smiled.

Brennan had been daily intelligence briefer for President Clinton; CIA station chief in Saudi Arabia; executive assistant and chief of staff to CIA Director Tenet. As the White House counterterrorism chief in Obama's first term, he had developed a strong relationship with the president, who rewarded him with the CIA directorship in his second term. Brennan was known as "The Answer Man." He read deeply in the intelligence reports, often asking to see agent reports and raw communications intercepts.

Mindful of the Iraq "mistake," Brennan ultimately concluded that the CIA had not done its job. The House of Broken Toys had dodged its responsibilities, insisting, "You need troops! You need troops!" Well, that was not the CIA's job. Their energy could better have been focused on what the CIA could do to present options. Given the magnitude of the mistake, Brennan concluded that the Saddam problem could have been solved with what he called "indirect assassination."

So as the North Korean problem escalated during the Obama presidency, Brennan developed an aggressive argument. The CIA should not seek regime change, but "man change," the elimination of Leader Kim Jong Un. Brennan concluded the Iraq Operations Group of the preinvasion period of 2002–03 had little guts, know-how and imagination. So the equivalent group for North Korea in the CIA operations directorate went to work. Was "indirect assassination" or "man change" possible? It was an option worth examining.

The CIA's North Korea group came up with the Peninsula Intelligence Estimate (PIE), which would provide warnings that the North was going to initiate an attack. The Pentagon's top secret contingency U.S. war plan, the response to an attack, was for regime change in North Korea and was called OPLAN 5027.

A tasking order assigned targets and missions of the air, naval and land forces. It was a massive plan designed to win the war and one of the most sensitive in the U.S. government.

The Time-Phased Force Deployment (TIPFID) showed that it would take 30 days to get all the forces in.

A simpler but vastly more risky option included strikes at the North Korean leadership targets, specifically Kim Jung Un, under a more refined war plan, OPLAN 5015.

The Air Force had several leadership attack options, including sending a stealth bomber attack in and out of North Korea before North Korea could do anything about it. This would require knowledge with "great clarity," as one general put it, to execute a pinpoint attack on leadership.

From October 17 to 19, 2017, the U.S. Air Force ran an elaborate series of simulated air strikes in the Missouri Ozarks. The region has a similar topography to North Korea.

The encrypted communications system between the bombers, the Airborne Early Warning aircraft, and the tankers was not working, so the pilots' communications were heard by locals who monitored the military frequencies.

One communication referred to a "possible DPRK [North Korea] leadership relocation site." In another, the pilot referred to "a command post possible DPRK leadership relocation site."

One airdrop exercise was from just 150 meters, which is dangerously low but designed for maximum underground destruction. In another related exercise the bomber carried a 30,000-pound MOP (Massive Ordnance Penetrator), the type used earlier in Afghanistan in April 2017. In the exercise simulations the map coordinates pinpointed a hangar at a Jefferson City airport. The pilots also discussed the timing of the bomb fuses to maximize impact on the targets.

By any reasoning, the exercise was serious preparation, but it was, at this point, one available contingency on the shelf being practiced.

McMaster sounded hawkish on North Korea, arguing internally in the White House that if Trump was going to attack, better to go early before the North improved its missiles and nuclear weapons.

Or before it built more. Time would make the threat greater. To those less inclined, McMaster asked, "Do you want to bet a mushroom cloud over Los Angeles over it?"

This question echoed the pre–Iraq invasion comment of Condoleezza Rice, Bush's national security adviser, that it was uncertain how quickly Saddam could acquire nuclear weapons. She added, "But we don't want the smoking gun to be a mushroom cloud."

General Kelly, the homeland security secretary and retired four-star Marine general, was furious when he learned that the White House was working on a compromise on immigration for "Dreamers"—a central issue in the immigration debate. Dreamers are immigrant children brought to the United States by their parents who as adults had entered illegally.

Under the 2012 legislation called DACA—Deferred Action for Childhood Arrivals—President Obama had given 800,000 Dreamers protection from deportation and made work permits available to them, hoping to bring them out of the shadow economy and give them an American identity.

Kelly, a hard-liner on immigration, was supposed to be in charge of these matters now. But Jared Kushner had been working a back-channel compromise. He had been inviting Senator Dick Durbin, the Illinois Democrat who was number two in his party's leadership, and Lindsey Graham to his office to discuss a compromise. Graham later asked Kelly, "Didn't Jared tell you we've been working on this for months? We've got a fix."

Kelly called Bannon. "If the son-in-law is going to run it, then have the son-in-law run it. I don't need to run it. I need to come see the president. I'm not doing this anymore. I'm not going to be up there and be blindsided and humiliated on something that I've got to be in the loop on."

Bannon believed the administration owned the hard-line immigration posture—except for Trump himself. "He's always been soft on DACA. He believes the left-wing thing. They're all valedictorians. They're all Rhodes Scholars. Because Ivanka over the years has told him that."

Kelly voiced his distress to Priebus, who along with Bannon feared Kelly might quit.

"Get Kelly some time on the calendar," Bannon proposed. "Let him come see the boss and light Jared up. Because this is Jared's shit, doing stuff behind people's back."

Priebus didn't do it.

"Get it on the fucking calendar," Bannon insisted.

Priebus continued to stall. It would expose disorganization in the White House.

"What are you talking about?" Bannon asked. This was laughable! Of course Priebus didn't have control of Jared. And people were always going behind someone's back.

So Bannon and Priebus both told Kelly, We'll take care of it. To go to the president would cause unnecessary consternation. We'll make sure it won't happen again and you're going to be in the loop.

Kelly, team player for the moment, didn't push it further. When he later mentioned it obliquely in the president's presence, Trump didn't respond.

Lindsey Graham wandered into Bannon's West Wing office. "Hey, here's the deal. You want your wall?" Trump would get wall funding in exchange for the Dreamers.

"Stop," Bannon said. A deal on the Dreamers was amnesty. "We will never give amnesty for one person. I don't care if you build 10 fucking walls. The wall ain't good enough. It's got to be chain migration."

Chain migration, formally called the family reunification policy, allowed a single legal immigrant to bring close family members into the United States—parents, children, a spouse and, in some cases, siblings. These family members would have a path to legal permanent residency or citizenship. They might be followed by a "chain" of their own spouses, children, parents or siblings.

Two thirds (68 percent) of legal permanent residents entered under family reunification or chain migration in 2016. This was at the heart of Trump's and Bannon's anti-immigration stance: They wanted to stop illegal immigration and limit legal immigration. Bannon wanted a new, stricter policy. Graham and he were not able to come close to agreement.

Ivanka and Jared invited Stephen Miller, the hard-liner on immigration, to their house for dinner along with Durbin and Graham.

"All you do is listen," Bannon instructed Miller. "Just go and receive. Don't fight them. I just want to hear it all."

Miller reported that Ivanka and Jared thought they had Trump on some sort of deal that included funding for the wall in exchange for amnesty for 1.8 million Dreamers. Bannon figured chain migration made the real number double or triple that—3 to 5 million new immigrants. "They can't think we're that dumb."

Some days, it seemed to Bannon that Senator Graham had moved into the West Wing. He heard his pitch on Dreamers at least three times. He thought that Graham wanted to replace McConnell as majority leader.

Bannon was at the height of his war with McConnell and saw Graham as his biggest ally. Graham and Bannon were on the phone nearly every day. Bannon believed everyone hated McConnell and wanted to put the shiv to him because he ran things too tight.

Graham did talk about finding a replacement for McConnell. "We've got to find our guy who'll replace him," Graham said. But Graham denied he wanted McConnell's leadership job.

Bannon believed Graham was the best deal maker for Republicans, but he was the establishment. Graham didn't like Bannon's nationalist agenda, telling him, "Bannon, that America First is bullshit. This is all bullshit."

In the true and practiced Trump White House style, Bannon was willing to ride any horse to achieve his purposes. He called Attorney General Sessions to the White House. Their problem on immigration was now Trump. "He's going to be listening to Jared and Ivanka. And Graham is the best salesman around there. He loves Graham. Graham can sell him anything. He's got Durbin. They're going to be loving up on him. We've got a fucking problem."

Bannon spoke with Kris Kobach, the secretary of state of Kansas, one of the biggest opponents of the Dreamers and a hero of the Right. Kobach's idea was that he and other state attorneys general would file suit claiming DACA was unconstitutional. Bannon and Sessions developed a plan not to defend the lawsuit. "It's over," Bannon said. "DACA's finished. All Trump had to say to Congress was, Hey, I work at 1600 Pennsylvania Avenue. If you've got an idea, come up and see me." Trump only had to stay neutral.

As Trump was laying plans to withdraw from the Paris Accord on climate change, Priebus had had it with Ivanka. The president's 35-year-old daughter and White House senior adviser effectively had free run of the West Wing. She had launched what amounted to a covert operation in support of the Paris Accord, a nonbinding international agreement to address climate change by voluntarily cutting greenhouse gas emissions that was reached in 2015 and involved 195 countries.

Obama had pledged to cut these emissions about 25 percent below the levels in 2005. This would be accomplished by 2025. He had committed $3 billion to aid underdeveloped countries in a Green Climate Fund.

Only $1 billion had been paid, and Obama had transferred half of that three days before he left office.

Ivanka strongly wanted her father to stick with the pro-environmental agreement. Priebus would be meeting in his office with a handful of aides from the economic team and the National Economic Council for 15 minutes and in would walk Ivanka. She would sit down and often say nothing.

Who is this person? Priebus marveled. What is she doing?

It was becoming impossible to manage the West Wing. At times it seemed Ivanka's presence—hours a day, days in a row—was nonstop. Jared had the same squatter's rights in the West Wing. They were like a posse of second-guessers, hovering, watching, interacting as family and senior advisers with the president. Ivanka planted seeds of doubt about policy and passed her father articles.

When Priebus voiced his dismay, Trump regularly joked, "They're Democrats." They were New Yorkers infected with the liberalism of their city roots. The president made no real effort to curtail their freelancing. Priebus believed he had run a very tight and organizationally sound Republican National Committee. The Trump White House seemed designed to upend any order or routine.

At one point Priebus had a decision memo for the president to review and sign on the U.S. withdrawal from the Paris Agreement.

Ivanka said to her father, "Mark Zuckerberg wants to talk to you." She had lined up a call between her father and the founder and CEO of Facebook. Zuckerberg was an outspoken climate change advocate. She did the same with Tim Cook, the Apple CEO, and others. At one point she slipped a personal message from former vice president Al Gore, one of the foremost Paris advocates, into a stack of papers on the president's desk.

Trump talked to Gore, who reported to others that he actually thought Trump seemed like he might stay in.

Ivanka and Jared gave a newspaper story to the president with highlighted quotes from an unnamed White House source. You know who this is? This is Steve Bannon, they said. In a West Wing filled with leakers, these tactics slowly but surely planted a distrust of Bannon with the president.

Porter noticed Scott Pruitt, the EPA administrator, in the West Wing lobby on April 5. He had been Pruitt's Sherpa when Pruitt was barely confirmed by the Senate 52 to 46. Pruitt had been Oklahoma attorney general for six years, where he ran a war against EPA regulations.

They made small talk. When Pruitt walked down to the Oval Office, Porter followed. Pruitt was not on the regular schedule. This was clearly an off-the-books meeting. That was evident when Bannon showed up in the Oval Office.

"We need to get out of Paris," Pruitt said, handing the president a plain sheet of paper he wanted him to read withdrawing from the Paris Accord. We need to get out, he said. "This was a campaign commitment."

"Yes, yes, yes," Bannon said several times. "We've got to do this now."

Make this statement, Pruitt said. This could be your press statement. Maybe read it to reporters in the Oval Office, and have the press secretary put it out as a written statement.

Porter was taken aback. As staff secretary he knew there had been no process. No one had been consulted. There had been no legal review. Pruitt and Bannon had snuck into the Oval Office and wanted an instant decision on the major international and national environmental issue of the day.

Porter knew the paper on the president's desk was incendiary. Trump could pick it up, decide to read it out loud to the press or take it to Press Secretary Sean Spicer and say, put this out. When he had a chance, Porter took Pruitt's draft statement from Trump's desk.

Later he told Bannon and Pruitt they could not just walk into the Oval Office this way. It was a huge process foul. It was unacceptable.

Gary Cohn gathered the principals for a meeting on the Paris Agreement in the Situation Room on April 27. Cohn's National Economic Council had sent around a For Official Use Only six-page memo proposing two options. The first was to withdraw from Paris. The second was: "Remain in the Paris Agreement, but Adopt a Pledge that Does Not Harm the Economy and Puts a Hold on Further Financial Commitments and Contributions."

"I want to turn first to the White House counsel," Cohn said, opening the meeting, "to walk us through some of the legal issues."

But Don McGahn was not yet there. His deputy, Greg Katsas, discussed technical issues until McGahn arrived.

"Great, McGahn's here," Cohn said. "Tee up the legal issues for us."

McGahn supported getting out, though he had not yet revealed his hand. "Well," he said, "we're going to have these court cases. And if we don't get out of Paris, then it's really going to jeopardize some of the regulatory rollback that we're likely to do at EPA.

"Paris was one of the justifications the Obama administration used as part of the regulatory record to justify the cost and benefits of the Clean Power Plan." That was an Obama-era 460-page rule to lower carbon dioxide emitted by power plants that the EPA estimated would save 4,500 lives a year. Pruitt was already moving to end the policy.

"So unless we exit Paris, all of these sorts of cases are going to be in jeopardy," McGahn said. He was for getting out immediately.

"You don't know what you are talking about," Tillerson said. "My State Department legal adviser, which was the office that negotiated this in the first place and has the relevant expertise, says we can't just announce that we are getting out."

The option paper clearly said the "United States cannot officially announce a withdrawal from the Paris Agreement until November 2019"—two and a half years away.

But the second option—remaining in the accord but doing nothing that harmed the economy and putting a hold on further financial contributions—would put the U.S. in good stead in terms of litigation, Tillerson said.

The secretary of state stood alone. Pruitt spoke strongly for getting out. Priebus, who saw the political benefits, was for getting out. Bannon saw Paris as one more globalist deal that screwed the United States.

At the end, Cohn said they obviously needed to get the legal issues squared away. "But I think we're starting to get a consensus." He was right. Paris was dead.

McMaster and Porter huddled before a 10 a.m., June 1 meeting with the president in the Oval Office on the Paris Accord. Trump was due to make an announcement that day. We've got to make a last-ditch effort, they agreed.

Withdrawing will damage our relationships with so many other countries, McMaster said. He was inundated with calls from his counterparts. "You guys aren't really thinking about doing this, are you?" Or more explicitly, "Please don't do this."

Porter had drafted some language for the president to use. "The United States will withdraw from the terms of the Paris Climate Accord, effective immediately." Porter read his proposal, "As of today the United States will not adhere to any financial or economic burden the Paris Accord purports to impose, including its nationally determined contribution."

Withdrawing from the "terms" would technically leave the United States in the accord. "This will read like it's tough enough," Porter argued to McMaster. "He'll feel like he's getting the political bang for the buck. He'll be fulfilling the campaign promise. It'll excite the base."

It was basically option two from the principals meeting—"Remain in the Paris Accord." Porter thought he had found a way to minimize the damage.

Porter and McMaster presented the proposed language to the president. They talked until they were blue in the face, but it was clear they'd lost the fight.

No, no, no, Trump said. He was withdrawing full-scale. "That's the only way that I can be true to my base."

As Trump worked over the speech draft, he toughened the language further.

In a late-afternoon Rose Garden appearance that day that included a brass band, the president praised the stock market and U.S. efforts to fight terrorism.

"On these issues and so many more, we're following through on our commitments. And I don't want anything to get in our way." Then unburying the lead, he said, "Therefore in order to fulfill my solemn duty to protect America and its citizens, the United States will withdraw from the Paris Climate Accord.

"As someone who cares deeply about the environment, which I do, I cannot in good conscience support a deal that punishes the United States—which is what it does—the world's leader in environmental protection, while imposing no meaningful obligations on the world's leading polluters.

"I was elected to represent the citizens of Pittsburgh, not Paris."

On June 15, 2017, *The Washington Post* ran a story by three of its top Justice Department and FBI reporters headlined "Special Counsel Is Investigating Jared Kushner's Business Dealings." Mueller wanted more and more records. Kushner hired Abbe Lowell, a top Washington criminal defense lawyer. Priebus could see the fires building around a string of troubled investments Jared was involved in. He decided to escalate, make a big play. He told Trump that Jared should not be in the White House in an official capacity. Nepotism laws existed for a reason. The Mueller investigation was going deeply into Jared's finances. And it will jump to your finances if it hasn't already.

Normally Trump would ignore or dismiss. This time he paused, slowed down, and became reflective. He looked at his chief of staff. The response was jarring, so different.

"You're right," the president said.

Priebus continued to tell Trump that as his son-in-law, Jared should not have an official position and office in the White House.

But this suggestion would ricochet right back and get him in trouble with Jared, who wanted to stay. Jared remained a mission Priebus failed to accomplish.

Having failed in efforts to control or curtail the president's tweeting, Priebus searched for a way to have practical impact. Since the tweets were often triggered by the president's obsessive TV watching, he looked for ways to shut off the television. But television was Trump's default activity. Sunday nights were often the worst. Trump would come back to the White House from the weekend at one of his golf resorts just in time to catch political talk on his enemy networks, MSNBC and CNN.

The president and the first lady had separate bedrooms in the residence. Trump had a giant TV going much of the time, alone in his bedroom with the clicker, the TiVo and his Twitter account. Priebus called the presidential bedroom "the devil's workshop" and the early mornings and dangerous Sunday nights "the witching hour."

There was not much he could do about the mornings, but he had some control over the weekend schedule. He started scheduling Trump's Sunday returns to the White House later in the afternoon. Trump would get to the White House just before 9 p.m. when MSNBC and CNN generally turned to softer programming that did not focus on the immediate political controversies and Trump's inevitable role in them.

Bannon realized that the cascade of NSC presentations about Afghanistan, Iran, China, Russia and North Korea was not really connecting with Trump. Without some organizing principle, it was too much for his attention span.

So he called Sally Donnelly, a key close adviser to Secretary Mattis. "Sally, you've got to talk to your boss. Here's the problem." One day the focus was Libya, the next it might be Syria. "I know this guy.

He's frustrated. It's too disjointed. Besides what we are doing with the Saudis, everything else is kind of hodgepodge.

"I've got something I want to talk to Mattis about, and I'll bring it over and diagram it for him." Bannon had come up with what he called "the strategy of the United States."

At 8 a.m. on a June Saturday, Bannon arrived at the Pentagon. He had coffee with Donnelly and Mattis's chief of staff, retired Rear Admiral Kevin Sweeney. They then gathered with Mattis around the small conference table in the secretary's office.

"Here's my problem," Bannon said. "You guys haven't thought about the Pacific at all. You haven't thought about China. There's no in-depth. You are so tied to CentCom"—the Central Command that covered the Middle East and South Asia.

Since Mattis had been the CentCom commander from 2010 to 2013, Bannon thought that Mattis had brought that mind-set to the job of secretary of defense. He reminded Mattis that Chinese policy leaders and intellectuals were split on their views of the United States. One group saw the U.S. as an equal partner, a co-hegemon. The other, the hawks, looked at the United States as a lesser power and treated it like one.

Mattis countered. Annihilating ISIS was the assignment President Trump had specifically given him.

"I'll basically cut a deal with you," Bannon proposed. If Mattis would support the containment of China, he would back off on the pressure to get the U.S. out of Afghanistan.

Afghanistan was a linchpin in the Chinese One Belt, One Road plan to expand its trading network to Europe.

"Steve," Mattis said, "I'm kind of one of those global trading guys. I think all that trade stuff's pretty good."

Bannon was appalled. Trump was right. The generals didn't know anything about business and economics. They never really cared about the cost of anything.

Over the weekend of July 8 and 9, *The New York Times* published two stories about a previously undisclosed meeting in Trump Tower in the middle of the campaign. Don Trump Jr., Manafort and Kushner had met with a Russian lawyer who, among other things, was offering dirt on Hillary Clinton. There were the usual denials, restatements and confusion among the participants. It was a huge story, suggesting—but not proving—some kind of subterfuge and clandestine cooperation with Russians.

The president was in orbit and called Dowd to complain about leaks and the press.

"Mr. President, it's horseshit," Dowd told him. And so what? Getting dirt on people was commonplace in campaigns and the nation's capital. It even had a name—"opposition research" or "investigative reporting." That's what half of Washington seemed to be paid for. Is there something wrong with that? No. Dowd knew that opposition research teams and investigative reporters would take dirt from anyone, even foreign governments. All the media posturing was disgusting. They were treating it like the crime of the century.

The New York Times and *The Washington Post* thought they were the special counsel and the law of the land. The stories were a big nothing burger, Dowd concluded.

On July 17 Trump tweeted: "Most politicians would have gone to a meeting like the one Don jr attended in order to get info on an opponent. That's politics!"

Dowd was determined not to be distracted by the daily drip from the media. He wanted hard evidence. McGahn religiously dictated all significant meetings or discussions with the president to his executive assistant, Annie Donaldson. She had 17 hours of notes relating to matters being investigated by Mueller and his team.

Dowd gave Mueller these notes and those of seven other lawyers. Nothing was held back. He told Mueller, "Bob, read Annie Donaldson's notes if you want to know what was in the head of the president."

All this was done with the president's blessing. Dowd would talk to him and say, look, here's the categories of documents. We're going to give him this. We're going to give him that. "Constitutionally he has no right" to the documents and testimony, "but just out of respect for law enforcement, since you're the chief, let's just let him do it. Not get in the fight." Dowd concluded that the president seemed fearless. He never said no.

Dowd told Mueller, "This is what I told the president, so don't make me look like an idiot, okay? And we're going to make you look good. You make us look good. But you've got to get it done."

Mueller received 1.4 million pages of documents from the Trump campaign and 20,000 pages from the White House. Dowd believed no documents had been destroyed. In all, 37 witnesses gave interviews to Mueller's team voluntarily.

McGahn, Priebus and the vice president's staff had put together a six-page White House summary of the entire Flynn matter from contemporaneous recollections. Dowd considered it the Bible on Flynn and delivered it to Mueller. He believed that no one, other than Flynn, had lied to investigators, and Mueller had not needed to pressure or jam anyone.

When Dowd was sending the campaign records to the congressional investigating committee, he told Mueller's deputy Quarles, "We're sending copies to the Hill. How about if I just deliver a copy to you?"

Quarles accepted. Dowd thought he and Quarles worked well together. They could meet and talk, whereas Mueller was so rigid, he sometimes seemed like marble.

On July 20 Bloomberg dropped an apparent bombshell: Mueller was investigating Trump's finances including "Russian purchases of apartments in Trump buildings . . . the 2013 Miss Universe pageant in Moscow and Trump's sale of a Florida mansion to a Russian oligarch in 2008."

Dowd called Quarles to ask about the story.

"Well," Quarles said, "Bob never comments."

"Give me a break, pal," Dowd replied angrily. "I'm taking care of you, now you take care of me." As they both knew, "a denial from the White House doesn't get anywhere." Dowd continued, "The deal was, with you guys, if you guys added to the investigation, we'd get a heads-up first."

"That's right."

"Because you gave us the subjects to cover," Dowd said. "And every once in a while you guys add things and we put it on a list. I didn't hear about condos in Florida or selling this estate." Dowd said he was aware of some matters under investigation in New York about Trump lawyer Michael Cohen and Felix Sater, who tried to develop a Trump Tower in Moscow. "You know, Jimmy," Dowd added, "when you ask me a question, I give it all to you. So I need a better explanation."

"John, let me put it this way," Quarles said. "I'm 99 percent sure that it's not us."

"I got it," Dowd said. He immediately called the president, knowing when that kind of story broke Trump could not focus on anything else. Trump was apoplectic.

"They're not investigating that stuff," Dowd said, trying to re-assure him. But Trump was not trusting at all and sounded like he could find no comfort.

Four days later Dowd met Quarles on a stone bench outside the Patriot Plaza where Mueller had his offices.

"Bob and I owe you one," Quarles said. "Bob says don't believe what you read in the papers."

"I got it," Dowd replied.

"We are really embarrassed," Quarles said.

"Why?"

"You've delivered more than you promised, and we're so pleased. We're moving along. We're getting it done. And there's a lot of stuff here to organize, but it came very well organized. We didn't have to go hunt and peck. You didn't drown us."

Dowd knew about a target of a tax investigation who had once told the FBI that the answer to their request was somewhere in two warehouses. The agents spent years searching.

"But let's agree going forward," Dowd said. "I don't want to play cat-and-mouse. You're not on my end of the stick. I got a guy that wants to know yesterday," and Trump's "instincts are it's bullshit." Dowd added that he had checked with the Trump Organization, and they had denied they were being separately investigated. They'd received no requests for documents or interviews—standard preliminary steps. "And they said, as far as we know, it's bullshit." All the organization's projects were eight or nine years old. There were no issues. Whatever Mueller wanted to see was out there in the public record someplace.

Dowd had told this to the president. "I know that, goddamn it!" Trump had said.

Dowd continued with Quarles. "Sometimes I've got to do this by phone and you've got to give me some direction. I'm not asking you to give away the store or reveal your hand. Just tell me are we going to get hit or not going to get hit. Or you have a request or you don't. It's not on your radar."

"I agree," Quarles said.

Dowd was careful not to stray, to ask about possible investigations of Jared's finances. Trump was his client, and it was key to be client-focused.

In July, the Freedom Caucus, a bloc of 30 strong conservatives in the House, threatened not to vote for the budget unless President Trump instituted some prohibition on paying for gender reassignment surgeries and hormone treatments for transgender people serving in the military.

Under Obama, transgender troops had no longer been banned from openly serving, although new recruits would not be allowed to join until July 1, 2017. On June 30, the day before the deadline, Mattis signed a memo delaying implementation by six months to review "the readiness and lethality of the force."

During the campaign, Trump had proclaimed himself a supporter of LGBT rights. Now he told Bannon, "What the fuck? They're coming in here, they're getting clipped"—a crude reference to gender reassignment surgery. Someone had told him that each surgery cost $250,000, an inflated number. "Not going to happen," he said.

Gender reassignment surgery can be expensive but also is infrequent. In a Pentagon-commissioned study, the RAND Corporation "found that only a few hundred of the estimated 6,600 transgender troops would seek medical treatment in any year. RAND found those costs would total no more than $8 million per year."

The interagency process had gone to work on the question. The general counsels of the departments and agencies had weighed in. The Deputies Committee had met, and there were several Principals Committee meetings. There was no agreement, but four options were developed.

On the morning of July 26, Priebus, Bannon and several lawyers reached the president on the speakerphone in the residence. He was not expected in the Oval Office for at least an hour.

Mr. President, Priebus said, we know you are going to come down soon but we wanted to give you a heads-up on a decision memo on transgender people in the military.

The four options: One was to retain the Obama policy that allowed transgender people to serve openly, two was to issue a directive to Secretary Mattis giving him leeway, three was a presidential order to end the program but come up with a plan for those transgender people already in the military, and four was to ban all transgender people from military service. The likelihood of being sued increased as they got to number four, Priebus explained. "When you come down, we want to walk you through on paper," Priebus said.

"I'll be down at 10," the president said. "Why don't you guys come and see me then? We'll figure it out."

Priebus thought they had found an orderly process on at least one controversial matter.

At 8:55 a.m., his phone signaled him that a presidential tweet had been sent. "After consultation with my Generals and military experts, please be advised that the United States Government will not accept or allow . . ."

In two more tweets following at 9:04 and 9:08 a.m., Trump finished his announcement: ". . . Transgender individuals to serve in any capacity in the U.S. Military. Our military must be focused on decisive and overwhelming victory and cannot be burdened with the tremendous medical costs and disruption that transgender in the military would entail. Thank you."

"What'd you think of my tweet?" the president asked Priebus later.

"I think it would've been better if we had a decision memo, looped Mattis in," Priebus answered.

Mattis was not happy with Trump's decision to tweet the news and the effect it would have on serving and deployed transgender troops. On vacation in the Pacific Northwest, he was caught by surprise.

The confusion played out in the press, with a Pentagon spokesman calling the Trump tweet "new guidance."

Trump spokesperson Sarah Huckabee Sanders said, "The president's national security team" was consulted and that Trump had made the decision the day before and "informed" Mattis immediately after. Several White House officials told the press that Mattis was consulted before the announcement and knew Trump was considering it.

Bannon knew that the generals, though hard-line on defense, had become progressive on social issues. "The Marine Corps is a progressive institution," Bannon said. "Dunford, Kelly and Mattis are the three biggest. They're more progressive than Gary Cohn and Kushner."

The commandant of the Coast Guard said publicly, "I will not break the faith" with transgender members of his service.

Dunford sent a letter to the service chiefs: "There will be no modifications to the current policy until the President's direction has been received by the Secretary of Defense and the Secretary has issued implementation guidance." In short, tweets were not orders. "In the meantime, we will continue to treat all of our personnel with respect . . . we will all remain focused on accomplishing our assigned missions."

Mattis aide Sally Donnelly called Bannon. "Hey, we've got a problem with the boss," she said. "We can't stand by this transgender decision. This is just not right. They are American citizens."

"These guys are coming over to get full surgery," Bannon said. "We're supposed to pay for that?"

Mattis was going to try to reverse the decision, she said.

"You've got to take one for the team," Bannon told her. Mattis would have to get in line.

The White House later issued formal guidance to the Pentagon. Mattis announced he would study the issue. In the meantime, transgender troops continued to serve. Lawsuits were filed, and four federal courts entered preliminary injunctions against the ban. On January 1, 2018, the Pentagon began accepting transgender recruits as required by the courts.

On June 2, Marc Kasowitz, Trump's longtime attorney, walked into the Oval Office. Trump was signing papers that Porter had brought him, carefully presenting each for signature and offering a few comments.

Wow, Kasowitz said. Your man Porter here is quite a hire. Harvard, Harvard Law School, Rhodes Scholar.

Trump had been dealing with Porter since he'd taken office.

"You've got a better résumé than Neil Gorsuch!" the president said. Gorsuch's nomination and confirmation to the Supreme Court was probably Trump's most notable accomplishment as president. He mentioned Gorsuch whenever he recounted his administration's achievements. "Who do you work for?" Trump asked after Kasowitz had left.

"I guess I work for . . ." Porter began.

"Who do you report to?"

"I guess I report to Reince, but I really work for you."

"Yeah, yeah, yeah," Trump said. He knew about the formal organization charts, and hated them. "Forget about Reince. He's like a little rat. He just scurries around. You don't even have to pay any attention to him. Just come talk to me. You don't have to go through him."

That day changed the Trump-Porter relationship. His staff secretary was practically a Neil Gorsuch clone.

Porter was shocked that Trump was so vicious about his chief of staff.

Priebus, Porter and others continued to try to persuade Trump to curtail his use of Twitter.

"This is my megaphone," Trump replied. "This is the way that I speak directly to the people without any filter. Cut through the noise. Cut through the fake news. That's the only way I have to communicate. I have tens of millions of followers. This is bigger than cable news. I go out and give a speech and it's covered by CNN and nobody's watching, nobody cares. I tweet something and it's my megaphone to the world."

"Going bananas" was the term Priebus used to describe Trump early on the morning of Thursday, June 29. Trump had aimed a pair of pre-6:00 a.m. tweets at the MSNBC cable show *Morning Joe*, starring former Republican congressman Joe Scarborough and his partner, Mika Brzezinski.

The two had been friendly and even supportive of Trump early in the presidential campaign, and Trump had called in to the show regularly during the primaries, but they were now regular detractors. Trump's tweet said, "How come low I.Q. Crazy Mika along with Psycho Joe came to Mar-a-Lago 3 nights in a row around New Year's Eve, and insisted on joining me. She was bleeding badly from a face-lift."

About 10:15 a.m. Trump was in the Oval Office reading the newspaper when Priebus walked in.

"I know what you are going to say," Trump said as Priebus crossed the threshold. "It's not presidential. And guess what? I know it. But I had to do it anyway."

Priebus knew not to ask why.

Hope Hicks, now the director of strategic communication, was horrified. She tried to take the lead on the tweets about Mika.

"It's not politically helpful," Hicks told the president. "You can't just be a loose cannon on Twitter. You're getting killed by a lot of this stuff. You're shooting yourself in the foot. You're making big mistakes."

Following the Mika tweet, a measurable storm of protest came from key Republicans who were necessary votes on repealing and replacing Obamacare and other legislation. Senator Susan Collins of Maine said, "This just has to stop." Senator Lisa Murkowski of Alaska: "Stop it!" Already on shaky ground with women, Trump's personal attack encouraged comparisons to his past history.

As an extreme measure, Hicks, Porter, Gary Cohn and White House social media director Dan Scavino proposed they set up a committee. They would draft some tweets that they believed Trump would like. If the president had an idea for a tweet, he could write it down or get one of them in and they would vet it. Was it factually accurate? Was it spelled correctly? Did it make sense? Did it serve his needs?

"I guess you're right," Trump said several times. "We could do that." But then he ignored most reviews or vetting and did what he wanted.

When Trump and North Korean leader Kim Jong Un amped up the rhetoric, he was warned, "Twitter could get us into a war."

"This is my megaphone," Trump said again. "Let's not call it Twitter. Let's call it social media." Though the White House had Facebook and Instagram accounts, Trump did not use them. He stuck to Twitter. "This is who I am. This is how I communicate. It's the reason I got elected. It's the reason that I'm successful."

The tweets were not incidental to his presidency. They were central. He ordered printouts of his recent tweets that had received a high number of likes, 200,000 or more. He studied them to find the common themes in the most successful. He seemed to want to become more strategic, find out whether success was tied to the subject, the language or simply the surprise that the president was weighing in. The most effective tweets were often the most shocking.

Later, when Twitter announced the number of permissible characters in a single tweet was being doubled from 140 to 280, Trump told Porter he thought the change made sense on one level. Now he would be able to flesh out his thoughts and add more depth.

"It's a good thing," Trump said, "but it's a bit of a shame because I was the Ernest Hemingway of 140 characters."

At the G20 summit in Hamburg, Germany, in early July Trump wanted to talk with Australian prime minister Malcolm Turnbull. In violation of security rules he invited Turnbull into his Sensitive Compartmented Information Facility (SCIF). Only those with the highest U.S. security clearances for Top Secret Sensitive Compartmented Information were allowed in the SCIF. It was an absolute rule, intended to prevent someone planting listening devices. This facility, a large steel room, had to be torn down after the meeting.

The relationship between the leaders had been difficult since the first week of the administration, when the two men spoke by phone. Trump wanted to get out of what he called a "stupid" deal that is "going to kill me" between the U.S. and Australia, made under President Obama. Under the agreement, certain refugees with questionable backgrounds waiting on an island off Australia would be allowed to enter the U.S. The transcript of their January 28, 2017, call had leaked. Trump had said, "It is an evil time. . . . Are they going to become the Boston bomber?"

As he went to the meeting with Trump in Germany, Turnbull was aware of the debate within the White House about possible tariffs on steel imported into the United States.

"If you do ever put steel tariffs on," Turnbull said, "you've got to exempt Australian steel. We do this steel that's specialty steel. We're the only one that produces it in the world. You've got to let us out.

You've got a $40 billion trade surplus with us. We're military allies with you. We're in every battle with you."

"Of course," Trump said, "we'll let you out. That makes total sense. You guys are great. We've got a big surplus with you guys"— the holy grail.

Gary Cohn, who was in the meeting, was pleased. Turnbull had previously been a partner at Goldman Sachs and had worked for Cohn when he was Goldman president.

Coming back from the G20 summit, Trump was editing an upcoming speech with Porter. Scribbling his thoughts in neat, clean penmanship, the president wrote, "TRADE IS BAD."

TRADE IS BAD

Though he never said it in a speech, he had finally found the summarizing phrase and truest expression of his protectionism, isolationism and fervent American nationalism.

Nearly eight months later, on February 23, 2018, Turnbull arrived at the White House to see the president.

In the prep session in the Oval Office for the meeting, Cohn reminded Trump of his pledge.

"Mr. President," Cohn said, "the first thing he's going to bring up is the steel tariffs. And he's going to remind you that you let him out."

"I don't remember," Trump said, sitting behind the Resolute Desk.

"Well, sir," Cohn said, "you had the conversation with him . . ."

"I'm going to deny it," Trump replied. "I never had that conversation with him."

"Okay, sir, just reminding you that it's going to come up."

Cohn had witnessed this for over a year—denial when needed or useful or more convenient. "He's a professional liar," Cohn told an associate.

At lunch Turnbull carefully stepped Trump through their time at the G20 the previous summer.

Remember we were in Hamburg?

Yes, Trump said.

You took me back in your secure facility?

"Oh, yeah, I remember that," Trump replied. "My security guys were so pissed. They couldn't believe I did it."

Remember what conversation we had?

Trump nodded.

We were talking about specialty steel that Australia exclusively produces.

A version of yes from Trump.

"We've got a $40 billion trade surplus?"

Yes, Trump knew that for sure.

And you agreed to let me out of any steel tariff?

"Oh, yeah," Trump answered, "I guess I remember that."

Cohn laughed.

Australian steel was later exempted, as were other nations. As of June 2018, Australia retained its exemption.

McMaster had drinks with Dina Powell, a senior deputy from his staff, and Porter on July 15.

"The team of two," McMaster said—Tillerson and Mattis—were making his position difficult and less and less tenable.

McMaster said that he believed Mattis and Tillerson had concluded that the president and the White House were crazy. As a result, they sought to implement and even formulate policy on their own without interference or involvement from McMaster, let alone the president.

Just the previous week, McMaster said that Tillerson had been in Qatar and signed an important Memorandum of Understanding with the Qatari foreign minister on counterterrorism and disabling the financing of terrorism.

McMaster said he had been completely in the dark about this. The secretary of state had not consulted or even informed him in advance. He had learned from press reports! In a news conference in Qatar, Tillerson had said the agreement "represents weeks of intensive discussions" between the two governments so it had been in the works for a while.

Porter said Tillerson had not gone through the policy process at the White House and had not involved the president either. Clearly Tillerson was going off on his own.

"It is more loyal to the president," McMaster said, "to try to persuade rather the circumvent." He said he carried out direct orders when the president was clear, and felt duty bound to do so as an Army officer. Tillerson in particular did not.

"He's such a prick," McMaster said. "He thinks he's smarter than anyone. So he thinks he can do his own thing."

In his long quest to bring order to the chaos, Priebus arranged for each of the key cabinet members to regularly check in. Tillerson came to his office at 5:15 p.m. on Tuesday, July 18.

McMaster had not been invited but joined the meeting anyway. He took a seat at the conference table. The national security adviser's silent presence was ominous and electric.

Tell me, Priebus asked Tillerson, how are things going? Are you on track to achieve your primary objectives? How is the relationship between the State Department and the White House? Between you and the president?

"You guys in the White House don't have your act together," Tillerson said, and the floodgates gushed open. "The president can't make a decision. He doesn't know how to make a decision. He won't make a decision. He makes a decision and then changes his mind a couple of days later."

McMaster broke his silence and raged at the secretary of state.

"You don't work with the White House," McMaster said. "You never consult me or anybody on the NSC staff. You blow us off constantly." He cited examples when he tried to set up calls or meetings or breakfasts with Tillerson. "You are off doing your own thing" and communicate directly with the president, Mattis, Priebus or Porter. "But it's never with the National Security Council," and "that's what we're here to do." Then he issued his most dramatic charge. "You're affirmatively seeking to undermine the national security process."

"That's not true," Tillerson replied. "I'm available anytime. I talk to you all the time. We just had a conference call yesterday. We do these morning calls three times a week. What are you talking about, H.R.? I've worked with you. I'll work with anybody."

Tillerson continued, "I've also got to be secretary of state. Sometimes I'm traveling. Sometimes I'm in a different time zone. I can't always take your calls."

McMaster said he consulted with the relevant assistant secretaries of state if the positions were filled.

"I don't have assistant secretaries," Tillerson said, coldly, "because I haven't picked them, or the ones that I have, I don't like and I don't trust and I don't work with. So you can check with whoever you want. That has no bearing on me." The rest of the State Department didn't matter; if you didn't go through him, it didn't count.

After the meeting, Tillerson, still steaming, came down to Porter's office. "The White House is such a disaster," he said. "So many of those guys upstairs, they just don't have a clue what's going on."

Tillerson said that Johnny DeStefano, the 39-year-old director of personnel, couldn't pick someone for a key State Department post if they hit him in the nose. DeStefano had worked as a Hill staffer and knew nothing about foreign policy. "You wouldn't believe this guy he sent over for me to interview" to be an assistant secretary of state.

"It was a joke. I don't know in what possible universe anybody could have thought that he could possibly be qualified for this job."

Priebus later said to Porter, "Oh wow, fireworks! It seems like Rex is really upset about a lot of stuff right now. He's just sort of ill-tempered."

Porter believed that McMaster absolutely had a point, though his meetings and calls could be tedious and not always necessary. But the breakdown between Tillerson and McMaster proved the general dysfunction.

On Wednesday, July 19, 2017, Trump granted an unusual interview to *The New York Times* and launched a head-spinning attack on Jeff Sessions.

He said he would never have appointed Sessions if he had known he would recuse himself from overseeing the Russia investigation. "Sessions should have never recused himself, and if he was going to recuse himself, he should have told me before he took the job and I would have picked somebody else. How do you take a job and then recuse yourself? If he would have recused himself before the job, I would have said, 'Thanks, Jeff, but I'm not going to take you.' It's extremely unfair—and that's a mild word—to the president."

Trump was still stewing about Sessions three days later, Saturday morning, July 22, when he boarded Marine One to head to Norfolk, Virginia. He was speaking at the commissioning ceremony of the USS *Gerald R. Ford* (CVN 78), a $13 billion warship.

Trump and Priebus were chatting. Trump said he had always admired Obama's attorney general, Eric Holder. Though he disagreed with their policies, of course, Holder had stuck with Obama no matter what came up or whatever the controversy for eight years. There had been no recusals and no dodging the political crossfire. Holder had been willing to take the hit for his president.

"Jeff isn't a guy that, through thick and thin, is willing to stick with me," he said.

Sessions, Trump said, could have declined to recuse himself in the Russia investigation by saying he had nothing to do with the day-to-day operations of the Trump campaign. He had been on the campaign plane and gone to rallies but he had nothing to do with strategy—the ground game, the persuasion mail or the digital operations.

He was also unhappy with Sessions's testimony before various congressional committees about meetings or discussions with Russians.

"Get his resignation," Trump ordered Priebus.

Stephen Miller, who was a former Sessions staffer and big supporter, later told Priebus, "We're in real trouble. Because if you don't get the resignation, he's going to think you're weak. If you get it, you're going to be part of a downward-spiral calamity."

Priebus spoke to Sessions several times. The attorney general did not want to resign. If the president doesn't want you to serve, Priebus said, then you ought not to serve.

No, he wouldn't go.

Eventually, Trump agreed to hold off. He did not want an immediate resignation because he said he wanted them to get through the Sunday talk shows the next day.

Two days later Trump continued the barrage on Sessions, calling him "our beleaguered A.G." on Twitter.

In an interview with *The Wall Street Journal*, he dismissed Sessions's endorsement during the presidential campaign. "When they say he endorsed me, I went to Alabama. I had 40,000 people. He was a senator from Alabama. I won the state by a lot, massive numbers. A lot of states I won by massive numbers. But he was a senator, he looks at 40,000 people and he probably says, 'What do I have to lose?' And he endorsed me. So it's not like a great loyal thing about the endorsement."

Bannon asked Sessions to come to the White House. Sessions took a chair in what Bannon called his war room, the walls lined with whiteboards listing Trump's campaign promises. The attorney general, small in stature, was nervous but pleasant.

"Look," Bannon said, "you were there through the whole time" of the campaign. "You knew this thing was a shit show, totally disorganized."

Sessions could not dispute that.

Bannon turned to what was perhaps the fondest memory of their political lives—when Trump had won the presidency on November 9. Victory was as sweet as it got.

"Is there any doubt in your mind on the 9th, when it was called, that it was the hand?" Bannon asked, dipping into a shared religious belief system. "That divine providence that worked through Trump to win this?"

"No," Sessions said.

"You mean that?"

Sessions said he did.

"It was the hand of God, right? You and I were there. We know there's no other way it could've happened than the hand of God."

"Yes."

"Fine," Bannon said. "You're never going to quit, are you?"

"I'm never quitting." Trump would have to fire him.

"You promise me you'll never quit?"

"Yeah."

"Because it's going to get worse."

"What do you mean?" Sessions asked.

"It's all a diversion."

"What do you mean?"

"Jared's testifying." Trump's son-in-law was appearing before the Senate Intelligence Committee on Monday and the House Intelligence Committee on Tuesday. "They didn't think they had enough cover."

"He wouldn't do that to me," Sessions said.

"He'd fucking do that to you in a second. He's doing it to you! You watch! When Jared finishes testifying, if they think it's good testimony, he'll stop tweeting."

On July 24 Kushner released a long, carefully lawyered statement ahead of his congressional appearance. "I did not collude, nor know of anyone else in the campaign who colluded, with any foreign government. I had no improper contacts. I have not relied on Russian funds to finance my business activities in the private sector."

The Trump attacks on Sessions subsided for a while. It was a sideshow, a diversion. He did believe Sessions had failed him, though, so it was a diversion with conviction.

Trump's attacks on Sessions awakened Republicans in the U.S. Senate. Graham said Sessions "believes in the rule of law." Other Republicans defended their former colleague and said it would not be easy to get a replacement confirmed by the Senate. Deputy Rod Rosenstein might resign. It could cascade into a Watergate-like situation reminiscent of the 1973 Saturday Night Massacre, when Nixon fired the special prosecutor and the attorney general and his deputy both resigned. Priebus worried that could make the Comey problem look like child's play.

Trump subjected Sessions to a withering attack in the Oval Office, calling him an "idiot." Despite his promise to Bannon, Sessions sent a resignation letter to Trump. Priebus talked the president out of accepting it.

Recusing himself made the attorney general a "traitor," Trump said to Porter. The president made fun of his Southern accent. "This guy is mentally retarded. He's this dumb Southerner." Trump even did a little impression of a Southern accent, mimicking how Sessions got all mixed up in his confirmation hearings, denying that he had talked to the Russian ambassador.

"How in the world was I ever persuaded to pick him for my attorney general?" Trump asked Porter. "He couldn't even be a one-person country lawyer down in Alabama. What business does he have being attorney general?"

Trump would not stop. He told Porter, "If he was going to recuse himself from this, why did he let himself be picked attorney general? That was the ultimate betrayal. How could he have done that?"

Porter had an answer, which he presented as gently as he could. "There are well-established rules and guidelines for when you have to recuse yourself. And he met those. This wasn't a political decision on his part. This wasn't something he wanted to do. He consulted the relevant experts at the Department of Justice and was told you meet the criteria, so you have to."

"Well," Trump said angrily, "he never should have taken the job. He's the attorney general. He can make these decisions on his own. He doesn't have to listen to his staff. If he was that smart of a lawyer and he knew he was going to have to recuse himself, he should've told me and I never would've picked him. But he's slow. He probably didn't even know."

Priebus called a full senior staff meeting at 8 a.m. on July 20 on immigration. Stephen Miller made a presentation. To some, it amounted to a shopping list of issues—the border wall, border enforcement, catch and release, immigration judges, the diversity lottery, sanctuary cities, Kate's Law—which would increase penalties for people who attempted to illegally reenter the U.S. after having been deported—and chain migration.

We need to select the winning issues, Miller said, the ones that are bad issues for the Democrats. We need to then convince the Senate to take on tough wedge issue votes such as defunding sanctuary cities.

Kushner strongly disagreed with Miller's strategy. We need to focus on bipartisan, constructive things, and even find things we could give the Democrats—"a few of our priorities, a couple of theirs." He wanted "a path forward so we can actually get something done."

Priebus disagreed with Kushner. "I know the Hill. I know what's going to be good in terms of these messaging votes." A real estate developer from New York City like Jared didn't know much about politics.

Jared protested. "I know how to get things done and be constructive and take people with disagreements and get them in the same
place."

Kushner said that most of the legislative discussions in the White
House involved Priebus acolytes from the combative Republican National Committee, or from former senator Sessions's office or from
Pence's stable of conservatives. None of them had experience negotiating bipartisan agreements or getting deals done. Extremists and people trying to score political points were running the legislative agenda.

Mattis and Gary Cohn had several quiet conversations about The
Big Problem: The president did not understand the importance of
allies overseas, the value of diplomacy or the relationship between
the military, the economy and intelligence partnerships with foreign
governments.

They met for lunch at the Pentagon to develop an action plan.

One cause of the problem was the president's fervent belief that
annual trade deficits of about $500 billion harmed the American
economy. He was on a crusade to impose tariffs and quotas despite
Cohn's best efforts to educate him about the benefits of free trade.

How could they convince and, in their frank view, educate the
president? Cohn and Mattis realized they were nowhere close to per-
suading him. The Groundhog Day–like meetings on trade continued
and the acrimony only grew.

"Let's get him over here to the Tank," Mattis proposed. The Tank
is the Pentagon's secure meeting room for the Joint Chiefs of Staff.
It might focus him.

"Great idea," Cohn said. "Let's get him out of the White House."
No press; no TVs; no Madeleine Westerhout, Trump's personal secretary, who worked within shouting distance of the Oval Office.
There wouldn't even be any looking out the window, because there
were no windows in the Tank.

Getting Trump out of his natural environment could do the trick.

The idea was straight from the corporate playbook—a retreat or off-site meeting. They would get Trump to the Tank with his key national security and economic team to discuss worldwide strategic relations.

Mattis and Cohn agreed. Together they would fight Trump on this. Trade wars or disruptions in the global markets could savage and undermine the precarious stability in the world. The threat could spill over to the military and intelligence community.

Mattis couldn't understand why the U.S. would want to pick a fight with allies, whether it was NATO, or friends in the Middle East, or Japan—or particularly with South Korea.

Just before 10 a.m. on July 20, a stifling, cloudless summer Thursday six months into his presidency, Donald Trump crossed the Potomac River to the Pentagon.

The Tank had its appeal. Trump loved the room. Sometimes known as the Gold Room for its carpet and curtains, it is ornate and solemn, essentially a private, high-security retreat reflecting decades of history.

Mattis and Cohn organized the presentations as part history lesson and part geostrategic showdown. It was also a belated effort to address the looming question: How does this administration establish its policy priorities and stick to them?

McMaster did not attend because he had a family obligation.

Maps depicting American commitments around the world—military deployments, troops, nuclear weapons, diplomatic posts, ports, intelligence assets, treaties and even trade deals—filled two large wall screens, telling the story of the United States in the world. Even countries where the U.S. had ports and flyover rights were shown, as were key radar and other surveillance installations.

"The great gift of the greatest generation to us," Mattis opened, "is the rules-based, international democratic order." This global architecture brought security, stability and prosperity.

Bannon sat off to the side, a backbencher with a line of sight to the president. He knew this globalist worldview too well. He viewed it as a kind of fetish. His own obsession was still America First.

This is going to be fun, Bannon thought, as Mattis made the case that the organizing principles of the past were still workable and necessary.

There it was—the beating heart of the problem, Bannon thought.

Secretary of State Rex Tillerson followed.

"This is what has kept the peace for 70 years," the former Texas oilman said.

It was more of the old world order to Bannon: expensive, limitless engagements, promises made and kept.

Trump was shaking his head, disagreeing, although he did not say anything.

Cohn spoke next. He made the case for free trade: Mexico. Canada. Japan. Europe. South Korea. He presented the import and export data. We're a huge exporter of agriculture products, about $130 billion a year, he noted. We need these countries to buy our agricultural products. The whole middle of the United States is basically farmers, he said.

Most of them were Trump voters.

U.S. arms deals abroad amounted to $75.9 billion in fiscal year 2017. It's no mistake that we've got a lot of military aircraft at the same airport in Singapore where they buy a lot of Boeing aircraft, Cohn said. It's no mistake that we've got enormous intelligence operations out of Singapore. It's no mistake that our naval fleet goes in and out of there to refuel and resupply.

Trade deficits were growing the U.S. economy, Cohn asserted.

"I don't want to hear that," Trump said. "It's all bullshit!"

Treasury Secretary Mnuchin, another Goldman veteran, spoke about the importance of the security allies and trading partners.

Trump turned to look at Bannon. Then he looked again. Bannon took this as a signal.

"Hang on for a second," Bannon said to everyone as he stood up. "Let's get real."

He picked one of the most controversial international agreements that bound the United States to this global order. "The president wants to decertify the Iranian deal and you guys are slow-walking it. It's a terrible deal. He wants to decertify so he can renegotiate." Trump would not just tear it up, as he'd promised in the campaign.

"One of the things he wants to do is" impose sanctions on Iran, the chief strategist said. "Is one of your fucking great allies up in the European Union" going to back the president? All this talk about how they are our partners. "Give me one that's going to back the president on sanctions?"

Mnuchin attempted to answer on the importance of the allies.

"Give me one guy," Bannon said. "One country. One company. Who's going to back sanctions?"

Nobody answered.

"That's what I'm talking about," Trump said. "He just made my point. You talk about all these guys as allies. There's not an ally up there. Answer Steve's question. Who's going to back us?"

Tillerson said, "The best we can tell, they're not in violation of anything." All the intelligence agencies agreed on this. It was the critical point. How could they impose new sanctions, if there was no violation of the agreement?

"They're all making money," Trump said, noting the European Union was trading and making big deals with Iran. "And nobody's going to have our back."

Trump flipped to Afghanistan, where he already had endured half a dozen recent NSC and smaller meetings. "When are we going to start winning some wars? We've got these charts. When are we going to win some wars? Why are you jamming this down my throat?"

Referring to the Afghanistan commander, General John Nicholson, who was not present, the president lashed out. "I don't think he knows how to win. I don't know if he's a winner. There's no victories."

Trump had not settled on an Afghanistan strategy, which was then still being debated.

"You should be killing guys. You don't need a strategy to kill people."

General Dunford, the chairman of the Joint Chiefs of Staff, sprang to Nicholson's defense.

"Mr. President," Dunford said, very polite, very soft-spoken, "there's not a mandate to win. That's not his orders." Under Obama, who had pulled out most of the troops—down to 8,400, from a high of 100,000—the strategy was effectively to achieve a stalemate.

Mattis and Dunford were proposing new rules of engagement for U.S. troops in Afghanistan, freeing them up to be more aggressive and lethal by lifting Obama-era restrictions on the local commanders. Tactics would no longer be announced to the enemy. Recent success against ISIS demonstrated the importance of these changes.

Trump recalled that General Nicholson had authorized the use of the 20,000-pound bomb, the GBU-43/B, known also as the MOAB, Mother of All Bombs. "He let that fucking big bomb off on them."

Yes, Dunford said, that was a decision made by the field commander, not in Washington.

Mattis tried to intervene politely, "Mr. President, Mr. President . . ."

"Mad Dog, Mad Dog," Trump replied, using his Marine nickname. "They're taking a free ride on us. What are we doing?" Trump questioned his generals as sharply as possible without shouting. "What about winning? The reason we're in this spot is because you've been recommending these activities."

The tension was increasing and soon they were back on Iran.

"They're complying," Tillerson said. "That's the deal. They're complying. You may not like it." The secretary of state had a logical way of walking through the details of the technical compliance of the deal.

"That's too establishment," Trump told him. They were arguing that all these things fit together—the trade agreements with China, with Mexico, the Iran nuclear deal, the troop deployments, the foreign aid. Trump's message was "no" on everything that had been presented.

"We can't do this," Trump said. "This is what's gotten us in that situation."

"When he says put sanctions in," Bannon said, addressing Mnuchin. "These great partners, what are they going to do on sanctions?"

Mnuchin seemed to hedge.

"No, stop," Bannon pressed. "Are they in or are they out?"

"They'll never support it," Mnuchin said.

"I rest my case," Bannon said. "There's your allies."

"The European companies," Trump said, pointing a finger at Mnuchin, "they're fucking worthless." Siemens, Peugeot, Volkswagen and other European household names were actively investing in Iran.

Trump said, "Rex, you're weak. I want to decertify."

Trump turned to one of his favorite issues. He wanted to slap tariffs on imported steel, aluminum and automobiles. He wondered why Mnuchin was not declaring China a currency manipulator as he wanted.

Mnuchin explained that China had, years ago, been a currency manipulator, but it no longer was.

"What do you mean?" Trump said. "Make the case. Just do it. Declare it."

Mnuchin explained that U.S. law was specific about what was required to prove currency manipulation, and he could not make the case.

"We're upside down" on trade deals, Trump said. "We're underwater on every one of these." The other countries are making money. "Just look at all this stuff up there. We're paying for it all." Those countries were "protectorates," he declared.

"It's actually good for our economy," Cohn said again.

"I don't want to hear that," Trump replied. "It's all bullshit."

As the meeting was winding down, Tillerson leaned back in his chair. He seemed to be speaking to the president but did not make eye contact with him. Instead he looked at Mattis.

"Your deal," the secretary of state said. "It's your deal."

It was a Texas walk-back—as if to say, I will obey and execute, but it is your design, not mine.

"We spend $3.5 billion a year to have troops in South Korea," Trump said angrily. The South could not decide if they wanted the THAAD antimissile system or not! And whether they are going to pay for it or not!

Some South Koreans believed the system could provoke war with North Korea and had protested the installation, arguing it was for the benefit of the U.S. and Japan.

"Pull the fucking thing out!" Trump said. "I don't give a shit."

"The South Koreans subsidize the hell out of us," Cohn said, challenging the president directly. The trade deal was good for the United States economy, he said again. "We buy the most amazing TVs in the world for $245. Which means that people are spending less money on TVs and more money on other products in the United States."

If the U.S. pulled its troops out, it would require more Navy carrier groups in that part of the world to feel comfortable. That might cost 10 times as much, Cohn stated.

Then there was the ultra-sensitive intelligence gained through the Special Access Programs South Korea allowed the U.S. to run. Trump seemed not to comprehend the value and the necessity.

"Like $3.5 billion, 28,000 troops," the president said. He was really hot. "I don't know why they're there. Let's bring them all home!"

"So, Mr. President," Cohn said, "what would you need in the region to sleep well at night?"

"I wouldn't need a fucking thing," the president said. "And I'd sleep like a baby."

Priebus called an end to the meeting. Mattis seemed completely deflated.

Trump got up and walked out.

All the air seemed to have come out of Tillerson. He could not abide Trump's attack on the generals. The president was speaking as if the U.S. military was a mercenary force for hire. If a country wouldn't pay us to be there, then we didn't want to be there. As if there were no American interests in forging and keeping a peaceful world order, as if the American organizing principle was money.

"Are you okay?" Cohn asked him.

"He's a fucking moron," Tillerson said so everyone heard.

Trump left the meeting with Priebus, Bannon and Kushner just before 12:45 p.m. He spent a few moments greeting service members lined up in the corridor.

"The meeting was great," Trump told reporters. "A very good meeting."

He moved toward the presidential limousine.

"I'm glad you fucking decided to say something," Trump said to Bannon. "I needed some backup."

"You were doing great," Bannon said.

Treasury Secretary Mnuchin had followed them out. He wanted to make sure it was clear he was with Trump on the European allies. "I don't know if they're allies or not," he said. "I'm with you."

In the car, Trump described his advisers, "They don't know anything about business. All they want to do is protect everybody—that we pay for."

He said that the South Koreans, our allies, won't cut a new deal with us on trade. "And they want us to protect them from that crazy guy in the North."

Cohn concluded that Trump was, in fact, going backwards. He had been more manageable the first months when he was a novice.

For Priebus, it was the worst meeting among many terrible ones. Six months into the administration, he could see vividly that they had a fundamental problem of goal setting. Where were they going?

The distrust in the room had been thick and corrosive. The atmosphere was primitive; everyone was ostensibly on the same side, but they had seemed suited up in battle armor, particularly the president.

This was what craziness was like, Priebus concluded.

A senior White House official who spoke contemporaneously with participants in the meeting recorded this summary: "The president proceeded to lecture and insult the entire group about how they didn't know anything when it came to defense or national security. It seems clear that many of the president's senior advisers, especially those in the national security realm, are extremely concerned with his erratic nature, his relative ignorance, his inability to learn, as well as what they consider his dangerous views."

A fter the meeting in the Tank, Tillerson, an Eagle Scout, left to attend the Boy Scout Jamboree in West Virginia and his son's wedding in Texas. He was thinking of resigning.

"Listen," Priebus said later in a call to him, "you can't resign right now. That's ridiculous. Come over to my office."

Tillerson came to see him. "I just don't like the way the president talks to these generals. They don't deserve it. I can't sit around and listen to this from the president. He's just a moron."

Priebus was surprised at his open hostility. He realized that Tillerson's real grievance was also the way the president talked to him. In many Situation Room meetings Tillerson would almost literally huff and puff, conspicuously telegraphing that he was more than just annoyed, masking the "moron" talk, but barely.

Priebus suggested that Tillerson tone it down. "You can't just be disrespectful. You can't talk to the president the way you do. You've got to find a way to communicate, say the same thing but find a way to say it that's not offensive."

Priebus admired Mattis's approach—avoid the confrontation,

demonstrate respect and deference, proceed smartly with business, travel as much as possible, get and stay out of town.

Tillerson returned to the generals. "I can't sit there and listen to the president dress down these generals. I just can't take it. It's not right."

Priebus later told Trump that he had spoken to Tillerson about being disrespectful to the president. He did not mention the "moron" comment.

Trump listened quietly, which was unusual, and did not disagree about what was going on. Priebus thought that the president did not want to acknowledge Tillerson's hostility because he was full of pride. As chief executive he should not allow clear insubordination from his secretary of state.

At times the NSC process worked. A Policy Coordination Committee, one level below the Deputies Committee, would convene and gather input from the Joint Staff, civilians at the Defense Department, the State Department, the intelligence agencies, Treasury and the Office of Management and Budget. A 30-page strategy paper might be drafted, with annexes. Disagreements would be ironed out. Then it would be sent up to the Deputies Committee, where deputies from various departments could make changes. When everyone agreed on a framework, when a roadmap was approved, a Principals Committee, chaired by McMaster and attended by cabinet secretaries, would be called.

Tillerson was senior and so talked first at principals meetings. He would walk in and say, I didn't see the NSC strategy paper. This is a tough issue. We have to put it in perspective. Here's how I'm looking at it.

He would distribute a package of briefing slides. Rather than send them prior to the meeting so others could read ahead, he went through each slide at the meeting, sometimes taking five minutes on just one. The members of the NSC were a captive audience. The principals meetings were often scheduled for an hour and 15 minutes, so sometimes Tillerson's was the only voice, certainly the main voice.

Tillerson wanted to have everyone agree with his definition of the problems and then go back and rework the strategy.

These Tillerson interventions—his desire to restart the entire interagency process based on his assessment of where policies needed to go—happened in one form or another on the strategies for Iran, Iraq, Lebanon and Hezbollah, Syria, China, North Korea and defeating ISIS.

Some at the Principals Committee meetings, including both those at the table and the backbenchers, were at times impressed with the reframing. Others thought his presentations conventional. Tillerson would argue for more economic integration, coordination of development assistance and the need to address the motivators of violence and actively use diplomacy.

What was often lacking or delayed was an execution plan assigning responsibility and accountability. Endgame goals were fuzzy or unstated. The result was often weeks or months of delay.

Around this time in July, Trump was on a small plane, still designated Air Force One, returning from Bedminster. He came back to the small staff area where Ivanka, Jared, McMaster and Porter were seated.

Iraq, Afghanistan and Syria, the three main war zones, were quagmires and he was tired of owning them, the president said in a lecturing tone. "The enormous resources that we continue to expend in those countries!" he said. "We should just declare victory, end the wars and bring our troops home."

McMaster seemed crestfallen. After six months as commander in chief, Trump wanted to sweep it all away and pull out.

After the president left, Jared and Ivanka seemed worried. They said they wanted to help McMaster. When we all get back, they said, why don't you sit down with Porter and figure out a strategy, some way to withdraw some troops but also leave some? Find some way to talk to the president.

On July 25, the president again berated McMaster. He had no interest in allies, Trump said. He didn't want any troops in South Korea even when reminded about the differential between the seven seconds to detect an ICBM launch from there as opposed to 15-minute detection from Alaska.

On the colonnade outside the Oval Office, McMaster spoke with Cohn and Porter.

McMaster said that at 6:03 a.m., Trump had tweeted: "Ukrainian efforts to sabotage Trump campaign—'quietly working to boost Clinton.' So where is the investigation A.G. [attorney general]"

It was clearly Russian propaganda, McMaster said. He and the NSC and intelligence experts had concluded that. But the president had picked it up and shot it out.

McMaster said he wasn't sure how long he could stay.

In the Oval Office later that day, McMaster had a sensitive order he wanted the president to sign relating to Libya.

I'm not going to sign it, Trump said. The United States should be getting oil. The generals aren't sufficiently focused on getting or making money. They don't understand what our objectives should be and they have the United States engaged in all the wrong ways.

Before the president went up to the residence at the end of each day, Porter handed him a briefing book with background papers, policy memos and his schedule for the next day.

The next morning he would come down to the Oval Office at 10 a.m. or 11 a.m., or even 11:30.

"What's on my schedule for the day?" he would ask, having perhaps glanced at the book, or maybe not at all. He conveyed the belief that improvising was his strength. He could read a situation. Or the room. Or the moment as he had during the presidential campaign.

Trump liked to do things spur of the moment, Porter concluded, to fly by the seat of his pants. He acted like doing too much advance preparation would diminish his skills in improvising. He did not want to be derailed by forethought. As if a plan would take away his power, his sixth sense.

What the president would bring up in the morning most often was what he had seen on television, especially Fox News, or something from the newspapers he read more thoroughly than the public generally knew.

Throughout the day Trump would seek opinions from anyone who might be around—from cabinet officials to security guards. It was his form of crowdsourcing.

He once asked Johnny McEntee, his 27-year-old body man, if he should send more troops to Afghanistan.

"It doesn't make any sense to me," McEntee said.

When Trump asked others in the West Wing, they often ducked: "I think you really ought to talk to H.R. about that because he's the expert."

"No, no, no," Trump said once, "I want to know what you think."

"I know what I read in the newspapers."

That was insufficient for the president. "No, I want to know what you think."

All presidencies are audience driven, but Trump's central audience was often himself. He kept giving himself reviews. Most were passionately positive. Much of his brain was in the press box.

The operations of the Oval Office and White House were less the Art of the Deal and more often the Unraveling of the Deal. The unraveling was often right before your eyes, a Trump rally on continuous loop. There was no way not to look.

In foreign affairs, it was about personal relationships, Trump explained to those who spent the most time in the Oval Office. "I have really good relations with Xi," he said about the Chinese president. "We have really good chemistry. Xi likes me. Xi rolled out the red carpet when I visited Beijing." In November 2017, he had said publicly, "I consider him a friend. He considers me a friend."

H. R. McMaster tried to explain that Xi was using the president. China was an economic aggressor, planning to become Number One in the world.

Trump said he understood all of that. But all of those problems were superseded by his rapport with Xi.

In the last four months of 2017, the United Nations Security Council had voted three times to impose stiffer economic sanctions on North Korea. On December 22, the vote was 15 to 0, including China. The sanctions were to cut the amount of petroleum that could be imported into North Korea by 89 percent. Trump was quite pleased.

"That's because I developed such a great relationship with President Xi," he said. "And because he respects me and I respect him. And isn't it good that I'm friendly when all you guys say that we should be adversarial with them. Because if I didn't have that great relationship with President Xi, they never would have done that." It was the chemistry, the trust. "So that I can get them to do things that they wouldn't otherwise do."

On matters in which Trump had developed decades of opinions, arguments were pointless. One of the most experienced West Wingers in 2017 and 2018 said, "There's some things where he's already reached the conclusion and it doesn't matter what you say. It doesn't matter what arguments you offer. He's not listening."

At one point Trump said he had decided to impose tariffs.

"Great," Cohn said. "The stock market will be down 1,000 or 2,000 points tomorrow, but you'll be happy. Right, sir?"

"No, no, meeting's over! Let's not do anything."

"Your biggest fear is being Herbert Hoover," Cohn said.

It was Groundhog Day on trade again. Same arguments, same points, same certainty—on both sides. The next week or next month, they would have the same discussion.

Trump repeatedly said he was going to get out of the trade deals and impose tariffs. Several times he said, "Let's do it," and asked for an order to sign.

"We've got to distract him from KORUS," Porter said to Cohn. "We've got to distract him from NAFTA." Cohn agreed.

At least twice, Porter had the order drafted as the president had directed. And at least twice Cohn or Porter took it from his desk. Other times, they just delayed.

Trump seemed not to remember his own decision because he did not ask about it. He had no list—in his mind or anywhere else—of tasks to complete.

On July 12, 2017, 15 former chairs of the Council of Economic Advisers, the high-powered, formal advisory group of academic economists, had sent a letter to Trump urging him not to "initiate the process of imposing steel tariffs" because it would harm relations with key allies and "actually damage the U.S. economy."

The letter's signers included an all-star cast of Republicans and Democrats—former Federal Reserve chairmen Alan Greenspan and Ben Bernanke, Laura Tyson, the top economic adviser in the Clinton administration, and Nobel Prize winner Joseph Stiglitz.

Across the top, in a handwritten note to Trump, Wilber Ross scrawled his disagreement: "Dear Mr. President, It is importantly the advice of the people on this list that resulted in our [trade] deficits. We cannot afford their policies. Best Regards, Wilbur."

The final 10 days of July 2017 left scars. On Thursday, July 27, Trump had hired Anthony Scaramucci, a brash investment banker and another Goldman Sachs alumnus, as communications director over Priebus's strong objections.

Scaramucci had done a victory lap of interviews and said publicly that Priebus would be asked to resign soon. "Reince is a fucking paranoid schizophrenic, paranoiac," he said.

Early the morning of Friday, July 28, Trump's promise to repeal and replace Obamacare had failed in Congress. Trump blamed Priebus. He was supposed to know the Hill and have close relationships with the Republican leaders. No matter how Priebus tried to explain, Trump would not buy it. "You didn't get it done."

That day, Trump flew to Long Island to give a speech. Priebus accompanied him. They had a talk in the private cabin at the front of Air Force One.

Priebus had submitted his resignation the night before. He was fed up and knew he had lost his usefulness to Trump.

Trump wondered who would be a good replacement and said he had talked to John Kelly, the secretary of homeland security and retired Marine four-star general. What do you think of Kelly? Trump asked.

General Kelly would be great, Priebus said.

Trump agreed and said he thought Kelly would be just right, but he said he had not offered Kelly the job.

Priebus was concerned about the optics of his departure. We can do it this weekend, he said, or we can do a press release. Or do it Monday. Whatever you want to do. "I'm ready to do it how you want to do it."

"Maybe we'll do it this weekend," Trump said. What are you going to do?

Priebus hoped to rejoin his old law firm.

Trump gave him a big hug. "We'll figure it out," he said. "You're the man."

Air Force One landed. Priebus walked off down the ramp. Rain dotted his black SUV, where Stephen Miller and Dan Scavino were waiting for him. He felt as good about the situation as possible.

He got an alert for a presidential tweet. He looked down at the latest from @realdonaldtrump: "I am pleased to inform you that I have just named General/Secretary John F Kelly as White House Chief of Staff. He is a Great American . . ."

"Unbelievable!" thought Priebus. "Is this serious?"

He had just talked to Trump about waiting.

No one had expected Trump's tweet. When Miller and Scavino saw it, they hopped out of Priebus's SUV to get into another car, leaving the former chief of staff alone.

As he shut the car door, Priebus wondered if maybe Trump had drafted a tweet and sent it accidentally. No, that had not happened. The conversation in the cabin was just one more lie.

That night General Kelly came to see Priebus. They had been in the foxhole together, but Kelly had privately criticized the disorder and chaos of the White House to Trump. Kelly had told the president he believed he could straighten the place out.

"Reince," Kelly said, "I'd never do this to you. I'd never been offered this job until the tweet came out. I would have told you."

It made no sense, Priebus realized, unless you understood the way Trump made decisions. "The president has zero psychological ability to recognize empathy or pity in any way."

Caught by surprise, Kelly had gone dark for several hours. He'd had to call his wife and explain that he had no choice but to accept after being offered one of the most important jobs in the world via tweet.

Kelly said in a statement that day, "I have been fortunate to have served my country for more than 45 years—first as a Marine and then as the Secretary of the Department of Homeland Security. I am honored to be asked to serve as the Chief of Staff to the president of the United States."

In some respects Priebus never got over the way his departure was handled. If you have no empathy or pity for anything or anybody, then that episode doesn't seem that abnormal, Priebus concluded. Which is why Trump could call him two days later: Reince, my man, what's going on? How you doing? Trump didn't think they had a problem, so he didn't view it as awkward.

As a general rule, in relations with Trump, the closer you were, the further away you got. You started with 100 points. You couldn't get more. Kelly had started with 100 points in his jar, and they'd gone down. Being close to Trump, especially in the chief of staff role, meant going down in points. It meant you paid.

The most important part of Trump's world was the ring right outside of the bull's-eye: the people that Trump thought perhaps he should have hired, or who had worked for him and he'd gotten rid of and now thought, Maybe I shouldn't have. It was the people who were either there or should have been there, or associates or acquaintances that owed nothing to him and were around him but didn't come in for anything. It was that outside circle that had the most power, not the people on the inside. It wasn't Kelly or Priebus or Bannon.

Months after his departure from the White House, Priebus made a final assessment: He believed he had been surrounded in the West Wing by high-ranking natural killers with no requirement to produce regular work products—a plan, a speech, the outline of a strategy, a budget, a daily and weekly schedule. They were roving interlopers, a band of chaos creators.

There was Ivanka, a charming huntress dipping in and out of meetings or the latest presidential business. Jared had the same rights. Theirs was a portfolio without experience.

Kellyanne Conway had, or took, license to weigh in on television or interviews almost at will, often without coordinating with the communications and press secretary offices that Priebus was supposed to control.

Then there was Bannon, who had snagged a key West Wing office near the Oval and lined his walls with whiteboards listing Trump's campaign promises. He was a strategist in an operation that had none. He came forward to enter discussions with his fire when the nationalist-populist agenda might be at risk, or seemingly at random or when he needed something to do.

Trump had failed the President Lincoln test. He had not put a team of political rivals or competitors at the table, Priebus concluded. "He puts natural predators at the table," Priebus said later. "Not just rivals—predators."

These were people who had no experience in government, an astonishingly common distinguishing characteristic. They had spent their lives dabbling in political opinions and in policy debates or were too young.

In some ways, these four—Ivanka, Jared, Conway and Bannon—had the same modus operandi. "They walk into the West Wing. You're not putting your weapon down," Priebus said. "I'm not either." Their discussions were not designed to persuade but, like their president, to win—to slay, crush and demean.

"If you have natural predators at the table," Priebus said, "things don't move." So the White House was not leading on key issues like health care and tax reform. Foreign policy was not coherent and often contradictory.

"Why?" asked Priebus. "Because when you put a snake and a rat and a falcon and a rabbit and a shark and a seal in a zoo without walls, things start getting nasty and bloody. That's what happens."

On a weekend in mid-August, in the seventh month of Donald Trump's presidency, hundreds of white supremacists came into violent conflict with protesters in Charlottesville, Virginia, vividly underscoring, once again, the racial divide in America.

Moving across the campus of the University of Virginia in a haunting nighttime torch walk on a steamy August 11 evening, echoing Germany of the 1930s, around 250 white nationalists chanted "Jews will not replace us" and the Nazi slogan "Blood and Soil."

The next day, following brawls between white nationalists protesting the removal of a statue of Confederate General Robert E. Lee and counterprotesters, one of the white nationalists drove his car into a crowd of protesters, killing a woman and injuring 19 others. Images of snarling, tiki-torch-bearing white men in polos and khakis and video of the vehicle brutally scattering pedestrians became a major television and news spectacle.

On Saturday, August 12, Trump was watching Fox News from his golf course in Bedminster. At 1 p.m. on Fox, a Virginia State Police spokeswoman described the melee: "In the crowds, on all sides, they were throwing bottles. They were throwing soda cans with cement in them. They were throwing paint balls. They were fighting. Breaking out and attacking one another. Launching chemicals into the crowd as well as smoke bombs."

At 1:19 p.m. Trump tweeted a call for calm. "We ALL must be united & condemn all that hate stands for. There is no place for this kind of violence in America. Lets come together as one!"

Later in the afternoon at a routine veterans bill signing, Trump had a script that was all condemnation that ended in the word "violence." Trump said, "We condemn in the strongest possible terms this egregious display of hatred, bigotry and violence." But he departed from his text and added, "On many sides. On many sides. It's been going on for a long time in our country. Not Donald Trump. Not Barack Obama. This has been going on for a long, long time." He then picked up the text: "It has no place in America."

Trump touched a nerve with the phrase "many sides" suggesting an equivalence between the neo-Nazis and those who opposed white supremacy. Biting criticism of the president spanned the political spectrum, including many Republican Party leaders.

"Very important for the nation to hear @potus describe events in #Charlottesville for what they are, a terror attack by #whitesupremacists," tweeted Senator Marco Rubio.

"Mr. President—we must call evil by its name," tweeted Cory Gardner, Republican senator from Colorado. "These were white supremacists and this was domestic terrorism."

"My brother didn't give his life fighting Hitler for Nazi ideas to go unchallenged here at home," tweeted Senator Orrin Hatch, normally a reliable Trump ally.

In a statement, Senator John McCain called Charlottesville "a confrontation between our better angels and our worst demons. White supremacists and neo-Nazis are, by definition, opposed to American patriotism and the ideals that define us."

House Speaker Paul Ryan tweeted, "White supremacy is a scourge. This hate and its terrorism must be confronted and defeated." Mitt Romney tweeted, "Racial prejudice, then hate, then repugnant speech, then a repulsive rally, then murder; not supremacy, barbarism."

Republican senator Lindsey Graham appeared on *Fox News Sunday* and said that the president needs "to correct the record here. These groups seem to believe they have a friend in Donald Trump in the White House," and "I would urge the president to dissuade these groups that he's their friend."

Vice President Pence added, "We have no tolerance for hate and violence from white supremacists, neo Nazis or the KKK. These dangerous fringe groups have no place in American public life and in the American debate, and we condemn them in the strongest terms."

News coverage zeroed in on Trump's clear reluctance to condemn the white supremacists. Some noted he had squandered an opportunity to snuff out suspicions that he harbored sympathy for the white supremacists.

Kelly had set up a senior staff meeting by secure teleconference for 8 a.m. on Monday, August 14. He was in Bedminster but most of the senior staff was at the White House in Washington. Something was wrong with the audio on the secure teleconference equipment and the start of the call was delayed.

"Fuck it!" Kelly said after about 30 seconds. "We're not going to do this." He stormed out, causing considerable chatter among the staff about his hot temper and hair trigger.

The next day there was another glitch.

"Screw this," Kelly said. "Fuck it. Take the people off the conference line. We're just going to have the meeting with the people who are here."

Rob Porter was in Bedminster with Trump and joined a coordinated effort to clean up the mess with a new speech on Charlottesville. A draft had been written by White House speechwriters and Porter had the draft for Trump to give at the White House the next day, Monday, August 14. The intent was to show the president as a constructive, calming force.

Porter handed the draft to Trump on the flight back to Washington on Air Force One. The two worked through it. The president did not like the tone. He didn't want to sound like he was capitulating to political correctness.

Porter and Sarah Huckabee Sanders, now the press secretary, had agreed that they needed to present a united front to get the president to give another speech.

"I think it's really important," Sanders told the president, "that you are able to speak directly to the American people, not through the media filter, so that you're not misunderstood on this. And so that people at CNN and MSNBC, whoever it is, aren't able to suggest that you say and mean something different than what you do. You need to be very clear about this. And the best way to do that is for you, without the media filter . . . to be very precise about it, very direct. And then that way you're able to do that without the media twisting it."

Trump defended what he had said. "It's not as if one side has any sort of [monopoly] on hatred or on bigotry. It's not as if any one group is at fault or anything like that. With the media, you're never going to get a fair shake. Anything that you say or do is going to be criticized."

"You need to fix this," Porter argued. "You don't want to be perceived the way in which you're being perceived now. You need to bring the country together." That was the moral obligation.

"There's no upside to not directly condemn neo-Nazis and those that are motivated by racial animus. There is a huge rift in the country." Porter played heavily to the president's ego and desire to be at the center. He said that the president could be a kind of healer in chief, consoler in chief.

"The country is counting on you rhetorically to help salve the wounds and point a direction forward," Porter said. The president could inspire and uplift. He could make this about him, the redeemer.

Trump did not push back but he didn't say yes.

Back at the White House, the West Wing was undergoing renova-
tion. Trump and Porter went up to the residence. Porter pulled up
the speech draft on his laptop. No printer was readily available.
So the president and Porter worked from the laptop. Trump, who
doesn't touch type or use a keyboard, sat behind his desk. Porter,
next to him, scrolled through the draft and they cut and pasted.

Trump said at one point, "I don't know about this."

The draft was an attack on racism, and referred to the necessity
of love and healing.

"I don't know if this feels right," the president said. It looked
weak. He didn't want to apologize. "This doesn't feel right to me."

Porter could see before him the two Donald Trumps—two impulses. He was clearly torn. He would not bend to political correctness, yet he did need to bring people together. He soon saw this and
did not object to the language.

"All right, okay," he said as Porter scrolled through the draft,
making changes that Trump approved. "All right," he finally said.
"We'll do this."

Porter could see the struggle. Not one to mask his emotions or
conclusions, it was clear that Trump wasn't thrilled. Yet he wasn't
upset. He wasn't angry. Porter had the final, approved version of
about 12 paragraphs loaded into the TelePrompTer. Trump was
going to give it from the Diplomatic Reception Room.

Shortly after 12:30 p.m. Trump walked to the podium set between the American flag and the presidential flag. He grabbed the
podium fiercely with both hands. He frowned. He looked grim, and
said he was here in Washington to meet with his economic team
about trade policy and tax reform. He touted the strong economy,
high stock market and low unemployment rate, and said he was
going to provide an update on Charlottesville.

The Department of Justice had opened a civil rights investigation, he told the national television audience. "To anyone who acted

criminally in this weekend's racist violence," Trump said, "you will be held fully accountable."

Looking stiff and uncomfortable, like someone coerced to speak in a hostage video, the president went on. "No matter the color of our skin, we all live under the same laws, we all salute the same great flag. We must love each other, show affection for each other and unite together in condemnation of hatred, bigotry and violence. We must rediscover the bonds of love and loyalty that bring us together as Americans.

"Racism is evil," he said, singling out the "KKK, neo-Nazis, white supremacists and other hate groups.

"We will defend and protect the sacred rights of all Americans" so every citizen "is free to follow their dreams in their hearts and to express the love and joy in their souls."

It was a five-minute speech that could have been given by President Reagan or Obama.

"Make sure you tell him how great it was," General Kelly told the senior staff. He had been chief of staff less than three weeks.

Steve Mnuchin and Gary Cohn were there to greet Trump at the elevator back to the residence. They showered praise on him. "That was a great speech," Cohn said. "This was one of your finest moments as president." It was in the grand tradition of unifying and taking the high road of racial healing. Later they told Porter they didn't know how he had managed to convince Trump.

Porter felt it was a moment of victory, of actually doing some good for the country. He had served the president well. This made the endless hours of nonstop work worth it.

Trump left to watch some Fox. Rob O'Neill, a former Navy SEAL Team Six leader and author, generally praised Trump for being specific but added, "That's almost an admission of okay, I was wrong. And I'm sort of negotiating on this."

Fox correspondent Kevin Corke said, "Some 48 hours into the biggest domestic challenge of his young presidency, Mr. Trump has made a course correction."

The suggestion that he had admitted doing wrong and was un-steady infuriated the president. "That was the biggest fucking mis-take I've made," the president told Porter. "You never make those concessions. You never apologize. I didn't do anything wrong in the first place. Why look weak?"

Though Porter had not written the original draft, he had spent almost four hours editing it with Trump, providing the accommo-dating language. But strangely Trump did not direct his rage at Por-ter. "I can't believe I got forced to do that," Trump said, apparently still not blaming Porter but venting directly to him. "That's the worst speech I've ever given. I'm never going to do anything like that again." He continued to stew about what he had said and how it was a huge mistake.

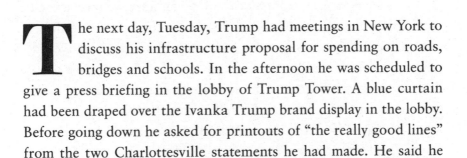

T he next day, Tuesday, Trump had meetings in New York to discuss his infrastructure proposal for spending on roads, bridges and schools. In the afternoon he was scheduled to give a press briefing in the lobby of Trump Tower. A blue curtain had been draped over the Ivanka Trump brand display in the lobby. Before going down he asked for printouts of "the really good lines" from the two Charlottesville statements he had made. He said he wanted the precise language he had used in case he was asked.

Don't take any questions, all the staff told him with urgency. Trump said he did not plan on taking any.

At the press briefing, he took questions, and the questions were about Charlottesville. He took out his Saturday statement. "As I said on—remember Saturday—we condemn in the strongest possible terms the egregious display of hatred, bigotry and violence." He left out the part about "both sides," but this time he added, "the alt-left came charging" at the rally. "You had a group on the other side that was also very violent. And nobody wants to say that, but I'll say it right now.

"Not all of those people were neo-Nazis, believe me. Not all of those people were white supremacists by any stretch. Many of those people were there to protest the taking down of the statue of Robert E. Lee. . . . I wonder, is it George Washington next week? And is it Thomas Jefferson the week after?" Both had been slave owners, he noted. "You really do have to ask yourself, where does it stop?"

He reverted to his earlier argument: "There is blame on both sides . . . you also had people that were very fine people on both sides. You had a lot of bad people in the other group too . . . there are two sides to a story."

David Duke, the well-known former Ku Klux Klan leader, tweeted, "Thank you President Trump for your honesty & courage to tell the truth about #Charlottesville."

The leaders of each branch of the U.S. military went on a social media offensive against their commander in chief in a stunning rebuke. Chief of Naval Operations Admiral John Richardson tweeted, "Events in Charlottesville unacceptable & musnt be tolerated @US-Navy forever stands against intolerance & hatred." Marine Corps Commandant General Robert B. Neller wrote that there is "No place for racial hatred or extremism in @USMC. Our core values of Honor, courage and Commitment frame the way Marines live and act." And Chief of Staff of the Army Mark Milley tweeted, "The Army doesn't tolerate racism, extremism, or hatred in our ranks. It's against our Values and everything we've stood for since 1775." The Air Force and National Guard chiefs followed with similar statements.

On CBS, Stephen Colbert joked darkly, "It's just like D-Day. Remember D-Day, two sides, Allies and the Nazis? There was a lot of violence on both sides. Ruined a beautiful beach. And it could have been a golf course."

Former General John Kelly had stood in the Trump Tower lobby as Trump took questions with a grim look on his face. Colbert said, "This guy is a four-star general. Iraq, no problem. Afghanistan, we can do it. Twenty-minute Trump press conference? A quagmire."

Porter had watched from the sidelines in the Trump Tower lobby. He was in a state of shock, shattered and in disbelief. Later, when Trump brought up the second speech to him, the staff secretary said, "I thought the second speech was the only good one of the three."

"I don't want to talk to you," Trump responded. "Get away from me."

Kelly later told the president that because he had made three statements, "now everybody has one to choose, and it might work in the president's favor. Maybe it's the best of all possible worlds." He said his wife liked Tuesday's statement and press conference, the third one, because it showed the president being strong and defiant.

Kenneth Frazier, the head of Merck, the giant pharmaceutical company, and one of the few African American CEOs of a Fortune 500 company, announced he was resigning from Trump's American Manufacturing Council, a group of outside business advisers to the president.

"America's leaders must honor our fundamental values by clearly rejecting expressions of hatred, bigotry and group supremacy. . . . As CEO of Merck and as a matter of personal conscience, I feel a responsibility to take a stand against intolerance and extremism," Frazier said in a statement.

Within an hour, Trump attacked Frazier on Twitter. Now that Frazier had resigned, Trump wrote, "he will have more time to LOWER RIPOFF DRUG PRICES!"

The CEOs of Under Armour and Intel followed Frazier, resigning from the council as well.

Still stewing, in a second Twitter swipe at Frazier, Trump wrote that Merck should "Bring jobs back & LOWER PRICES!"

On Tuesday, August 15, Trump tweeted, "For every CEO that drops out of the Manufacturing Council, I have many to take their place." He called those who had resigned "grandstanders."

Trump's press conference proved too much for the members of the president's Strategic & Policy Forum, a second advisory board, and the Manufacturing Council. Throughout the day, the CEOs of 3M, Campbell Soup and General Electric announced their resignations from the Manufacturing Council, as did representatives from the AFL-CIO and the Alliance for American Manufacturing president.

Jamie Dimon, CEO of JPMorgan Chase, told employees that the Strategic & Policy Forum had decided to disband. Trump preempted further resignations by abolishing both groups via Twitter: "Rather than putting pressure on the businesspeople of the Manufacturing Council & Strategy & Policy Forum, I am ending both. Thank you all!"

Most significant, however, were the private reactions from House Speaker Ryan and Senate majority leader McConnell. Both Republicans called some of the CEOs and privately praised them for standing up.

On Friday, August 18, Gary Cohn flew by helicopter from East Hampton, Long Island, to Morristown, New Jersey, where it was raining heavily. He had to wait on the tarmac to get clearance to Bedminster. He was carrying a resignation letter. This was too much. Someone had put a swastika on his daughter's college dorm room.

He headed to the clubhouse where Trump was going to address a member-guest tournament. Walking in to applause, Trump shook hands and made remarks, reminding everyone he had won the member-guest before. Trump and Cohn took food from the buffet and slipped into a private dining room.

"Mr. President," Cohn said when they were alone, "I'm very uncomfortable with the position you have put me and my family in. I don't want this to be a contentious discussion."

"You don't know what you are talking about," Trump said.

They debated what Trump had said and what he had not said.

"Before you say anything further," the president said, "I want you to go back and listen to it again."

"Sir," Cohn replied, "I've listened to it like 30 times. Have you seen the video, sir?" Cohn said.

"No, I haven't seen the video."

"I want you to watch the video, sir," Cohn said. "I need you to watch the video of a bunch of white guys carrying tiki torches saying, 'Jews will not replace us.' I cannot live in a world like that."

"You go listen and you go read," Trump said. "I'll go watch the video."

They agreed to discuss it after they had done their listening and watching.

"I said nothing wrong," Trump said. "I meant what I said."

"The Monday statement was great," Cohn said. "Saturday and Tuesday were horrible."

The next Monday at the White House, Cohn appeared at the Oval Office. Ivanka was sitting on one of the couches. Kelly was standing behind a chair.

Cohn was halfway into the Oval Office when Trump said, "So you're here to resign?"

"Yes, sir, I am."

"I've done nothing wrong," Trump repeated. He was leaving "because of your liberal Park Avenue friends. This must be your wife," Trump said, blaming Cohn's wife. Trump launched into a story about a great golfer. The golfer's wife complained because he was gone every weekend. So he listened to her, and now Trump said the once-great golfer is selling golf balls and making no money, completing his blame-the-wife narrative.

"Everyone wants your position," Trump continued. "I made a huge mistake giving it to you."

The president continued with venom. It was chilling. Cohn had never been talked to or treated like that in his life. *"This is treason,"* Trump said.

Trump turned to trying to make Cohn feel guilty. "You are driving our policy and if you leave now, taxes are over. You can't do this." Cohn had spent months working a tax cut plan and was in the middle of negotiations on the Hill, a massive, complex undertaking. "How could you leave me hanging like that?"

"Sir, I don't ever want to leave you hanging. I don't want anyone to ever think I betrayed them. I have a reputation I care more about than anything in the world. I'm working for free here in the White House. It's not about money. It's about helping the country. If you think I'm betraying you, I will never do that." And relenting, he added, "I will stay and get taxes done. But I can't stay here and say nothing."

Vice President Pence walked in and stood next to Cohn and touched him affectionately. They needed to keep Cohn, Pence said, but he understood the position Cohn was in. Yes, Cohn should say something publicly.

"Go out there and say whatever you want," Trump said. "Mnuchin said something."

Mnuchin had put out a statement: "I strongly condemn the actions of those filled with hate. . . . They have no defense from me nor do they have any defense from the president or this administration." He quoted and commended Trump's initial response to Charlottesville and added, "As someone who is Jewish . . . while I find it hard to believe I should have to defend myself on this, or the president, I feel compelled to let you know that the president in no way, shape or form believes that neo-Nazi and other hate groups who endorse violence are equivalent to groups that demonstrate in peaceful and lawful ways."

Trump cited others who had distanced themselves from him.

"I don't have a platform," Cohn replied.

"What do you mean?" asked Trump.

The cabinet secretaries had press departments, Cohn said. "They can go out and make statements whenever they want. I'm an assistant to the president. I'm not supposed to be making press statements."

"I don't care," Trump said. "Go to the podium right now, and make a statement." He was inviting Cohn to go to the podium in the press room of the White House.

"I'm not going to do that, sir. That's embarrassing. That's not what you do. Let me do it my way."

"I don't care what way you do it," Trump said. "I just don't want you leaving until taxes are done. And you can say whatever you need to say."

"Do you want to see it before I say it?"

Trump seemed to be of two minds. "Nope," Trump replied at first. "Say whatever you want to say." But then he asked what it might be. "Could we see it first?"

Cohn said he would work with the White House communications department.

On the way out of the Oval Office, General Kelly, who had heard it all, pulled Cohn into the Cabinet Room. According to notes that Cohn made afterward, Kelly said, "That was the greatest show of self-control I have ever seen. If that was me, I would have taken that resignation letter and shoved it up his ass six different times."

A few minutes later, Pence showed up in Cohn's West Wing office. He reiterated his support. Say whatever you need and want to say, and continue to serve your country, he said, thanking him for everything.

Cohn chose to make his views known in an interview with the *Financial Times*. "This administration can and must do better. . . . I have come under enormous pressure both to resign and to remain. . . . I also feel compelled to voice my distress . . . citizens standing up for equality and freedom can never be equated with white supremacists, neo-Nazis and the KKK."

Cohn could tell that Trump was angry because the president would not talk to him for a couple of weeks. At regular meetings, Trump would ignore him. Finally one day, Trump turned to him and asked, "Gary, what do you think?"

The inner administration shunning was over, but the scar remained.

———

To Rob Porter, Charlottesville was the breaking point. Trump rejected the better judgment of almost all of his staff. He had done that before. His perverse independence and irrationality ebbed and flowed. But with Charlottesville the floodgates just opened. For just the sake of a few words, he had drawn a stark line. "This was no longer a presidency," Porter said. "This is no longer a White House. This is a man being who he is." Trump was going ahead no matter what.

As Porter saw it from up close—perhaps as close as anyone on the staff except Hope Hicks—the Trump election had rekindled the divide in the country. There was a more hostile relationship with the media. The culture wars were reinvigorated. There was a racist tinge. Trump accelerated it.

Porter wondered if trying to repair any of those divisions after Charlottesville was almost a lost cause. There was no turning back. Trump had crossed the point of no return. To the Trump opponents and haters, he was un-American, racist. There was so much fuel on that fire already, and Trump had added so much more. The fire was going to burn, and it was going to burn brightly.

It was now an almost permanent state of suspicion, disbelief and hostility. "It's just all-out war now."

CHAPTER

31

In the midst of the Charlottesville controversy, Bannon called Kelly. "I know this guy," he said. "If you don't start having people in the White House covering" for Trump, there would be trouble. "You've got to cover for him."

Republican senator Bob Corker had told reporters "the president has not yet been able to demonstrate the stability nor some of the competence" needed to succeed in office. And *Politico* had run a long piece on Trump's anger issues, calling Trump "driven by his temper" and saying "anger serves as a way to manage staff, express his displeasure or simply as an outlet that soothes him."

"Not one guy in the White House at the senior level has come out and defended him," Bannon said.

Bannon felt that Trump should be winning the messaging war. "President Trump, by asking, 'Where does this all end'—Washington, Jefferson, Lincoln—connects with the American people. The race-identity politics of the left wants to say it's all racist. Just give me more . . . I can't get enough of it."

Vice President Mike Pence had dutifully retweeted some of Trump's more benign remarks and added, "As @POTUS Trump said, 'We have to come together as Americans with love for our nation . . . & true affection for each other.' #Charlottesville."

Bannon told Kelly, "If he gets boxed in, you're going to have free shots on goal from the guys on Capitol Hill. You have to start protecting this guy."

"Do you fucking want to take this job?" Kelly asked.

"Excuse me?"

"Do you want to be fucking chief of staff?"

"What are you talking about?" Bannon replied. "Don't pull that on me. You know you're the only guy to do it."

"Listen," Kelly said, "my problem right now is I think I'm going to lose half the guys here, and I could lose a third of the cabinet. You don't understand. This thing's on a knife's edge. People are not going to just tolerate this. This has got to be condemned. If you think you've got a solution . . ."

Bannon did not. But he did tell Kelly he was going to resign.

"Look, I'm going to leave on Friday," Bannon said. Tomorrow would be his last day.

I think that may be best, said Kelly.

But Bannon was worried about Trump's upcoming weekend at Camp David that would include the final NSC meeting before the Afghanistan decision.

"Just make sure the president gets every option and detail."

"I'll make sure that happens," Kelly said. That was his standard line—the president would get the full story and the full range of options.

"Make sure Pompeo gets a full chance to make his pitch."

Kelly said he would.

Bannon knew Trump was heading toward a globalist decision. The forces of the national security establishment, led by McMaster, were setting him up. They were creating a record that Trump had been briefed fully about the potential Afghanistan threat as a base for future 9/11-style terrorism. If the threat materialized, they would leak to *The Washington Post* or *The New York Times* that Trump had ignored the warning.

Under the plan for the NSC meeting on August 18, Sessions and Kellogg would advocate pulling out of Afghanistan. CIA Director Pompeo would argue for expanding the CIA paramilitary role instead of additional troops, a position he and Bannon had crafted. McMaster would argue for staying the course, which meant adding 4,000 troops.

Sessions began by noting that he had been on the Senate Armed Services Committee since 9/11. I've always heard the same thing. We're six months to 18 months from turning Afghanistan around. Time and time again, the same. You guys have always been wrong. Look at the major decisions to add tens of thousands of troops by Obama, he hammered. A major turnaround promised and expected. Always wrong. That's why we've been here for 16 years. The Taliban now control more than half the country. Withdraw now. Give it up.

Kellogg concurred. "Got to come home."

Pompeo had gone through some come-to-Jesus sessions at Langley. The old hands reminded him that Afghanistan was the graveyard not just of empires but of careers. The agency had spent years in a subsidiary role with the CTPT paramilitary teams, avoiding full responsibility. Afghanistan was the Army's problem, the agency old hands advised; keep it that way. Another consideration: Under Pompeo's proposed plan, the Army would be in charge of the CTPT and would never give the CIA real control. There was no guarantee, or reasonable expectation, of success, and somebody's going to get blamed down the road.

When it came time for Pompeo to make the case for the middle course, he rained all over his own alternative. It would take us about two years for the CIA to get ready to expand its CTPT counterterrorist effort, he said. We're not physically ready and don't have the infrastructure. We don't have the ability to step in and co-run such an ambitious undertaking with Special Forces. The CIA assets in Afghanistan have atrophied. It's not a viable alternative today.

McMaster was then up to make the case for staying the course and adding up to 4,000 troops. His key argument was that a major strategic objective was to prevent al Qaeda or other terrorists from hitting the U.S. homeland or other allies.

"I'm tired of hearing that," Trump said, "because you guys could say that about every country in the world. You keep talking about there's ISIS all over. They could be organizing an attack on us. We can't be everywhere."

Trump exploded, most particularly at his generals. You guys have created this situation. It's been a disaster. You're the architects of this mess in Afghanistan. You created these problems. You're smart guys, but I have to tell you, you're part of the problem. And you haven't been able to fix it, and you're making it worse.

And now, he added, echoing Sessions, you're wanting to add even more troops to something I don't believe in. I was against this from the beginning.

He folded his arms. "I want to get out," the president said. "And you're telling me the answer is to get deeper in."

Mattis, with his quiet style, had immense impact on the decision. He was not a confronter. As he often did, he adopted the approach that less was more.

I think what you're saying is right, he told Trump, and your instincts are right on the money. But a new approach could work—ending artificial Obama-style timelines and lifting restrictions on the on-the-ground commanders. Leaving could precipitate the collapse of the Afghan state. U.S. withdrawal from Afghanistan had left the vacuum for al Qaeda to create a terrorist sanctuary leading to the 9/11 attacks. The problem is that a new terrorist attack, especially a large one, originating from Afghanistan would be a catastrophe.

He argued that if they pulled out, they would create another ISIS-style upheaval. ISIS already had a presence in Afghanistan.

What happened in Iraq under Obama with the emergence of ISIS will happen under you, Mattis told Trump, in one of his sharpest declarations. It was a barb that several present remembered.

"You all are telling me that I have to do this," Trump said grudgingly, "and I guess that's fine and we'll do it, but I still think you're wrong. I don't know what this is for. It hasn't gotten us anything. We've spent trillions," he exaggerated. "We've lost all these lives." Yet, he acknowledged, they probably could not cut and run and leave a vacuum for al Qaeda, Iran and other terrorists.

After the meeting, Sessions called Bannon. "He spit the bit," Sessions said, using a term for an exhausted, worn-down racehorse's rejection of its rider's control.

"Who?" Bannon asked.

"Your boy, Pompeo."

"What are you talking about?"

"That was the worst presentation I ever saw," Sessions said. He and Kellogg had done their best. "I couldn't have been any better. Kellogg was fantastic. McMaster was actually better than he's ever been, because you weren't around. The president actually said afterwards that I and Kellogg made the best presentation. But clearly the president was looking for the middle option as an alternative."

"How bad was Pompeo?"

"His heart wasn't in it."

"How could it not be?"

Bannon called Pompeo. "What the fuck happened? We set this whole thing up for you to come and own it."

"I can take that building only so far," Pompeo said of the CIA. "I've got other fights I've got to win."

Pompeo reported what the senior officials at Langley were telling him: What are you doing? Pompeo was getting excellent reviews and Trump liked his style. You're on a roll. But you're going to be held accountable for this.

One person at Langley had told him, We spent 10 years in Washington making sure we weren't held accountable for anything in Afghanistan. Why are you volunteering? We never volunteer for anything. Don't worry about Bannon. He is a clown. He's crazy. This is the Pentagon trying to trap us because they want out, too.

Pompeo described the CIA's position. "We don't have the apparatus to take command of this. This is something the Army's got to do. You're saying make it a joint venture. We don't have those kinds of resources. We don't have that kind of expertise on the scale they're talking about. We're not going to take responsibility. Are you going to take responsibility for Afghanistan? Because we're not going to win. You understand we're not going to win!" And that would be hard because Trump was saying, "How come we're not winning? How come they're [the Taliban] blowing up guys?"

Bannon talked to Trump by phone. "You know where I stand on this," Bannon said. "I think eventually you're going to come to see the middle ground."

"You didn't hear the whole thing," Trump said. "There's really a new strategy in there, and we're going to win."

At the August 18 NSC meeting, Trump approved McMaster's four Rs. Summarized in a 60-page strategy memo dated August 21 signed by McMaster, they were formalized as, Reinforce: "provide more equipment and training but leverage support with conditions to drive reforms"; Realign: "US civilian assistance and political outreach will be realigned to target key areas under government control with contested areas considered on case by case basis"; Reconcile: "diplomatic efforts will urge government to undertake broader efforts to foster inclusivity and political accommodation, promote elections, and conduct outreach of ethnic and regional powerbrokers"; and Regionalize: "work with regional actors."

The memo said the meeting established that the goal in Afghanistan was to "reshape the security environment" to limit the Taliban's military options and "encourage them to negotiate a political settlement that reduces violence and denies safe haven to terrorists."

Trump authorized Mattis to designate the Taliban and the terrorist Haqqani Network in Pakistan as hostile forces.

Buried in the 19-page section on integrated strategy was an admission: "Stalemate likely to persist in Afghanistan" and "Taliban likely to continue to gain ground."

In the tradition of concealing the real story in a memo, "Win is unattainable" was the conclusion signed by McMaster.

"You're the first person I called," Trump told Graham. "I just met with the generals. I'm going to go with the generals."

"Well, Mr. President that's probably the smartest thing any president could have done."

"That was a hard one," Trump said. "It's the graveyard of empires." It was a reference to a book by Seth G. Jones on Afghanistan.

"It's my luck the only book you ever read was that one," Graham joked.

Trump laughed along.

"Off the record," Trump said to his senior staff on Air Force One, though there was no press present on Friday, August 18, "I just fired Bannon. Did you see what he said about North Korea and having no military option? Motherfucker!"

Bannon had just given an interview to Robert Kuttner of the liberal *American Prospect* suggesting that Trump's belligerent language to North Korea threatening "fire and fury" was a bluff.

"There's no military solution here," Bannon said. "They got us." He added, "Until somebody solves the part of the equation that shows me that 10 million people in Seoul don't die in the first 30 minutes from conventional weapons, I don't know what you're talking about."

Trump was worried about a prolonged war of words with Bannon and upset that he wasn't going quietly.

A nationally televised Afghanistan strategy speech was set for Monday night, August 21, in front of a military audience at Fort Myer in Virginia. This was a big deal—one of Trump's first formal announcements of a policy before a large audience.

"My original instinct was to pull out—and historically, I like following my instincts," Trump said. Three times he said the goal was to "win" and said, "We will not talk about numbers of troops or our plans for further military."

With that, Trump dodged Bush's and Obama's Achilles' heel. His strategy had the effect of pushing the Afghanistan War debate away, off the front page and out of the news unless there was a major act of violence.

John McCain commented, "I commend President Trump for taking a big step in the right direction with the new strategy for Afghanistan." Democratic senator and Clinton running mate Tim Kaine said the U.S. needed to "make sure that Afghanistan is not a breeding ground for things that can come back and hurt us."

Bannon spoke with Stephen Miller. "What the fuck was that speech about?" Bannon said. "First of all, it just went around in circles."

The speech did not really go in circles. It was both new and more of the same Obama strategy. Bannon's chief objection was the lack of realism. "You can't have him sitting there talking about victory. There's not going to be a victory."

Trump clung to the rhetoric of winning. He had given the military, Mattis and McMaster, just enough. The military had saved face and did not have to admit defeat.

The day after the president's speech, Tillerson found another way to declare that a win was not attainable. He addressed the Taliban at a press briefing: "You will not win a battlefield victory. We may not win one, but neither will you."

Stalemate.

Kelly and Porter spent several weeks at Bedminster with the president during the August congressional recess. The new chief of staff was of the view that the White House was a muddle. Priebus and Bannon had been amateurs. He would instill some order and discipline.

"We've sort of tried to do this a little bit," Porter said. He told Kelly how Priebus had taken a run at establishing order. Several months earlier Priebus had the top staffers—McMaster, Cohn, Bannon, Kellyanne Conway and Porter—for a meeting in a strategy room in the Executive Office Building.

"We need a strategy," Priebus had said. "What are the priorities? How are we going to sequence them?" He wrote the ideas on whiteboards that lined the walls of the strategy room. It was like a SCIF for the most highly classified discussions. It was filled with computers and video teleconferencing equipment.

Ideas from the session were never taken seriously. The president often made decisions with only one or two or three people involved. There was no process for making and coordinating decisions. Chaos and disorder were inadequate to describe the situation. It was a free-for-all. The president would have an idea and say, "I want to sign something." And Porter would have to explain that while Trump had broad authority to issue executive orders, for example, a president was frequently restricted by law. Trump had no understanding of how government functioned. At times he would just start drafting orders himself or dictating. The basic tactic Porter had employed from the Priebus days until now was to stall and delay, mention the legal roadblocks and occasionally lift the drafts from the Resolute Desk.

Porter had been "screaming bloody process" as he called it every day for months. They needed an iron grip on what was signed and ordered. If not iron, they needed at least something, a thread of control.

On August 21, Kelly and Porter issued two memorandums to all cabinet officers and senior White House assistants. "The White House staff Secretary [Porter] serves as both the inbox and outbox for all presidential materials." Every single piece of paper, including decision memos, every memo, press releases, even news articles had to go through Porter.

Executive orders would take "at least two weeks to complete" including required review by the White House counsel and the Justice Department Office of Legal Counsel, which provided legal interpretation to the White House.

"All paper leaving the Oval Office must be submitted to the Staff Secretary . . . for compliance with the Presidential Records Act."

A second memo (underlined in the original) said "Decisions are not final—and therefore may not be implemented—until the Staff Secretary secures a cleared Decision Memoranda that has been signed by the President." This included all new policy initiatives such as "budget, health care, trade initiatives" and government operations such as "diplomatic, intelligence or military operations."

"A decision made following an oral briefing is not final until" there was a formal decision memo.

It was a fantasy.

President Donald J. Trump, first lady Melania Trump and their son Barron, age 11, at the White House on April 17, 2017.

After the *Access Hollywood* tape was released in October 2016, Mike Pence, Trump's running mate, released a tough statement, and some believed he was prepared to take Trump's place as the Republican presidential candidate with former Secretary of State Condoleezza Rice as his running mate.

Trump named former ExxonMobil CEO Rex Tillerson as Secretary of State in December 2016, telling aides that Tillerson looked the part he would play on the world stage. Tillerson had spent 40 years at Exxon and was untainted by government experience. "A very Trumpian-inspired pick," campaign manager Kellyanne Conway said on television, promising "big impact."

Tillerson and Trump clashed regularly. He called the president a "moron" and was later fired on March 13, 2018.

Retired Marine General and Secretary of Defense James Mattis helped top White House Economic Adviser Gary Cohn and Staff Secretary Rob Porter underscore to Trump the necessity of staying in a crucial trade deal with South Korea. "Mr. President," Mattis said, "Kim Jong Un poses the most immediate threat to our national security. We need South Korea as an ally. It may not seem like trade is related to all this, but it's central. We're not doing this for South Korea. We're helping South Korea because it helps us."

Chairman of the Joint Chiefs General Joseph Dunford argued in favor of NATO and against leaving the South Korean trade deal. When Trump asked for a new war plan for a military strike on North Korea, Dunford was shaken. "We need better intelligence before I give the president a plan," Dunford said.

CIA Director Mike Pompeo, a former Republican congressman, became a Trump favorite. Pompeo initially tried to find a middle ground for the war in Afghanistan. Could the CIA paramilitary force be expanded, making a large troop increase unnecessary? Persuaded by old hands at the Agency that the CIA should avoid overcommitting to Afghanistan, Pompeo told the president the CIA was not a viable alternative to conventional forces in Afghanistan.

He was later named as Tillerson's replacement as secretary of state.

Trump felt Attorney General Jeff Sessions had failed him by recusing himself from the Mueller investigation into Russian meddling in the 2016 presidential election. "Jeff isn't a guy that, through thick and thin, is willing to stick with me," Trump said. Sessions was an "idiot," a "traitor," and "mentally retarded" for recusing himself. "How in the world was I ever persuaded to pick him for my attorney general?" Trump asked. "He couldn't even be a one-person country lawyer down in Alabama.

"What business does he have being attorney general?"

Reince Priebus, Trump's first chief of staff, believed the White House was not leading on key issues like health-care and tax reform, and that foreign policy was not coherent and often contradictory. The Trump White House did not have a team of rivals but a team of predators, he concluded. "When you put a snake and a rat and a falcon and a rabbit and a shark and a seal in a zoo without walls, things start getting nasty and bloody. That's what happens." In July 2017, Priebus was replaced by Homeland Security Secretary John Kelly.

9

Homeland Security Secretary and retired Marine General John Kelly privately criticized the disorder and chaos of the White House. Kelly told the president he believed he could straighten the place out. But he was taken by surprise when Trump announced that he had named him his new chief of staff via Twitter in July 2017. Kelly was soon sidelined by Trump, although he remained in his post.

Retired General Michael Flynn resigned as Trump's first national security adviser on February 13, 2017, for lying about his conversations with
Russian Ambassador Sergey Kislyak. Flynn later plead guilty to lying to
the FBI but denied emphatically that he had committed treason.

Lieutenant General H. R. McMaster, Trump's second national security
adviser, considered Secretary of Defense Mattis and Secretary of State
Tillerson "the team of two" and found himself outside their orbit. He
believed Mattis and Tillerson had concluded that the president and the
White House were crazy. They sought to implement and even formulate
policy on their own without interference or involvement from McMaster, let alone the president. "It is more loyal to the president," McMaster
said, "to try to persuade rather than circumvent."

Trump clashed with his national security adviser, H. R. McMaster; his chief of staff, retired General John Kelly; and his secretary of state, Rex Tillerson. In contrast, his vice president, Mike Pence, kept a low profile, avoiding conflict.

13

National Economic Council Chairman Gary Cohn formed an alliance with Staff Secretary Rob Porter and at times Secretary of Defense Jim Mattis to curb some of Trump's most dangerous impulses. "It's not what we did for the country," Cohn said. "It's what we saved him from doing."

Jared Kushner, the president's son-in-law and a senior White House adviser, almost single-handedly engineered Trump's first overseas visit. The May 2017 summit in Saudi Arabia solidified relations among the Saudi Kingdom, other Gulf allies and Israel.

This was done in the face of resistance from Trump's foreign policy advisers.

Steve Bannon became the Chief Executive Officer of Trump's campaign in August 2016. Bannon had three campaign themes: "Number one, we're going to stop mass illegal immigration and start to limit legal immigration to get our sovereignty back. Number two, you are going to bring manufacturing jobs back to the country.

"And number three, we're going to get out of these pointless foreign wars."

Ivanka Trump, the president's 36-year-old daughter, was a senior White House adviser whose influence with her father was resented and resisted by others in the White House. Chief strategist Steve Bannon got into a screaming match with her. "You're a goddamn staffer!" Bannon yelled. "You're nothing but a f---ing staffer! You walk around this place and act like you're in charge, and you're not. You're on staff!"

Ivanka shouted back, "I'm not a staffer! I'll never be a staffer. I'm the first daughter."

Kellyanne Conway became Trump's campaign manager in August 2016 and coined the phrase "the hidden Trump voter. . . . There's not a single hidden Hillary voter in the entire country. They're all out and about."

Hope Hicks served as Trump's press secretary during the campaign and became White House strategic communications director. Like many others, she tried and failed to rein in the president's tweeting. "It's not politically helpful," she told Trump. "You can't just be a loose cannon on Twitter. You're getting killed by a lot of this stuff. You're shooting yourself in the foot. You're making big mistakes." Hicks is pictured here with Press Secretary Sarah Huckabee Sanders.

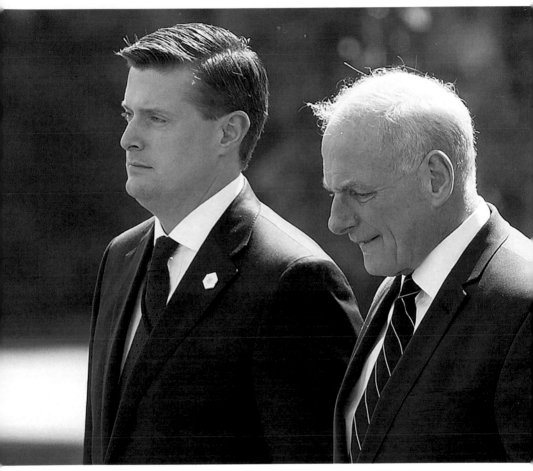

As Staff Secretary, Rob Porter briefed Trump on decision memos and other important presidential documents. In alliance with Gary Cohn, he attempted to block Trump's most dangerous economic and foreign policy impulses.

Porter told an associate, "A third of my job was trying to react to some of the really dangerous ideas that he had and try to give him reasons to believe that maybe they weren't such good ideas."

Peter Navarro, a 67-year-old Harvard PhD in economics, received a White House post from Trump. Both Trump and Navarro were passionate believers that trade deficits harmed the U.S. economy. Navarro agreed with Trump on steel and aluminum tariffs though few others did.

Senator Lindsey Graham (R-SC) pushed Trump to take a hard line on North Korea. "You don't want it on your résumé that North Korea, a nuclear power, got a missile that could reach the United States on your watch," Graham told Trump.

"If they have a breakout and have a missile that will reach the United States, you've got to whack them."

FBI director James Comey was fired by Trump in May 2017. "Don't try to talk me out of it," Trump told his White House counsel, Don McGahn, and his chief of staff, Reince Priebus. "Because I've made my decision, so don't even try." He believed Comey was a grandstander and out of control.

Trump seized on allegations that Comey had mishandled the investigation into Hillary Clinton's e-mails as grounds for his firing.

Former FBI director Robert Mueller was appointed as special counsel to investigate Russian election meddling and any connection to the Trump presidential campaign. Trump rejected him as Comey's replacement for FBI director.

"He was just in here and I didn't hire him for the FBI," Trump said. "Of course he's got an ax to grind with me."

John Dowd joined Trump's legal team in May 2017. He convinced the president not to testify in the Mueller investigation, but resigned in March 2018 when Trump changed his mind and Dowd could not dissuade him.

"Mr. President, I cannot, as a lawyer, as an officer of the court, sit next to you and have you answer these questions when I full well know that you're not really capable," Dowd told Trump.

White House counsel Don McGahn wanted the president to assert executive privilege in the Mueller investigation and resist handing over documents. Trump's lawyer John Dowd disagreed and cooperated with Mueller in order to speed up the investigation.

"We'd get a hell of a lot more with honey than we would with vinegar."

Trump and first lady Melania Trump with Chinese president Xi Jinping and first lady Peng Liyuan. Trump believed China's support for sanctions against North Korea was a result of his personal relationship with Xi. "Isn't it good that I'm friendly when all you guys say that we should be adversarial with them," he said, despite warnings that Xi was using him. "Because if I didn't have that great relationship with President Xi, they never would have done that. So that I can get them to do things that they wouldn't otherwise do."

North Korean Leader Kim Jong Un, 34, was a more effective leader of North Korea's nuclear weapons and missiles programs than his father, Kim Jong Il, according to U.S. intelligence. The younger Kim accepted that weapons and missile testing would inevitably lead to failures. He did not order officials and scientists shot after failures as his father had. Trump believed the building conflict between the U.S. and North Korea was a contest of wills.

"This is all about leader versus leader. Man versus man. Me versus Kim."

Kelly and Porter sat down with the president to explain the re-vamped process.

"You can't make decisions unless you sign a decision memo," Porter said. The memo did not have to be long. "I'll keep it to a page." Porter noted that decision memos would have supporting materials, "but I won't ever make you read more than a page on any decision. I'll come in and I'll brief you on it as well, so we can talk through it. Sometimes you'll need to have a full meeting with five or six or seven advisers. A lot of times we can just do it on the basis of a decision memo."

Okay, Trump said.

For the first weeks the new system annoyed the president. Eventually Porter developed a routine and would bring in two to 10 decision memos for him to sign each day. Trump liked signing. It meant he was doing things, and he had an up-and-down penmanship that looked authoritative in black Magic Marker.

Kelly was very chummy with the president in the first weeks, Porter noticed. They were peers. Kelly always seemed to have a smile on his face when he was around the president. He would joke around with Trump. He would give advice and offer his reaction. "Mr. President I think we ought to do this." He was deferential. "I'm just a staffer. You're the boss. We want to try to get you the best information." The perfect chief of staff. "You're the decider. And I'm not trying to sway you one way or the other."

The honeymoon was soon over. Beginning in September, Kelly and Porter would be together alone, or with a few senior staffers.

"The president's unhinged," Kelly said. There would be something, especially about trade agreements or the U.S. troops in South Korea. "We all need to try to talk him out of it," Kelly said. They needed to stand up to the president. He wasn't listening.

Oval Office business and decision making became increasingly haphazard. "The president just really doesn't understand anything about that. He doesn't know what he's talking about," Kelly said.

As Trump redoubled on withdrawing from trade agreements or

costly foreign policies, Kelly would say, "I can't believe he's thinking about doing this." He made a personal appeal to Porter.

"Rob, you've got to put a stop to this. Don't write that [order] up. Don't go down and do that. Can you go in and talk to him and just see if you can make any progress? I was on the phone with him this morning. I made these arguments. Can you go see what good you can do?"

The U.S. troop presence in South Korea continued to be a constant theme with Trump. We are subsidizing South Korea, he insisted. "It doesn't make any sense."

Porter reminded him that Mattis and many others had told him these were possibly the best national security dollars that the United States spent. The troop presence provided the indispensable top secret intelligence that was vital to detecting and deterring North Korean missile launches.

On August 25, the president decided he was going to make a sweeping decision on NAFTA, KORUS and the World Trade Organization. "We've talked about this ad nauseam," Trump said. "Just do it. Just do it. Get out of NAFTA. Get out of KORUS. And get out of the WTO. We're withdrawing from all three."

Cohn and Porter enlisted Kelly, who didn't want trade to roil national security. Kelly and Porter went to the Oval Office. "South Korea is an ally," Kelly told Trump. "The KORUS deal is actually better than you think."

Porter presented some studies showing that KORUS kept the trade deficit down.

"This is a really important time with North Korea and that whole region," Kelly said. "We don't want to do anything on the trade side, especially given how peanuts this is in the grand scheme of things. It's going to blow things up." He recommended that the president call Tillerson. Tillerson made the same arguments.

Tillerson, Mattis, McMaster, Kelly—everyone on the national security side—agreed that if the trade deficit with South Korea had been 10 times greater, it still wouldn't justify withdrawing. It was insane to even be thinking of that, they agreed.

"All right," Trump finally said on Friday, September 1, "we're not going to do the KORUS 180-day thing today. It's not that we're not going to do it, but all right, we won't do it today."

Porter put out the word to the legislative staff, the White House lawyers and the NSC staff to rest easy for at least that day. He made sure there was nothing drafted that the President could sign.

Four days later, on September 5, Cohn, Porter and the others went to the Oval Office. Trump had in his hands a draft letter giving notice of the required 180 days that the United States was withdrawing from KORUS. Porter had not written it and he was never sure who had, probably Navarro or Ross, but he never found out for sure.

"I've got a draft," Trump said. "We're going to withdraw from this. I just need to wordsmith this and we're going to get it on official stationery and send this off. We need to do it today."

McMaster made the national security arguments. Cohn and Porter made the trade and economic arguments.

"Until I actually take some action to demonstrate my threats are real and need to be taken seriously," Trump said, "then we're going to have less leverage in these things." He then left the Oval Office.

Now that the president had gone outside of the staff secretary process that Porter controlled to get a new draft letter, Cohn was really worried. He removed it from the president's desk.*

For the first several months of his job as chief of staff, it seemed that Kelly sat in the Oval Office almost all day, in every meeting. He didn't say much, acting more as an observer and monitor. He tried to make sure that the door was closed between the Oval Office and the little outer office where Madeleine Westerhout sat. She was 27, a former RNC aide, and looked like Hope Hicks with her long brown hair and big smile. The stated reason was to provide more privacy

---

* See Prologue, page xvii–xxii.

and security. Kelly also wanted to keep people from wandering in and out as they had done regularly in the past.

"No, no, leave it open," the president would say. "I need to be able to see Madeleine so that I can call out to her."

Rear Admiral Ronny Jackson, the president's White House physician, stopped by to see the president most days, certainly several times a week.

"How are you doing today, Mr. President?" he would say, sticking his head out of his office as the president passed by. It would usually be a 30-second check-in, often about something like a nasal spray.

Several times Dr. Jackson visited Kelly. "The president's been under a lot of stress recently," Jackson said at one point. "We may need to figure out some way to dial things back, or to ease up on his schedule."

Another time, Jackson was more specific. "Seems like the president's under more stress than usual. We may just want to try to cut back on the schedule tomorrow."

Kelly's solution was to give the president more "Executive Time." Trump normally set his own schedule on when to start the day and often had flexibility when he returned to the residence.

Kelly tried to respond to Jackson. Which meetings were essential? Could they give Trump an extra half hour or an hour in the mornings or clear his schedule an hour earlier in the evenings? They tried. But the nonstop presidency did not abate and Trump often got everyone, himself included, spun up.

Trump assembled a group in the residence to discuss steel tariffs. Ross, Navarro, Lighthizer, Cohn, McMaster and Porter attended. Trump said he was tired of the debate and wanted to sign a decision memo to implement 25 percent steel tariffs across the board, with no exemptions for any country.

They had the usual Groundhog Day round of arguments, until Mnuchin said that tax reform had to be the number-one priority. A Republican-held House, Senate and White House was a once-in-a-lifetime opportunity to pass tax reform, he said. It had not been done since Reagan's presidency more than 30 years earlier.

Mnuchin warned that many of the Republican senators he would need for tax reform were free traders and strongly opposed steel tariffs.

Mr. President, you could lose them, he said.

Cohn seconded this, and Porter agreed. McMaster, who had been arguing on national security grounds that steel tariffs would severely damage relations with key allies, agreed about taxes and Republican senators.

"Yeah, you're right," Trump finally said. "As important as this is, we can't jeopardize the tax bill for this. So we'll hold off. But as soon as we're done with taxes, we're going to move to trade. And one of the first things that we need to do is put these steel tariffs on."

With Bannon out of the White House, Trump and Sessions came up with another solution for immigration on September 5. Trump announced the end of the Obama-era DACA program. He labeled it an "amnesty-first approach" and said Congress should find a replacement in six months.

Two days later he tried to calm everyone down. On September 7, Trump tweeted: "For all those (DACA) that are concerned about your status during the 6 month period, you have nothing to worry about — No action!"

Bannon, who still had access to Trump, called to remind him of the importance of hard-line anti-immigration.

"Do you understand this almost destroyed the Republican Party in the summer of 2013?" Bannon recalled asking the president. "This is the central reason you're president. The one thing that can destroy the Republican Party. It's been haunting us, this amnesty issue."

Stephen Miller passed word from the White House to Bannon that this whole debate was now about chain migration. He calculated that the current policy would add 50 million new immigrants in 20 years if it continued.

Miller told Bannon, "The Democrats will never give up on chain migration. It's changed the country. Chain migration is everything. That's how they get the family unification."

Miller turned out to be correct. Trump might continue to talk as if he would compromise, but there was no deal with Democrats.

"I don't have any good lawyers," Trump said one day in the Oval Office. "I have terrible lawyers." He singled out White House Counsel Don McGahn. "I've got a bunch of lawyers who are not aggressive, who are weak, who don't have my best interests in mind, who aren't loyal. It's just a disaster. I can't find a good lawyer." He included the personal lawyers he had handling the Mueller investigation.

Porter went to Kelly's office to give him a heads-up. It was just the two of them. "I've seen this movie before," Porter said. "I'm concerned, because there have been some times in the past, including especially after the appointment of the special counsel—the Comey, Mueller period—where the president got so consumed and distracted that it was a challenge to continue to do the work and make the decisions—effectively to be president. And to give the direction that the rest of us needed to be able to carry on the work of the government.

"Thankfully we got through it. I'm concerned that there are going to be those kinds of flare-ups again, especially as the investigation takes its course. As things come to a head. I don't know what the catalyst is going to be."

It could even be something from the Senate and House Russia investigations. "Or who knows what. But we need to be cognizant of this. If we don't do a better job of partitioning things, of giving him time and space to deal with some of the Mueller stuff where the president could get his head in a better place, then it is going to infect the rest of the White House." Trump needed time "to vent and sort of emotionally stabilize himself."

Porter urged Kelly to give this some thought, "so that you can be prepared, so that we can continue to function and this doesn't lead to an incapacitation of the entire West Wing for days if not weeks, like it kind of did in the past."

Kelly nodded. "Yeah, I've seen little bits and pieces of that. And I can imagine it being that bad."

"We barely got by the last time it happened," Porter said. "It could be even worse than before. So we need to start to game out a plan for how we handle that."

Kelly agreed that made sense. "Let's try," he said. But neither had an immediate idea.

CHAPTER

33

It was not just the distraction of a wide-ranging Mueller investigation hanging over his head, but the constant media coverage
that Trump had colluded with the Russians and/or obstructed
justice, a real feeding frenzy—vicious, uncivil. The result, Porter
said, "In some moments it was almost incapacity of the president to
be president."

McMaster noticed it. Trump normally wouldn't listen long or
very carefully to his national security adviser but it had gotten much
worse, McMaster told Porter. "It's like I can't even get his attention."

"Don't take it personally," Porter advised. "He's clearly distracted.
He's been like that all day. Because he's focused on this news about
Russia."

Gary Cohn told Porter, "It's pointless to even talk to him today."

Hope Hicks was worried. "He's worked up about this," she told
Porter. She wanted the president to settle down, avoid doing or saying anything rash or that he would later regret. She would try to get
Trump to talk about other things, get his attention away from the
television, even try to make light of things.

They would get him on Air Force One to a rally. Leaving the plane for one rally, he said, "I think I'm going to spend the first 10 minutes just attacking the media."

On several occasions, Trump asked Porter if he was interested in being White House counsel. Porter declined.

When Trump's personal attorney came to talk about matters relating to Special Counsel Mueller, Trump at times asked Porter to join in.

"Rob, I want you to stay. You've got to be a part of this."

"I'm not your lawyer," Porter said. "I'm not acting as a lawyer. But even if I was, I'd be a government lawyer, not one of your personal lawyers and that would break attorney-client privilege. And so I can't be in here."

"No, no, no," Trump said, "that doesn't matter."

It would take one of Trump's personal lawyers, like John Dowd, saying, "Rob needs to go."

"I don't know how much longer I can stay," Gary Cohn told Porter, "because things are just crazy here. They're so chaotic. He's never going to change. It's pointless to prepare a meaningful, substantive briefing for the president that's organized, where you have a bunch of slides. Because you know he's never going to listen. We're never going to get through it. He's going to get through the first 10 minutes and then he's going to want to start talking about some other topic. And so we're going to be there for an hour, but we're never going to get through this briefing."

Porter tried to prepare organized briefing papers with relevant information, different viewpoints, costs/benefits, pros and cons and consequences of a decision. It didn't work.

Gary Cohn and Robert Lighthizer, the U.S. trade representative, had worked for months to get Trump to agree to authorize an intellectual property inquiry into China's trade practices. It was a case where Trump could flex his antitrade muscle without blowing up a trade agreement. The authority came from section 301 of the Trade Act of 1974, which gave the president power to unilaterally institute punitive trade restrictions on countries that engage in unfair trading with the U.S.

The Chinese broke every rule. They stole everything, from tech companies' trade secrets to pirated software, film and music, and counterfeited luxury goods and pharmaceuticals. They bought parts of companies and stole the technology. They stole intellectual property from American companies that had been required to move their technology to China to operate there. Cohn considered the Chinese dirty rotten scoundrels. The administration estimated China had committed $600 billion in intellectual property theft.

A 301 investigation, 301 for short, would give Lighthizer one year to determine whether the office of the U.S. Trade Representative should open a formal investigation of China. If so, Trump would have the authority to impose tariffs, sanctions and other measures against China.

The Europeans, Japanese and Canadians would join the United States in a massive, coordinated effort against Chinese intellectual property violations. This would be the first trade enforcement by Trump.

Trump had finally agreed to sign a memo and announce in a speech a year-long investigation of China's intellectual property violations. It had been a long march to provide him with clear definable action on the trade front.

During an August meeting in the residence with his economic and trade teams, Trump balked. He had just talked to President Xi. He didn't want to target China. "We're going to need their help for North Korea," he said. "It's not just one U.N. Security Council vote. We'll need their help on an ongoing basis. I want to take all the references to China out of the speech." He did not want to jeopardize his great relations with President Xi.

Porter said the short two-page memo mentioned China five times, and only China. It was all about China as they had been discussing for months.

"No, no, no," Trump said. "I don't want to make it China-specific. Let's just do it for the whole world."

Under the law, these investigations have to be about particular unfair trade practices by a specific country.

"In this case it's China," Porter said. "We can't get around the fact."

"Well, okay," the president said, "I can sign whatever, but I don't want to mention China in the remarks."

"We can't explain what this is without mentioning that we're targeting China."

Okay, Trump said. In his public remarks, he said, "The theft of intellectual property by foreign countries costs our nation millions of jobs and billions and billions of dollars each and every year. For too long, this wealth has been drained from our country while Washington has done nothing. . . . But Washington will turn a blind eye no longer." He made one mention of China.

Cohn and Porter hoped signing the memo authorizing a 301 investigation would divert Trump from imposing steel and aluminum tariffs immediately.

Whenever either of them would challenge Trump's conviction on the importance of trade deficits and the need to impose tariffs, Trump was immovable. "I know I'm right," he said. "If you disagree with me, you're wrong."

Cohn knew the real battle was going to be over tariffs, where Trump had the most rigid views and where he could do the most damage to the U.S. and world economies. He shoveled all the data he could to the president about how tariffs on imported steel would be a disaster and hurt the economy.

A 17-page document that Cohn sent contained a chart showing the minuscule revenue earned in 2002–03 when President Bush had imposed steel tariffs for similar reasons. It showed that the revenue that came in was $650 million. That was .04 percent of the total federal revenue of $1.78 trillion.

The estimated revenue from a 25 percent steel tariff would now be $3.4 billion, or .09 percent of expected total revenue of $3.7 trillion for 2018.

Tens of thousands of U.S. jobs had been lost in industries that consumed steel, Cohn said, and produced a chart to prove it.

Trump had three allies who agreed with him that trade deficits mattered: Secretary of Commerce Wilbur Ross, Peter Navarro and Bob Lighthizer, the U.S. trade representative.

Navarro said that the data did not include the jobs created in the steel mills under the Bush tariffs of 2002–03.

"You're right," Cohn said. "We created 6,000 jobs in steel mills."

"Your data is just wrong," Navarro said.

Trump was determined to impose steel tariffs. "Look," Trump said, "we'll try it. If it doesn't work, we'll undo it."

"Mr. President," Cohn said, "that's not what you do with the U.S. economy." Because the stakes were so high, it was crucial to be conservative. "You do something when you're 100 percent certain it will work, and then you pray like hell that you're right. You don't do 50/50s with the U.S. economy."

"If we're not right," Trump repeated, "we roll them back."

NAFTA was another enduring Trump target. The president had said for months he wanted to leave NAFTA and renegotiate. "The only way to get a good deal is to blow up the old deal. When I blow it up, in that six months, they'll come running back to the table." His theory of negotiation was that to get to yes, you first had to say no.

"Once you blow it up," Cohn replied, "it may be over. That's the most high-risk strategy. That either works or you go bankrupt."

Cohn realized that Trump had gone bankrupt six times and

seemed not to mind. Bankruptcy was just another business strategy. Walk away, threaten to blow up the deal. *Real power is fear.*

Over the decades Goldman Sachs had not done business with the Trump Organization or Trump himself, knowing that he might stiff anyone and everyone. He would just not pay, or sue. Early in Cohn's time at Goldman there had been a junior salesperson who did a bond trade for a casino with Trump.

Cohn told the young trader that if the trade didn't settle, he would be fired. Fortunately for the trader, Trump did pay.

Applying this mind-set from his real estate days to governing and deciding to risk bankrupting the United States would be a different matter entirely.

In another discussion with the president, Cohn unveiled a Commerce Department study showing the U.S. absolutely needed to trade with China. "If you're the Chinese and you want to really just destroy us, just stop sending us antibiotics. You know we don't really produce antibiotics in the United States?" The study also showed that nine major antibiotics were not produced in the United States, including penicillin. China sold 96.6 percent of all antibiotics used here. "We don't produce penicillin."

Trump looked at Cohn strangely.

"Sir, so when mothers' babies are dying of strep throat, what are you going to say to them?" Cohn asked Trump if he would tell them, "Trade deficits matter"?

"We'll buy it from another country," Trump proposed.

"So now the Chinese are going to sell it [antibiotics] to the Germans, and the Germans are going to mark it up and sell it to us. So our trade deficit will go down with the Chinese, up with the Germans." U.S. consumers would be paying a markup. "Is that good for our economy?" Navarro said they would buy it through some country other than Germany.

Same problem, Cohn said. "You're just rearranging deck chairs on the *Titanic*."

The U.S. automobile industry was another Trump obsession. China was hurting the industry dramatically and U.S. workers even more, he alleged.

Cohn assembled the best statistics that could be compiled. Trump would not read, so Cohn brought charts to the Oval Office. The numbers showed that the American auto industry was fine. One big chart showed Detroit's Big Three were producing 3.6 million fewer cars and light trucks since 1994, but the rest of the U.S., mostly in the Southeast, was up the same 3.6 million.

The entire BMW 3 series in the world were made in South Carolina, Cohn said. The Mercedes SUVs were all made in the United States. The millions of auto jobs lost in Detroit had moved to South Carolina and North Carolina because of right-to-work laws.

What about the empty factories? Trump asked. "We've got to fix this."

Cohn had put another document, "U.S. Record in WTO Disputes," in the daily book that Porter compiled for the president at night. But Trump rarely if ever cracked it open.

"The World Trade Organization is the worst organization ever created!" Trump said. "We lose more cases than anything."

"This is in your book, sir," Cohn said, and brought out another copy. The document showed that the United States won 85.7 percent of its WTO cases, more than average. "The United States has won trade disputes against China on unfair extra duties on U.S. poultry, steel and autos, as well as unfair export restraints on raw materials and rare earth minerals. The United States has also used the dispute settlements system to force China to drop subsidies in numerous sectors."

"This is bullshit," Trump replied. "This is wrong."

"This is not wrong. This is data from the United States trade representative. Call Lighthizer and see if he agrees."

"I'm not calling Lighthizer," Trump said.

"Well," Cohn said, "I'll call Lighthizer. This is the factual data.

There's no one that's going to disagree with this data." Then he added, "Data is data."

Cohn occasionally sought Vice President Pence's help, always in private conversations. He made his case on steel and aluminum tariffs. "Mike, I need your help on this."

"You're doing the right thing," Pence said. "I'm just not sure what I can do."

"Mike, there's no state going to be hurt worse than Indiana on steel and aluminum tariffs. Elkhart, Indiana, is the boat and RV capital of the world. What goes into boats and RVs? Aluminum and steel. Your state is going to get killed on this."

"Yeah, I got it."

"Can you help me?"

"Doing everything I can."

As usual, Pence was staying out of the way. He didn't want to be tweeted about or called an idiot. If he were advising Pence, Cohn would have had him do exactly that—stay out of it.

Kelly concluded that Peter Navarro was the problem. Navarro would get into the Oval Office and spin Trump up on the trade deficits. Since he was preaching to the converted, Trump would soon be in full activist mode, declaring, I will sign today.

Cohn took every chance he could get to tell Kelly how Navarro was an absolute disaster. Get rid of him, Cohn argued, fire him. This place is never going to work as long as he is around.

Kelly asked Porter for his opinion. "The current status quo is unsustainable," Porter said. "I don't think you can get rid of Peter, because the president loves him. He'd never allow for that." You can't promote Navarro, like he wants, because that would be absurd. "Peter needs to be responsible to someone, other than feeling like he's got a direct report to the president. A lot of times I'm able to block him."

Kelly decided he was going to assert control, and called a meeting of the combatants for September 26. It was like a duel. Navarro was allowed to bring in a second and he chose Stephen Miller. Cohn brought Porter.

Navarro started off arguing that during the campaign he was promised to be an assistant to the president. Now he was only a deputy assistant. This is a betrayal. He said he couldn't believe it had lasted this long. He had talked to the president, who did not really know the difference between an assistant to the president and a deputy assistant. The president thought special assistant sounded a lot better, not realizing it was an even lower position.

Navarro said that the president had told him he could have whatever title and reporting structure he wanted. He and his Trade Council represented the American worker, the manufacturing base, the forgotten man.

"Peter's out there going rogue," Cohn responded. "He's creating these problems. He's telling the president lies. He's totally unchecked. He's the source of all the chaos in this building."

"Gary doesn't know what he is talking about," Navarro replied. "Gary's just a globalist. He's not loyal to the president." And Porter was always fiddling with the process and manipulating to delay everything so Navarro couldn't get in to see the president.

"All right," Kelly said. "I can't deal with this anymore. Peter, you're going to be a member of the National Economic Council, and you're going to report to Gary. And that's just how it's going to be. And if you don't like it, you can quit. Meeting over."

"I want to appeal this," Navarro said. "I want to talk to the president."

"You're not talking to the president," Kelly said. "Get out of my office."

Months went by. "Where the hell is my Peter?" the president asked one day. "I haven't talked to Peter Navarro in two months." But, as was often the case, he did not follow up.

CHAPTER

34

Trump's face-off with Kim Jong Un was growing increasingly personal.

On Air Force One when tensions were ramping up, Trump said, in a rare moment of reflection, "This guy's crazy. I really hope this doesn't end up going to a bad place."

He delivered contradictory comments on North Korea from provocative and bombastic to assertions that he wanted peace. In May he said he would be "honored" to meet with Kim "under the right circumstances." In August he told the press, "North Korea best not make any more threats to the United States. They will be met with fire and fury like the world has never seen."

With no resolution, McMaster issued a new strategy outlining a North Korea Pressure Campaign. The plan, put forward in a signed document, was designed to pressure North Korea and China to negotiate the North's nuclear weapons program and cease development of their ICBMs. Treasury would work on sanctions. State would work on engagement with China to pressure the North.

The Defense Department was to make military incursions such as overflights, going into their airspace in exercises called Blue Lightning, and engage in limited cyber activity to demonstrate capability and show the threat. But these actions were not to trigger an unintended conflict.

McMaster kept repeating in the NSC that Trump could not accept a nuclear North Korea.

But the president summed up his position on almost everything in an interview with *The New York Times*. "I'm always moving. I'm moving in both directions."

Joint Chiefs of Staff Chairman Dunford formed a strategic communications cell in his Operations Directorate, J3, to look at the messaging opportunities in North Korea. What actions could be taken that were just threatening enough to be a deterrent?

When there were three aircraft carriers in the vicinity, Mattis voiced discomfort. Could this trigger an unanticipated response from Kim? Could the United States start the war they were trying to avoid? He showed more concern about this than many others in the Pentagon and certainly in the White House.

Mattis was a student of historian Barbara Tuchman's book *The Guns of August* about the outbreak of World War I. "He's obsessed with August 1914," one official said, "and the idea that you take actions, military actions, that are seen as prudent planning, and the unintended consequences are you can't get off the war train." A momentum to war builds, "and you just can't stop it."

Mattis did not want war. The status quo and a no-war strategy, even amid powerful, overwhelming tensions, were a win/win.

The official summed it up: "Mattis and Dunford's view is that North Korea can be contained. Dunford actually said, 'This was my advice to the president.'"

On September 19, 2017, President Trump gave his first address to the United Nations General Assembly. For the first time, he dubbed the North Korean Leader "Rocket Man." He said the United States, if forced to defend itself, "will have no choice but to totally destroy North Korea."

Kim fired back three days later. "A frightened dog barks louder," and said Trump is "surely a rogue and a gangster fond of playing with fire. I will surely and definitely tame the mentally deranged U.S. dotard."

In a tweet on September 23 Trump called Kim "Little Rocket Man."

Trump and Rob Porter were together in the president's front cabin on Air Force One. Fox News was on the TV.

"Little Rocket Man," Trump said proudly. "I think that may be my best ever, best nickname ever."

"It is funny," Porter said, "and it certainly seems to have gotten under Kim's skin." But, he asked, "What's the endgame here? If we continue to amp up the rhetoric and get into a war of words and it escalates, what are you hoping to get out of this? How does this end?"

"You can never show weakness," Trump replied. "You've got to project strength. Kim and others need to be convinced that I'm prepared to do anything to back up our interests."

"Yes, you want to keep him on his toes," Porter said. "And you want some air of unpredictability from you. But he seems pretty unpredictable. And we're not sure, is he even well? Is he all mentally there? He doesn't have the same political constraints that other people do. He seems very much to want to be taken seriously on the international stage."

"You've got to show strength," the president repeated.

"I wonder," Porter plowed on, "if embarrassing him is more likely to sort of get him into submission or if it could also provoke him?"

Trump didn't respond. His body language suggested that he knew Kim was capable of anything. Then he offered his conclusion: It was a contest of wills. "This is all about leader versus leader. Man versus man. Me versus Kim."

At the end of September, General Kelly asked Graham to come to the White House for an upcoming tabletop exercise on North Korea.

Contradictory messages from Trump and Tillerson were flooding the news. For weeks, Tillerson had been out publicly with what he called the "Four Nos": The United States was not seeking regime change; or a collapse of the regime; was not looking for an accelerated reunification of the North and South; and did not want an excuse to send troops into the North.

"We've got the guy guessing," Kelly said to Graham, referring to Kim Jong Un.

Graham made a dramatic proposal to Kelly and McMaster. "China needs to kill him and replace him with a North Korean general they control," Graham said. China had at least enough control so the North would not attack. "I think the Chinese are clearly the key here and they need to take him out. Not us, them. And control the nuclear inventory there. And wind this thing down. Or control him. To stop the march to a big nuclear arsenal. My fear is that he will sell it."

He proposed that Trump tell China: "The world is a dangerous place. I am not going to let this regime threaten our homeland with a nuclear weapon."

Graham said Trump had told him he would not let this happen. He had done everything but take an ad out in the newspaper telling the world what Trump had told him to his face.

On October 1, months after Tillerson had begun publicly reaching out to North Korea to open a dialogue, Trump tweeted: "I told Rex Tillerson, our wonderful Secretary of State, that he is wasting his time trying to negotiate with Little Rocket Man. Save your energy Rex, we'll do what has to be done!"

The bellicose tweet was widely interpreted as undermining the nation's top diplomat.

Trump had apparently been seized by an impulse. During the presidential campaign, Trump himself had extended an olive branch voicing a willingness to negotiate with Kim over a hamburger.

But overlooked was that Trump had a way of appearing to strengthen his own hand by creating a situation, often risky, that did not previously exist. Threatening the volatile North Korean regime with nuclear weapons was unthinkable, but he had done it. It turned out to be only the beginning. The go-along, get-along presidency of the past was over.

Trump was soon tugging harder on Kelly's leash and after several months the Kelly mystique of controlling Trump faded. It was clear that Trump didn't like outsider control emotionally, as if to say, I can't deal with this anymore. I feel cocooned. I feel I'm no longer in charge.

In November, Trump saw Chris Crane, the head of the Immigration and Customs Enforcement (ICE) union, complaining on Fox News about access to Trump. He said Trump was letting them down. The union had endorsed Trump six weeks before the election, the first time the National ICE Council, as it was called, had endorsed a presidential candidate.

Trump went through the roof.

Kelly and Chris Crane had an intense dislike for each other. When Kelly had been secretary of homeland security, he had blocked ICE agents from a hard-line crackdown on some immigration violations.

Trump invited Crane to the Oval Office without informing Kelly. Kelly's cut off all our access, Crane said. We put ourselves on the line for you. We endorsed you. We support all your policies. Now we can't even communicate with you.

Kelly heard Crane was in the Oval Office and strode in. Soon Crane and Kelly were cursing each other.

"I can't believe you'd let some fucking guy like this into the Oval Office," Kelly told Trump. If this was the way it was going to work, he said, "then I quit!" And he stormed out.

Trump later told others that he thought Kelly and Crane were going to get into a fistfight.

Kelly urged the president to select Kirstjen Nielsen, a 45-year-old lawyer who had been Kelly's Department of Homeland Security deputy, as the new secretary.

"Kirstjen is the only person who can do this," Kelly argued to the president. "She knows DHS, she was my chief of staff, she's terrific at all this stuff."

The nomination was sent to the Senate on October 11.

The president saw that Fox News commentator Ann Coulter called Nielsen "an open borders zealot" who opposed Trump's border wall. Lou Dobbs piled on, saying Nielsen was pro-amnesty, not a true believer, not an immigration hard-liner, and served in the George W. Bush administration. At her confirmation hearing she had said, "There is no need for a wall from sea to shining sea," and Dobbs, a strong Trump supporter, called this comment "outrageous."

"Everybody's saying that she's terrible," Trump said later to Kelly in the Oval Office. "It's a joke. She's a Bushie. Everybody hates her. How could you have possibly made me do this?"

"She's the best," Kelly said. "She's the best of the best. I can personally vouch for her. She's the first woman to lead the department. I know she's a good person. She's going to do a great job. She will be very effective. She is on your team. She was my right-hand person when I was there. She knows the department."

"That's all bullshit," Trump said. "She's terrible. You're the only one that thinks she's any good. Maybe we'll have to withdraw her nomination."

Kelly threw up his hands. "Maybe I'm just going to have to resign." And he stormed out.

Porter later took Nielsen's commission for Trump to sign that would officially make her secretary.

"I don't know if I really want to sign this right now," Trump said. "I'm just not sure about her."

"She's been confirmed," Porter said. The Senate had approved her nomination 62 to 37. "You're going to attend her swearing-in."

Trump signed.

Kelly appeared on Fox News's Bret Baier show and said that Trump had gone through "an evolutionary process" and "changed his attitude toward the DACA issue and even the wall."

At the White House, Trump went through the roof.

"Did you see what Kelly said?" he asked Porter. "I evolved? I've changed on this? Who the fuck does he think he is? I haven't changed one bit. I'm exactly where I was. We're going to build the wall. We're going to build it across the entire border."

Zach Fuentes, Kelly's assistant, warned the senior staff in the West Wing that Kelly had a short attention span and was easily distracted.

"He's not a detail guy," said Fuentes, who had also been Kelly's assistant at Homeland Security. "Never put more than one page in front of him. Even if he'll glance at it, he's not going to read the whole thing. Make sure you underline or put in bold the main points." However there were some subjects, particularly about the military, Fuentes said, that would engage Kelly's full attention and he might want to have a long conversation.

Normally, Fuentes said, "you'll have 30 seconds to talk to him. If you haven't grabbed his attention, he won't focus."

Kelly held regular senior staff meetings of the 20 top people from the White House every Monday, Wednesday and Friday in the Roosevelt Room. He frequently reviewed his conversations with the president.

"I talked with the president over the weekend," Kelly recounted at one meeting. "He's really hot on getting us out of the Korean Peninsula altogether. Forcing the South Koreans to pay for THAAD. I've just been going back and forth with him, and I've really laid into him and told him he couldn't do this."

As Kelly himself got caught in the Washington political crossfire and was criticized in the media, he spoke more and more about the press and his own role at the senior staff meetings.

"I'm the only thing protecting the president from the press," Kelly said at one meeting. "The press is out to get him. They want to destroy him. And I'm determined to stand in the way, taking the bullets and taking the arrows. Everyone's out to get us.

"The press hates him. They hate us. They're never going to give us a break on anything. It's active hostilities. And so that's why we're taking all this incoming. They're also turning on me because I'm the one guy standing in front of the president trying to protect him."

In a small group meeting in his office one day, Kelly said of the president, "He's an idiot. It's pointless to try to convince him of anything. He's gone off the rails. We're in crazytown.

"I don't even know why any of us are here. This is the worst job I've ever had."

Kelly began to have less control, less involvement. Trump called members of Congress when Kelly wasn't around. He called Chuck Schumer, Tom Cotton, Lindsey Graham, Dick Durbin or cabinet members, underscoring that he was his own chief of staff and his own legislative affairs director.

"Madeleine," he would call out, "get Speaker Ryan on the phone."

Trump's questions started. "How's Kelly doing?" he asked Porter. "He's tough but it kind of seems like he's too tough. I don't know that the staff really likes him that much."

"I think he's helped," Porter answered. "Better to be feared than loved. But he's got his limitations. I think he just needs to recognize them. And you do too." Porter said he thought Kelly's weakness was on legislative matters. "You really need a good political affairs director because that's not Kelly's background. And if you want your chief of staff to be your chief political adviser, it shouldn't be Kelly."

Tillerson complained to Kelly many times about Porter getting Trump to sign decision memos without a sign-off from the secretary of state.

"I know you've been trying to loop Rex in," Kelly told Porter, "but now you cannot take a decision memo to the president—you can't brief the president on something like that—unless you have explicit sign-off." Kelly made clear that feedback from State in general or from Tillerson's chief of staff would not be sufficient. No decisions, Kelly instructed, "until you've talked or emailed with Rex specifically."

Trump heard about the conflicts. He liked aggressive disagreements. They smoked out a wide variety of opinions. Harmony could lead to groupthink. He embraced the chaos and churn beneath him.

At about 9 p.m., Monday, November 27, more than four months after Priebus left the White House, the president reached him on his cell phone. They talked for 10 minutes.

What about the upcoming Senate race in Alabama? Trump asked. How was the ocean cruise that Priebus had just been on? Trump said it was amazing how much they got done together in the first six months. What about tax reform? And the Republican senators who were holding out on tax reform? Trump said that the stories *The New York Times* had that week were nuts.

How do you think Rex is doing? Trump asked. You think he gets it?

Priebus was careful. He thought Tillerson should have been great, but he was hard with the president. And the president didn't like hard.

But the call was not heavy, as if Trump wanted someone to shoot the shit with. Kelly was all business. Kelly would not sit and BS.

The president invited Priebus to lunch at the White House for Tuesday, December 19. Now as a private attorney his proximity to the president and his well-publicized meetings were useful with his private clients. The world knew Priebus was still a player for sure. However, the president's questions about Tillerson reminded Priebus of all the times he learned that Trump had sounded out others about him: How do you think Reince is doing?

It was a bad memory. Trump was always asking everyone their opinions of everyone else, seeking a report card. It was corrosive and could become self-fulfilling—undermining and eating at the reputations and status of anyone and everyone.

"The president's MO is to put people back on their heels," Priebus said. "Put all the chips on the table. And then slowly but surely pick off each chip individually." It could be a person, a policy, a country, a foreign leader, a Republican, a Democrat, a controversy, an investigation—Trump would try to leverage anyone, by any means, and at times he would succeed. "He uses leverage in a way I've never seen before."

N ow that he had agreed to stay to do tax reform, Gary Cohn had to deliver. The current U.S. corporate tax rate was 35 percent, one of the highest in the world. Reducing it had been a rallying point for Republicans and businesspeople for years.

It was all Trump had wanted to talk about at first. During the Bush and Obama years, dozens of large companies had moved their headquarters overseas to take advantage of lower foreign tax rates. This process was known as inversion because it typically entailed creating a new parent company in a low-tax country like Ireland and making the existing American company its subsidiary. This was a big issue with Trump's business friends. Lowering the corporate tax rate could bring trillions of dollars back to the United States.

"The corporate rate's got to be 15 percent," Trump said.

"Sir," Cohn said, "we'll try and get that." Treasury Department calculations showed very few corporations paid the full 35 percent because of various loopholes and special tax breaks that Congress had passed.

Cohn agreed that the U.S. was out of sync with the rest of the world. Some countries, like Ireland, had a corporate tax rate as low as 9 percent. "So bring the money back home," Cohn agreed. "Trillions of dollars are parked offshore to avoid U.S. higher tax rates."

About $4 trillion, Trump said, even more—possibly $5 trillion.

Cohn had a chart that showed it was $2.6 trillion.

At one point the president proposed raising the top income tax rates—currently 39.6 percent at the highest bracket—for earners in exchange for drastically lowering the corporate rate.

"I'll take the personal top rate to 44 percent if I can get the corporate rate to 15 percent," Trump said.

Cohn knew that was crazy, though he realized Trump, with all his real estate and other deductions, had probably never, or rarely, paid the full 39.6 percent.

"Sir," Cohn continued, "you can't take the top rate up. You just can't."

"What do you mean?"

"You're a Republican," explained Cohn, who was a Democrat. Republicans were always for lower personal income tax rates. Republicans were the party of Reagan, who had lowered the top federal income tax rate from 70 percent to 28 percent. "You will get absolutely destroyed if you take the top rate up."

Trump seemed to understand.

Cohn had a packet of Goldman Sachs–style charts and tables to educate the president on taxes. Trump was not interested and did not read it.

At a meeting in the Oval Office, Trump wanted to know what the new individual income tax rates would be.

"I like these big round numbers," he said. "Ten percent, 20 percent, 25 percent." Good, solid numbers that would be easy to sell.

Mnuchin, Cohn and Office of Management and Budget Director Mick Mulvaney said there needed to be analysis, study and discussion on the impact on revenue, the deficit and the relation to expected federal spending.

"I want to know what the numbers are going to be," Trump said, throwing out numbers again. "I think they ought to be 10, 20 and 25."

He dismissed any effort to crunch the numbers. A small change in rates could have a surprising impact on taxes collected by the U.S. Treasury.

"I don't care about any of that," Trump said. Solid, round numbers were key. "That's what people can understand," he said. "That's how I'm going to sell it."

The central feature of Cohn's tax reform packet was on the first page: "Increasing economic growth from 2 percent to 3 percent" would create $3 trillion in budget savings over 10 years.

"Sir, if we can get from 2 to 3 percent, that's all we've got to do, we could pay for the tax plan," Cohn said. The more economic growth, the more taxes the government would collect. Simple in theory, but it would be hard, perhaps impossible, to get 3 percent growth—often a Republican fantasy.

Trump liked the idea. He was infatuated with the simplicity and started using variations of high economic growth in speeches.

Cohn tried to explain that during the Reagan era the U.S. economy had been very competitive and other countries had begun cutting their taxes. There was plenty of history and technical detail.

"I don't give a shit about that," Trump said.

On Monday nights, Speaker Paul Ryan hosted an Italian buffet in his conference room for the six main tax reform players representing Congress and the administration. Known as the "Big Six," they were Ryan, McConnell, House Ways and Means Committee chairman Kevin Brady, chairman of the Senate Finance Committee Orrin Hatch, Mnuchin and Cohn. The group was a Democrat's nightmare—five conservative Republicans and the former president of Goldman Sachs revising the tax code.

The group came up with four principles: simplification of the tax code, tax relief for middle-income families, job creation and wage growth, and bringing back and taxing the trillions of corporate dollars stashed overseas.

Cohn's approach to the congressional leadership was to treat them like gold. In his decades in the client service business at Goldman, everyone was treated as the most important client. He had told his clients there, "I'm available 24/7. You want to talk, we talk." The customer was always first, and only the customer counted. Now the congressional leadership was, for the moment, the only customer.

Mnuchin had alienated some Republican House members early on in the administration by insisting they had to vote for certain continuing budget resolutions and for the debt ceiling, the limit on how much the government could borrow.

OMB director Mick Mulvaney, who had served six years in the House, reported to Cohn that one Republican told Mnuchin: Mr. Secretary, the last time someone told me what I had to do, I was 18. It was my dad. And I never listened to him again, either.

Later, Mnuchin proposed capping the amount of business income a taxpayer could pay at the lower personal income tax rates—known as "pass-throughs." He said some 95 percent of the pass-through tax returns were below $350,000 in annual income.

No, Ryan and Brady said. That was the dumbest idea they had ever heard. Mnuchin had not accounted for the other 5 percent of pass-through tax returns, which included huge mega-donors to the Republican Party like the Koch brothers.

Mnuchin went behind Ryan's and Brady's backs to try to enlist some House Republicans.

Mulvaney threw a note on Cohn's desk: If you want to get tax reform done, keep Mnuchin out of the Capitol.

Cohn reported this to Kelly. As the tax negotiations intensified in November, Mnuchin went on a tour of the country, speaking and selling the tax plan alongside Ivanka in California on November 5 and 6 and New Jersey on November 13, and on his own in Ohio on November 14.

On the Senate side, Finance Committee chair Orrin Hatch put together a group made up of Senators Pat Toomey of Pennsylvania, Rob Portman of Ohio, Tim Scott of South Carolina and John Thune of South Dakota to handle the negotiations on his behalf, since he had a relatively limited knowledge of tax policy. Cohn was on the phone nonstop with these senators.

Cohn discovered how challenging tax reform could be. One of his charts was titled, "The Federal Income Tax System Is Very Progressive." He believed it was another important chart; it showed the big picture, told the whole story. Forty-four percent of Americans did not pay federal income tax.

During the 2012 presidential campaign, when the percentage was higher immediately following the Great Recession, Republican nominee Mitt Romney was recorded saying disparagingly, "There are 47 percent who are with [President Barack Obama], who are dependent upon government, who believe that they are victims, who believe the government has a responsibility to care for them, who believe that they are entitled to health care, to food, to housing, to you-name-it—that that's an entitlement. And the government should give it to them. And they will vote for this president no matter what. . . . These are people who pay no income tax. . . . My job is not to worry about those people. I'll never convince them they should take personal responsibility and care for their lives."

While most of the 44 percent paid payroll taxes on their wages that went toward Social Security and Medicare, as well as state, local, property and sales taxes, they paid zero dollars in federal income tax. That meant the federal government brought in revenue for its budget from only 56 percent.

Many low-income people paid less than zero, Cohn's slide showed. Their income was so low that not only did they owe the government no federal income tax, they cost the federal government revenue because it gave them refundable tax credits—money from the government—like the Earned Income Tax Credit and the Child Tax Credit.

Ivanka Trump worked with Senators Marco Rubio and Mike Lee to increase the Child Tax Credit from up to $1,000 per child to $2,000. Rubio and Lee would not vote for the final tax package unless this was included. "We had to buy their votes," Cohn said. "We'd been extorted by Lee and Rubio." He believed the federal government had conflated taxes and welfare, and, of course, was using tax legislation to help the poor.

The corporate tax rate was still a key question. Trump was stuck on 15 percent. Cohn and Mnuchin finally got him to agree to 18 percent. Then Speaker Ryan, the tax expert, called and urged Trump to move to 20 percent. Orrin Hatch's group of senators and Cohn came up with a rate of 21 percent.

Cohn called Trump. He gave the president a complicated technical description of the advantages of this corporate tax rate. A tax lawyer might understand the nuances of the various percentages or of certain loopholes Trump could not possibly understand or care about.

"Go for it," Trump said.

Cohn saw that he could do anything on the tax reform bill as long as Trump could call it a win.

Trump had a marketing idea: "Call it the 'Cut, Cut, Cut Bill.'" He loved the idea, and had a long phone call with Ryan and Brady to sell this name. After the phone call, Trump was under the impression that it would be called the "Cut, Cut, Cut Bill" in the House.

The House called it "The Tax Cut and Jobs Act." But because of ancient Senate rules, that title was too short, and rather unbelievably it was finalized as "An Act to Provide for Reconciliation Pursuant to Titles II and V of the Concurrent Resolution on the Budget for Fiscal Year 2018."

Cohn found out that getting votes in the Senate was all about giving individual senators their favorite loopholes or tax breaks. "It's
a candy store," he said. Senators Chuck Grassley, John Thune and
Dean Heller were among those who wanted credits for alternative
fuel, including windmills. Susan Collins insisted on a deduction for
schoolteachers who bought supplies for their classrooms. She would
not vote for the bill if the deduction was not included. Ron Johnson
of Wisconsin was concerned about pass-through businesses. McConnell made other promises including one to Jeff Flake on immigration.

The final bill was a dizzying labyrinth of numbers, rules and categories. There was no doubt that it was a Republican tax bill, bene-
fiting corporations and the wealthy most. The bill, however, would
reduce taxes for all income groups in 2018, and according to the
Tax Policy Center, after-tax income would go up an average of 2.2
percent.

Most in the middle class—Americans earning taxable income
ranging from $19,000 to $77,000—would go from the 15 percent
tax bracket to the new lower 12 percent tax bracket, saving the average person hundreds of dollars. These individual tax cuts, however,
would decrease each year and end altogether in 2025.

The business benefits included the reduction in the corporate tax
rate from 35 to 21 percent. Another was that so-called pass-through
enterprises such as partnerships and small businesses like the Trump
Organization could get an effective 20 percent tax deduction.

Around 1 a.m. on December 20, 2017, Vice President Pence was
in the chair if they needed his vote to break a tie in the Senate.

It passed, 51 to 48.

A senior Democratic senator with whom Cohn was good friends
came up to him. He seemed to be the most agitated person walking
off the Senate floor.

"This will do damage for the next decade," the senator said.
"We'll be undoing this for the next decade."

Cohn urged him to relax. "We had to get competitive in the corporate world," he said. "We just had to. And when you see that chart
of our competitors—look, we're in a competitive world."

The individual income tax rates were pegged at 10, 12, 22, 24, 32, 35 and the top rate, 37 percent. The drop from 39.6 percent was standard Republican tax cutting.

In the end, the law would add an estimated $1.5 trillion to the annual deficit over 10 years.

Republican leaders and Trump celebrated with self-congratulatory speeches on the South Portico of the White House. Trump said, "Ultimately what does it mean? It means jobs, jobs, jobs."

Tax reform was the only major legislation passed his first year.

CHAPTER

36

Early in 2018, the president unleashed a full take-down of Bannon, who had clearly spoken to journalist Michael Wolff as a main source for his unflattering book *Fire and Fury*.

In a long statement, rather than a tweet, Trump said, "Steve Bannon has nothing to do with me or my Presidency. When he was fired, he not only lost his job, he lost his mind. . . . Now that he is on his own, Steve is learning that winning isn't as easy as I make it look."

From his point of view, Bannon believed Trump had largely failed as a change agent. The old order in national security certainly won in Trump's first year, Bannon believed. Perhaps the only exception was a toughening stance on China and an awareness that China was the true rival in international affairs.

Bannon was appalled by the National Security Strategy, a 55-page document published in December 2017. The Middle East section said the policy was designed to "preserve a favorable regional balance of power."

What the fuck is that? Bannon asked. It was a retread of the old-world, Kissingeresque order, seeking political stability. The whole

purpose of Trump's 2017 Riyadh summit had been to form an alliance to shut down Iranian expansion and hegemony. "Balance of
power" in Bannon's view meant the U.S. was comfortable with the
status quo and Iran's "short-of-war" strategy that took confrontation
to the brink but left Iran owning the gray zone.

Bannon believed that Trump wanted to roll Iran back—get Iran
out of Iraq, out of Syria, out of Lebanon and out of the peninsula in
Yemen. The alliance to do that was the U.S., Saudi Arabia, the Gulf
states and Israel.

China was the real enemy. Russia was not the problem. The Russian economy was the size of New York State's economy—about $1.5
trillion—and the Chinese economy would soon be bigger than that
of the United States, perhaps within a decade.

Bannon still believed the forces of the populist-nationalist movement were powerful. But the old order was able to blunt all that in
the first year of the Trump presidency. The old order was not going
to roll over.

The populist movement had shown that it didn't have the force
to break through the permanent political class. Trump had been the
armor-piercing shell that could pierce the Clinton part, but not the
rest.

The Republican establishment had brought Trump to heel, he
believed. The tax cut was a 100 percent corporate interest tax cut.
The budget, adding $1.5 trillion to the deficit, was the worst part of
the permanent political-class, boomtown mentality where every lobbyist got their deal for their clients. There was no wall. The swamp
had won.

The Deep State was not the problem. It was the up-in-your-face
state.

Most compromising for Trump, in Bannon's view, was the January 26, 2018, speech that Trump gave at the World Economic Forum
in Davos, Switzerland. The *New York Times* headline had been,
"Trump Arrived in Davos as a Party Wrecker. He Leaves Praised as
a Pragmatist."

It had been a Chamber of Commerce speech, Bannon believed. Trump had looked at the establishment and essentially embraced it.

Trump's critique of Attorney General Jeff Sessions was particularly galling to Bannon. He was sure Trump would never get a better guy confirmed by the Senate.

Grievance was a big part of Trump's core, very much like a 14-year-old boy who felt he was being picked on unfairly. You couldn't talk to him in adult logic. Teenage logic was necessary.

During Trump's first six months in the White House, few understood how much media he consumed. It was scary. Trump didn't show up for work until 11:00 in the morning. Many times he watched six to eight hours of television in a day. Think what your brain would be like if you did that? Bannon asked.

Bannon claimed he used to say to Trump, "Cut the fucking thing off."

At Mar-a-Lago, Trump would come back from playing golf. It'd be a Saturday afternoon in February or March. Absolutely stunningly beautiful. One of the most beautiful things in the world. Melania would be in the room right next door. He would watch CNN's D-team of panelists, whom Bannon considered super-haters, and get worked up. Bannon would say, "What are you doing? Why do you do this? Cut this off. It's not meaningful. Just enjoy yourself."

Trump's response would often go like this: "You see that? That's a fucking lie. Who the fuck's . . ."

Bannon would say, "Go play some slap and tickle with Melania." Trump also did not spend much time with his son Barron, then age 11.

Bannon felt he was not friends with Trump. Trump didn't have genuine friends. He was a throwback to a different time—1950s America. He was a man's man and a guy's guy.

The #TimesUp and #MeToo movements of women and feminists would create an alternative to end the male-dominated patriarchy, Bannon believed.

"Trump is the perfect foil," he summarized. "He's the bad father, the terrible first husband, the boyfriend that fucked you over and wasted all those years, and [you] gave up your youth for, and then dumped you. And the terrible boss that grabbed you by the pussy all the time and demeaned you."

President Trump's tweets may have come close to starting a war with North Korea in early 2018. The public never learned the full story of the risks that Trump and North Korean leader Kim Jong Un took as they engaged in a public battle of words.

It began on New Year's Day in an address by Kim, reminding the world, and the American president, of his nuclear weapons.

"It's not a mere threat but a reality that I have a nuclear button on the desk in my office," Kim declared. "All of the mainland United States is within the range of our nuclear strike." It was an ugly and provocative threat.

Lingering after receiving his President's Daily Brief on January 2, President Trump said, "In this job I'm playing five hands of poker simultaneously, and right now we're winning most of the hands. Iran is busting up and the regime is under intense pressure. Pakistan is terrified of losing all of our security aid and reimbursements. And South Korea is going to capitulate to us on trade and talks with North Korea." He seemed on top of the world but he didn't mention the fifth poker hand.

Real power is fear.

The answer on North Korea was to scare Kim Jung Un. "He's a bully," Trump told Porter. "He's a tough guy. The way to deal with those people is by being tough. And I'm going to intimidate him and I'm going to outfox him."

That evening, Trump sent a taunting, mine-is-bigger-than-yours tweet that shook the White House and the diplomatic community: "North Korean Leader Kim Jong Un just stated that the Nuclear Button is on his desk at all times," Trump wrote on Twitter at 7:49 p.m. "Will someone from his depleted and food starved regime please inform him that I too have a Nuclear Button, but it is a much bigger & more powerful one than his, and my Button works!"

It played on Kim's insecurities. In the last six years, 18 of Kim's 86 missile tests had failed, according to the Center for Nonproliferation Studies.

The president of the United States was practicing a scene out of *Dr. Strangelove*. The Internet lost its collective mind.

The Washington Post's Twitter account rushed to clarify: "There is no button."

Colin Kahl, Obama's former deputy assistant secretary of defense, tweeted, "Folks aren't freaking out about a literal button. They are freaking out about the mental instability of a man who can kill millions without permission from anybody."

Many on Twitter wondered if Trump had violated the platform's terms of service by threatening nuclear war. Others recalled Hillary Clinton's line from her July 2016 convention speech: "A man you can bait with a tweet is not a man we can trust with nuclear weapons."

Trump's tweet was not without supporters. A writer for the conservative *Washington Examiner* concluded: "One of former President Barack Obama's central challenges was the foreign perception—by friends and foes alike—that he was reluctant to employ the full range of U.S. power. . . . I believe Trump is right to roll the dice and take the opposite approach."

Trump was not done. Nor was he satisfied that it sufficed for the United States, the top nuclear power in the world, to issue an unprecedented threat.

Within the White House but not publicly, Trump proposed sending a tweet declaring that he was ordering all U.S. military dependents—thousands of the family members of 28,500 troops—out of South Korea.

The act of removing the dependents would almost certainly be read in North Korea as a signal that the United States was seriously preparing for war.

On December 4, McMaster had received a warning at the White House. Ri Su-yong, the vice chairman of the Politburo, had told intermediaries "that the North would take the evacuation of U.S. civilians as a sign of imminent attack."

Withdrawing dependents was one of the last cards to play. The possible tweets scared the daylights out of the Pentagon leadership— Mattis and Dunford. A declaration of intent to do so from the U.S. commander in chief on Twitter was almost unthinkable.

A tweet about ordering all military dependents out of South Korea could provoke Kim. The leader of a country like North Korea that only recently had acquired nuclear weapons and had many fewer nukes than a potential adversary could be trigger-happy. A use-it-or-lose-it mind-set could take hold.

The tweet did not go out. But Trump wouldn't drop the matter, and raised the issue of withdrawing U.S. military dependents with Senator Graham.

On December 3, before Trump and Kim's war of words, and after a North Korean ICBM test, Graham had advocated removing military families from South Korea. "It's crazy to send spouses and children to South Korea," he said on CBS's *Face the Nation*. He suggested making South Korea an unaccompanied tour for service members and said, "I think it's now time to start moving American dependents out of South Korea."

Now, a month later, when Trump called, Graham seemed to have had a change of heart.

"You need to think long and hard before you make that decision," Graham said. "Because when you make that decision, it is hard to go back. The day you do that is the day you rock the South Korean stock market and the Japanese economy. That is a big frigging deal."

"You think I should wait?" Trump asked.

"Mr. President," Graham said, "I don't think you should ever start this process unless you're ready to go to war."

Trump had stayed his Twitter finger for the moment, but the issue of U.S. military dependents in South Korea did not go away. The U.S. military, however, continued to send dependents to South Korea.

G eneral Kelly informed the president that his two top foreign
policy advisers, McMaster and Tillerson, were in a fero-
cious fight over who would negotiate with Saudi Arabia to
get $4 billion. The money was in part to fund operations in Syria,
including a top secret CIA project for the Syrian rebels code-named
TEAK.

Getting foreign governments to fund U.S. military and CIA operations in foreign countries remained one of Trump's biggest goals.
Damn H.R., Trump said. This pointy-head academic has no sense of
business or how to negotiate.

Kelly agreed, McMaster was not the guy for the job and so far
had not been very successful with the Saudis. They were often willing to write big checks for a variety of projects in Syria. According to
Tillerson, McMaster had stepped in and said, "I'm reaching out to
my counterparts in Saudi. I'm going to negotiate directly with them."

The president was furious. Even with a multitude of problems
with Tillerson, at least he had experience cutting deals with the Saudi
royal family for years as the Exxon CEO. Tillerson also knew the
Saudis could not be trusted and for Trump, not trusting the people

on the other side of the table was a first principle of haggling, of beating them down to get a better bargain. You had to be tough and say no to get to yes. Why the hell would McMaster take this away from Tillerson? It doesn't make any sense, he said.

But there was a more pressing matter that day, January 19, 2018, one day short of Trump's first full year.

In several secure phone conversations with President Moon Jae-in of South Korea, Trump had intensified his criticism of the KORUS trade agreement between the two countries. He would not let go of the $18 billion trade deficit and the $3.5 billion expense of stationing 28,500 U.S. troops. The refrain was jeopardizing relations with Moon, whom he disliked. Trump's obsessive and unfiltered venting had brought him to the edge once again.

Trump told Moon he wanted to send a 180-day termination letter and destroy the trade relationship.

You guys are ripping us off, he said. He wanted the trade and security issues separated. I'm done just giving you guys free money!

Moon replied that trade and security were intertwined. We want to work with you, the South Korean president said. He was conciliatory. You're one of our allies, one of our partners. There may be some misunderstanding about the economic relationship. We want to come to an understanding.

Trump was amped up. You've got to pay for the THAAD anti-ballistic missile system. Why do we need to have any of our anti-ballistic system there?

He belittled the KORUS trade agreement, South Korea and its new leader. This barely concealed rage at an ally was magnificently undiplomatic, the way the president often liked it. He was on the verge of blowing up the relationship.

Kelly, McMaster, Tillerson and Mattis joked darkly that it was inexplicable that the president was voicing more ire at South Korea than our adversaries—China, Russia, Iran, Syria and North Korea.

The senior White House staff and national security team were appalled. They didn't know what the president might say or do. This was an important relationship, especially at that moment. They had to shut this down. There was a consensus that something needed to be done before Moon decided he'd had enough.

McMaster set up a National Security Council meeting in the Situation Room for January 19, 2018. The meeting was billed as a discussion of issues related to South Korea among the president and the principals—Tillerson, Mattis, Kelly, McMaster, Dunford, Cohn.

Trump got right to his point. "What do we get by maintaining a massive military presence in the Korean Peninsula?" he asked, returning to his obsession with the money and the troops.

"And even more than that," he went on, "what do we get from protecting Taiwan, say?" He had always seen this as a worldwide problem: the United States paying for the defense of others in Asia, the Middle East and NATO. Why are we even friends with South Korea? he wanted to know. What do we get out of this? He had been fuming for a year. The answers were insufficient.

Mattis and General Dunford once more explained that the benefit was immense. We get a stable democracy in a part of the world where we really need it, Mattis said. South Korea was one of the strongest bastions—free elections and a vibrant capitalism.

South Korea had a population of 50 million people, the 27th-largest country in the world but with an economy that was the 11th-largest and a GDP of $1.5 trillion, the same as Russia's.

Trump had been informed about the edge the Special Access Program intelligence operations gave the United States in detecting a North Korean missile launch—seven seconds versus 15 minutes from Alaska. There was also an offensive cyber attack capability. It had mixed results sabotaging North Korean missiles before or after launch.

Mattis showed signs that he was tired of the disparaging of the military and intelligence capability. And of Trump's unwillingness to comprehend their significance.

"We're doing this in order to prevent World War III," Mattis said. He was calm but stark. It was a breathtaking statement, a challenge to the president, suggesting he was risking nuclear war. Time stopped for more than one in attendance.

One person present said Mattis's message was clear: Stop fuck-ing around with this. We're doing this because we've got to prevent World War III. This isn't some business gamble where if you happen to go bankrupt or whatever, it's not a big deal.

It seemed Mattis and others were at the end of their rope with the president. How are you possibly questioning these things that are obvious and so fundamental? It was as if Mattis were saying, God, stop it!

Mattis was not finished. "We have the ability to defend the home-land with forward deployment" of the 28,500 troops. He was reluc-tant to mention the Special Access Programs in such a large meeting.

Mattis explained, without the intelligence capability and the troops, the risk of war would vastly increase. The means of defend-ing South Korea and Japan would be decreased. If there was a war without these assets, "The only option left is the nuclear option. We can't achieve the same deterrent effect" in any other way. "And we can't do it as cost effectively." The arrangement with South Korea was one of the great national security bargains of all time. Mattis tried to speak the president's language of cost/benefit analysis.

"But we're losing so much money in trade with South Korea, China and others," Trump countered. "I'd rather be spending money on our own country." The United States was subsidizing others with the trade imbalances.

"Other countries," Trump went on, "who've agreed to do secu-rity things for us only do it because they're taking so much of our money." They were almost stealing from us.

"Forward-positioned troops provide the least costly means of achieving our security objectives, and withdrawal would lead our allies to lose all confidence in us," Mattis replied.

Chairman Dunford jumped in, seconding all these points with some passion.

"We're spending massive amounts for very rich countries who aren't burden sharing," Trump said, hammering his point.

Then, out of the blue, he raised what Kelly had told him about the McMaster and Tillerson feud over who would negotiate with the Saudis to get the $4 billion for operations in Syria and elsewhere.

He said he had heard McMaster had urged Tillerson to back off. He laid into his national security adviser. "Why would you do that?" he asked McMaster. "The Saudis are confused. This is $4 billion. Rex is going to do this. H.R., stay out of it. I have no idea why you possibly would've thought that it was wise for you to take it away from Rex, but steer clear. Rex is going to do this. He's going to handle it."

McMaster took the dressing-down in stride. He had been insulted in front of the National Security Council he was supposed to lead and coordinate.

McMaster, a chain-of-command general, replied, "Yes, sir."

Tillerson, on the other hand, turned back to the main issue: the value of forward deployment. "It's the best model. The global system. Joining together in trade and geopolitics leads to good security outcomes."

Dunford again supported his argument. "Our forward-deployed cost in South Korea is roughly $2 billion. South Korea reimburses us for over $800 million of that. We don't seek reimbursement for the cost of our troops" such as their pay. The chairman also said that other countries were paying the U.S. an annual subsidy for activities we would engage in anyway for our own protection. "We're getting $4 billion a year subsidy in our efforts to protect the homeland," Dunford said.

"I think we could be so rich," Trump said, "if we weren't stupid. We're being played [as] suckers, especially NATO." Collective defense was a sucker play.

Citing a number often used by Bannon for the financial sacrifice and cost of all the wars, military presence and foreign aid in the Middle East, the president summed up, "We have [spent] $7 trillion in the Middle East. We can't even muster $1 trillion for domestic infrastructure."

The president left. Among the principals there was exasperation with these questions. Why are we having to do this constantly? When is he going to learn? They couldn't believe they were having these conversations and had to justify their reasoning. Mattis was particularly exasperated and alarmed, telling close associates that the president acted like—and had the understanding of—"a fifth or sixth grader."

When I first learned of the details of this NSC meeting, I went back to a transcript of what President Obama had told me in 2010 about what he worried about the most.

"A potential game-changer," Obama said, "would be a nuclear weapon . . . blowing up a major American city. . . . And so when I go down the list of things I have to worry about all the time, that is at the top, because that's one area where you can't afford any mistakes. And right away, coming in, we said, how are we going to start ramping up and putting that at the center of a lot of our national security discussion? Make sure that that occurrence, even if remote, never happens."

The pressure campaign on North Korea was effectively put on hold while the 2018 Winter Olympics were held in South Korea from February 9 to 25.

General Dunford learned that the Air Force had planned some research and design tests of its nuclear-capable ballistic missiles from California into the Pacific Ocean, scheduled right before and after the Olympics.

They were the kind of tests that the United States was pressuring North Korea to stop. They were provocative. He stepped in and the Air Force held off on the tests.

Early in 2018, the CIA concluded that North Korea did not have the capability to accurately deliver a missile into the United States mainland with a nuclear weapon on top. According to the intelligence and the information on the testing of North Korean rockets, they did not have the reentry of missiles perfected. But they were marching toward that goal. The CIA, for the moment, seemed to convince Trump that the North was not yet there.

Afghanistan continued to frustrate Trump. Months earlier, in late September, he had hosted a reception at the United Nations annual meeting in New York. Azerbaijan president Ilham Aliyev and his wife posed for a picture with the Trumps. The Azerbaijan leader passed word that the Chinese were mining substantial amounts of copper from Afghanistan.

Trump was furious. Here was the United States paying billions for the war, and China was stealing copper!

Afghan president Ghani had dangled the possibility that the United States would have exclusive access to vast mineral wealth, untouched in the Afghanistan mountain ranges. His argument: There's so much money to be made. Don't walk away. Rare earth minerals, including lithium, a main ingredient in the latest batteries. Some exaggerated estimates held that all minerals in Afghanistan might be worth as much as several trillion dollars.

Trump wanted the minerals. "They have offered us their minerals!" he said at one meeting. "Offered us everything. Why aren't we there taking them? You guys are sitting on your ass. The Chinese are raiding the place."

"Sir," said Gary Cohn, "it's not like we just walk in there and take the minerals. They have no legal system, no land rights." It would cost billions of dollars to build the mining infrastructure, he added.

"We need to get a company in there," Trump said. "Put it out for bid." This was a giant opportunity, capitalism, building and development at its best. "Why aren't we in there taking it?"

"Who's we?" Cohn asked.

"We should just be in there taking it," Trump said, as if there were a national mining company to move into Afghanistan.

At a subsequent meeting in the Oval Office, Trump asked, "Why hasn't this been done?"

"We're running it through the NSC process," McMaster said.

"I don't need it done through a fucking process!" Trump yelled. "I need you guys to go in there and get this stuff. It's free! Who wants to do this?" It was a free-for-all. Who wanted this bonanza?

Commerce Secretary Wilbur Ross volunteered. "I'll take care of it, sir. I'll do it," he said as if it were a Commerce Department issue.

Trump approved.

Kelly didn't say much but took McMaster, Ross and Cohn to his office.

McMaster was ripshit at Kelly for not intervening. "You just chopped my legs out from me. You knew I was running a process." He was going by the textbook as usual, was working with the State and Defense Departments and any other departments or agencies with an interest. "You hung me out to dry in front of the president!"

There was little that appealed to Trump more than the idea of getting money from others to pay for national security commitments made by previous U.S. administrations—NATO, Afghanistan, Iraq. The only other appealing prospect was making a good deal, and he thought this was one.

The State Department assessed the mineral rights. Analysts concluded this would be a great propaganda boon to worldwide extremists: The United States is coming to rape your land and steal your wealth from the ground. They sought legal opinions in hopes of slowing it down.

On February 7, 2018, McMaster convened a small group of principals in the Situation Room to hear Commerce Secretary Ross's report. He had talked with the acting minister of mining in Afghanistan that morning. "The Chinese are not getting anything out. They have these big concessions, as they do worldwide, and they sit on them. They're in it for the long term. They don't need to make immediate money off it."

So there was nothing to worry about. Afghanistan did not have the infrastructure or transportation, the regulatory or environmental controls, he said. No private company would make an investment.

"It's fake news," Ross said, to mild laughter.

McMaster added that most of these minerals would be impossible to reach because a lot of them were in Taliban-controlled areas. It was a war zone, and a military perimeter defense would have to be established before mining. At best, he said, it would take 10 years if everything went right.

Ross said he would follow up to explain this to the president.

Kelly seemed to be just trying to keep the ship from sinking. At a senior staff meeting in early 2018, he announced with pride, "I now know that I will not be the shortest-serving chief of staff. I've now surpassed Reince." Priebus had served 189 days, the shortest tenure of any White House chief of staff in history.

Early in 2018, *60 Minutes* broadcast a piece on the Afghanistan War, noting that Kabul was so violent that the U.S. commander could not be safely driven to his headquarters through the city. General Nicholson flew the two miles by helicopter. He made it clear he had adopted Trump's victory-driven approach. "This is a policy that can deliver a win," Nicholson said.

Nicholson's intelligence and operational maps showed that the U.S.-led coalition controlled about 50 percent of the country. Within knowledgeable Pentagon and State Department circles it was known that Nicholson had claimed, "I'll get to 80 percent in two years."

He was determined to enhance the coalition's and Afghan Army's capability to claw back what would amount to 75,000 square miles. It was unattainable, even preposterous, to many who had served in Afghanistan.

A secondary goal of Nicholson's was that after four years, the Taliban would realize they could not win and would come to the negotiating table. This was the same Taliban that had been fighting for 16 years.

The DNI intelligence expert briefed Trump on Afghanistan in early 2018: No gains by the U.S. in territory. Nothing clawed back. No improvement from last year; actually, some areas were getting worse. Part of the explanation was that the U.S. and Afghans had to guard Kabul as the Taliban mounted attack after attack on the capital. In the last nine days of January, 130 people were killed in four attacks. This left little coalition military capacity to take back territory.

The analysts had more grim conclusions. Pakistan was not playing ball or responding to pressure. Any settlement was premised on Pakistani participation.

The immediate prospect was more insurgency, maybe even civil war if the U.S. pulled out. Jihadists were coming out of Syria and heading to Afghanistan: the new promised land for bomb makers and bomb throwers.

The coalition probably only had until the spring of 2019 to keep the status quo. The political fabric seemed to be coming apart. A perfect storm was coming, and a practical problem like weather might be the tipping point. The mountains had little to no snow, so no water was coming down to the fields. A drought was coming, and with it a crisis of food insecurity. Around the same time, Pakistan was likely to send one to two million refugees over the border into Afghanistan, many of them Afghans who had crossed the border into Pakistan after the Russian invasion of 1979. Some two million had lived in Pakistan for decades, never in their native Afghanistan, but they would be coming.

Still, General Nicholson kept saying that he would "win" in Afghanistan. Mattis didn't like it. "The secretary is very unhappy with what he [Nicholson] just said, and we're trying to rein him in," one Pentagon official privately confided.

If the language of the commander in chief was about "winning," it was hard to criticize the ground commander for using it. But the intelligence indicated that it was heading to worse, not better, next year.

In early 2018, one key participant said, "The military seemed to want a South Korea–style permanent presence. If so, Iran, Russia and China will ramp up their antagonism because all of a sudden we now have a permanent presence in their backyard. But the military may have got its way here because getting out would be a huge walk-down. [The president] said we're going to win. And you can't define that as a stalemate forever. At some point people are going to recognize you can't succeed there."

Quietly and nervously, some officials at State and the intelligence community began some extremely sensitive scenario planning, a Plan B. "The military does scenario planning all the time. Why not the civilians?"

The analyst described the outcome of this Plan B. "It's not a withdrawal and a collapse and civil war. It's not a liberal democracy, deeply centralized. What's in the middle? Federalist, more realistic, more sustainable? To give potentially the Taliban a role? The sort of wild card is the president's short attention span and his questioning all these assumptions that people keep throwing out. And smelling and calling bullshit when he sees it." For example, saying things will work out with Pakistan. "But Pakistan has not changed since 9/11 and they won't. The only option, then, is to get out."

In summary, Afghanistan was a new House of Broken Toys. Political instability. Fraying of the Afghan government. Congressional and public criticism in the United States. Few, if any, military gains. Drought. Massive food insecurity. Refugees.

Trump blamed two people in particular. First he had a special scorn for former president George W. Bush, who had started the Afghanistan War in 2001 and then the Iraq War in 2003. "A terrible president," he told Porter. "He was a warmonger. He wanted to exert American influence and take democracy all throughout the world and wanted to be the world's policeman and started all these wars." It was foolhardy and a mistake. Even though Trump had made the decision to add several thousand troops, he said he was not going to continue the status quo.

The other person Trump blamed was McMaster. He used Iraq as his evidence. "I don't know how they've [the Iraqis] managed to fool McMaster, but he's not a businessman. They [U.S. generals] don't understand the cost/benefit analysis. I can't believe I let him talk me into putting more troops in there." He believed that McMaster had been co-opted.

In a searing insult to McMaster, Trump did an imitation of his national security adviser. The president puffed up his chest and started noticeably exaggerated breathing. He said in loud staccato, *"I know the president of Iraq. He's a good man, sir! I know he has our best interest at heart."*

Returning to his normal voice, Trump said, "That guy's just full of shit. I met this guy. McMaster doesn't know what he's talking about." Trump had met the Iraqi prime minister, Haider al-Abadi, at the White House in March 2017.

"These military guys, they don't get business. They know how to be soldiers and they know how to fight. They don't understand how much it's costing."

On Afghanistan, Trump told Porter, "It's a disaster there. It's never going to be a functioning democracy. We ought to just exit completely."

Trump and Senator Graham played golf at the Trump International Golf Club in West Palm Beach two weeks before Christmas, December 10, 2017. In a tweet Graham said the golf course was "spectacular," a comment sure to please Trump. It was nothing compared to the praise Graham lavished on Trump during their round.

"You're a very good commander in chief," he told Trump. The president was listening to his military commanders and the changes in the rules of engagement in the Middle East and Afghanistan were paying off.

This was Graham's pitch to Trump: "You can do something nobody else did. You're cleaning up the mess that Obama left you. You're doing a damn good job of cleaning it up. You're rebuilding the military. You're taking a wet blanket off the economy. You're really unshackling the military and the economy. God bless you for undoing the damage done in the last eight years. Where do you want to go? What do you want to be your legacy? Your legacy is not just undoing what he did, but it's putting your stamp on history."

Trump seemed to love the adulation but said to Graham, "You're a middle-of-the-road guy. I want you to be 100 percent for Trump."

This resembled the loyalty pledge that then FBI director James Comey said that Trump had asked of him. According to Comey, Trump had said, "I need loyalty. I expect loyalty," during their now famous one-on-one Green Room dinner in the White House during the first week of the Trump presidency.

"Okay, what's the issue?" Graham asked, "and I'll tell you whether I'm 100 percent for you or not."

"You're like 82 percent," Trump said.

"Well, some days I'm 100 percent. Some days I may be zero."

"I want you to be a 100 percent guy."

"Why would you want me to tell you you're right when I think you're wrong? What good does that do for you or me?" Graham asked. "Presidents need people that can tell them the truth as they see it. It's up to you to see if I'm full of shit."

On December 29, 2017, Trump's tweet had summarized his position on DACA: "The Democrats have been told, and fully understand, that there can be no DACA without the desperately needed WALL at the Southern Border and an END to the horrible Chain Migration . . . We must protect our Country at all cost!"

The president called a meeting in the Cabinet Room with 20 senators and House members to discuss an immigration plan for the Dreamers. Trump directed that the Tuesday, January 9, meeting be televised, all 55 minutes. He was in full performance mode, promising legislation. "Truly, it should be a bill of love, and we can do that."

The president was engaging and fun. Graham was astounded at Trump's apparent shift on one of the most polarizing issues before them. The anti-immigration hard-liners would be aghast. Trump had once been their leader. Graham hoped this was the president at his deal-making best.

Graham had never felt better about Trump's ability to get an immigration deal done. He had worked on immigration for years, attempting to broker compromises with Democrats like Ted Kennedy, Chuck Schumer and Dick Durbin. With Trump, he saw the potential to finally succeed. In a statement, he was exuberant, saying, "Most fascinating meeting I've been involved with in twenty plus years in politics."

The headlines reinforced Graham's optimism. *The New York Times*: "Trump Appears to Endorse Path to Citizenship for Millions of Immigrants." *The Washington Post*: "At the table: Trump tried to negotiate and prove stability."

The next day Trump phoned Graham.

"I thought you were masterful," Graham said. "Don't let all these people"—Republican hard-liners—"scare you away. You're on track here. This is the guy that I try to tell people about when we play golf. This is the Donald Trump that I'm all-in for. Only you can do it. Bush tried. Obama couldn't do it. You can do this."

To Graham's surprise, Trump put Melania, the first lady, on the phone. "I just wanted to tell you I like what you said," the first lady said in her soft accent. "And the way you handled yourself, and the way you speak. I thought it was very nice."

"Well, thank you, ma'am, you made my day," Graham replied. He was impressed with her grace. It was the first time he had ever really talked to her. It was pretty clear she, an immigrant herself, was sympathetic to the DACA children.

"Can we change the libel laws?" Trump asked, rapidly shifting the tenor of the conversation to one of his pet peeves.

"No," Graham, the lawyer, said.

"Why?"

We are not England, Graham said, where the libel laws were stricter.

People were writing "bullshit," Trump said.

"I don't doubt it," Graham agreed. "But no, we can't change the libel laws and don't worry about it." In the landmark 1964 decision *New York Times v. Sullivan*, the U.S. Supreme Court had set the libel bar about as high as possible: Something was libelous only if published or said knowing that it was false and with reckless disregard for the truth.

"Well, I don't intend to become like England," Trump said.

"There's no more bigger punching bag in all the world than the president of the United States," Graham said. "And you've gotten more than your fair share of unfounded criticism, but that's just the hand you're dealt. And the way you beat them, Mr. President, is you produce. And the way you put your critics in a box is you don't sue them, you just deliver. Prove all these guys wrong."

Graham felt it had been one of his best conversations with the president. He had done most of the talking.

About 11 a.m. the next day, Senator Dick Durbin, the number-two Democrat in the Senate, called Graham.

"I just got off the phone with Trump," said Durbin, who had joined Graham in the efforts for a compromise on immigration. "He likes what we did. He wants you and me to come down."

Graham called the White House to try to set up a meeting. Kelly came to Graham's office to go over details.

Kelly, the immigration hard-liner, was edgy. He had told the West Wing staff and even some on the Hill that the president didn't understand what DACA was, that he was ignorant of both the policy and the mechanics. The president had deputized Kelly to handle DACA, and he viewed part of that job as making sure Trump didn't do anything or meet with anyone on DACA, like Graham and Durbin, without him there. The president can't do this on his own, he'd told West Wing colleagues, because if he does it on his own, he's going to screw it up.

"All I'm asking for is a chance to explain to the president," Graham said. Graham's plan was simple, he repeated. Trump would go along with legislation for Dreamers in exchange for funding for the wall. "Let him make up his own mind," Graham said. He was repeating Kelly's mantra on all issues. He wanted the facts presented to the president, who could then decide.

So Graham and Durbin showed up at the White House, thinking they would meet alone with Trump. Instead there was a group of anti-immigrant senators, congressmen and staffers, including Kelly and Stephen Miller. Graham thought it looked like a lynch mob lined up on chairs in the Oval Office.

Graham began walking through the plan, which included the money Trump had asked for on border security.

It was not enough, Trump said, condescending.

Graham said he was sure they could do more but this was where they had started. And he mentioned 25,000 visas from mostly African countries. He turned to the visas for places such as Haiti and El Salvador because of earthquakes, famine and violence.

"Haitians," Trump said. "We don't need more Haitians." At that and the mention of immigrants from African countries, Trump said, "Why are we having all these people from shithole countries come here?" He had just met with the prime minister of Norway. Why not more Norwegians? Or Asians who could help the economy?

Durbin was sickened. Graham was floored.

"Time out," Graham said, signaling for a halt with his hands. "I don't like where this thing's going." America is an ideal, he said. "I want merit-based immigration from every corner of the globe, not just Europeans. A lot of us come from shitholes."

Trump snapped back to reasonable, but the damage was done.

Durbin went public, revealing Trump's comments about "shithole countries," and Graham backed Durbin up.

Two days later, Saturday, Trump called Graham, who thought Trump was calling to take his temperature. How mad was he?

Trump said he was playing golf at his club in West Palm Beach.

"Well, hit 'em good," Graham said.

"I didn't say some of the things that he said I said," Trump said, referring to Durbin.

"Yeah, you did," Graham insisted.

"Well, some people like what I said."

"I'm not one of them," Graham said. "I want to help you. I like playing golf with you. But if that's the price of admission, count me out. Good luck. Hit 'em good."

The idea of "shithole countries" was not a new one for Trump. During the 2016 campaign, Trump had visited Little Haiti in Miami. Former Haitian leaders had come to the microphones and accused the Clintons of corruption and stealing from Haiti.

After the event, in private, Trump seemed down. "I really felt for these people. They came from such a shithole."

With Bannon out of the White House, Stephen Miller was the driving force behind the White House's hard-line DACA policy. Trump often still expressed sympathy for young people in the DACA program, saying, a lot of times these kids came here through no fault of their own. They're sympathetic. He also pointed out the political appeal of the Dreamers.

Miller would inject the hard line. Look, everybody calls them the kids and the Dreamers but, he argued, they weren't kids anymore. Many were 24 or 26 or 27. Miller's position was absolute: In exchange for a compromise on DACA, we want full border wall funding for a decade—not just one year—plus an end to chain migration and the diversity lottery that dispersed up to 50,000 green cards per year to immigrants from nations that otherwise had low immigration rates to the U.S. We're not accepting anything less than all three.

On January 21, Graham attacked Miller publicly. "As long as Stephen Miller is in charge of negotiating immigration, we are going nowhere. He's been an outlier for years. I've talked to the president—his heart is right on this issue. He's got a good understanding of what will sell, and every time we have a proposal it is only yanked back by staff members."

On Friday morning, February 23, 2018, Trump spoke at the Conservative Political Action Conference (CPAC), the most important conservative audience in the country. Relaxed and brimming with self-confidence, the president spoke for over an hour. At times he stuck to his prepared text, but he went exuberantly "off the glass" at points, speaking spontaneously.

"You're getting the wall," he said. "Don't worry. Had a couple of these characters in the back say, oh, he really doesn't want the wall. He just used that for campaigning. I said, are you—can you believe it? You know, I say every time I hear that, the wall gets 10 feet higher, you know that, every single time. Okay, now, we're going to have the wall."

On immigration he said, "I don't want people that are going to come in and be accepting all the gifts of our country for the next 50 years and contribute nothing . . . And I want people that love us . . . I don't want people coming in the way they do now."

He then repeated one of his favorite stories, a rhyming poem about a woman who took in a snake.

On her way to work one morning, down the path along the
   lake,
a tender-hearted woman saw a poor, half-hearted frozen snake.
His pretty colored skin had been all frosted with the dew.
"Poor thing," she cried. "I'll take you in. And I'll take care of you."
"Take me in, oh tender woman, take me in for heaven's sake;
"take me in, oh tender woman," sighed the vicious snake.
She wrapped him up all cozy in a comforter of silk,
and laid him by her fireside with some honey and some milk.
She hurried home from work that night, and soon as she arrived,
she found that pretty snake she had taken in had been re-
   vived. . . .

She stroked his pretty skin again, and kissed and held him tight.
But instead of saying thank you, that snake gave her a vicious
    bite. . . .
"I saved you," cried the woman. "And you've bitten me, heavens
    why?
"You know your bite is poisonous and now I'm going to die."
"Oh, shut up, silly woman," said the reptile with a grin.
"You knew damn well I was a snake before you took me in."

"And that's what we're doing with our country, folks," Trump said. "We're letting people in. And it is going to be a lot of trouble. It is only getting worse."

Trump had just approved a two-year spending bill for $8.6 trillion that had no money—not one red cent—for the wall.

Trump's relationship with his secretary of state was irrevocably fractured. There were months of speculation that Tillerson was about to quit or be fired. He was in Africa when Kelly warned him in March 2018 to cut his trip short. "You may get a tweet," Kelly said. The morning of March 13 Trump tweeted that CIA Director Pompeo was going to be the next secretary of state. "Thank you Rex Tillerson for his service!" was all he said about Tillerson.

Trump told reporters on the South Lawn of the White House, "Rex and I have been talking about this for a long time. . . . We disagreed on things. . . . We were not really thinking the same. . . . Really, it was a different mind-set, a different thinking."

Trump was continuing to complain to his attorney Dowd that the Mueller investigation was hampering his ability to act as president. He passed on some classified anecdotes that Dowd, who had a security clearance, could pass to Mueller and Quarles, who also had the proper clearances.

Cautioning Dowd that it was very sensitive, Trump said one had occurred in April when he had personally negotiated the release of a charity worker, Aya Hijazi, 30, a U.S. citizen who had been imprisoned in Cairo for three years.

Trump relayed his conversation with Egyptian president Abdel Fattah el-Sisi, who had an abysmal human rights record including mass detentions, security forces' killing protesters and military trials of civilians. "Dowd, remember who I'm talking to," he said. "The guy's a fucking killer. This guy's a fucking killer! I'm getting it done. He'll make you sweat on the phone. And right before we make the deal, el-Sisi says," and Trump assumed a deep gravelly voice, "Donald, I'm worried about this investigation. Are you going to be around? Suppose I need a favor, Donald." It was "like a kick in the nuts. It's awful," Trump said.

In November, Kelly called Dowd. "The president said you're going to see Mueller."

"Yeah, we're going to see him in a couple hours."

"Mattis has told the president that Putin and the Russians are just getting too dangerous, and that we're going to have to deal with them. And I want you to convey that to Bob. Bob knows Mattis." Mueller and the secretary of defense had both been Marines.

Dowd described to Mueller how everything Trump did with Russia was suspect. "Bob, I know you know General Mattis." Mueller had met with Mattis during a visit to Kandahar in January 2002 when he was FBI director. Dowd reported that Mattis was worried about Russia. "And by the way, you want to check it? Pick up the phone and call him. He knows who you are. He knows you're a Marine."

Dowd reminded Mueller that he'd said he wouldn't let grass grow under him. "The grass is about a foot high, pal. We keep defending you with the president."

Mueller said he was dead serious about finishing the investigation.

"Well, I got to tell you, Bob, I don't know how long I'm going to last. I defend you guys all the time. I stand up for what you're doing. But you know, we got people being interviewed over and over again."

With Mueller, Dowd pushed gently.

With Quarles, he complained. "Enough is enough!"

Dowd had other problems. Ty Cobb started giving interviews to the media saying that the investigation would be over by the end of 2017. "I'd be embarrassed if this is still haunting the White House by Thanksgiving," he told Reuters, "and worse if it's still haunting him by year end." The media ran stories with Cobb's picture. Dowd now thought Cobb looked like an old Western sheriff with a handlebar mustache out of the Western novel and miniseries *Lonesome Dove* and he was astonished. He was the lead lawyer for the president. Was Cobb having separate conversations with Quarles?

No, Cobb insisted. "My wife wants me out of this," he said. "And so I've been trying to nudge it along publicly."

"There's interviews scheduled in December," Dowd said. "And frankly, they're all favorable to the president so we're going to let them go."

Kelly asked Dowd, "Where'd you find this fucking friend Ty?" Cobb had started off on the wrong foot with Kelly, going behind the chief of staff's back to the president to get an office in the West Wing. He told Cobb, "Don't you ever go behind my fucking back again."

Dowd assured the president that their strategy of dealing with Mueller was "to cooperate and grind them down until we had a 3D picture of what was in their heads." Based on this picture and the cooperation of 37 witnesses and all the documents turned over, he repeated several times, "I don't see a case."

Under Article II of the Constitution, Dowd explained to him, the president solely ran the executive branch. And all of his actions, particularly pertaining to Comey, were within those powers. "I will never tell you that your instincts are wrong about these guys and what they're up to. We've been treated very nicely. But we treated them very nicely."

In December a story ran in the German financial daily *Handels-blatt* saying the Mueller investigation had subpoenaed records from Deutsche Bank, the largest in Germany, and the primary lender to Trump.

The president called Dowd at 7 a.m. He was furious.

"I know my relationships with Deutsche Bank," he said. He maintained the bank loved him and always got paid. "I know what I borrowed, when I borrowed, when I paid it back. I know every goddamn one." He could recall whom he had dealt with and other details with specificity. "I'm telling you, this is bullshit!"

Dowd pushed Quarles. "Hey, Jim, there's no secrets here. This is bullshit."

A conference call was scheduled with lawyers from all the relevant law firms. Everyone sounded like they were talking in code.

"Look, would you please," Dowd said. "My guy does not talk in code."

Finally Quarles reported, "There's nothing there. We had subpoenas to Deutsche Bank way back in the summertime, but it doesn't involve the president or his finances."

At 10 a.m. on December 21, Dowd went to see Mueller in an attempt to turn the tables. Often the best defense was to go on the offense.

"All the records have been produced," Dowd said. "All the witnesses have been interviewed except one or two. The entire inquiry appears to be the product of a conspiracy by the DNC, Fusion GPS—which did the Steele dossier—and senior FBI intelligence officials to undermine the Trump presidency. The failure to investigate Comey's role precipitating the inquiry is a travesty. Comey's aberrant and dishonorable conduct demands scrutiny." The Justice Department Inspector General was investigating Comey's actions in the Clinton email case. "Kicking the can to the IG undermines confidence in your inquiry," Dowd claimed.

Mueller did not reply.

Mueller and Quarles kept pushing. They wanted to interview the president. On January 8, 2018, Mueller dictated a list of 16 topics they wanted to ask. Nearly all dealt with Flynn, Comey or Sessions.

Dowd advised the president that list was not specific. "What I'd like to do is I'd like to push it even further so you have a better picture. You know, 16 topics, you're kind of guessing as to what they're going to ask you."

"What are you going to do?" Trump asked.

"Well, my idea is we're going to write him a letter answering these." They would present the facts as they saw them, and make legal arguments especially about the president's Article II powers. "And do it like a Supreme Court brief."

"We've given them everything," Trump insisted. Why wasn't it enough? He added, "I don't mind talking to him."

Dowd and Jay Sekulow spent the next two weeks drafting the letter. Sekulow, a frequent commentator on the Christian Broadcasting Network and Fox News, had represented conservative, religious and antiabortion groups over a 30-year career.

"How you coming?" Trump eventually asked Dowd. "Can I see it?"

Dowd came to the White House residence on Saturday, January 27, 2018, around 1 p.m.

The president gave him a brief tour including the Lincoln Bedroom. "You and I fit in this bed," he joked.

"We could see ourselves in the mirror," Dowd joked back.

"If you win this case," Trump said, "I'll give you the A tour. Takes hours. In my opinion, this is the most beautiful mansion in the world. There's nothing like it."

Trump's son, Barron, came in with a friend.

"Dad," Barron said, "he wants his picture taken with you. Is that all right?"

Sure. The picture was snapped.

Trump and Dowd sat at a table with a view of the Washington and Jefferson Memorials.

"I would like to give you sort of a feel of what testimony could be like," Dowd said. They would do a practice session. "And we'll talk about a couple of these subjects. Maybe Comey and Flynn. Just lightly. You don't have to do anything to prepare. Just come in cold.

"I want you to read our letter. I'm ready to sign it, but I will not sign it until you feel good about it. Because it is a major submission. This tells Bob where we are and where we think he is and why you should not—why he doesn't deserve to ask you questions.

"If the questions seem harmless, don't treat them that way. And I want you thoroughly focused on listening to the words. I'm not a windy examiner. I like the short, sweet questions. And I like to build

it. I'm very patient. And I'll give you the standard advice—just answer the question. Okay? Got it?"

Yes.

"When did you first learn that there was a problem with General
Flynn?"

"I'm not sure. I think when McGahn had talked to Sally Yates.
But John, I'm not sure." Trump said that the acting attorney general
had said that Flynn had told the vice president something that wasn't
correct.

"What'd you do about it?"

Trump said he didn't think he had done anything. "I think Don
took ahold of it. And they worked . . ."

"Did you call Flynn in?"

"No."

"Did you talk to Flynn at all?"

"I don't know. There's something in my mind that . . . He and
Priebus called me."

"Well, Mr. President, did you ever ask him if he talked about
sanctions with [Russian ambassador] Kislyak?"

"No."

"Are you sure about that, Mr. President? We have some evidence
that there may have been such a conversation. Are you sure about
that?"

Dowd was aware that Priebus had given testimony favorable to
the president. In one version with Priebus in the room Flynn had
said in front of the president that he had never discussed his Kislyak
conversations with the president.

Trump wandered off with a long answer that didn't mean much.

"Look, let's get back to brass tacks," Dowd said.

"Oh."

"Did there come a time when you had to let him go?" Dowd
asked about Flynn.

"Yeah."

"Do you remember how that happened?"

"No. I think he had a letter of resignation. I don't mind telling you I felt very bad for him. He had his shortcomings, but he was a hell of a nice guy and I admired him. As you know, I love military guys. So that was the recommendation, and that's what I did." Priebus and McGahn had recommended that Flynn be fired.

"Did they ever tell you about an FBI interview?"

"I don't know. I can't remember."

Dowd felt that Trump really couldn't remember. As he asked more questions there was a lot that Trump said he couldn't remember. He found this understandable, given the demands of the presidency.

So Dowd went back to December 2016, just after the election, and asked more about Flynn. "Well, was he making contact with diplomats, etcetera?"

"I assume he was."

"Did he talk to Kislyak?"

"You know, I don't know. I know there were a lot of conversations among the staff. I think I tweeted out some things."

On March 31, Trump had tweeted, "Mike Flynn should ask for immunity in that this is a witch hunt (excuse for big election loss), by media & Dems, of historic proportion!"

"What was your position on the sanctions Obama approved?" Dowd asked. Obama had expelled 35 Russian diplomats, sanctioned several individuals and entities, and closed two Russian compounds in January 2017.

"Well, my position was it gave me leverage."

"Oh!" Dowd said. "Because everybody thinks you would be against them, because you wanted good relations with Putin."

"No, I looked at them as leverage," Trump repeated.

Based on the testimony that Dowd had reviewed, this was accurate. Dowd figured he was cruising pretty well. The six-page memo the White House and Dowd had compiled on Flynn had much more information than Trump was now recalling. Dowd had given the day-by-day account of how the White House discovered that Flynn had lied to Mueller and Quarles, who had complimented the memo for its thoroughness.

"Well," Dowd asked, "why did you tell Director Comey that—you kind of asked him to take it easy on Flynn. What was that all about?"

"I never said," Trump said.

"He made a contemporaneous memorandum of it," Dowd said. "Reported it to his buddies."

"I didn't say that," Trump replied. "John, I absolutely didn't say that."

"Well, he says . . ."

"He's a liar," Trump said. He went full tilt on Comey. "The guy's a crook, he's a liar. He bounces between the Clinton [email] thing and making memos and leaking."

The president had his critique down pat. He delivered it all, unleashed, nonstop. Dowd tried to interject. No way. Trump went the whole nine yards.

"Look," Dowd said after the storm had briefly subsided, "you can't answer a question that way. That is what they say is off-putting. It's not good. Okay? Be polite about it."

"Well, goddamn it!"

"Did he tell you that you weren't under investigation" on January 6?

"Yes he did."

"He just meant on the salacious part, not collusion, right?" Dowd asked. That was one theory in Mueller's team.

"That's bullshit! He never said that to me."

Dowd believed him since Comey had corroborated that there had been no investigation on anything at that point.

The next 30 minutes were useless. "This thing's a goddamn hoax!" Trump reprised everything he had tweeted or said before. Dowd could get nowhere. Trump was raging. Dowd worried that if he had been Mueller that Trump probably would have fired him on the spot. It was almost as if Trump were asking, Why am I sitting here answering questions? "I am the president of the United States!"

What a mess. Dowd shrugged his shoulders at the waste of time, but he saw the full nightmare. It was quite a sight seeing the president of the United States fuming like some aggrieved Shakespearean king.

Trump finally came down from the ceiling and began to regain his composure.

"Mr. President, that's why you can't testify," Dowd said. "I know you believe it. I know you think it. I know you experienced it. But when you're answering questions. When you're a fact witness, you try to provide facts. If you don't know the facts, I'd just prefer you to say, Bob, I just don't remember. I got too much going on here. Instead of sort of guessing and making all kinds of wild conclusions."

Then Dowd handed Trump the draft of the letter addressed to Mueller. The subject read "Request for Testimony on Alleged Obstruction of Justice."

A raw assertion of presidential power was printed in boldface: **"He could, if he wished, terminate the inquiry, or even exercise his power to pardon if he so desired."**

Trump read the 22-page letter carefully, pausing to read several paragraphs out loud. He said he loved the letter. "You know, I've got a hell of a case here. I love the way it's organized." He admired the 59 footnotes.

"This is just one of the best days I've ever had in this thing," he went on. His capacity to cycle between emotions, from low to high, was on full display. "It really is beautiful. I guess it's everything I ever thought of and better. Now I get it. I see what you're doing."

Yeah, Dowd said.

"Let's push them to the wall. But you don't want me to testify?"

"No," Dowd replied. "Why don't we exhaust this thing? Maybe if push comes to shove, I'll suggest to Bob, give me the questions. We will answer them. And we'll make a script. You can come over, ask your questions and he'll read the answers. How can you complain about that when you've trusted us on everything we've given? Plus the president cannot possibly remember all this. And by the way, he would love to meet you and talk through this thing, but he needs the assistance [of a script]."

"By God, I'll do that," Trump said. "That's great."

"Well," Dowd said, "just imagine if you didn't have the script."

"I don't know, John. We just went through that. You think I was struggling?"

"Yeah, you are. But Mr. President, I don't blame you. It's not that you're lying or you're bad or anything like that. Given your daily intake—just look what we've done this afternoon."

There had been during their conversation several interruptions, two short briefings on world problems and some classified documents for Trump to sign. How could he remember everything?

"You know," Dowd continued, "that gets in the way of trying to recollect what happened six months ago or nine months ago."

"That's great," Trump said. "I'm with you. I don't really want to testify."

The day after the practice session in the White House, Trump called Dowd. "I slept like a rock," Trump said. "I love that letter. Can I have a copy?"

"No," Dowd said.

Dowd had the president where he wanted him.

On Monday, January 29, 2018, Dowd and Sekulow signed the letter. Dowd then arranged to deliver the letter to Quarles on February 1. It would be just like in the movies, Dowd thought. Quarles was to walk down the street and hop into Dowd's parked car.

They exchanged a few pleasantries and asked about each other's kids.

"Well, here's your letter," Dowd said.

"What's this?"

"In response to your 16 topics," Dowd said. "And we kind of make our case. I leave the door open. I'm going to push for some specific questions. Think about it. You want to talk about it, tell Bob let's get together."

In a meeting in January 2018, Navarro, Ross, Cohn and Porter
gathered in the Oval Office. After months of arguing about tariffs from entrenched positions, debates had become heated and
sharp.

Cohn, backed by Porter, rehashed the economic arguments and
the geopolitical national security arguments. He talked about how
tariffs risked roiling the markets and jeopardizing a lot of the stock
market gains. He said the tariffs would be, in effect, a tax on American consumers. Tariffs would take away a lot of the good that Trump
had done through tax and regulatory reform.

You're the globalist, Trump said. I don't even care what you think
anymore, Gary.

Trump shooed him away. Cohn retreated to a couch.

Navarro and Porter picked up the debate, with Ross interjecting
on Navarro's side from time to time. Navarro argued that tariffs
would raise revenues and be beloved by businesses and unions. He
said it would be a great way for Trump to get union support and help
his base in advance of the 2018 midterm election.

Porter brought up the Bush tariffs and the net job loss that had occurred. In the years since, Porter argued, downstream industries that consumed and relied on steel—builders and pipelines and the auto industry—had expanded, while there was little potential for expansion of steel manufacturing and production jobs. The job losses under new tariffs would be even more pronounced than the ones during the Bush administration.

Porter said Navarro's belief that tariffs would be met with widespread acclaim was "just dead wrong." Many businesses would oppose tariffs because they were buyers and consumers of steel.

"The automakers are going to hate this," Porter said. "They have narrow margins, and this is going to raise their costs." Pipeline makers too. "We're opening up all of these new federal public lands and offshore drilling. It requires people building pipelines.

"And the unions," Porter said. "Well, that's crazy. Sure, the steel union is going to love this, but the United Auto Workers isn't going to like this. The Building and Construction Trades isn't going to like this. It's going to up their costs."

Porter ordinarily tried to remain an honest broker who facilitated the discussion. When he had a strong view, he tended to wait until he was one-on-one with the president. Now he was outing himself as a free trader.

Navarro countered each argument as strenuously as Porter made it. Chief of Staff John Kelly walked into the room midway through the meeting. The president was watching the back-and-forth avidly.

What are you, an economist now? Trump asked Porter after he and Navarro had taken verbal swings at each other for nearly half an hour. What do you know about economics? You're a lawyer.

Porter said he had studied and tutored others in economics while he was at Oxford as a Rhodes Scholar. He pointed out that many of his arguments weren't strictly economic.

"I always knew Gary was a fucking globalist," Trump said. "I didn't know you were such a fucking globalist, Rob."

Trump turned to Kelly. Get a load of this guy. He's a globalist!

Kelly nodded and smiled. He wanted this meeting wrapped up.

The meeting broke up without a real resolution except to remind Trump that he had signed a decision memo to move forward on the 301 investigation with China and announced it. That had to come before steel tariffs. That was the strategy and agreement.

Porter left the White House on February 7 after two ex-wives went public with allegations that he had physically abused them. One released a photo showing a black eye that she said Porter gave her. Each, one to the press and one in a blog post, gave graphic descriptions of domestic abuse.

Porter quickly concluded it would be best for all—his former spouses, his family and close friends, the White House and himself—to resign. He wanted to focus on repairing relationships and healing.

The New York Times wrote, "Abuse Claims End Star's Rise in White House" and "Aide's Clean-Cut Image Belied His Hot Temper, Former Colleagues Say."

In a statement, Porter said, "I took the photos given to the media nearly 15 years ago, and the reality behind them is nowhere close to what is being described."

"Peoples lives are being shattered and destroyed by a mere allegation," Trump tweeted.

The *Washington Post* editorial board accused the White House of "shrugging off domestic violence" and *The New York Times* said "Trump Appears to Doubt the #MeToo Movement."

Cohn saw that one of the main restraining influences on Trump was now gone.

After 6:30 on the night of Wednesday, February 28, Commerce Secretary Wilbur Ross and Peter Navarro went to the Oval Office and convinced the president to move ahead with steel tariffs before the 301 investigation was complete, imploding the whole trade strategy. Ross had earlier produced a study maintaining that the rising imports of steel and aluminum were a threat to the national security, giving Trump the authority to impose them without Congress.

Ross and Navarro had arranged for the main U.S. steel executives to come to the White House the next day.

When Cohn got word of the plan, he called Kelly around 10 p.m.

"I don't know anything about a meeting," Kelly said. "There's no meeting."

"Oh, there's a meeting."

"What are you talking about, Gary?"

Cohn tried to kill the meeting, and for a while he thought he had succeeded. But then it was back on.

More than a dozen executives showed up the next day. At a meeting in the Cabinet Room, Trump announced that he had decided to impose a 25 percent tariff on foreign-made steel and 10 percent on aluminum.

"You will have protection for the first time in a long while," Trump told the executives. "And you're going to regrow your industries," he said, even though all the data Cohn had gathered showed it was not practical or even possible.

Cohn believed if they had completed the work on the intellectual property case against China, they would have had the allies on board for a blockbuster trade case. It would have been most of the world against China. Their economic rival would be isolated. Steel tariffs upended all of that.

Cohn concluded that Trump just loved to pit people against each other. The president had never been in a business where he had to do long-term strategic thinking. He went to see Trump to explain that he was resigning.

"If this is the way you're going to run the place," Cohn said, he was going to leave. "I can deal with losing a battle in the White

House as long as we follow proper protocol and procedure. But when two guys get to walk in your office at 6:30 at night and schedule a meeting that the chief of staff and no one knows about, I can't work in that environment."

Cohn knew the importance of Hope Hicks, who had been elevated to White House communications director. Cohn often asked her to join him when he was heading into a tough conversation with Trump, saying, "Hope, come on in with me." He found Hicks softened the president and that Trump treated Cohn differently when she was there.

On Tuesday, March 6, he went to see Hicks. They crafted a statement for the president to issue with Cohn's resignation.

"Gary has been my chief economic adviser and did a superb job in driving our agenda, helping to deliver historic tax cuts and reforms and unleashing the American economy once again. He is a rare talent, and I thank him for his dedicated service to the American people."

They fiddled with the language, then took a printed copy into the Oval Office. They took seats at the Resolute Desk.

"Mr. President," Cohn said, "today's probably the right day for me to put out my resignation."

"Gary's been so great," Hicks said, soothing the moment. "We're going to miss him so much. This is a shame. We've got to find a way to bring him back."

"Of course," the president said, "we're going to bring him back."

It was a false show to the end. Cohn realized again what he had said before to others about the president: "He's a professional liar."

"I've got a quote here that I've okayed with Gary," Hicks said. "I want you to okay it."

Trump took the piece of paper and tweaked a word, but otherwise let the statement stand.

"It's a huge loss," Trump said. "But we'll be fine. And he's coming back."

"Gary Cohn to Resign as Trump Adviser After Dispute Over Tariffs," *Bloomberg* reported. "Gary Cohn Resigns Amid Differences with Trump on Trade," said *The Washington Post*. "Gary Cohn Resigns, Apparently Over Tariffs," read *The Atlantic*. "Gary Cohn Resigns as White House Economic Adviser After Losing Tariffs Fight," said *The Wall Street Journal*.

Later, after he resigned, Cohn worried about instability in the economy that would come from tariffs and the impact on the consumer. The U.S. is a consumer-driven economy. And if the consumer is unsure of what the economy will look like and what their disposable income will look like, that will be seen very quickly in the economy and in the stock market.

Trump's action and mounting threats on tariffs were jarring. Cohn thought that Trump had to know. "But he's not man enough to admit it. He's never been wrong yet. He's 71. He's not going to admit he's wrong, ever."

Tom Bossert, the president's adviser for homeland security, cyber security and counterterrorism, went to the Oval Office in the spring of 2018 and found Trump in his private dining room.

"Sir, do you have a minute?" Bossert, a 43-year-old lawyer and security expert, asked.

"I want to watch the Masters," Trump said. He had TiVo'd the Augusta National Golf Club tournament, the most famous in the world, and was glued to it.

Bossert, another high-flying aide with Oval Office access even in the Kelly era, invited himself to sit down and watch.

The lawyer knew the United States was already in a constant state of low-intensity cyber war with advanced foreign adversaries such as China, Russia, North Korea and Iran. These countries had the ability to shut down the power grid in United States cities, for example, and the only deterrent was to make clear that a massive cyber attack would not just be met with cyber-for-cyber symmetry.

The full force of the U.S. military, including nuclear weapons, would have to be a central part of the deterrent. Bossert liked to say, and he said it regularly, that the use of any element of national power would be justified. The United States had too much to lose in a high-consequence cyber attack. Bossert had repeated it so often that the president seemed to understand, but the import of this—nuclear weapons as a cyber deterrent—had not quite become part of the public debate.

"What's going on?" Trump finally asked.

"I'm coming at you one more time," Bossert said. "I'm going to do TV"—the upcoming ABC Sunday show *This Week*. "But this China trade issue is going to come up again." So would cyber.

"You and your cyber," Trump said, "are going to get me in a war—with all your cyber shit."

"That's the point, sir. I'm trying to use other elements of national power to prevent bad behavior online. And that's going to put me right in the middle of all of the decisions you're making. That's why I'm here. You're now in the middle of a personal negotiation with President Xi. You just upped the ante to $150 billion" in tariff threats with China. "Fine. How do you want me to handle it on TV? I don't want to go out and say something that's going to then piss you off."

Trump jumped at the invitation to provide some television coaching, to mainline some performance wisdom. It was pure delight.

"So here's how you do it," Trump said, his fingers flying in the air. "Tom, are you ready? You go up there. You say . . ." He wanted to formulate it just right. "You tell them you've never seen—no wait. First you tell them, 'Trump's dead serious.' That's what you tell them. Are you ready?"

Trump's hands and fingers went up again. "You tell them $150 billion. Wait! You tell them $150 billion is nothing. He's ready to go to $500 billion because he's tired of not being treated fairly. That's what you tell them!"

Trump continued with animated fingers. "You ready? That's what you tell them."

"Okay," Bossert said, "you want me to go hard?"

"You go hard!" Trump said with enthusiasm. "If it weren't Sunday, you'd shut the markets down, that's how fucking hard you fucking go!"

Fingers up again. "Hold on! Wait! Then you say, 'Don't worry about it.' See here, watch, here's what you do." Trump offered some stage direction, one hand up again for dramatic emphasis. "Then you say, 'It'll all be all right because the relationship Trump has with Xi is so . . .'" A pause. A refinement. "It's the best." Wait! "You've never seen such a good relationship between two presidents in your life. Maybe ever.

"Are you ready?" the president asked.

Bossert thought he would remember the script and the Trump show, perhaps for the rest of his life. It was Trump's way of saying, go hard, Trump's willing to go to the mat. We're being treated unfairly.

"And don't worry about soybeans," Trump said. The Chinese had announced they would retaliate with tariffs on American agriculture and other goods. Speaking in the third person, Trump said, "He'll buy more goddamn soybeans if Trump has to. He'll buy his own damn soybeans from his own farmers before the Chinese push him around. But then you tell them, 'It'll be all right. He and Xi will work out a deal. It'll be a beautiful deal. The best deal you've ever seen.'"

"So you want me to go hard and soft?" Bossert now asked—hard on determination and soft on the relationship with Xi.

"Yeah."

Bossert raised cyber again.

"Oh, for Christ's sake," Trump said, "if you have to hit the cyber thing, fine."

Bossert saw that Trump wanted him to stick to trade. "Boss, here's how I do it: It's a trade dispute, it's not a trade war. There's a trade deficit. In the '80s we had a trade dispute with Japan and we were close allies with them at the same time."

"Perfect!" Trump said. "You got it. You throw that crap in there, sounds good, then you tell them what I said. And then you're good." Apparently trying to tamp down any anxiety, he added, "Tom, you'll be fine."

Afterward, Bossert stuck his head in Kelly's office, just as a courtesy, to say he had just been prepping for TV with the president and had nothing unusual to report. Kelly waved him off. It seemed to Bossert that the chief of staff was greatly diminished, resigned and had largely given up.

Bossert was ready with his talking points, but on ABC, host Martha Raddatz focused on border security. Trump had said he wanted to send 2,000 to 4,000 National Guard troops to the southern border. It was the topic of the day, driven by Trump's comment. She never asked about China.

Bossert was disappointed because he was "Ready!" to pass along the president's message of determination and the extraordinary bonding with President Xi of China.

CHAPTER

42

The rest of February, Dowd didn't hear much. He thought Mueller and Quarles were slow-rolling it. A meeting was finally arranged for 2 p.m. on Monday, March 5, at Mueller's office.

Mueller was accompanied by Quarles and three other prosecutors.

Dowd came with Sekulow and another lawyer. It quickly became clear that they had different views about the purpose of the meeting.

"Well," Mueller said, "I guess that's it."

"What are you talking about?" Dowd asked. "Where are the questions?"

"You know, I don't know," Mueller said, a poker player in midgame.

"Jim said that's what was going to happen here."

"Well, you know, I don't know," Mueller said again. "Seems to me you're not going to testify."

"Under the circumstances, exactly right."

"Well, you know," Mueller said, "I could always get a grand jury subpoena."

"You go right the fuck ahead and get it!" Dowd said, striking the table with his hand. "I can't wait to file a fucking motion to quash. And I want to hear you tell the U.S. district judge what the crime is. And I want you to explain."

Dowd said Mueller had all the evidence he could possibly need. "My motion to quash is going to have everything we've given you, including the testimony of 37 witnesses. Including the 1,400,000 documents with the highlights on the most intimate conversations of the president. I want you to tell that judge why you need a grand jury subpoena. Which by the way, has never been issued in the history of the country to any president. And by the way, there is no president, all the way back to Thomas Jefferson, who's ever been so transparent."

Dowd continued, "You want to go to war? Let's go to war. And by the way, I will tell the president that you have now threatened us with a grand jury subpoena. 'So Mr. President, if you don't testify, I'm going to haul your ass in front of the public and we're going to have a grand jury subpoena. We're going to have a hearing.' And by the way, Bob, none of this evidence is before the grand jury. So I want you to explain that to the federal judge, why none of this is before his or her grand jury yet."

Dowd believed all the main evidence was in the interviews and documents. And only in rare cases had that sort of evidence been presented to the grand jury.

"John, it's okay," Mueller said, trying to calm Dowd.

"Bob, you threatened the president of the United States with a grand jury subpoena when he's not a target. And barely a subject. He's essentially a goddamn witness. And I'm going to tell the judge that. So he has no criminal liability as of March 5, 2018," the date they were meeting. "Nothing. And I'm going to tell the judge I'm not going to let you play gotcha. I'm not going to have you start testing the recollection of this president over something that—there is no crime. And Bob, I've asked you. You're the one that wanted to engage. Talk about reciprocity. You guys tell me where the collusion is. And don't give me that chickenshit meeting in June," Dowd said, referring to Donald Trump Jr.'s meeting with a Russian lawyer in Trump Tower.

"That's a nothing. There's no collusion. And the obstruction? It's a joke. Obstruction's a joke. Flynn? I mean, Yates and Comey didn't think he lied. And by the way, he told—in the memo of the White House counsel, he told them the agents had said they closed his file. I mean, Flynn believed that he had no jeopardy. Yeah. None."

Dowd continued. "I can't wait to read your papers. Well, my papers are going first. And by the way, just give me the subpoena. I'll take it."

"John," Mueller said, "I'm not trying to threaten you. I'm just thinking of the possibilities here."

Dowd pivoted to the good-old-boy approach. "The other possibility is, give me the questions. We have a relationship of mutual trust. We've trusted you guys. You've trusted us. And we've never failed you. Bob, isn't really the important thing that you get whatever the truth is? And you've got us working for you."

Dowd decided to take an extraordinary step. "I have no secrets with you guys," Dowd said. "I'm going to tell you about my conversation with the president of the United States on the subject of testimony." He mentioned three of the questions he had taken Trump through up in the White House residence. On the third he had no clue. "He just made something up. That's his nature."

Dowd realized he had Mueller's full attention.

"Jay," he said to Sekulow, "you play the president. I'll play Mueller. Okay?" They would role-play what Dowd had witnessed with the president. "Let's talk about Comey." Dowd asked about one of Trump's Comey conversations. Sekulow's answer was classic Trump—an answer spun out of thin air, with contradictions, made-up stuff, anger. A perfect performance. A perfect Trump.

"Gotcha! Gotcha, 1001!" Dowd said slamming the table, referring to the section of the U.S. Code that deals with false statements. "Gotcha, 1001!"

Dowd asked another simple question of Sekulow, still playing Trump.

"I don't know," Sekulow said. "I don't know. I don't know."

"Jay," Dowd said, "how many times did he say I don't know when we talked to him?"

"Oh, a dozen, twenty."

"Bob," Dowd said to Mueller, "here's my point. You're asking me to sit next to a president who'll get to the third question, screw it up and thereafter, because I'm going to counsel him, he just doesn't know and he doesn't remember. So he's going to say I don't remember 20 times. And I'm telling you, Bob, he doesn't remember. And by the way, if you'd like I will get General Kelly in here to tell you he doesn't remember. And the reason he doesn't remember is very simple. One, these facts and these events are of little moment in his life." Most had taken place early in his presidency.

"All of a sudden he's the boss. But he's getting information from all quarters, including the media every day. That is like tonnage. And the fact is, I don't want him looking like an idiot. And I'm not going to sit there and let him look like an idiot. And you publish that transcript, because everything leaks in Washington, and the guys overseas are going to say, I told you he was an idiot. I told you he was a goddamn dumbbell. What are we dealing with that idiot for? He can't even remember X, Y, Z with respect to his FBI director."

Dowd was aware that he had illustrated the president was "clearly disabled."

"John, I understand," Mueller said.

"Well, Bob, what do you want to know? Give me one question that no one has answered."

"Well, I want to know if he had corrupt intent."

"Bob, do you think he's going to say yes? Because on his behalf, I'm telling you no. And if you want me to get an affidavit from the president that he had no corrupt intent, I'll give it to you."

"Let me think about it," Mueller said. "I hate to think that you would be playing us."

"Wait a minute," Dowd said. "Give me a fucking break. I've got a track record here that is unimpeachable. You ask Jim Quarles if I've ever played him. Is there anything that I've ever said to you that wasn't correct?"

No, Quarles answered. "John's one of the best lawyers we deal with."

Dowd began to think that Mueller didn't know the facts of the case.

Under the joint defense agreement with some 37 witnesses, Dowd had received debriefings from the lawyers for them.

"Did anyone lie?" Dowd asked.

"No," Mueller said.

"Did anyone destroy documents?"

"No," Mueller said.

"Am I right that you want good, reliable answers?"

"Yes."

"Get me the questions," Dowd said, "and I will take them and tell you whether we can answer them." He would provide the answers—a line or two to each question. "Fair swap," he continued. "You give me the questions so I know what's on your mind."

General Kelly could get Mueller, his team and a court reporter into the White House without anyone knowing. "We'll have a script." The president would be under oath. "We'll get it just the way we want it. But we're telling you that's the truth as we know it. The president's saying that's the truth as he knows it, with the assistance of counsel. So either that or you sit there while we interrupt him for six hours or he plays, 'I don't know.'"

Mueller's team were shaking their heads and made it clear that had never been done before. No way. It was unheard of.

"Let me think about whether to give you some questions," Mueller said.

Dowd reminded Mueller that in July or August, when Trump had attacked Mueller and Sessions, Mueller had contacted Dowd to say, "I got a problem, can you come by? You said, I got people refusing to testify that don't need to refuse to testify. They don't have any culpability at all. But I'm afraid that the atmosphere, they feel like they're disloyal if they testify."

And Dowd had told him, "Well, I'll go public and say we want everyone to cooperate. The president's cooperating. We're cooperating 100 percent. And we encourage everyone to do that." Dowd and Cobb had been quoted in the press saying Trump and the White House would "continue to fully cooperate."

As he had at each meeting, Dowd said, "What's at stake is the country." The president needed to do his job, and did not have time for this investigation. There were serious, even dramatic tensions in the world—North Korea, Iran, the Middle East, Russia, China.

"I'm very sensitive to that," Mueller replied. "I'm doing the best I can."

"Why don't you just give us the questions?" Dowd pressed.

Mueller didn't like it.

Dowd knew he was gambling and daring Mueller by threatening to fight a grand jury subpoena. That was his design, sending a message that if Mueller wanted to go the grand jury route, this was what it would look like. He would fill his motions with exhibits. And the district judge would spend two weeks reading them.

Dowd had laid it out as strongly as he could to Mueller. "And you're going to have to stand in the well of the court and tell the judge why you want to put the president of the United States in the grand jury. Bob, as you know, I have handled cases like this. And I wouldn't go near the grand jury with the president of the United States."

He had a final argument. The perjury trap was what Mueller's team did, he charged. "You did it to Flynn, you did it to Gates, you did it to [George] Papadopoulos," a former campaign aide. "You guys, that's the games you played." Rick Gates, a Manafort business associate and Trump's deputy campaign chairman, had one of the best lawyers sitting next to him and had still lied. "You guys gave him no time to prepare. And now he's got a felony. Bob, that's exactly what I told the president: that's what they're going to do to you in an interview."

Dowd thought it possible, even likely, that there was something he didn't know. "Bob, you guys are all wound up about something. There must be something here." Maybe you disapprove of the president's behavior. "But you don't have a case." Whatever they had, Dowd said, "Go tell it to the mountain and go tell it to the Hill. I don't care."

Mueller sat stone-faced—marble, nonresponsive. Such control. The meeting was over.

At 5 p.m. Dowd and Sekulow went to see the president in the dining room off the Oval Office.

"How'd it go?" Trump asked.

"Mr. President," Dowd said, "this is ridiculous."

"Oh, my God," Trump said. Dowd's reaction to the Mueller meeting seemed so negative that Trump looked worried that he was now really in trouble.

"No," Dowd said. "You've never truly respected Mueller. You've got really good instincts, but I've never bought into it. But I've got to tell you, I think your instincts might be right. He really wasn't prepared. Why are we coming back here with nothing?"

A week later, March 12, Dowd and his team went again to see Mueller and his team. He hoped against hope that Mueller was going to say he was inclined to decline prosecution and say he needed the president's testimony just to write a report to Rosenstein, the deputy attorney general.

Mueller's team, Quarles and three others, dictated 49 questions and Jay Sekulow took notes. Nearly all concerned Trump's attitude, opinions, decision making or conclusions about major players such as Flynn, Comey and Sessions. Some inquired about Donald Jr. and the famous meeting at Trump Tower, and the offer from a Russian lawyer to provide dirt on Hillary Clinton. Others concerned real estate development in Russia.

The broad range of subjects validated what the news was reporting on what Mueller was investigating.

This is horseshit, Dowd thought. Second-year-law-school questions. Many had been answered. To have Trump answer them, of course, would be a catastrophe because Trump could erupt and say absolutely anything. On one level, Dowd thought the broad range of questions suggested that Mueller had nothing and wanted to go on a giant fishing expedition. Setting a perjury trap for the volatile Trump would be child's play.

"There's no case here," Dowd told Mueller.

"I need the president's testimony," Mueller said. "What was his intent on Comey?"

"I'm not sure constitutionally you can question that," Dowd told him. The Article II powers of the president were long acknowledged, even by Comey.

"I want to see if there was corrupt intent," Mueller said again. This was the very heart of the matter. The obstruction statutes did not make specific acts alone unlawful. The acts had to be done "corruptly" or "willfully," with the intent of obstructing justice. State of mind was the key. Why had the president acted the way he had? That was why Mueller wanted the president's testimony, Dowd believed.

"Do you have some evidence that he was paid off?" Dowd asked. Payment for illegal action, suborning perjury or destroying evidence are normally the elements needed to show obstruction. Tapes, sworn testimony of a witness or documents are the best evidence. Unless the prosecutors had it out of the mouth of the subject of the investigation, unless someone torpedoed himself as Dowd was certain the president would do.

"Your own deputy attorney general is a witness for the president," Dowd said. Rosenstein had written the memo urging that Comey be fired for his conduct in the Clinton email case.

"Matter of fact, he [Rosenstein] took the president's four-page letter and rewrote it. I rest my case. Then you've got the attorney general. Then you've got the vice president. Then you've got McGahn, everybody around the president. And then you've got Comey's behavior, which both the deputy and the AG had condemned in the Clinton case.

"Intent," Dowd continued, "all the documents and testimony" answer that. "You asked witnesses what he [the president] said and

what he did and when he did it. I submit all that stuff is in real time."
That was all that was needed to show the president's intent.

Mueller was not buying.

Dowd and Sekulow left the building.

"What do you think?" Sekulow asked.

"He ain't testifying," Dowd said. It had been a complete fantasy
to think that Mueller would decline prosecution.

Dowd believed he could use the Court of Appeals decision in
the independent counsel investigation of Bill Clinton's agriculture
secretary Mike Espy. The court had ruled that executive privilege
applied to the president and to his advisers. Prosecutors who wanted
to overcome the privilege must show the materials sought contain
important evidence that isn't available elsewhere.

The court ruled that prosecutors had to show a matter under
investigation was a serious crime and that no one other than the
subpoenaed witness could answer.

Dowd and Sekulow reported back to Trump.

"I have a completely different picture of Mueller now," Dowd
told Trump. The president had been right. "I don't trust him."

The 49 questions troubled Dowd. Why not just five?

Why no deference to the president of the United States, who
didn't have time to prepare and then answer questions in the middle
of so many world problems? Dowd said this reinforced the decision
that the president should not testify.

"Yeah," Trump said. "They got answers to all of them."

Cobb began saying publicly that the president really wanted to
testify and answer a few questions.

"Mr. President," Dowd said, "it ain't a few. There's 49 of them.
That's not my advice."

"What are people going to say?" Trump asked. "How's it going
to look in the press?"

"Mr. President, it's a trap. They don't have a legal or constitutional reason to talk to you." He mentioned lawyers who had represented Trump in the past. "If you don't want to take my word for
it," call them.

Trump called Dowd from Air Force One later in March.

"Mr. President, you just need to take my advice," Dowd said. "Otherwise we're going to have a major disaster. There's no way you can get through these. You remember our meeting when you read our letter? You remember you were comfortable, you understood the strategy? Mr. President, we have won this thing hands down. The 49 questions, you agree, have already been answered. You've got people here that answered them. You've got lawyers that answered them. You've got staff. I mean, Priebus, Bannon, all of them gave testimony acceptable to the special counsel. He has no quarrel with it.

"Mr. President, there's no poison in the well. No one has lied. No documents are missing. There's no president in our history that's done what you've done. Why can't I get you to just be proud of that and sit on it?

"And Mr. President, what I recommend is we just make all that public. We politely tell Bob you're not going to sit for an interview, for the obvious reasons and for the constitutional reasons, and you're protecting the office for your successors. If you testify, then we're going to go through decades of gotcha and let's get the president under oath. It's just the new game. Particularly when there's no crime and no basis, you know?"

The investigations of Reagan in Iran-contra, Clinton in Whitewater-Lewinsky and Nixon in Watergate all involved criminal activity, he said. "And by the way, if there was criminal activity where your White House could help out, I have no doubt you would respond. And that you would—if someone asked you about someone on your staff that had misbehaved and you witnessed something, you'd be a good witness. You'd testify. But that's not the case here. This is a case where all of the questions have been answered.

"Mr. President, you're just cutting my legs off. I'm trying to be a good lawyer."

"You're a good lawyer," Trump said. "You're a great lawyer."

"Mr. President, I cannot, as a lawyer, as an officer of the court, sit next to you and have you answer these questions when I full well know that you're not really capable."

Dowd wanted to dress it up as much as possible, to say, it's not your fault. It's the burden of the office. He knew in this confrontation he could not be insulting. He could not say what he knew was true: "You're a fucking liar." That was the problem.

So Dowd said, "You do have trouble staying on the subject. And that can defeat you. Then you try to catch yourself, and you misstate something, and bam. It's like Mike Flynn not remembering the conversation with Kislyak."

Once more on Air Force One, Trump called his lawyer.

"Are you happy?" the president asked.

"No," Dowd said. "I'm not happy, Mr. President. This is a goddamn heartbreak. I feel like I failed. I've failed as your lawyer. I've been unable to persuade you to take my advice. I'm no different than a doctor. I know what ails you. I know what your difficulty is. I've given a prescription that I know will keep you out of harm's way. Remember the first rule, Mr. President, is do no harm. That's where we are. And if I go and sit with you and let you do something that I think is bad for you and will get you in further trouble, then I ought to lose my license. Maybe there are lawyers that just sort of blink at all that."

"I know that. John, I know you're frustrated."

"I am. I don't mind telling you, I regret the day I ever recommended Ty Cobb. And I can't believe that he undermined me."

"Well," Trump said, "I asked him" to speak out and show the president was not afraid to testify.

"He should have declined. He's a government employee. And by the way, they can call him as a witness. He has no privilege with you."

"Jesus," Trump said, sounding worried, "I've talked a lot with him."

"I wish I could persuade you," Dowd said. "Don't testify. It's either that or an orange jump suit. If it's decision time, you're going to go forward, I can't be with you."

"You're walking away," Trump said. "How can you quit on me?"

It was a matter of principle, Dowd said, and the lawyer's obligation to try to protect his client.

"I wish you'd stay. You're a great lawyer."

Dowd knew it was bullshit. But that was one of the Trump paradoxes. They could have a hell of an argument, but when they were done, on the phone or in person, Trump would say, thank you. I appreciate everything you're doing.

In a lifetime of law, Dowd maybe had only five clients who had so graciously expressed their thanks.

Sekulow and Cobb called Dowd to complain that the president was not responding to them, blowing them off. They needed Dowd to call the president.

"Mr. President," Dowd said in a call on the night of March 21 around 10 p.m.

"Hi, John," the president said. He was very nice. Calm.

"Mr. President," Dowd said, "I'm sorry to bother you. But Ty and Jay have called me." They wanted him to address the question about testifying.

Trump said he had decided to testify. He could handle Mueller. "John, that's just where I am. Sorry you don't agree."

"Well, it's not my job to agree. It's my job to look after you. And if you start taking your own advice, you get in trouble. Mr. President, I don't take my own advice."

"You have lawyers?"

"Absolutely. All the crap I've been through? Of course I have lawyers."

"John, that's where I'm at," Trump repeated. "I think the president of the United States cannot be seen taking the Fifth."

"Mr. President, we can make a far better presentation than that. By the way, I would add something. I think we ought to brief the key leaders on the Hill first, before we go public." Take all the testimony and documents, and make the case to them before getting involved in a court battle. "Tell them why we're not testifying. If we show them all this stuff . . ."

"That's not a bad idea," Trump said. "But, John, the guys out there are not going to be happy if I don't testify." He did not say who "the guys" were—but Dowd knew he meant the Trump base, the crowds at his rallies, the Fox News watchers, the deplorables.

"What are they going to think when Mueller requests an indictment for 1001 violations?" Dowd asked, referring to false statements.

"No, no, I'm a good witness. I'll be a real good witness."

Dowd knew this was self-delusion, total bullshit. He had earlier told the president an anecdote from a lawyer friend in Florida who had once taken Trump's deposition. When the lawyer had asked him what he did for a living, it had taken Trump about 16 pages to answer the question.

"You are not a good witness," Dowd said again. Some people simply were not. Dowd offered an example. "Mr. President, you remember Raj Rajaratnam?"

"The hedge fund guy," Trump recalled. Dowd had represented Rajaratnam, the billionaire founder of Galleon Group who was found guilty in 2011 of insider trading and sentenced to 11 years in prison.

"Brilliant guy," Dowd said. "If you just sat down at a table and talked to him, you'd say, he was one of the most gifted, eloquent guys I ever met. He can talk about anything. Mr. President, when I got him ready to testify, just for five minutes on a motion, he wet himself. He suddenly became so nervous—I mean, he couldn't . . . And then when I got him on direct, he could barely answer his own name. It's just the nature of the beast, and I am an expert in that beast.

"Mr. President, I'm afraid I just can't help you," Dowd said.

He told the president he had every right to be pissed off at Mueller.

"They're not going to impeach you. Are you shitting me? They're a bunch of cowards, the whole town. The media, the Congress. They're gutless. What's the impeachment going to be, for exercising

Article II? Huh? Hello? Hello, I want to hear Speaker Ryan take that one up before the Rules Committee and the Judiciary Committee."

It is the press, Trump said. "They're kicking the crap out of me."

"Mr. President, you're the one that didn't give up your tax returns. You've already won round one. They're sore as hell. They hate you. They hate your guts."

What does the press want? Trump asked.

"I'd pull all their credentials. I'd throw them the fuck out of here. I don't think they have any right to come into the White House and behave the way they do."

Trump said that was his sentiment. "But I always get overruled, John. They"—Hope Hicks and Kelly—"overrule me every time I want to pull someone's credentials."

The press, Mueller, Congress, Dowd said, "We ought to tell them to go fuck themselves. And let's get back to being president of the United States. Because compared to what you do every day, this is a gnat on an elephant's ass. And we've got to treat it that way and get going." Dowd considered it his closing argument.

"You're a great guy," Trump said. "I thank you. I'm sorry to keep you up so late."

The next morning Dowd told his wife, Carole, "I'm gone." He called the president and said he was resigning. "I'm sorry I am resigning. I love you. I back you. And I wish you the very best. But if you're not going to take my advice, I cannot represent you."

"I understand your frustration," the president said. "You've done a great job."

"Mr. President, anything else I can do for you, call me anytime."

"Thank you."

Two minutes later, *The New York Times* called Dowd, and *The Washington Post* called. Dowd could see Trump picking up the phone and imagined him calling Maggie Haberman at the *Times*. "Maggie? Fucking Dowd just resigned." Trump always liked to be the first to deliver the news.

At least Dowd felt he'd gotten ahead of it, had resigned before being fired and getting his ass trashed.

Dowd remained convinced that Mueller never had a Russian case or an obstruction case. He was looking for the perjury trap. And in a brutally honest self-evaluation, he believed that Mueller had played him, and the president, for suckers in order to get their cooperation on witnesses and documents.

Dowd was disappointed in Mueller, pulling such a sleight of hand.

After 47 years, Dowd knew the game, knew prosecutors. They built cases. With all the testimony and documents, Mueller could string together something that would look bad. Maybe they had something new and damning as he now more than half-suspected. Maybe some witness like Flynn had changed his testimony. Things like that happened and that could change the ball game dramatically. Former top aide comes clean, admits to lying, turns on the president. Dowd didn't think so but he had to worry and consider the possibility.

Some things were clear and many were not in such a complex, tangled investigation. There was no perfect X-ray, no tapes, no engineer's drawing. Dowd believed that the president had not colluded with Russia or obstructed justice.

But in the man and his presidency Dowd had seen the tragic flaw. In the political back-and-forth, the evasions, the denials, the tweeting, the obscuring, crying "Fake News," the indignation, Trump had one overriding problem that Dowd knew but could not bring himself to say to the president: "You're a fucking liar."

Acknowledgments

This is my 19th book with Alice Mayhew, my editor at Simon & Schuster, over the last 46 years. Alice understood immediately, in the midst of the Trump presidency with all its controversies and investigations, the importance of finding out what Trump actually did as president in foreign and domestic policy. It was Alice's full and brilliant engagement on the concept for the book, the pace, structure and tone.

Jonathan Karp, president and publisher of Simon & Schuster Adult Publishing, is at the top of his game. He devoted time and his keen intellect to this book. He helped edit and thought through the opportunities, responsibilities and dilemmas of publishing a book about President Trump in this convulsive era. I owe him much. He used to be the Boy Wonder; now he is the Middle Age Wonder but still has the Boy Wonder's energy.

I thank Carolyn K. Reidy, the CEO at Simon & Schuster, who for decades has sponsored and promoted my work.

At Simon & Schuster I thank the following: Stuart Roberts, Alice Mayhew's talented, energetic and thoughtful assistant, and Richard Rhorer, Cary Goldstein, Stephen Bedford, Irene Kheradi, Kristen Lemire, Lisa Erwin, Lisa Healy, Lewelin Polanco, Joshua Cohen, Laura Tatum, Katie Haigler, Toby Yuen, Kate Mertes and Elisa Rivlin.

My special thanks to Fred Chase, traveling counselor and extraordinary copy editor, who spent a week in Washington with Evelyn and myself. Fred loves words and ideas. In that week he went through the manuscript three times with meticulous care and wisdom. We call Fred the Fixer, which he does on nearly every page with his sharp red and green pencils.

I wish I had taken careful notes over the last two years of my regular conversations with Carl Bernstein, my Nixon-Watergate partner, as we discussed Trump. We did not always agree but I loved those talks and the deep insights he has about the presidency, Washington and the media. The friendship and affection for Carl is one of the half-dozen joys of my life.

The Washington Post has generously kept me on as an associate editor. I associate very little these days because I rarely go to the *Washington Post* in downtown Washington but work out of my office at home. And my editing might, at most, be a phone conversation with a reporter who has a query, often about the past. Associate editor is a wonderful title, however, and allows me to keep connected to my journalist roots. The *Post* has been my institutional home and family for 47 years. It is run exceptionally well these days, doing some of the best, most aggressive and necessary journalism of the Trump era. My thanks to Marty Baron, the executive editor, Cameron Barr, the managing editor, Jeff Leen, the investigations editor, Robert Costa, Tom Hamburger, Rosalind Helderman, David Fahrenthold, Karen Tumulty, Philip Rucker, Robert O'Harrow, Amy Goldstein, Scott Wilson, Steven Ginsberg, Peter Wallsten, Dan Balz, Lucy Shackelford and countless others at the *Post*.

I thank many old colleagues and friends there at the *Post* or once there: Don Graham, Sally Quinn, David Maraniss, Rick Atkinson, Christian Williams, Paul Richard, Patrick Tyler, Tom Wilkinson, Leonard Downie Jr., Marcus Brauchli, Steve Coll, Steve Luxenberg, Scott Armstrong, Al Kamen, Ben Weiser, Martha Sherrill, Bill Powers, Carlos Lozada, Fred Hiatt, John Feinstein and publisher Fred Ryan.

Many thanks to Michael Kranish and Marc Fisher, who assembled a group of reporters from the *Post*, including myself, to report on Trump before the election. The result was Michael and Marc's book, *Trump Revealed*, one of the best sources on the president-to-be. It includes more than 20 hours of interviews with Trump.

All those still employed by or connected to the *Post* have reason to be thankful that Jeff Bezos, the Amazon founder and CEO, is owner of the *Post*. He has spent time and a great deal of money to give the newspaper the extra reporting and editing resources to make in-depth examinations. The independent newspaper culture fostered, and rigorously supported, by Katharine Graham and Don Graham is alive and well.

A book on the sitting president owes much to the journalism, writing and books that have gone before. There is so much on Trump already in the vortex of the 24/7 daily news. It is no longer a cycle but a steady stream. This book is based on my own reporting but it is inevitable that ideas or information were supplied directly or indirectly from other publications and news accounts. I owe an immense debt to all who have written on Trump and this political era, especially from *The Washington Post*, *The New York Times*, *The Wall Street Journal*, *Axios* and *Politico*.

Robert B. Barnett, my lawyer, counselor and friend, once again did his marvelous work. Wedded to the concept of total devotion to his clients, he delivered the full support package. Bob knows Washington politics and New York publishing like no one else, and uses that knowledge with ingenuity and devotion to his clients.

Evelyn and I are fortunate for the presence, care and kindness of Rosa Criollo and Jackie Crowe.

Deep appreciation and love to Tali Woodward, my oldest daughter, who is the director of the Master of Arts program at Columbia Journalism School. She regularly provided wise counsel. And my love to her husband, Gabe Roth, and their two children, Zadie and Theo—my grandchildren.

Diana Woodward, our youngest daughter, is entering her senior year at Yale where she majors in humanities and psychology. When she returns during college breaks she brings that spark and joy we miss so much around the house.

This book is dedicated to Elsa Walsh, my wife, known widely as the Kindness Lady because she lives by Henry James's words on the importance and centrality of kindness. For Elsa this is not just unselfish appreciation for each person but reverence for each. This is the 15th book in the 37 years we have been together. A former reporter for *The Washington Post* and staff writer for *The New Yorker*, Elsa loves people, ideas and books. She applied her natural, well-practiced and demanding editing skills to this book. I am forever grateful. I cannot thank her enough for her love and support. Over the years, I have developed a permanent respect for her judgment. I often ask, How does she know? Where does this intellect come from? I have never found the complete answer to those questions. But I get to see her magic in daily life. I cherish her—partner and the love of my life.

Source Notes

PROLOGUE

The information in this chapter comes primarily from multiple deep background interviews with firsthand sources.

xviii *But now there was the letter:* Author obtained document.
xxii *"More than anything else, it's":* On-the-record interview with Donald J. Trump, March 31, 2016.

CHAPTER 1

The information in this chapter comes primarily from multiple deep background interviews with firsthand sources. See also *Let Trump Be Trump* by Corey Lewandowski and David Bossie (New York: Hachette, 2017).

2 *Trump had once given Bannon:* "Bannon's 'Victory Sessions' Goes National," *Breitbart*, February 23, 2012.

CHAPTER 2

The information in this chapter comes primarily from multiple deep background interviews with firsthand sources.

8 *"The Failing Inside Mission":* Alexander Burns and Maggie Haberman, "The Failing Inside Mission to Tame Trump's Tongue," *The New York Times*, August 14, 2016, p. A1. (Available online at https://www.nytimes.com/2016/08/14/us/politics/donald-trump-campaign-gop.html.)

11 *The* Times *article about the failure:* Ibid.

13 *Trump had appeared on a series:* David A. Fahrenthold and Frances Stead Sellers, "How Bannon Flattered and Coaxed Trump on Policies Key to the Alt-Right," *The Washington Post*, November 15, 2016.

15 *In an August 8 speech:* Donald J. Trump, "Remarks to the Detroit Economic Club," August 8, 2016. Online by Gerhard Peters and John T. Woolley, *The American Presidency Project.* http://www.presidency.ucsb .edu/ws/?pid=119744.

18 *It had been great when Trump released:* Louis Nelson, "Trump Outlines 10-Point Plan to Reform Veterans Affairs Department," *Politico*, July 11, 2016.

CHAPTER 3

The information in this chapter comes primarily from multiple deep background interviews with firsthand sources.

20 *But the New York* Daily News *had:* Jennifer Fermino, "Senior Donald Trump Adviser Appears to Be Fan of NYC Bondage, Swinger's Club," New York *Daily News*, April 12, 2016.

21 *"I need you to look at something":* Andrew E. Kramer, Mike McIntire and Barry Meier, "Secret Ledger in Ukraine Lists Cash for Donald Trump's Campaign Chief," *The New York Times*, August 14, 2016.

22 *The* Times *article on Manafort:* Ibid.

23 *For all the abuse:* Bob Cusack, "Trump Slams RNC Chairman, Calls 2016 Process 'A Disgrace,'" *The Hill*, April 12, 2016.

24 The New York Times *reported:* Jonathan Martin, Jim Rutenberg and Maggie Haberman, "Donald Trump Appoints Media Firebrand to Run Campaign," *The New York Times*, August 17, 2016.

26 *On August 22,* Time *magazine:* View the cover online at http://time.com /magazine/us/4447970/august-22nd-2016-vol-188-no-7-u-s/.

CHAPTER 4

The information in this chapter comes primarily from multiple deep background interviews with firsthand sources.

The in-depth and wide-ranging 2017 *Yahoo News/Huffington Post* oral history project "64 Hours in October: How One Weekend Blew up the Rules of American Politics" was a helpful resource throughout this chapter. It was reported by Michael Isikoff, Dylan Stableford, Hunter Walker, Holly Bailey, Liz Goodwin, Lisa Belkin, Garance Franke-Ruta and Gabby Kaufman, and written by Dylan Stableford. Read it here: https://www.huffingtonpost.com/entry /yahoo-64-hours-october-american-politics_us_59d7c567e4b072637c43dd1c.

27 *The first showed up:* Pam Fessler, "10 Months After Election Day, Feds Tell States More About Russian Hacking," NPR, September 22, 2017.

28 *In July of 2016, WikiLeaks:* Eric Lipton, David E. Sanger and Scott Shane, "The Perfect Weapon: How Russian Cyberpower Invaded the U.S.," *The New York Times*, December 13, 2016; Ellen Nakashima, "Cybersecurity Firm Finds Evidence That Russian Military Unit Was Behind DNC Hack," *The Washington Post*, December 22, 2016.

28 *The next day, August 5:* Michael J. Morell, "I Ran the C.I.A. Now I'm Endorsing Hillary Clinton," *The New York Times*, August 5, 2016.

29 *At 3 p.m. on Friday:* Joint Statement from the Department of Homeland Security and Office of the Director of National Intelligence on Election Security, Department of Homeland Security [archived], October 7, 2016.

29 *But one hour later:* David A. Fahrenthold, "Trump Recorded Having Extremely Lewd Conversation About Women in 2005," *The Washington Post*, October 8, 2016.

30 *"I expected it to be something":* Yahoo News Staff, "64 Hours in October: How One Weekend Blew Up the Rules of American Politics," *Yahoo News/ Huffington Post*, October 6, 2017.

30 *Trump issued a brief statement:* David A. Fahrenthold, "Trump Recorded Having Extremely Lewd Conversation About Women in 2005," *The Washington Post*, October 8, 2016.

30 *After midnight—and hours:* "Transcript of Donald Trump's Videotaped Apology," *The New York Times*, October 8, 2016.

33 *Just before 1 p.m., Pence:* Yahoo News Staff, "64 Hours in October: How One Weekend Blew Up the Rules of American Politics," *Yahoo News/Huffington Post*, October 6, 2017.

34 *Two hours later, Melania Trump:* Ibid.

34 *At 3:40 p.m., Trump tweeted:* Ibid.

36 *Will you stay in the race?:* Ibid.

36 *Priebus, Christie, even the reliable:* Brent Griffiths, "Trump Campaign Manager Reemerges to Show Support for GOP Nominee," *Politico*, October 9, 2016; *State of the Union* transcript, CNN, October 9, 2016.

36 *Giuliani gave, or tried: Meet the Press* transcript, NBC, October 9, 2016.

36 *The "transformational" presidential campaign: Fox News Sunday* transcript, Fox News, October 9, 2016.

36 *When CNN's Jake Tapper: State of the Union* transcript, CNN, October 9, 2016.

36 *He had pulled out every stop: This Week* transcript, ABC, October 9, 2016.

CHAPTER 5

The information in this chapter comes primarily from multiple deep background interviews with firsthand sources.

The in-depth and wide-ranging 2017 *Yahoo News/Huffington Post* oral history project "64 Hours in October: How One Weekend Blew Up the Rules of American Politics" was a helpful resource throughout this chapter.

38 *Giuliani had said twice: State of the Union* transcript, CNN, October 9, 2016; *Meet the Press* transcript, NBC, October 9, 2016.
39 *Just before 7:30 p.m.:* Yahoo News Staff, "64 Hours in October: How One Weekend Blew Up the Rules of American Politics," *Yahoo News/Huffington Post*, October 6, 2017.
39 *At 7:26, Trump tweeted:* Ibid.
39 *Early on, CNN's Anderson Cooper:* Presidential Debate at Washington University in St. Louis, Missouri, transcript, Commission on Presidential Debates, October 9, 2016.
44 *They were using Pence well:* Pence's campaign appearances were recorded by the nonpartisan P2016: *Race for the White House,* http://www.p2016 .org/trump/pencecal1116.html.
44 *Two days before the election: Fox News Sunday* transcript, Fox News, November 6, 2016.
45 *"If we don't win":* Donald J. Trump, "Remarks at J. S. Dorton Arena in Raleigh, North Carolina," November 7, 2016. Online by Gerhard Peters and John T. Woolley, *The American Presidency Project.* http://www .presidency.ucsb.edu/ws/?pid=122536.
45 *According to Clinton's book:* Hillary Clinton, *What Happened* (New York: Simon & Schuster, 2017), p. 378.
45 *The state was called:* Lauren Easton, "Calling the Presidential Race State by State," AP, https://blog.ap.org/behind-the-news/calling-the-presidential -race-state-by-state.
45 *It was announced he had won:* Ibid.
46 *The AP called Wisconsin:* Ibid.
46 *"Now it's time for Americans":* Donald J. Trump, "Remarks in New York City Accepting Election as the 45th President of the United States," November 9, 2016. Online by Gerhard Peters and John T. Woolley, *The American Presidency Project.* http://www.presidency.ucsb.edu/ws/?pid=119495.
46 *The president-elect dwelled:* Ibid.
48 *The press release listed:* Donald J. Trump, "Press release—President-Elect Donald J. Trump Announces Senior White House Leadership Team," November 13, 2016. Online by Gerhard Peters and John T. Woolley, *The American Presidency Project.* http://www.presidency.ucsb.edu/ws/?pid =119641.

CHAPTER 6

The information in this chapter comes primarily from multiple deep background interviews with firsthand sources.

54 *When he was nominated as secretary:* Trump announced at a Cincinnati rally on December 1, 2016, that he would nominate Mattis for secretary of defense.

54 *"A very Trumpian-inspired":* Chris Cillizza, "Here's Why Donald Trump Picked Rex Tillerson as Secretary of State," *The Washington Post*, December 13, 2016. Conway gave her comments on a December 12, 2016, episode of MSNBC's *Andrea Mitchell Reports*.

CHAPTER 7

The information in this chapter comes primarily from multiple deep background interviews with firsthand sources.

58 *Cohn didn't mention a report:* Christine Giordano, "Trump's Business Credit Score Is 19 Out of a Possible 100," Fox Business, October 20, 2016.

59 *Five minutes later while Cohn:* Donald J. Trump, "Press release—President-Elect Donald J. Trump to Nominate Steven Mnuchin as Secretary of the Treasury, Wilbur Ross as Secretary of Commerce and Todd Ricketts as Deputy Secretary of Commerce," November 30, 2016. Online by Gerhard Peters and John T. Woolley, *The American Presidency Project*. http://www.presidency.ucsb.edu/ws/?pid=119711.

60 *The day after Christmas:* Interview with Michael Flynn, December 26, 2016.

61 *Flynn was being widely criticized:* Rosalind S. Helderman and Tom Hamburger, "Trump Adviser Flynn Paid by multiple Russia-Related Entities, New Records Show," *The Washington Post*, March 16, 2017.

CHAPTER 8

The information in this chapter comes primarily from multiple deep background interviews with firsthand sources.

62 *An unclassified, scaled-back version:* Read the unclassified version of the intelligence community's January 6, 2017, report on the Director of National Intelligence (DNI) website at https://www.dni.gov/files/documents/ICA_2017_01.pdf.

63 *Steele had shared portions:* Max Greenwood, "McCain Gave Dossier Containing 'Sensitive Information' to FBI," *The Hill*, January 11, 2017.

64 *On the second page it said:* Ken Bensinger, Miriam Elder and Mark Schoofs, "These Reports Allege Trump Has Deep Ties to Russia," BuzzFeed News, January 10, 2017.

64 *This was designed to obtain:* Ibid.

65 *On December 9, Trump said:* Nahal Toosi, "Trump Team Rejects Intel Agencies' Claims of Russian Meddling," *Politico*, December 9, 2016.

65 *He later told Fox News:* "Trump: Claims of Russian Interference in 2016 Race 'Ridiculous,' Dems Making Excuses," Fox News, December 11, 2016.

65   *He tweeted, "Unless you catch":* View Trump's tweet at https://twitter
.com/realdonaldtrump/status/808300706914594816.

65   *Angry at the criticism:* Martin Matishak and Connor O'Brien, "Clapper:
Trump Rhetoric on Intel Agencies Alarming U.S. Allies," *Politico*, January
5, 2017.

65   *The next day, Kellyanne Conway:* Louis Nelson, "Conway 'Disappointed'
in Media Leaks Before Intel Briefing," *Politico*, January 6, 2017.

65   *In a telephone interview:* Michael D. Shear and David E. Sanger, "Putin
Led a Complex Cyberattack Scheme to Aid Trump, Report Finds," *The
New York Times*, January 6, 2017.

66   *In his book, Comey offers:* James Comey, *A Higher Loyalty* (New York:
Flatiron Books, 2018), p. 218.

67   *Russia has had a long-standing desire:* Read the unclassified version of the
intelligence community's January 6, 2017, report on the DNI website at
https://www.dni.gov/files/documents/ICA_2017_01.pdf.

67   *Trump was a "clear preference":* Ibid.

68   *Comey later wrote, "I figured":* James Comey, *A Higher Loyalty* (New
York: Flatiron Books, 2018), p. 224.

68   *In* A Higher Loyalty, *Comey wrote:* Ibid., p. 216.

69   *This is what Comey wrote:* Ibid., p. 225.

69   *After the briefing Trump released:* Louis Nelson, "Trump Says Hacking
Had 'No Effect on the Outcome of the Election,'" *Politico*, January 6,
2017.

69   *Four days later, January 10:* Ken Bensinger, Miriam Elder and Mark
Schoofs, "These Reports Allege Trump Has Deep Ties to Russia," Buzz-
Feed News, January 10, 2017.

70   *In* Facts and Fears, *Clapper:* James R. Clapper, *Facts and Fears* (New York:
Penguin, 2018), p. 4.

70   *In* A Higher Loyalty, *published:* James Comey, *A Higher Loyalty* (New
York: Flatiron Books, 2018), p. 216.

71   *On January 15, five days: Fox News Sunday* transcript, Fox News, January
15, 2017.

71   *Later that afternoon Trump tweeted:* View Trump's tweet at https://
twitter.com/realdonaldtrump/status/820723387995717632.

CHAPTER 9

The information in this chapter comes primarily from multiple deep background interviews with firsthand sources.

73   *A lot went wrong:* For some of the best public accounts of this event,
see Eric Schmitt and David E. Sanger, "Raid in Yemen: Risky from the
Start and Costly in the End," *The New York Times*, February 1, 2017;
and Thomas Gibbons-Neff and Missy Ryan, "In Deadly Yemen Raid, a

Lesson for Trump's National Security Team," *The Washington Post*, January 31, 2017.

73 *Owens's father, Bill Owens:* Julie K. Brown, "Slain SEAL's Dad Wants Answers: 'Don't Hide Behind My Son's Death,'" *Miami Herald*, February 26, 2017.

73 *He later also said*: Ibid.

74 *"I can understand people saying"*: Nolan D. McCaskill, "Trump Deflects Responsibility on Yemen Raid: 'They Lost Ryan,'" *Politico*, February 28, 2017.

74 *In an interview on Fox*: Ibid.

74 *To the congressional audience:* Donald J. Trump, "Address Before a Joint Session of the Congress," February 28, 2017. Online by Gerhard Peters and John T. Woolley, *The American Presidency Project*. http://www.presidency.ucsb.edu/ws/?pid=123408.

76 *As a private citizen Mattis:* Carla Marinucci, "Ex-Military Leaders at Hoover Institution Say Trump Statements Threaten America's Interests," *Politico*, July 15, 2016.

76 *Senator John McCain, displaying:* Emma Loop, "John McCain Says the Recent Yemen Raid Was a 'Failure,'" BuzzFeed News, February 7, 2017.

78 *Under the Brexit referendum:* Great Britain's Brexit referendum was held on June 23, 2016.

79 *In his speech in Munich:* "Intervention by Secretary of Defense Mattis, Session One of the North Atlantic Council," NATO Defense Ministerial, February 15, 2017.

79 *Nonetheless he said:* "U.S. Defense Chief Says NATO Is 'Fundamental Bedrock,'" Reuters, February 15, 2017.

79 *At a news conference:* Donald J. Trump, "The President's News Conference with Secretary General Jens Stoltenberg of the North Atlantic Treaty Organization," April 12, 2017. Online by Gerhard Peters and John T. Woolley, *The American Presidency Project*. http://www.presidency.ucsb.edu/ws/?pid=123739.

79 *When Trump met the European leaders:* Donald J. Trump, "Remarks at the Dedication Ceremony for the Berlin Wall Memorial and the 9/11 and Article 5 Memorial in Brussels, Belgium," May 25, 2017. Online by Gerhard Peters and John T. Woolley, *The American Presidency Project*. http://www.presidency.ucsb.edu/ws/?pid=125840.

CHAPTER 10

The information in this chapter comes primarily from multiple deep background interviews with firsthand sources.

80 *What the hell! Priebus thought:* Greg Miller, Adam Entous and Ellen Nakashima, "National Security Adviser Flynn Discussed Sanctions with

Russian Ambassador, Despite Denials, Officials Say," *The Washington Post*, February 9, 2017.

81 *The* Post *story, carrying the bylines:* Ibid.

81 *According to a six-page internal:* Author obtained document.

82 *President-elect Trump praised Putin:* View Trump's tweet at https://twitter .com/realdonaldtrump/status/814919370711461890.

82 *Flynn's resignation was announced:* Greg Miller and Philip Rucker, "Michael Flynn Resigns as National Security Adviser," *The Washington Post*, February 14, 2017.

82 *His statement said, "I accept":* Carol D. Leonnig, Adam Entous, Devlin Barrett and Matt Zapotosky, "Michael Flynn Pleads Guilty to Lying to FBI on Contacts with Russian Ambassador," *The Washington Post*, December 1, 2017.

84 *Trump had raised hell about McCabe's wife:* D'Angelo Gore, "Clinton's Connection to FBI Official," FactCheck.org, October 25, 2016.

84 *She had received $675,288:* Ibid.; see also D'Angelo Gore, "Trump Wrong About Campaign Donations," FactCheck.org, July 26, 2017.

84 *He had not let go of the issue:* View Trump's tweets at: https://twitter .com/realdonaldtrump/status/889792764363276288; https://twitter.com /realdonaldtrump/status/890207082926022656; https://twitter.com/real donaldtrump/status/890208319566229504.

84 *"You know this story in* The New York Times?*":* Michael S. Schmidt, Mark Mazzetti and Matt Apuzzo, "Trump Campaign Aides Had Repeated Contacts with Russian Intelligence," *The New York Times*, February 14, 2017.

85 *About a week later on February 24:* Jim Sciutto, Evan Perez, Shimon Prokupecz, Manu Raju and Pamela Brown, "FBI Refused White House Request to Knock Down Recent Trump-Russia Stories," CNN, February 24, 2017.

85 *Four months later on June 8:* Michael S. Schmidt, Mark Mazzetti and Matt Apuzzo, "Comey Disputes New York Times Article About Russia Investigation," *The New York Times*, June 8, 2017.

CHAPTER 11

The information in this chapter comes primarily from multiple deep background interviews with firsthand sources.

89 *"I just wanted to announce":* Donald J. Trump, "Remarks on the Appointment of Lieutenant General H. R. McMaster (USA) as National Security Adviser in Palm Beach, Florida, and an Exchange with Reporters," February 20, 2017. Online by Gerhard Peters and John T. Woolley, *The American Presidency Project*. http://www.presidency.ucsb.edu/ ws/?pid=123396.

CHAPTER 12

The information in this chapter comes primarily from multiple deep background interviews with firsthand sources.

91   *Dispelling any doubt:* Christine Kim, "Voice of Triumph or Doom: North Korean Presenter Back in Limelight for Nuclear Test," Reuters, September 4, 2017.

92   *The North's nuclear weapons center:* Matt Clinch, "Here's the Full Statement from North Korea on Nuclear Test," CNBC, September 9, 2016.

92   *To compound the potential:* See the CNS North Korea Missile Test Database, available for download at http://www.nti.org/analysis/articles/cns-north-korea-missile-test-database/.

95   *Former U.S. negotiator Robert Gallucci:* Panel discussion on U.S. policy on North Korea at George Washington University, August 28, 2017, Washington, D.C. Video is available at https://www.c-span.org/video/?433122-1/us-policy-north-korea.

95   *Trump had a history of public statements:* Rebecca Shabad, "Timeline: What Has Trump Said About North Korea over the Years?" CBS News, August 10, 2017.

95   *In a 2016 campaign speech:* Ibid.

95   *In May of 2016, he told Reuters:* Ibid.

95   *As president, in 2017:* Ibid.

97   *He condemned the North's:* Barack Obama, "Statement on North Korea's Nuclear Test," September 9, 2016. Online by Gerhard Peters and John T. Woolley, *The American Presidency Project.* http://www.presidency.ucsb.edu/ws/?pid=118931.

98   *To maximize shock value:* Elizabeth Weise, "Sony Pictures Entertainment Hacked," *USA Today*, November 24, 2014.

CHAPTER 13

The information in this chapter comes primarily from multiple deep background interviews with firsthand sources.

99   *Former vice president Joe Biden:* Bob Woodward, *Obama's Wars* (New York: Simon & Schuster, 2010), p. 62.

100   *He'd called Trump a "jackass":* Nicholas Fandos, "Lindsey Graham Destroys Cellphone After Donald Trump Discloses His Number," *The New York Times*, July 22, 2015.

100   *He endorsed Jeb Bush:* Cheri Cheng, "Lindsey Graham Endorses Presidential Candidate Jeb Bush," *News EveryDay*, January 15, 2016.

100   *Graham and McCain had released:* "Statement by Senators McCain and Graham on Executive Order on Immigration," January 29, 2017.

102   *Just days before, on March 5:* See the CNS North Korea Missile Test

Database, available for download at http://www.nti.org/analysis/articles/cns-north-korea-missile-test-database/.

103 *The week prior, on March 4:* View Trump's tweets at https://twitter.com/realdonaldtrump/status/837989835818287106; https://twitter.com/realdonaldtrump/status/837993273679560704; https://twitter.com/realdonaldtrump/status/837994257566863360; https://twitter.com/realdonaldtrump/status/837996746236182529.

104 *In 2015, Trump had made:* Jonathan Martin and Alan Rappeport, "Donald Trump Says John McCain Is No War Hero, Setting Off Another Storm," *The New York Times*, July 18, 2015.

105 *During a spring meeting:* Adriana Diaz, "U.S. THAAD Missile System a Factor in South Korea's Presidential Election," CBS News, May 8, 2017.

106 *Trump later told Reuters:* Stephen J. Adler, Jeff Mason and Steve Holland, "Exclusive: Trump Vows to Fix or Scrap South Korean Trade Deal, Wants Missile System Payment," Reuters, April 27, 2017.

107 *He told Chris Wallace on Fox News:* "McMaster Says U.S. Will Pay for THAAD Antimissile System in South Korea," Fox News, April 30, 2017.

107 *As a first step:* "South Korea Trade Ministry Says Ready to Begin Renegotiating U.S. Trade Pact," Reuters, December 17, 2017.

CHAPTER 14

The information in this chapter comes primarily from multiple deep background interviews with firsthand sources.

110 *McMaster, angry with Harvey:* McMaster fired Harvey on July 27, 2017.

114 *When it looked like they were:* Julie Hirschfeld Davis, "Trump Meets Saudi Prince as U.S. and Kingdom Seek Warmer Relations," *The New York Times*, March 14, 2017.

114 *Trump finally gave the go-ahead:* Mark Landler and Peter Baker, "Saudi Arabia and Israel Will Be on Itinerary of Trump's First Foreign Trip," *The New York Times*, May 4, 2017.

114 *He announced $110 billion:* Aaron Mehta, "Revealed: Trump's $110 Billion Weapons List for the Saudis," *DefenseNews*, June 8, 2017.

114 *The next month Saudi king Salman:* Sudarsan Raghavan and Kareem Fahaim, "Saudi King Names Son as New Crown Prince, Upending the Royal Succession," *The Washington Post*, June 21, 2017.

CHAPTER 15

The information in this chapter comes primarily from multiple deep background interviews with firsthand sources.

115 *Beginning in 2011, four years:* View Trump's tweet at https://twitter.com/realdonaldtrump/status/122396588336349184.

115   *In March 2012, he tweeted:* View Trump's tweet at https://twitter.com /realdonaldtrump/status/179270017064513536.

115   *In January, it was, "Let's get out":* View Trump's tweet at https://twitter .com/realdonaldtrump/status/289807790178959360.

115   *In March, "We should leave":* View Trump's tweet at https://twitter.com /realdonaldtrump/status/307568422789709824.

115   *In April, "Our gov't is so pathetic":* View Trump's tweet at https://twitter .com/realdonaldtrump/status/324590961827143681.

115   *And in November, "Do not allow":* View Trump's tweet at https://twitter .com/realdonaldtrump/status/403511109942247424.

116   *And in December 2015, Trump tweeted:* View Trump's tweet at https:// twitter.com/realdonaldtrump/status/679000573241393154.

116   *White House coordinator:* Bob Woodward, *Obama's Wars* (New York: Simon & Schuster, 2010), p. 361.

117   *President Bush had publicly cited:* Transcript, "President Bush Discusses the War in Iraq," CQ Transcripts Wire, March 20, 2006.

122   *In a May 31 op-ed in* The Wall Street Journal: Erik D. Prince, "The Mac-Arthur Model for Afghanistan," *The Wall Street Journal*, May 31, 2017.

123   *For years the CIA had run:* Bob Woodward, *Obama's Wars* (New York: Simon & Schuster, 2010), p. 8.

123   *On July 18, Trump had lunch:* Ben Jacobs, "In Town Pool Report #3," 1:12 p.m., July 18, 2017, http://www.presidency.ucsb.edu/report.php?pid=2365.

124   *The National Security Council gathered:* Author review of contemporaneous notes by a participant.

126   *Later in the day those:* Ibid.

126   *That evening, Priebus hosted:* Ibid.

CHAPTER 16

The information in this chapter comes primarily from multiple deep background interviews with firsthand sources.

129   *In February, Trump had called it:* Donald J. Trump, "The President's News Conference with Prime Minister Benjamin Netanyahu of Israel," February 15, 2017. Online by Gerhard Peters and John T. Woolley, *The American Presidency Project*. http://www.presidency.ucsb.edu/ws/?pid=123361.

129   *As a candidate in 2016, he had said:* Donald J. Trump, "Remarks at the AIPAC Policy Conference in Washington, DC," March 21, 2016. Online by Gerhard Peters and John T. Woolley, *The American Presidency Project*. http://www.presidency.ucsb.edu/ws/?pid=116597.

130   *He directed that the short letter:* "Tillerson: Iran Remains a Leading State Sponsor of Terror," Breitbart News, April 20, 2017.

130   *In a five-minute presentation, Tillerson:* See Tillerson's comments as part of the transcript of *The Lead with Jake Tapper*, CNN, April 19, 2017, http://transcripts.cnn.com/TRANSCRIPTS/1704/19/cg.01.html.

CHAPTER 17

The information in this chapter comes primarily from multiple deep background interviews with firsthand sources.

134 *At a rally in June 2016*: Full transcript: "Donald Trump's Jobs Plan Speech," *Politico*, June 28, 2016.
134 *"This is the president's vision"*: Peter Coy, "After Defeating Cohn, Trump's Trade Warrior Is on the Rise Again," Bloomberg, March 8, 2018.
138 *Each month Cohn brought:* JOLTS numbers are publicly available at https://www.bls.gov/jlt/.
138 *He came into the job with five-star:* Foremost among those recommending him was Brett Kavanaugh, who had been staff secretary to President George W. Bush. Bush appointed Kavanaugh to a judgeship on the powerful District of Columbia Court of Appeals. He was nominated to the Supreme Court by President Trump on July 9, 2018.

CHAPTER 18

The information in this chapter comes primarily from multiple deep background interviews with firsthand sources.

144 *Bannon was convinced that Jared:* See Emily Crane and Cheyenne Roundtree, "Donald's Eruption in the Oval Office: Video Emerges of Trump's 'Furious Argument' with Top Adviser Steven Bannon as Ivanka and Jared Look On, Hours Before President Made Phone Tapping Claims," *Daily Mail*, March 5, 2017.
145 *For his part, he was convinced:* See Michael S. Schmidt, Matthew Rosenberg and Matt Apuzzo, "Kushner and Flynn Met with Russian Envoy in December, White House Says," *The New York Times*, March 2, 2017.
146 *The later event for Modi:* Max Bearak, "Modi's 'No Frills' Visit to Washington Masks a Potential Minefield," *The Washington Post*, June 26, 2017.
147 *In 2014 he said, "We mark":* Barack Obama, "Statement on the Elimination of Syria's Declared Chemical Weapons Stockpile," August 18, 2014. Online by Gerhard Peters and John T. Woolley, *The American Presidency Project*. http://www.presidency.ucsb.edu/ws/?pid=106702.
147 *"We got 100 percent of the chemical":* John Kerry interview with David Gregory, *Meet the Press*, NBC, July 20, 2014.
147 *In 2016, DNI Clapper said publicly:* Peter Baker, "For Obama, Syria Chemical Attack Shows Risk of 'Deals with Dictators,'" *The New York Times*, April 9, 2017.
149 *In a public statement on April 4:* Donald J. Trump, "Statement on the Chemical Weapons Attack in Khan Sheikhoun, Syria," April 4, 2017.

Online by Gerhard Peters and John T. Woolley, *The American Presidency Project*. http://www.presidency.ucsb.edu/ws/?pid=123681.

152 *Graham knew Trump-speak:* The next day Putin called the attack an "illegal act of aggression" and canceled an agreement to prevent midair incidents between U.S. and Russian jets over Syria called deflection.

153 *The next morning, Senator John McCain:* "Sen. John McCain, R-Ariz, Is Interviewed on MSNBC's 'Morning Joe,'" Federal News Service, April 7, 2017.

153 *Anne-Marie Slaughter, who had been:* View Slaughter's tweet at https://twitter.com/slaughteram/status/850263058756673540.

CHAPTER 19

The information in this chapter comes primarily from multiple deep background interviews with firsthand sources.

156 *An emergency meeting was called:* Author review of contemporaneous notes by a participant.

158 *Sonny Perdue gave a presentation:* Author review of contemporaneous notes by a participant.

159 *A New York Times headline read:* Gina Chon and Pete Sweeney, "China Surrenders Little to U.S. in First Round of Trade Talks," *The New York Times*, May 12, 2017.

160 *The president held a meeting:* Author review of contemporaneous notes by a participant.

CHAPTER 20

The information in this chapter comes primarily from multiple deep background interviews with firsthand sources.

163 *He brought a three-page memo:* Rosenstein's memo is available at https://assets.documentcloud.org/documents/3711188/Rosenstein-letter-on-Comey-firing.pdf.

164 *He had muddied the waters:* "Partial Transcript: NBC News Interview with Donald Trump," CNN, May 11, 2017, https://www.cnn.com/2017/05/11/politics/transcript-donald-trump-nbc-news/index.html.

164 *The evening of Tuesday, May 16:* Michael S. Schmidt, "Comey Memo Says Trump Asked Him to End Flynn Investigation," *The New York Times*, May 16, 2017.

164 *On CNN that evening:* Derek Hawkins, "'I Think We're in Impeachment Territory,' Says David Gergen, Former Aide to Nixon and Clinton," *The Washington Post*, May 17, 2017.

CHAPTER 21

The information in this chapter comes primarily from multiple deep background interviews with firsthand sources.

168 *First, he had been blindsided:* "Attorney General Sessions Statement on Recusal," U.S. Department of Justice, March 2, 2017.

169 *Dowd examined the one-page Rosenstein order:* The order is publicly available at https://www.documentcloud.org/documents/3726408-Rosenstein-letter-appointing-Mueller-special.html.

169 *Perhaps the most troubling pieces:* Comey's June 8, 2017, testimony to the Senate Select Committee on Intelligence is available at https://assets.documentcloud.org/documents/3860393/Comey-Opening-Statement-June-8.pdf. Comey's memos are available at https://assets.documentcloud.org/documents/4442900/Ex-FBI-Director-James-Comey-s-memos.pdf.

172 *In a celebrated July 27 news conference:* Donald J. Trump, "News Conference in Doral, Florida," July 27, 2016. Online by Gerhard Peters and John T. Woolley, *The American Presidency Project.* http://www.presidency.ucsb.edu/ws/?pid=118047.

173 *He later tweeted, "If Russia":* View Trump's tweet at https://twitter.com/realdonaldtrump/status/758335147183788032.

173 *The next day he said:* Nick Gass, "Trump on Russia Hacking Comments: 'Of Course I'm Being Sarcastic,'" *Politico*, July 27, 2016.

CHAPTER 22

The information in this chapter comes primarily from multiple deep background interviews with firsthand sources.

177 *Within the intelligence and military world:* Bob Woodward, *Obama's Wars* (New York: Simon & Schuster, 2010), p. 56.

178 *Just over a month later:* See the CNS North Korea Missile Test Database, available for download at http://www.nti.org/analysis/articles/cns-north-korea-missile-test-database/.

179 *That afternoon, McMaster chaired:* Author review of contemporaneous notes by a participant.

181 *Less than two months later:* Michelle Ye Hee Lee, "North Korea's Latest Nuclear Test Was So Powerful It Reshaped the Mountain Above It," *The Washington Post*, September 14, 2017.

181 *During the campaign, on February 10:* Matt Stevens, "Trump and Kim Jong Un, and the Names They've Called Each Other," *The New York Times*, March 9, 2018.

182 *He was captured nine months later:* Saddam Hussein was tried for crimes against humanity, found guilty and hanged three years later.

184 *From October 17 to 19, 2017:* David Cenciotti, "Here Are Some Inter-
esting Details About the Way U.S. B-2 Bombers Trained Over the U.S. to
Strike North Korea," *The Aviationist*, October 30, 2017.

185 *This question echoed:* Wolf Blitzer, "Search for the 'Smoking Gun,'"
CNN, January 10, 2003.

186 *Chain migration, formally called:* William A. Kandel, "U.S. Family-Based
Immigration Policy," Congressional Research Service, February 9, 2018,
https://fas.org/sgp/crs/homesec/R43145.pdf.

186 *Two thirds (68 percent):* Ibid.

CHAPTER 23

The information in this chapter comes primarily from multiple deep background interviews with firsthand sources.

191 *Gary Cohn gathered the principals:* Author review of contemporaneous
notes by a participant.

194 *In a late-afternoon Rose Garden:* Donald J. Trump, "Remarks Announcing
United States Withdrawal from the United Nations Framework Convention on Climate Change Paris Agreement," June 1, 2017. Online by Gerhard Peters and John T. Woolley, *The American Presidency Project.* http://
www.presidency.ucsb.edu/ws/?pid=125881.

194 *On June 15, 2017,* The Washington Post: Sari Horwitz, Matt Zapotosky
and Adam Entous, "Special Counsel Is Investigating Jared Kushner's Business Dealings," *The Washington Post*, June 15, 2017.

194 *Priebus continued to tell Trump:* In early 2018, Jared's interim Top Secret
security clearance was taken away as the FBI continued a very aggressive
background investigation. But in May, the FBI granted Jared a permanent
Top Secret clearance, suggesting his troubles in the special counsel probe
were over—a startling turn in his favor.

CHAPTER 24

The information in this chapter comes primarily from multiple deep background interviews with firsthand sources.

197 *Over the weekend of July 8 and 9:* The first article was by Jo Becker, Matt
Apuzzo and Adam Goldman, "Trump Team Met with Lawyer Linked to
Kremlin During Campaign," *The New York Times*, July 8, 2017. The sec-
ond, by the same reporters, was "Trump's Son Met with Russian Lawyer
After Being Promised Damaging Information on Clinton," *The New York
Times*, July 9, 2017.

198 *On July 17 Trump tweeted:* View Trump's tweet at https://twitter.com/real
donaldtrump/status/886950594220568576.

198 *McGahn, Priebus:* Author obtained document.

199 *On July 20 Bloomberg dropped:* Greg Farrell and Christian Berthelsen, "Mueller Expands Probe to Trump Business Transactions," Bloomberg, July 20, 2017.

201 *In a Pentagon-commissioned study:* Tom Vanden Brook, "Military Tells Transgender Troops They Can Still Serve and Get Medical Treatment Until Further Notice," *USA Today*, July 27, 2017. Read more on the study at https://www.rand.org/content/dam/rand/pubs/research_briefs/RB9900 /RB9909/RAND_RB9909.pdf.

202 *"After consultation with my Generals":* View Trump's tweet at https:// twitter.com/realdonaldtrump/status/890193981585444864.

202 *In two more tweets following:* View Trump's tweets at https://twitter .com/realdonaldtrump/status/890196164313833472; https://twitter.com /realdonaldtrump/status/890197095151546369.

202 *The confusion played out:* Leo Shane III and Tara Copp, "Trump Says Transgender Troops Can't Serve in the Military," *MilitaryTimes*, July 26, 2017.

202 *Trump spokesperson Sarah Huckabee Sanders:* "Press Briefing by Press Secretary Sarah Sanders," The White House, July 26, 2017.

203 *Several White House officials:* Rachel Bade and Josh Dawsey, "Inside Trump's Snap Decision to Ban Transgender Troops," *Politico*, July 26, 2017.

203 *The commandant of the Coast Guard:* Chris Kenning, "Retired Military Officers Slam Trump's Proposed Transgender Ban," Reuters, August 1, 2017.

203 *Dunford sent a letter:* Rebecca Kheel, "Joint Chiefs: No Change in Transgender Policy Until Trump Sends Pentagon Direction," *The Hill*, July 27, 2017.

203 *The White House later issued:* Richard Sisk, "Pentagon Ready to Accept Transgender Recruits Starting Jan. 1," Military.com, December 30, 2017.

CHAPTER 25

The information in this chapter comes primarily from multiple deep background interviews with firsthand sources.

205 *Trump had aimed a pair:* View Trump's tweets at https://twitter.com/real donaldtrump/status/880408582310776832; https://twitter.com/realdonald trump/status/880410114456465411.

206 *Following the Mika tweet:* Glenn Thrush and Maggie Haberman, "Trump Mocks Mika Brzezinski; Says She Was 'Bleeding Badly from a Face-Lift,'" *The New York Times*, June 29, 2017.

207 *Trump wanted to get out of:* Greg Miller, Julie Vitkovskaya and Reuben Fischer-Baum, "'This Deal Will Make Me Look Terrible': Full Transcripts

of Trump's Calls with Mexico and Australia," *The Washington Post*, August 3, 2017.

207 *Trump had said, "It is an evil time":* Ibid.

208 *Scribbling his thoughts:* Author obtained document.

CHAPTER 26

The information in this chapter comes primarily from multiple deep background interviews with firsthand sources.

210 *Just the previous week:* Tom Finn, "U.S., Qatar Sign Agreement on Combating Terrorism Financing," Reuters, July 10, 2017.

210 *In a news conference in Qatar:* Ibid.

211 *In his long quest:* Author review of contemporaneous notes by a participant.

213 *On Wednesday, July 19, 2017:* Peter Baker, Michael S. Schmidt and Maggie Haberman, "Citing Recusal, Trump Says He Wouldn't Have Hired Sessions," *The New York Times*, July 19, 2017.

214 *Two days later Trump continued:* View Trump's tweet at https://twitter .com/realdonaldtrump/status/889467610332528641.

214 *In an interview with* The Wall Street Journal: Michael C. Bender, "Trump Won't Say if He Will Fire Sessions," *The Wall Street Journal*, July 25, 2017.

215 *On July 24 Kushner released:* Annie Karni, "Kushner Defends His Russia Contacts: 'I Did Not Collude,'" *Politico*, July 24, 2017.

215 *Graham said Sessions:* Rebecca Savransky, "Graham Defends Sessions: Trump Tweets 'Highly Inappropriate,'" *The Hill*, July 25, 2017.

216 *Priebus talked the president:* Chris Whipple, "'Who Needs a Controversy over the Inauguration?' Reince Priebus Opens Up About His Six Months of Magical Thinking," *Vanity Fair*, March 2018.

CHAPTER 27

The information in this chapter comes primarily from multiple deep background interviews with firsthand sources.

217 *Priebus called a full senior staff meeting:* Author review of contemporaneous notes by a participant.

221 *"They're all making money," Trump said:* The 2015 nuclear deal had been a bonanza for the European Union countries. EU imports from Iran had grown an astonishing 347 percent in 2016 over the previous year. (Source: Congressional Research Service, October 25, 2017.) One French company had made a $4.7 billion gas deal in Iran. Trump, of course, made the point without the details.

222 *Trump recalled that General Nicholson:* MOAB officially stands for Massive Ordnance Air Blast.

225 *Trump left the meeting:* Jordan Fabian, "In-Town Pool Report #2—Troop Greeting & Another Comment on Afghan," 12:51 p.m., July 20, 2017, http://www.presidency.ucsb.edu/report.php?pid=2357.

226 *A senior White House official who spoke contemporaneously:* Author review of contemporaneous notes by a participant.

CHAPTER 28

The information in this chapter comes primarily from multiple deep background interviews with firsthand sources.

230 *McMaster said that at 6:03 a.m.:* View Trump's tweet at https://twitter.com/realdonaldtrump/status/889788202172780544.

232 *In November 2017, he had said:* Donald J. Trump, "The President's News Conference with Prime Minister Shinzo Abe of Japan in Tokyo, Japan," November 6, 2017. Online by Gerhard Peters and John T. Woolley, *The American Presidency Project*. http://www.presidency.ucsb.edu/ws/?pid=128510.

232 *On December 22, the vote was 15 to 0:* Rick Gladstone and David E. Sanger, "Security Council Tightens Economic Vise on North Korea, Blocking Fuel, Ships and Workers," *The New York Times*, December 22, 2017.

234 *"Reince is a fucking paranoid":* Ryan Lizza, "Anthony Scaramucci Called Me to Unload About White House Leakers, Reince Priebus and Steve Bannon," *The New Yorker*, July 27, 2017.

234 *He looked down at the latest:* View Trump's tweet at https://twitter.com/realdonaldtrump/status/891038014314598400.

235 *Kelly said in a statement:* Cristiano Lima, "Kelly 'Honored' to Serve as White House Chief of Staff," *Politico*, July 28, 2017.

CHAPTER 29

The information in this chapter comes primarily from multiple deep background interviews with firsthand sources.

238 *At 1 p.m. on Fox:* The spokeswoman's comments may be viewed on YouTube at https://youtu.be/UshUxz7Lt0w.

239 *At 1:19 p.m. Trump tweeted:* View Trump's tweet at https://twitter.com/realdonaldtrump/status/896420822780444672.

239 *Later in the afternoon:* Donald J. Trump, "Remarks on Signing the VA Choice and Quality Employment Act of 2017 in Bedminster, New Jersey," August 12, 2017. Online by Gerhard Peters and John T. Woolley, *The American Presidency Project*. http://www.presidency.ucsb.edu/ws/?pid=128032; and author review of contemporaneous notes by a participant.

239 *"Very important for the nation"*: Kristine Phillips, "Trump Didn't Call Out White Supremacists. He Was Rebuked by Members of His Own Party," *The Washington Post*, August 13, 2017.

239 *"Mr. President—we must call evil"*: Ibid.

239 *"My brother didn't give his life"*: Ibid.

239 *In a statement, Senator John McCain:* Ibid.

239 *House Speaker Paul Ryan tweeted:* Ibid.

239 *Mitt Romney tweeted:* Ibid.

240 *Republican senator Lindsey Graham appeared: Fox News Sunday* transcript, Fox News, August 13, 2017.

240 *Vice President Pence added:* Philip Rucker, "Pence: 'We Have No Tolerance for . . . White Supremacists, Neo-Nazis or the KKK," *The Washington Post*, August 13, 2017.

242 *Shortly after 12:30 p.m.:* Donald J. Trump, "Remarks on the Situation in Charlottesville, Virginia," August 14, 2017. Online by Gerhard Peters and John T. Woolley, *The American Presidency Project.* http://www.presidency.ucsb.edu/ws/?pid=128019.

243 *Rob O'Neill, a former Navy SEAL:* "Trump Condemns Hate Groups Amid Uproar over Initial Response," transcript, Fox News, August 14, 2017.

CHAPTER 30

The information in this chapter comes primarily from multiple deep background interviews with firsthand sources.

245 *At the press briefing:* Donald J. Trump, "Remarks on Infrastructure and an Exchange with Reporters in New York City," August 15, 2017. Online by Gerhard Peters and John T. Woolley, *The American Presidency Project.* http://www.presidency.ucsb.edu/ws/?pid=126765.

246 *David Duke, the well-known former Ku Klux Klan leader:* View Duke's tweet at https://twitter.com/drdavidduke/status/897559892164304896.

246 *The leaders of each branch:* Ben Watson, "How U.S. Military Leaders Are Reacting to Charlottesville," *Defense One*, August 16, 2017.

246 *On CBS, Stephen Colbert joked darkly:* Emily Yahr, "'Clinically Insane,' '7th Circle of Hell': Late-Night Hosts Process Trump's News Conference," *The Washington Post*, August 16, 2017.

247 *Kenneth Frazier, the head of Merck:* Nolan D. McCaskill, "Trump Attacks Merck CEO for Quitting Manufacturing Council over Charlottesville," *Politico*, August 14, 2017.

247 *Now that Frazier had resigned:* Ibid.

247 *Still stewing, in a second Twitter swipe:* Ibid.

247 *On Tuesday, August 15, Trump tweeted:* View Trump's tweet at https://twitter.com/realdonaldtrump/status/897478270442143744.

248 *Trump preempted further resignations:* View Trump's tweet at https://twitter.com/realdonaldtrump/status/897869174323728385.

248 *On Friday, August 18:* Author review of contemporaneous notes.

249 *The next Monday at the White House:* Ibid.

250 *Mnuchin had put out a statement:* "Statement by U.S. Treasury Secretary Steven T. Mnuchin," U.S. Department of the Treasury, August 19, 2017.

251 *Cohn chose to make his views known:* "Transcript: Gary Cohn on Tax Reform and Charlottesville," *Financial Times*, August 25, 2017.

CHAPTER 31

The information in this chapter comes primarily from multiple deep background interviews with firsthand sources.

253 *Republican senator Bob Corker:* "Republican Senator Says Trump Yet to Demonstrate Needed Stability," Reuters, August 17, 2017.

253 *And* Politico *had run a long piece:* Nancy Cook and Josh Dawsey, "'He Is Stubborn and Doesn't Realize How Bad This Is Getting,'" *Politico*, August 16, 2017.

253 *"President Trump, by asking":* Jeremy W. Peters, Jonathan Martin and Jack Healy, "Trump's Embrace of Racially Charged Past Puts Republicans in Crisis," *The New York Times*, August 16, 2017.

253 *Vice President Mike Pence:* View Pence's tweet at https://twitter.com/vp/status/896471461669605376.

259 *"Off the record," Trump said:* Author review of contemporaneous notes by a participant.

259 *Bannon had just given an interview:* Robert Kuttner, "Steve Bannon, Unrepentant," *The American Prospect*, August 16, 2017.

259 *A nationally televised Afghanistan strategy speech:* Donald J. Trump: "Address to the Nation on United States Strategy in Afghanistan and South Asia from Joint Base Myer-Henderson Hall, Virginia," August 21, 2017. Online by Gerhard Peters and John T. Woolley, *The American Presidency Project*. http://www.presidency.ucsb.edu/ws/?pid=126842.

260 *John McCain commented:* "McCain on the New Strategy for Afghanistan," August 21, 2017.

260 *Democratic senator and Clinton running mate:* "Kaine: U.S. Must Be 'Invested' in Afghanistan," *Talking Points Memo*, August 21, 2017.

260 *He addressed the Taliban:* Aaron Blake, "Rex Tillerson Totally Undercut Trump's 'We Will Win' Rhetoric on Afghanistan," *The Washington Post*, August 22, 2017.

CHAPTER 32

The information in this chapter comes primarily from multiple deep background interviews with firsthand sources.

265 *Trump had in his hands:* Author obtained document.

266 *Trump assembled a group:* Author review of contemporaneous notes by a participant.

267 *Trump announced the end:* Michael D. Shear and Julie Hirschfeld Davis, "Trump Moves to End DACA and Calls on Congress to Act," *The New York Times*, September 5, 2017.

267 *Two days later he tried to calm:* View Trump's tweet at https://twitter.com /realdonaldtrump/status/905788459301908480.

CHAPTER 33

The information in this chapter comes primarily from multiple deep background interviews with firsthand sources.

272 *Trump had finally agreed to sign:* Donald J. Trump, "Memorandum on Addressing China's Laws, Policies, Practices, and Actions Related to Intellectual Property, Innovation, and Technology," August 14, 2017. Online by Gerhard Peters and John T. Woolley, *The American Presidency Project.* http://www.presidency.ucsb.edu/ws/?pid=128023.

273 *In his public remarks:* Donald J. Trump, "Remarks on Signing a Memorandum on Addressing China's Laws, Policies, Practices, and Actions Related to Intellectual Property, Innovation, and Technology and an Exchange with Reporters," August 14, 2017. Online by Gerhard Peters and John T. Woolley, *The American Presidency Project.* http://www.presidency.ucsb .edu/ws/ ?pid=128022. Note that Trump delivered these remarks on August 14, the same day as his second set of remarks on Charlottesville. His Charlottesville speech was at 12:40 p.m. and his remarks on China were at 3:06 p.m.

278 *Kelly decided he was going to assert:* Author review of contemporaneous notes by a participant.

CHAPTER 34

The information in this chapter comes primarily from multiple deep background interviews with firsthand sources.

279 *In May he said he would be:* Ashley Parker and Anne Gearan, "President Trump Says He Would Be 'Honored' to Meet with North Korean Dictator," *The Washington Post*, May 1, 2017.

279 *In August he told the press:* Donald J. Trump, "Remarks Prior to a Briefing on the Opioid Crisis and an Exchange with Reporters in Bedminster, New Jersey," August 8, 2017. Online by Gerhard Peters and John T. Woolley, *The American Presidency* Project. http://www.presidency.ucsb.edu /ws/?pid=127991.

280 *But the president summed up his position:* "Excerpts from Trump's Interview with the Times," interview conducted by Michael S. Schmidt, *The New York Times*, December 28, 2017.

280 *On September 19, 2017, President Trump gave:* Donald. J. Trump, "Remarks to the United Nations General Assembly in New York City," September 19, 2017. Online by Gerhard Peters and John T. Woolley, *The American Presidency Project.* http://www.presidency.ucsb.edu/ws/?pid=128326.

281 *Kim fired back three days later:* "Full Text of Kim Jong-un's Response to President Trump," *The New York Times*, September 22, 2017.

281 *In a tweet on September 23:* View Trump's tweet at https://twitter.com /realdonaldtrump/status/911789314169823232.

282 *For weeks, Tillerson had been:* Arit John and Mark Niquette, "Tillerson Vows 'Peaceful Pressure Campaign' Against North Korea," Bloomberg, September 17, 2017.

282 *On October 1, months after Tillerson:* View Trump's tweets at https://twitter .com/realdonaldtrump/status/914497877543735296; https://twitter.com /realdonaldtrump/status/914497947517227008.

283 *In November, Trump saw Chris Crane:* See Crane's letter summarizing the ICE agents' complaints at https://jicreport.com/wp-content/uploads /2017/11/POTUS-Ltr-11_13_2017.pdf.

284 *The nomination was sent to the Senate:* Ashley Parker and Matt Zapotosky, "Trump Taps Kirstjen Nielsen to Lead Department of Homeland Security," *The Washington Post*, October 11, 2017.

284 *The president saw that Fox News:* Andrew Restuccia and Eliana Johnson, "Advisers Bad-Mouth Nielsen as a 'Never Trumper,'" *Politico*, May 11, 2018.

284 *At her confirmation hearing:* Ibid.

285 *Kelly appeared on Fox News's Bret Baier:* Sophie Tatum, "Kelly on Immigration: Trump 'Has Changed the Way He's Looked at a Number of Things,'" CNN, January 17, 2018.

285 *"I talked with the president":* Author review of contemporaneous notes by a participant.

286 *"I'm the only thing protecting the president":* Ibid.

286 *In a small group meeting in his office:* Ibid.

CHAPTER 35

The information in this chapter comes primarily from multiple deep background interviews with firsthand sources.

290 *Cohn knew that was crazy:* A leaked copy of Trump's 2005 tax return showed he had paid $38 million on more than $150 million income for that year—a rate of about 25 percent. View the document at https:// www.nytimes.com/interactive/2017/03/14/us/politics/document-Donald-Trump-2005-Tax.html.

292 *As the tax negotiations intensified:* Saleha Mohsin, "Mnuchin Crosses the U.S. Trying to Sell the GOP Tax Plan," Bloomberg, November 16, 2017.

293 *During the 2012 presidential campaign:* Molly Moorhead, "Mitt Romney Says 47 Percent of Americans Pay No Income Tax," *PolitiFact*, September 18, 2012.

293 *While most of the 44 percent:* Roberton C. Williams, "A Closer Look at Those Who Pay No Income or Payroll Taxes," Tax Policy Center, July 11, 2016.

293 *Their income was so low:* In 2013 the EITC cost the federal Treasury $63 billion, according to PolitiFact. The Child Tax Credit cost $57 billion in 2013 according to the Committee for a Responsible Federal Budget.

295 *The bill, however, would reduce taxes:* Howard Gleckman, "How the Tax Cuts and Jobs Act Evolved," Tax Policy Center, December 28, 2017.

296 *Republican leaders and Trump celebrated:* Donald J. Trump, "Remarks on Congressional Passage of Tax Reform Legislation," December 20, 2017. Online by Gerhard Peters and John T. Woolley, *The American Presidency Project*. http://www.presidency.ucsb.edu/ws/?pid=129018.

CHAPTER 36

The information in this chapter comes primarily from multiple deep background interviews with firsthand sources.

297 *In a long statement, rather than a tweet:* Donald J. Trump, "Statement on Former White House Chief Strategist Stephen K. Bannon," January 3, 2018. Online by Gerhard Peters and John T. Woolley, *The American Presidency Project*. http://www.presidency.ucsb.edu/ws/?pid=128962.

297 *Bannon was appalled by:* The National Security Strategy may be viewed online at https://www.whitehouse.gov/wp-content/uploads/2017/12/NSS -Final-12-18-2017-0905.pdf.

298 *Most compromising for Trump:* Donald J. Trump, "Remarks and a Question and Answer Session at the World Economic Forum in Davos, Switzerland," January 26, 2018. Online by Gerhard Peters and John T. Woolley, *The American Presidency Project*. http://www.presidency.ucsb .edu/ws/?pid=128980.

298 *The* New York Times *headline had been:* Peter S. Goodman and Keith Bradsher, "Trump Arrived in Davos as a Party Wrecker. He Leaves Praised as a Pragmatist," *The New York Times*, January 26, 2018.

300 *"It's not a mere threat":* Peter Baker and Michael Tackett, "Trump Says His 'Nuclear Button' Is 'Much Bigger' Than North Korea's," *The New York Times*, January 2, 2018.

300 *Lingering after receiving:* Author review of contemporaneous notes by a participant.

300 *That evening, Trump sent a taunting:* Peter Baker and Michael Tackett,

"Trump Says His 'Nuclear Button' Is 'Much Bigger' Than North Korea's," *The New York Times*, January 2, 2018.

301   The Washington *Post's Twitter account rushed:* View the *Post*'s tweet at https://twitter.com/washingtonpost/status/948380549156098052.

301   *Colin Kahl, Obama's former deputy:* View Kahl's tweet at https://twitter .com/colinkahl/status/948395216213626881.

301   *Others recalled Hillary Clinton's:* Hillary Clinton, "Address Accepting the Presidential Nomination at the Democratic National Convention in Phila- delphia, Pennsylvania," July 28, 2016. Online by Gerhard Peters and John T. Woolley, *The American Presidency Project.* http://www.presidency.ucsb .edu/ws/?pid=118051.

301   *A writer for the conservative* Washington Examiner*:* Tom Rogan, "Trump's 'Nuclear Button' Tweet About North Korea Was Good," *Washington Ex- aminer,* January 3, 2018.

302   *On December 3, before Trump and Kim's war:* "Transcript: Sen. Lindsey Graham on 'Face the Nation,'" December 3, 2017.

CHAPTER 37

The information in this chapter comes primarily from multiple deep back- ground interviews with firsthand sources.

305   *McMaster set up a National Security Council meeting:* Author review of contemporaneous notes by a participant.

308   *When I first learned of the details:* Interview with President Barack H. Obama, July 10, 2010.

CHAPTER 38

The information in this chapter comes primarily from multiple deep back- ground interviews with firsthand sources.

309   *Azerbaijan president Ilham Aliyev:* "President of Azerbaijan Ilham Aliyev Met President Donald Trump," U.S. Embassy in Azerbaijan, September 21, 2017, https://az.usembassy.gov/president-azerbaijan-ilham-aliyev-met -president-donald-trump/.

311   *On February 7, 2018, McMaster convened:* Author review of contempora- neous notes by a participant.

311   *Early in 2018,* 60 Minutes *broadcast:* "16 Years Later, Afghan Capital Under Siege," *60 Minutes,* CBS, January 11, 2018.

312   *In the last nine days:* Pamela Constable, "A String of Deadly Attacks in Afghanistan Exposes Government Weakness, Limits of U.S. Training Ef- fort," *The Washington Post,* January 29, 2018.

315   *On Afghanistan, Trump told Porter:* In April 2018, in order to win an

important vote for Mike Pompeo to become secretary of state, Trump had this to say to Senator Rand Paul, Republican of Kentucky. According to Paul, "The president told me over and over again in general we're getting the hell out of there."

CHAPTER 39

The information in this chapter comes primarily from multiple deep background interviews with firsthand sources.

316 *In a tweet Graham said:* View Graham's tweet at https://twitter.com /LindseyGrahamSC/status/939988068823715842.

317 *According to Comey, Trump had said:* Comey's June 8, 2017, testimony to the Senate Select Committee on Intelligence is available at https://assets.document cloud.org/documents/3860393/Comey-Opening-Statement-June-8.pdf.

317 *On December 29, 2017, Trump's tweet:* View Trump's tweet at https:// twitter.com/realdonaldtrump/status/946731576687235072.

317 *The president called a meeting:* Donald J. Trump, "Remarks in a Meeting with Members of Congress on Immigration Reform and an Exchange with Reporters," January 9, 2018. Online by Gerhard Peters and John T. Woolley, *The American Presidency Project.* http://www.presidency.ucsb .edu/ws/?pid=128934.

318 *In a statement, he was exuberant:* View Graham's tweet at https://twitter .com/LindseyGrahamSC/status/950800026401492992.

318 The New York Times: *"Trump Appears":* Julie Hirschfeld Davis and Sheryl Gay Stolberg, "Trump Appears to Endorse Path to Citizenship for Millions of Immigrants," *The New York Times,* January 9, 2018.

318 The Washington Post: *"At the table":* Ashley Parker and Philip Rucker, "55 Minutes at the Table: Trump Tries to Negotiate and Prove Stability," *The Washington Post,* January 9, 2018.

320 *Durbin went public:* John Byrne and Katherine Skiba, "Sen. Dick Durbin: President Trump Used 'Hate-Filled, Vile and Racist' Language in Immigration Meeting," *Chicago Tribune,* January 12, 2018; Josh Dawsey, "Trump Derides Protections for Immigrants from 'Shithole' Countries," *The Washington Post,* January 12, 2018.

321 *On January 21, Graham attacked Miller:* Elana Schor, "Graham Tees Off on Stephen Miller over Immigration," *Politico,* January 21, 2018.

322 *On Friday morning, February 23, 2018:* Donald J. Trump, "Remarks at the Conservative Political Action Conference in Oxon Hill, Maryland," February 23, 2018. Online by Gerhard Peters and John T. Woolley, *The American Presidency Project.* http://www.presidency.ucsb.edu/ws/?pid=129472.

322 *He then repeated one of his favorite:* The story is an appropriation of lyrics by radical black singer, songwriter and activist Oscar Brown Jr. done repeatedly on the campaign trail to the harsh criticism of the Brown family.

323 *He was in Africa:* Peter Baker, Gardiner Harris and Mark Landler, "Trump Fires Rex Tillerson and Will Replace Him with CIA Chief Pompeo," *The New York Times*, March 13, 2018.

323 *The morning of March 13:* Ibid.

323 *Trump told reporters on the South Lawn:* Donald J. Trump, "Remarks on the Nomination of Director of the Central Intelligence Agency Michael R. Pompeo to Be Secretary of State, the Termination of Rex W. Tillerson as Secretary of State, and the Nomination of Gina C. Haspel to be Director of the Central Intelligence Agency and an Exchange with Reporters Upon Departure for San Diego, California," March 13, 2018. Online by Gerhard Peters and John T. Woolley, *The American Presidency Project.* http://www.presidency.ucsb.edu/ws/?pid=129510.

CHAPTER 40

The information in this chapter comes primarily from multiple deep background interviews with firsthand sources.

325 *"I'd be embarrassed if this is still haunting":* Karen Freifeld, "White House Lawyer Cobb Predicts Quick End to Mueller Probe," Reuters, August 18, 2017.

326 *In December a story ran:* "Mueller's Trump-Russia Investigation Engulfs Deutsche," *Handelsblatt*, December 5, 2017.

330 *On March 31, Trump had tweeted:* View Trump's tweet at https://twitter.com/realdonaldtrump/status/847766558520856578.

331 *"He made a contemporaneous memorandum":* Comey's memos are available at https://assets.documentcloud.org/documents/4442900/Ex-FBI-Director-James-Comey-s-memos.pdf.

CHAPTER 41

The information in this chapter comes primarily from multiple deep background interviews with firsthand sources.

334 *In a meeting in January 2018:* Author review of contemporaneous notes by a participant.

336 *Each, one to the press and one in a blog:* MJ Lee and Kevin Liptak, "Former White House Aide's Ex-Wives Detail Abuse Allegations," CNN, February 8, 2018; Colbie Holderness, "Rob Porter Is My Ex-Husband. Here's What You Should Know About Abuse," *The Washington Post*, February 12, 2018; Felicia Gans, "Jennifer Willoughby Called Rob Porter's Alleged Abuse 'Insidious' Last Year," *Boston Globe*, February 10, 2018.

336 The New York Times *wrote:* Maggie Haberman and Katie Rogers, "Abuse Claims End Star's Rise in White House," *The New York Times*, February

8, 2016, p. A1; Katie Rogers, "Aide's Clean-Cut Image Belied His Hot Temper, Former Colleagues Say," *The New York Times*, February 20, 2018, p. A14.

336 *In a statement, Porter said:* Josh Dawsey, Beth Reinhard and Elsie Viebeck, "Senior White House Official to Resign After Ex-Wives' Allegations of Abuse," *The Washington Post*, February 7, 2018.

336 *"Peoples lives are being shattered":* View Trump's tweet at https://twitter .com/realdonaldtrump/status/962348831789797381.

336 *The* Washington Post *editorial board:* "The White House Shrugged Off Domestic Violence. It's Not Alone," *The Washington Post*, February 8, 2018; Mark Landler, "Trump, Saying 'Mere Allegation' Ruins Lives, Appears to Doubt #MeToo Movement," *The New York Times*, February 10, 2018.

337 *More than a dozen executives showed up:* Donald J. Trump, "Remarks at a Listening Session with Steel and Aluminum Industry Leaders and an Exchange with Reporters," March 1, 2018. Online by Gerhard Peters and John T. Woolley, *The American Presidency Project*. http://www .presidency.ucsb.edu/ws/?pid=129484.

339 *"Gary Cohn to Resign as Trump Adviser":* Justin Sink, Jennifer Jacobs, Dakin Campbell and Shannon Pettypiece, "Gary Cohn to Resign as Trump Adviser After Dispute over Tariffs," Bloomberg, March 6, 2018.

339 *"Gary Cohn Resigns Amid Differences":* Damian Paletta and Philip Rucker, "Gary Cohn, Trump's Top Economic Adviser, to Resign Amid Differences on Trade Policy," *The Washington Post*, March 7, 2018.

339 *"Gary Cohn Resigns, Apparently over Tariffs":* Derek Thompson, "Gary Cohn Resigns, Apparently over Tariffs," *The Atlantic*, March 6, 2018.

339 *"Gary Cohn Resigns as White House":* Nick Timiraos, Peter Nicholas and Liz Hoffman, "Gary Cohn Resigns as White House Economic Adviser After Losing Tariffs Fight," *The Wall Street Journal*, March 6, 2018.

340 *"You just upped the ante to $150 billion":* Bob Davis, "Trump Weighs Tariffs on $100 Billion More of Chinese Goods," *The Wall Street Journal*, April 5, 2018. Bossert and Trump met on April 6, 2018.

341 *The Chinese had announced they would retaliate:* Ibid.

342 *Bossert was ready with his talking points:* "Transcript of *This Week*," ABC News, April 8, 2018.

CHAPTER 42

The information in this chapter comes primarily from multiple deep background interviews with firsthand sources.

348 *Dowd and Cobb had been quoted:* Michael S. Schmidt, Matt Apuzzo and Maggie Haberman, "Mueller Is Said to Seek Interviews with West Wing in Russia Case," *The New York Times*, August 12, 2017.

348 *"You did it to Flynn, you did it to Gates":* Jeremy Herb, Evan Perez, Marshall Cohen, Pamela Brown and Shimon Prokupecz, "Ex-Trump Campaign Adviser Pleads Guilty to Making False Statement," CNN, October 31, 2017; Carrie Johnson, "Rick Gates Pleads Guilty and Begins Cooperating with Mueller's Russia Investigation," NPR, February 23, 2018.

349 *Mueller's team, Quarles and three others:* Read Mueller's questions, obtained by *The New York Times* in April 2018, at https://www.nytimes.com/2018/04/30/us/politics/questions-mueller-wants-to-ask-trump-russia.html.

355 *Dowd had represented Rajaratnam:* Peter Lattman, "Galleon Chief Sentenced to 11-Year Term in Insider Case," *The New York Times*, October 13, 2011.

Photography Credits

Index

al-Abadi, Haider, 314
ABC, 32–35, 40, 340, 342
abortion, 24–25
Access Hollywood tape, 29–37, 39, 43
Afghanistan/Afghanistan War,
    115–28, 254–60
  Bannon and, 122–23, 124, 125,
    126, 127, 195–96, 254
  CIA and, 119, 123, 126, 255, 257–58
  civilian scenario planning on,
    313–14
  decision on policy regarding,
    254–60
  enlisted soldiers, Trump's meeting
    with, 123–24
  Graham on, 121–22, 123, 126–28,
    259, 316
  Harvey on, 108, 109
  as House of Broken Toys, 314
  India on, 125
  Kabul, extent of violence in, 311,
    312
  Mattis and, 50, 51, 123, 124, 125–
    26, 196, 256, 258, 260, 313
  McMaster on, 117–21, 122, 123–
    26, 254, 255–56, 257, 258, 259,
    260, 310–11, 314

  mineral wealth of, 125, 309–11
  MOP used in, 184
  Nicholson on, 311–13
  NSC meetings and strategizing,
    117–21, 124–26, 254–60
  under Obama, 116, 117–18, 120,
    127, 128
  poppy fields, 125
  as quagmire, 229, 246
  R4s (reinforce, realign, reconcile,
    and regionalize), 121, 123, 258
  South Korea compared, 313
  strategy in, 115–28, 221–22, 254–60
  Taliban, 116, 118–19, 121–23,
    125–27, 255, 258, 260, 311–13
  Trump asking McEntee about, 231
  Trump briefed on, 124–26
  Trump's desire to pull out of,
    229–30, 314–15
  Trump's opposition to war,
    115–16, 120, 314
  "victory" in, 260, 311–13
AFL-CIO, 248
African countries, immigrants from,
    320
agricultural products, trade in,
    158–61, 220, 341

Ailes, Roger, 12–13
Air Force One, 145, 229, 234, 241,
    259, 271, 279, 281, 352, 353
Airborne Early Warning aircraft, 184
al Qaeda, 51, 72–75, 108, 112, 116,
    256, 257
al-Abadi, Haider, 314
al-Assad, Bashar, 131, 146–47,
    149–53
Aliyev, Ilham, 309
Alliance for American
    Manufacturing, 248
aluminum tariffs, 223, 273, 277,
    337
American Manufacturing Council,
    247–48
antibiotics produced by China, 275
apologies
    Access Hollywood tape and, 30,
        32, 33, 34, 36
    of Flynn for leading "Lock Her
        Up" chant, 60
    of Graham for Republican
        majority, 101
    Trump's difficulties with making,
        34, 242, 244, 249
Apple, 190
The Apprentice (TV show), 2
arms deals, 220
Article II powers of president, 326,
    328, 350, 356
al-Assad, Bashar, 131, 146–47,
    149–53
assassination ban, 181
assassination/replacement of Kim
    Jong Un, proposals regarding,
    181–84, 282
The Atlantic, 339
Augusta National Golf Club, Masters
    Tournament at, 339
Australia
    refugee agreement, 207
    steel tariffs exemption for, 207–9
automotive industry, 58, 142, 175,
    223, 276–77, 335

autonomous vehicles, economic
    impact of, 58
Azerbaijan, 309

B-2 stealth bombers, 178
Baier, Bret, 285
Baker, James A., III, 54
Baltics, Russia on war in, 132
Banana Republic, 136
bankruptcies of Trump, 274–75
Bannon, Steve (Stephen K.)
    Access Hollywood tape and, 31–33,
        34, 35, 37
    Afghanistan War and, 122–23, 124,
        125, 126, 127, 257, 259, 260
    appearance and demeanor of, 8
    Bossie and, making inquiries about
        Trump candidacy, 1–7
    campaign strategy of, 25–26
    Charlottesville, media view of
        Trump after, 253, 254
    as "chief strategist," 48
    Christie and, 35, 37
    Comey, firing of, 162, 163, 165
    on election night, 45, 46, 47,
        214–15
    in final ten days of campaign,
        43–44, 45
    foreign policy, on lack of
        organizing principle for,
        195–96
    foreign policy, Pentagon lunch and
        Tank meeting on, 218–26
    Graham and, 186–88
    on immigration, 185–88, 267–68,
        321
    Kelly and, 253–54, 261
    Kushner and Ivanka Trump,
        problems with, 144–45, 186
    Mannafort, meeting with, 20–22
    McMaster, appointment of, 86–87,
        88, 89, 90
    on Melania Trump, 32, 299
    on Middle East, 297–98, 307
    on military families, and Trump, 75

money for transition team and,
40–41, 42
Mueller investigation, testimony
in, 352
on North Korea, 259
on Paris Climate Accord, 190, 191,
192
presidential campaign, takeover of,
8–16, 19–24
Priebus and, 48, 144, 145, 236–37
Priebus on, 236–37
resignation of, 254, 259, 267, 321
on Saudi Arabia, 114, 298
second presidential debate and,
38–39
Sessions, Trump's attack on,
214–15
on Syrian air strike, 148, 149–50, 151
#TimesUp and #MeToo
movements, 299–300
on trade/trade agreements/trade
deficit, 140
on transgender troops, 201, 203
Trump, breakdown in relationship
with, 190, 297–301
Trump presidency as viewed by,
297–300
White House staffing in transition
period and, 51, 55
Yemen strike and, 72–73, 75
Bedminster, Trump National Golf
Club at, 12, 51, 229, 238, 240,
248, 261
Beirut, bombing of Marine Barracks
in (1983), 52
Bernanke, Ben, 233
Biden, Joe, 99, 122
bin Laden, Osama, 108, 116
bipartisanship, 99, 103, 217, 218
Blackwater (defense contractor), 122
Bloomberg, 199, 339
Blue Lightning, 279
Blue Room (White House), 104
Bolton, John, 87–88
Bortnikov, Alexander, 28

Bossert, Tom, 339–42
Bossie, David, 1–7, 40, 145
Boston bombers, 207
Brady, Kevin, 291, 292, 294
Brazile, Donna, 30
Breitbart News, 8, 9, 22, 39
Breitbart News Daily (radio show), 13
Brennan, John O., 28, 62, 63, 64,
68, 182–83
Britain. *See* United Kingdom
Broaddrick, Juanita, 38, 39
Brzezinski, Mika, 205, 206
Building and Construction Trades, 335
Bunker, Archie, Trump compared to,
3, 25
Bureau of Labor Statistics, 138
Bush, George H. W., 76
Bush, George W., 31, 64, 76, 93,
105, 116, 117, 137, 182, 185,
260, 274, 314, 318
Bush, Jeb, 17, 100
BuzzFeed, 69

Cabinet Room (White House), 251,
317, 337
Camp David, 146, 254
Campbell Soup, 248
Canada
case for free trade with, 220
Chinese intellectual property
violations and, 272
NAFTA, 135, 142, 155–58, 160,
233, 264, 274
Caslen, Robert, 88–89
CBS, 246, 302
CBS This Morning, 65, 181
Central Intelligence Agency (CIA)
Afghanistan War and, 119, 123,
126, 255, 257–58
intelligence standards, 63–64
Iran nuclear deal and, 132
Iraq, WMD allegations against, 64
North Korea and, 180, 183, 308
permanent government institutions,
power of, 162

Central Intelligence Agency (*cont.*)
  Russian meddling in election and,
    28–29, 62–71
  Saddam Hussein, efforts to remove,
    182–83
  on Saudis, 111
  Syria, Saudi Arabia funding
    operations in, 303
chain immigration (family
    reunification policy), 186–87,
    268, 321
change agent, Trump as, 15, 297
Charlottesville, 238–52
  CEO comments on, 247–48
  Cohn's response to, 248–51
  Congressional comments on, 239–40
  media coverage of Trump and,
    253–54
  military comments on, 246
  Mnuchin on, 250
  Porter's response to presidential
    comments about, 247, 252
  Trump comments on, 239,
    240–47, 249
  video watched by Trump, 248–49
  white supremacist march in, 238–39
chemical weapons attack on Syrian
    rebels, air strike in retaliation
    for (April 2017), 146–54
Cheney, Dick, 49
Child Tax Credit, 293–94
China
  Afghanistan's mineral wealth and,
    125, 309, 311
  agricultural trade with, 158–61,
    220, 341
  antibiotics produced by, 275
  Bannon on, 196, 297, 298
  Bossert on trade with, 339–42
  as currency manipulator, 223
  cyber wars with, 339–40, 341
  economy of, compared to U.S., 298
  intellectual property violations,
    301 investigation into, 272–73,
    336, 337

jobs lost to, 6, 15
McMaster on, 232
North Korea and, 97, 102, 105,
  179, 180, 272, 282
presidential election interference
  and, 65, 69
Syrian air strike and, 151, 153
tariffs and, 135, 159, 174
Tillerson on, 229
U.S., policy leaders' views on, 196,
  297
U.S. in Afghanistan and, 313
WTO disputes with, 276
Christian Broadcasting Network,
  328
Christie, Chris, 12, 13, 32, 33, 34,
  35, 36, 37, 42
CIA. *See* Central Intelligence Agency
Citizens United, 1
Clapper, James, 27, 29, 62–64, 65,
  67–68, 70, 93, 96–97, 147
Clean Power Plan, 192
climate change, Paris Accord on,
  189–94
Clinton, Bill, 30, 32–33, 38, 39, 84,
  93, 105, 164, 165, 181, 183,
  321, 351, 352
Clinton, Hillary
  Comey, firing of, 163, 164
  on election night, 45–46, 47
  email investigations, 163, 172–73,
    327, 331, 350
  Haitians accusing Clintons of
    corruption, 321
  "Lock Her Up" chant against, 43,
    60
  Jill McCabe campaign donations
    attributed by Trump to, 84
  North Korea and, 92
  in presidential campaign, 9, 10, 13,
    15–16, 17, 24, 25, 26, 29, 30,
    33, 35, 36, 38, 39, 44, 134
  Russian election meddling and, 60,
    63, 67, 84, 172–73, 197, 349
  on Trump and nuclear threat, 301

Ukraine presidential campaign
  sabotage in favor of, Russian
  propaganda about, 230
CNN, 17, 36, 38, 39, 85, 164, 165,
  195, 205, 241, 299
Coats, Dan, 110, 180
Cobb, Ty, 171, 325–26, 348, 351,
  353, 354
Cohen, Michael, 172, 199
Cohen, William, 181
Cohn, Gary
  on Afghanistan's mineral wealth, 310
  bankruptcies of Trump and,
    274–75
  Charlottesville, response to, 243,
    248–51
  China's intellectual property
    violations and, 272–73
  as Democrat, 55–56, 60
  disorder and disruption in White
    House and, 261, 264, 265, 266,
    270, 271
  on economy, 55–60, 274
  foreign policy, Pentagon lunch and
    Tank meeting on, 218–26
  jobs offered by Trump to, 58–60
  KORUS, Trump's desire to
    terminate, xvii, xviii–xix, xx–
    xxi, 233, 264, 265, 305
  on NAFTA, 156, 158, 274
  Navarro and, 277–78
  NEC director, appointment as,
    59–60
  Paris Climate Accord and, 191–93
  Pence and, 277
  resignation of, 337–39
  Russian election meddling/
    collusion/Mueller investigation
    and, 165, 230
  Syrian air strike and, 150
  on tariffs, 158, 160, 175, 208–9,
    232–33, 266–67, 273–74, 277,
    334, 335, 336, 337
  on tax reform, 57, 249–50, 251,
    267, 289–95

  on trade/trade agreements/trade
    deficit, 135–38, 140, 141, 143,
    273–78
  Twitter, efforts to control
    president's use of, 206
Cohn, Lisa, 60
Colbert, Stephen, 246
Collins, Susan, 206, 295
collusion with Russia. *See* Mueller
  investigation; Russia, collusion
  with
Colombia, Hezbollah in, 109
Comey, James
  Hillary Clinton email
    investigations and, 163, 327,
    331, 350
  firing of, 162–66, 169, 216
  Flynn investigation, Trump urging
    Comey to drop, 164, 169–70,
    173
  A Higher Loyalty, 66–67, 68–69,
    70
  on loyalty pledge, 317
  Mueller investigation and, 326,
    327, 328, 331, 345, 349, 350
  Russia, intelligence report on, 62,
    63, 66–67, 68–69, 70–71, 85
Congress. *See also specific members
  of Congress by name*
  apologies of Graham for
    Republican majority, 101
  Charlottesville, comments on,
    239–40
  free traders in, 267
  Freedom Caucus, 43, 201
  Gang of Eight briefings, 29, 62
  Graham on state of, 101, 102
  House Ethics Committee, 170
  immigration, possible deal on,
    317–23
  immigration and, 186–87
  Senate Armed Services Committee,
    65, 99, 105, 255
  tax reform and, 267, 291–93, 294,
    295

Conservative Political Action
  Conference (CPAC), 322–23
Constitution, Article II powers of
  president in, 326, 328, 350,
  356
Conway, Kellyanne, 16–18, 24–25,
  32, 33, 34, 35, 36, 40, 46, 54,
  65, 236, 237, 261
Cook, Tim, 190
Cooper, Anderson, 39
Corke, Kevin, 243
Corker, Bob, 253
corrupt intent, as focus of Mueller
  investigation, 346, 350
Costa, Bob, xiii, xxii
Cotton, Tom, 286
Coulter, Ann, 284
Counterterrorism Pursuit Teams
  (CTPT), 123, 255
CPAC (Conservative Political Action
  Conference), 322–23
Crane, Chris, 283
crowdsourcing by Trump, 231
CTPT (Counterterrorism Pursuit
  Teams), 123, 255
culture wars, 252
currency manipulation, 223
cyber attacks and cyber security, 92,
  93, 97–98, 280, 339–40, 341

DACA (Deferred Action for
  Childhood Arrivals), 185–88,
  267, 285, 317, 318, 319, 321
Daily Mail (United Kingdom), 145
DCLeaks, 28
debt ceiling, 58, 292
decision memos, xix, 143, 190, 201,
  202, 262–63, 266, 287, 336
Deferred Action for Childhood
  Arrivals (DACA), 185–88, 267,
  285, 317, 318, 319, 321
Demilitarized Zone (DMZ; between
  North and South Korea), 94
Democratic National Committee
  (DNC), 28, 30, 327

Democratic National Convention,
  24, 74, 301
Democrats. *See also individual*
  Democrats by name
  donations by Trump to, 5
  in Gang of Eight, 29, 62
  Graham on bipartisanship, 103
  on immigration, 217, 268, 317,
    318, 319
  Kushner and Ivanka described by
    Trump as, 144, 190
  on Mueller investigation team, 169
  tariffs and, 233
  tax reform and, 291
  Trump's relationship to, 103
  Virginia Democratic Party, 84
Deng, Wendi, 20
"deplorables," 35, 355
Dereliction of Duty (McMaster), 86,
  87, 117
DeStefano, Johnny, 132, 212
Deutsche Bank, records subpoenaed
  from, 326–27
Devos, Betsy, 123
Dimon, Jamie, 248
Diplomatic Reception Room (White
  House), 242
diversity lottery, 321
DMZ (Demilitarized Zone; between
  North and South Korea), 94
DNC (Democratic National
  Committee), 28, 30, 327
Dobbs, Lou, 284
domestic abuse allegations against
  Porter, 336
Donaldson, Annie, 198
donations to political parties/
  candidates by Trump, 5, 6
Donilon, Tom, and Donilon memo, 53
Donnelly, Sally, 195–96, 203
"dotard" remark of Kim Jong Un, 281
Dover Air Force Base, Delaware, 73
Dowd, Carole, 356
Dowd, John, 167–72, 173, 197–98,
  199–201, 271, 324–33, 343–57

Dr. Strangelove (film), 301

Dreamers and DACA, 185–88, 267, 285, 317, 318, 319, 321

Duke, David, 246

Dunford, Joseph, 76, 77, 86, 99–100, 124, 132, 203, 222, 280, 302, 305, 306, 307, 308

Durbin, Dick, 185, 187, 188, 286, 318, 319–20

Earned Income Tax Credit, 293

economy. *See also* jobs; trade/trade deficits/trade agreements
autonomous vehicles, economic impact of, 58
Cohn's initial meeting with Trump on, 55–60
conservative approach urged by Cohn, 274
financial crisis of 2008 (Great Recession), 137, 293
Graham on Trump's success with, 316
of Russia, China, and U.S. compared, 298
of South Korea, 305
stock market, 194, 232, 242, 302, 334, 339
tariffs, effect of, 339
tax reform, increased economic growth as means of paying for, 291
U.S. as consumer-driven economy, 339
U.S. as trade-based economy, 56
World Economic Forum, Trump speech at (January 2018), 298–99

Egypt, release of U.S. charity worker imprisoned in, 324

El Salvador, immigrants from, 320

election campaign. *See* presidential election campaign

election night, 45–47

el-Sisi, Abdel Fattah, 324

emails
Clinton email investigations, 163, 172–73, 327, 331, 350
from DNC server, 28
from Podesta's personal account, 30, 36

employment. *See* jobs

England. *See* United Kingdom

Espy, Mike, 351

Europe/European Union. *See also* *specific countries*
Brexit referendum, 78
case for free trade with, 220
Chinese intellectual property violations and, 272
economic growth rate in, 78
Iran, trade with, 221, 223

executive privilege and presidential testimony in Mueller investigation, 351

"Executive Time" for Trump, 266

F-22s, 178

Face the Nation (TV show), 302

Facebook, 33, 39, 190, 206

Facts and Fears (Clapper), 70

Fahrenthold, David, 29

fake news, concept of, 164, 311, 357

family reunification policy (chain immigration), 186–87, 268, 321

FBI. *See* Federal Bureau of Investigation

fear, as real power, xiii, 175, 275, 300

Federal Bureau of Investigation (FBI)
firing of Comey and, 162
intelligence standards, 63
Kushner financial records sought by, 163
Mueller as director, 168, 170
Russian meddling in election and, 27, 62–71, 83–85, 330

fighting/pushing back, Trump's belief in, 166, 174, 175, 176

financial crisis of 2008 (Great Recession), 137, 293

Financial Times, 8, 251
Fire and Fury (Wolff), 297
FISA (Foreign Intelligence
      Surveillance Act), 174
Flake, Jeff, 295
Flynn, Michael
   Comey, firing of, 164
   Comey on Trump asking him to
      drop investigation of, 164,
      169–70, 173
   lies and lying, 82, 198, 330, 345
   as national security advisor to
      presidential campaign, 46
   resignation of, 82, 330
   Russia, interview with Woodward
      on, 60–61
   Russian election meddling/
      collusion/Mueller investigation,
      80–82, 169, 170, 173, 198,
      327–30, 345, 348, 349, 353,
      357
   treason, denial of, 82
Foreign Intelligence Surveillance Act
      (FISA), 174
foreign policy. *See also specific
      countries and issues*
   lack of organizing principle for,
      195–96
   Pentagon lunch and Tank meeting
      on, 218–26
   personal relationships, Trump's
      belief in, 231–32
foreign wars, Trump on, 15,
      229–30, 314. *See also specific
      engagements*
Fox News, 13, 49, 65, 87–88, 101,
      107, 165, 231, 238, 242, 281,
      283, 284, 328, 355
Fox News Sunday, 44, 71, 240
Frazier, Kenneth, 247
free trade and free trade agreements.
      See trade/trade deficits/trade
      agreements
Freedom Caucus, 43, 201
FSB (Russia), 28, 64

Fuentes, Zach, 285
"full Ginsburg," 36
Fusion GPS, 327

G20, 179, 207–9
Galleon Group, 355
Gallucci, Robert, 95
Gang of Eight, 29, 62
Gap, 136
Gardner, Cory, 239
Gates, Rick, 348
Gates, Robert, 54
GBU-43/B (Mother of All Bombs or
      MOAB), 222
Geffen, David, 20
gender reassignment surgery for
      military personnel, 201–3
General Electric, 248
U.S.S *Gerald R. Ford* (CVN 78), 213
Gergen, David, 164
Germany
   American relationship with, 96
   Deutsche Bank, Mueller
      investigation subpoenaing
      records from, 326
   G20 summit in, 207
   NATO spending, 76
   trade deficit with, 275
Ghani, Ashraf, 126, 309
Ginsburg, William H., 36
Giuliani, Rudy, 4, 12, 13, 32, 33, 34,
      36–37, 38
globalists and globalism, 51, 134, 143,
      192, 220, 254, 278, 334, 335
Gold Star families, 73–75
Goldman Sachs, xvii, 26, 36, 41, 55,
      135, 208, 234, 275, 290, 291
golf and golfing, 12, 13, 30, 106,
      140, 166, 195, 238, 246, 249,
      299, 316, 318, 320–21, 339
Gore, Al, 190
Gorsuch, Neil, 204
Graham, Lindsey
   on Afghanistan War, 121–22, 123,
      126–28, 259, 316

Biden on, 99
cell phone number given out by
    Trump, 100, 101
on Charlottesville, 240
on immigration, 185–88, 317–21
on libel laws, 318–19
on North Korea, 99–105, 281–82,
    302
on removing U.S. dependents from
    South Korea, 302
on Sessions, 215
on Syrian air strike, 151–52
Trump calling, without going
    through Kelly, 286
Trump praised by, 316–17, 318–19
Grassley, Chuck, 295
Gray, C. Boyden, 76, 77, 78
Great Britain. *See* United Kingdom
Great Recession (financial crisis of
    2008), 137, 293
Green Room (White House), 317
Greenspan, Alan, 233
Gridiron Dinner, 175–76
Gulf Cooperation Council, 114
Gulf War, 77, 117
The Guns of August (Tuchman), 280

Haberman, Maggie, 356
Haiti, 320, 321
Haley, Nikki, 179
"hammerheads," 33
Handelsblatt, 326
Hanoi Hilton, 77
Haqqani Network, in Pakistan, 258
Harvey, Derek, 108–14, 147–48,
    151, 154
Harward, Bob, 51–52
Hatch, Orrin, 239, 291, 293, 294
Heller, Dean, 295
Hezbollah, 54, 109–10, 113, 154,
    229
Hicks, Hope, 20, 66, 165, 206, 252,
    265, 270, 338, 356
"the hidden Trump voter," 24–25
Hijazi, Aya, 324

Hiroshima, 181
Hitler, 239
Holbrooke, Richard, 127
Holder, Eric, 213
Holt, Lester, 164
Hoover, Herbert, 233
Hoover, J. Edgar, 63, 71
House Ethics Committee, 170
House of Broken Toys
    Afghanistan as, 314
    Iraqi Operations Group as, 182, 183
Huckabee Sanders, Sarah, 202–3,
    241
human trafficking, 104–5
Hussein, Saddam, 65, 181–82, 185
Hwasong-14 (North Korean ICBM),
    178

ICBMs (Intercontinental Ballistic
    Missiles), xviii, 60, 178–80,
    230, 279, 302
ICE (Immigration and Customs
    Enforcement) union, 283
Ignatius, David, 153
immigration
    Australian refugee agreement, 207
    border security, 320, 342
    chain immigration (family
        reunification policy), 186–87,
        268, 321
    Cohn on U.S. as immigration
        center, 56
    diversity lottery, 321
    Dreamers and DACA, 185–88,
        267, 285, 317, 318, 319, 321
    Graham on, 185–88, 317–21
    Mexicans called "rapists" by
        Trump, 11
    Muslim ban, 100
    Nielsen on, 284
    possible deal on, 317–23
    in presidential campaign, 15
    "shithole countries" remark,
        320–21
    strategy on, 217

immigration (*cont.*)
  Trump's rhyming snake story on, 322–23
  wall, 175–76, 186, 284, 285, 317, 322, 323
Immigration and Customs Enforcement (ICE) union, 283
impeachment
  of Bill Clinton, 181
  Trump and Comey firing, 164–65
  Trump and Mueller investigation, 355–56
India
  Afghanistan and, 121, 125, 127
  Modi and Trump, 125, 146
  Pakistan, as counterweight to, 146
inflation, 57, 58
Instagram, 206
Intel, 247
intellectual property violations by China, 272–73, 336, 337
intelligence community. *See also specific agencies*
  on chemical weapons in Syria, 147
  North Korean nuclear proliferation, secretiveness about, 177–81
  Russia, first Trump briefing on, 62–71
  on Saudis, 111–12
  Trump's war with, 65, 68, 71
Intercontinental Ballistic Missiles (ICBMs), xviii, 60, 178–80, 230, 279, 302
The Interview (film), 98
inversion (relocation of corporation's legal home to low-tax company), 57–58, 289
Iran
  Bolton on, 87
  cyber wars with, 339
  European trade with, 221, 223
  Harvey and Kushner on, 109, 111, 113, 114
  Hezbollah and, 109, 154

Iraq and, 182, 209
  Mattis and, 50, 52–54, 83
  National Security Strategy and, 298, 300
  nuclear deal with, 111, 129–33, 221–23
  Syria and, 154
  Tillerson on, 229
  Trump on state of regime in, 300
  U.S. in Afghanistan and, 313
  Yemen and, 72
Iran-contra, 165, 352
Iraqi Operations Group (The House of Broken Toys), 182, 183
Iraqi Republican Guard, 117, 181
Iraq/Iraq War
  Afghanistan compared, 128
  Bolton's support for Iraq War, 87
  under George W. Bush, 314
  Dunford, in Iraq War, 100
  Gulf War, 77, 117
  Harvey as director for Middle East on, 108
  Iran and, 182, 209, 298
  Mattis and, 50, 51, 54
  McMaster and, 117, 314
  under Obama, 256
  paying for commitments in, 310
  Rice on, 185
  Saddam Hussein, efforts to remove, 181–83
  Tillerson on, 229
  Trump's desire to pull out of, 229
  WMD allegations, 64
ISIS, 39, 51, 61, 83, 196, 222, 229, 256
Israel, 51, 109–11, 113, 114, 131, 298

J. P. Morgan/JPMorgan Chase, 136, 248
Jackson, Ronny, 266
Japan
  American relationship with, 96, 179, 219
  case for free trade with, 220

Chinese intellectual property
violations and, 272
Hiroshima, 181
North Korean nuclear-proliferation
and, 92, 93, 179, 224, 302, 306
TPP and, 139
trade with, 179, 220
Jarrett, Valerie, 122
Jefferson, Thomas, 246, 253
Jefferson Memorial, 328
Jeffersonian democracy, 127
Job Openings and Labor Turnover
Survey (JOLTS), 138
jobs
agricultural products, trade in,
158–61, 220
in automotive industry, 276
China, jobs lost to, 6, 15
employment statistics under
Trump, 175
in presidential campaign, 15
service economy versus industrial/
manufacturing jobs, 136–38
tariffs affecting, 274, 335
tax reform and, 292, 296
trade agreements affecting,
Trump's views on, 134, 135,
137
Johnson, Jeh, 29, 30
Johnson, Ron, 295
Johnson, Woody, 10
JOLTS (Job Openings and Labor
Turnover Survey), 138
Jones, Paula, 38, 39
Jones, Seth G., 259

Kahl, Colin, 301
Kaine, Tim, 260
Kasowitz, Marc, 167, 168, 169, 204
Katsas, Greg, 192
Keane, Jack, 49–51
Keating Five ethics investigation, 168
Kellogg, Keith, 77, 88, 126, 255, 257
Kelly, John F.
on Afghanistan, 254, 310, 311

on Charlottesville, 240, 243, 246,
247, 249, 251, 253–54
as chief of staff, 234–36, 311
on Cobb, 326
Chris Crane and, 283
on disorder and disruption of
White House staff, 261,
262–64, 265–66, 268, 269
on immigration, 185–86, 285, 319, 323
KORUS, Trump's desire to
terminate, 264, 265, 304, 306
on McMaster versus Tillerson, 303
media and, 285–86, 356
Mueller investigation and, 325,
326, 342, 346, 347
on NAFTA, 156
Navarro and, 277–78
Nielsen suggested as secretary of
homeland security by, 284
on North Korea, 281–82
in Oval Office meetings, 265–66
Porter and, 261–63, 268–69
senior staff meetings of, 285–86
short attention span of, 285
tariffs and, 335–36, 337
tax reform and, 292
Tillerson warned about imminent
removal by, 323
on transgender troops, 203
Trump, relationship with, 263,
265–67, 268–69, 283–87
Kennedy, Ted, 318
Kenya, Hezbollah in, 109
KEY2ACT, 42–43
Khans (Gold Star parents), 74
Kim Jong Il, 93
Kim Jong Un, 93, 95, 97, 98, 180, 181,
183, 184, 206, 279, 280–81, 282,
300–302
Kislyak, Sergey, 80, 81, 329, 330, 353
Kissinger, Henry, 297
KKK (Ku Klux Klan), 243, 246, 251
Kobach, Kris, 188
Koch brothers, 292
Korean War, 96

KORUS (United States–[South]
    Korea Free Trade Agreement),
    Trump's desire to terminate,
    xvii–xxii, xxiii, 105–7, 142,
    224, 233, 264–65, 300, 304–8
Ku Klux Klan (KKK), 243, 246, 251
Kushner, Jared
  Bannon and Priebus, problems
    with, 144–45, 186, 194–95,
    195–96, 237
  finances investigated, 163, 194–95
  foreign policy, Pentagon lunch and
    Tank meeting on, 218–26
  foreign wars, Trump's desire to
    pull out of, 229–30
  on immigration, 185–88, 217
  KORUS, Trump's desire to
    terminate, xx
  McMaster and, 88, 89, 229–30
  Middle East interests of, 109
  on NAFTA, 155, 156, 157
  on NATO, 78
  on Paris Climate Accord, 190
  political acumen of, 217–18
  in presidential election campaign,
    20, 22, 26, 32, 33, 39, 40–41
  Priebus resignation and, 236, 237
  Russian election interference/
    collusion/Mueller investigation,
    145, 165, 194–95, 197, 215
  on Saudi Arabia, 110, 111–14
  Sessions attack by Trump as
    smokescreen for Russian
    testimony of, 215
  Syrian air strike and, 144–45, 150,
    154
  on trade/trade agreements/trade
    deficit, 138–39
  in transition-period economy
    meeting, 55, 59
Kuttner, Robert, 259

Lavoy, Peter, 116, 120
leader's command-and-control
    targeting, 181–84

leaking
  Bannon and Kushner, conflict
    between, 144–45, 190
  hacked Democratic Party emails, 28
  Podesta emails, 30, 36
  in presidential campaign, 14
Lebanon
  Beirut, bombing of Marine
    Barracks in (1983), 52
  Hezbollah, 54, 109–10, 113, 154, 229
  National Security Strategy and, 298
  Tillerson interventions on, 229
Lee, Mike, 294
Lee, Robert E., 238, 246
Lewinsky, Monica, 36, 165, 352
LGBT rights, 201–3
libel laws, 318–19
Libya, 195, 230
lie detectors, 64
lies and lying
  Hillary Clinton coming across as
    lying, 16
  Comey accused of, 169, 331
  by Flynn, 82, 198, 330, 345
  by Gates, 348
  Mueller investigation and, 4, 299,
    347, 348, 352
  in polls, 45
  Trump, as liar, 208–9, 235, 320,
    338, 353, 357
  Trump accusations of, 4, 169, 299,
    331
  to Woodward, about North Korea,
    177–78, 181
Lighthizer, Robert E. (Bob), 142–43,
    160, 266, 272, 274, 276
Lincoln, Abraham, 123, 237, 253
Lincoln Bedroom (White House), 328
Lindsey, Lawrence B., 137
lithium, 309
"Little Rocket Man"/"Rocket Man,"
    280, 281, 282
"Lock Her Up" chant, 43, 60
Lonesome Dove (novel/miniseries), 325
Lowell, Abbe, 194

loyalty, importance to Trump of, 66,
    138–39, 176, 268, 317
Lujan, Fernando, 117–18
Lute, Douglas, 116

M16 (United Kingdom), 63
"Make America Great Again" slogan,
    15, 115
Manafort, Kathleen, 21
Manafort, Paul, 9, 10, 13–14, 16,
    20–22, 21–22, 26, 172, 197, 348
Mar-a-Lago, 86, 88, 150, 151, 205, 299
Marine One, 213
Massive Ordnance Penetrator
    (MOP), 184
Masters Tournament, 339
Mattis, James
    on Afghanistan, 50, 51, 123, 124,
        125–26, 196, 256, 258, 260, 313
    approach to working with Trump,
        227–28
    on coordination of foreign policy,
        195–96
    foreign policy, Bannon's efforts to
        deal on, 196
    foreign policy, Pentagon lunch and
        Tank meeting on, 218–26
    on Iran nuclear deal, 130, 132, 133
    KORUS, Trump's desire to terminate,
        264, 304, 305–6
    as "Mad Dog," 50, 222
    McMaster and, 86, 154, 210, 211
    on NATO, 76–79
    on North Korea, xxi, xxii, 100,
        106, 179, 180, 280, 302
    recruitment as secretary of defense,
        50–54
    on Russian election interference,
        collusion, and Mueller
        investigation, 82–83, 325
    on Saudi Arabia, 110, 112, 114
    Sunday talk shows, refusal to
        appear on, 133
    on tariffs, 160
    Tillerson and, 132, 210–11

    on trade/trade agreements/trade
        deficits, 139, 146, 148, 149–50,
        153, 154
    on transgender troops, 202, 203
    on Trump, 83
    waiver to become secretary of
        defense, 139
    Yemen, strike on, 72, 74
MBN (Mohammed bin Nayef), 111–12
MBS (Mohammed bin Salman), 111, 112
McAuliffe, Terry, 84
McCabe, Andrew, 63, 83–85
McCabe, Jill, 84
McCain, Cindy, 104–5
McCain, John
    on Afghanistan, 260
    on Charlottesville, 239
    dinner with Trump, 104–5
    dislike of Trump, 104
    Dowd's representation of,
        in Keating Five ethics
        investigation, 168
    Graham and, 99, 100, 104–5
    on North Korea, 105
    as presidential candidate, 17
    Steele dossier and, 63
    on Syrian air strike, 153
    Trump on Vietnam War
        experience of, 76–77, 104
    Yemen raid criticized by, 76–77
McCain, Admiral John, 77
McConnell, Mitch, 11, 104, 159,
    187, 248, 291, 295
McEntee, Johnny, 231
McGahn, Donald, 80, 81, 162–63,
    165, 170, 172, 192, 198, 268,
    329, 330, 350
McMaster, H. R.
    on Afghanistan, 117–21, 122,
        123–26, 254, 255–56, 257,
        258, 259, 260, 310–11, 314
    coordination failures in White
        House and, 261, 264, 265, 266
    Dereliction of Duty, 86, 87, 117
    on Iran nuclear deal, 131, 132, 133

McMaster, H. R. (*cont.*)
  Iraq and, 117, 314
  KORUS, Trump's desire to terminate,
    264, 265, 303–4, 305, 307
  on NAFTA, 156
  on North Korea, 91, 101, 102, 103,
    106–7, 184–85, 279–80, 282
  NSC process and, 228
  on Paris Climate Accord, 193
  Priebus and, 145–46
  recruitment as national security
    advisor, 86–90
  on Saudi Arabia, 110–14
  Saudi Arabian money, feud with
    Tillerson over, 303–4, 307
  on Syrian air strike, 145–46, 147,
    148–49, 150, 151, 153, 154
  Tank meeting at Pentagon not
    attended by, 219
  on tariffs, 266–67
  Tillerson and Mattis, difficulties
    with, 154, 210–12, 228–29,
    303–4, 307
  Trump, relationship with, 145–46,
    230, 270
  Trump's view of foreign wars and,
    229–30, 314–15
  on Xi Jinping and China, 232
Meadows, Mark, 43–44
media. *See also specific outlets*
  Charlottesville and, 253–54
  Cobb interviews in, 325–26
  on Comey firing, 164
  credentials, Trump's desire to pull,
    356
  fake news, concept of, 164, 311, 357
  Hicks's views on, 66
  Kelly and, 285–86, 356
  McMaster's appointment as
    national security advisor and,
    86–90
  on Mueller investigation, 165, 174,
    197–98
  oppositional defiance syndrome
    attributed to, 66

  Trump heavily influenced by, 195,
    231, 291
  Trump's views on, 14, 86, 195, 356
Mercer, Bob, 10, 13
Mercer, Rebekah, 9–10, 13
Merck, 247
#MeToo, 299–300, 336
Mexico
  case for free trade with, 220
  jobs lost to, 134, 135
  Mexicans called "rapists" by
    Trump, 11
  NAFTA, 135, 142, 155–58, 160,
    233, 264, 274
Middle East. *See also specific countries*
  Harvey as director for, 108–14
  Hezbollah in, 54, 109–10, 113,
    154, 229
  importance of U.S. alliances in, 219
  ISIS in, 39, 51, 61, 83, 196, 222,
    229, 256
  Mattis and, 50, 83, 219
  National Security Strategy on,
    297–98, 316
  Trump briefings, 110
  U.S. payment for defense of,
    Trump on, 305
military
  arms deals, 220
  Charlottesville, comments on, 246
  SEALs, 51, 72–75, 243
  Syria, Saudi Arabia funding
    operations in, 303, 307
  transgender troops in, 201–3
  Trump's ability to relate to families
    of, 73–75
Miller, Jason, 20
Miller, Stephen, 126, 133, 140, 187,
  213–14, 217, 234, 235, 260,
  268, 278, 320, 321
Milley, Mark, 89, 246
mineral wealth of Afghanistan, 125,
  309–11
Mnuchin, Steve
  on Charlottesville, 243, 250

economy, meeting on, 55–57, 59
foreign policy, Pentagon lunch and
    Tank meeting on, 218–26
on NAFTA, 156
on North Korea, 180
in presidential campaign, 26, 41–42
on tax reform, 267, 290, 291, 292,
    294
on trade/trade agreements/trade
    deficit, 55–57, 59, 140, 143
MOAB (Mother of All Bombs; GBU-
    43/B), 222
Modi, Nahendra, 125, 146
Mohammed bin Nayef (MBN), 111–12
Mohammed bin Salman (MBS), 111,
    112
Moon Jae-in, 304
MOP (Massive Ordnance
    Penetrator), 184
Morell, Mike, 28–29
Morning Joe (TV show), 153, 205
moron, Tillerson describing Trump
    as, 225, 227, 228
Mossad, 110
Mother of All Bombs (MOAB; GBU-
    43/B), 222
Mozambique, Hezbollah in, 109
MSNBC, 165, 195, 205, 241
Mueller, Robert (Bob)
    appointment of Mueller as special
        counsel, 165, 168
    conflict of interest raised by
        Trump, 166
    Dowd and, 170–72, 325
    Dowd's negotiations with, 324–33,
        343–56
    as FBI director, 168, 170
    Mattis and, 325
    silence of, 171, 349
Mueller investigation
    anger and agitation of Trump
        regarding, 165–66, 168–69,
        173–74, 268–69, 270–71, 331–32
    appointment of Mueller as special
        counsel, 165, 168

Article II powers of president and,
    326, 328, 350, 356
authority of, 169, 171
collusion (*See* Russia, collusion
    with)
Comey and, 326, 327, 328, 331
conclusion of, 325
corrupt intent as focus of, 346, 350
Deutsche Bank, records
    subpoenaed from, 326–27
documentation submitted to,
    171–73, 198–99
Dowd's recommendation that
    Trump not testify, 332–33,
    351–56
Dowd's resignation and, 356–57
Dowd's strategies for dealing with,
    324–33, 343–56
executive privilege and, 351
Flynn and, 169, 170, 173, 198,
    327–30
grand jury subpoena of president
    threatened, 343–45, 348
hindering ability to act as
    president, Trump's complaints
    about, 324–25
on Kushner finances, 194
legal representation of Trump in,
    167–73
lies and lying, 4, 299, 347, 348,
    352, 357
obstruction of justice, 169, 173,
    345, 350, 357
perjury traps set by, 348, 350, 357
presidential campaign, alleged
    meetings with Russians during,
    172–73, 197–98
presidential testimony sought
    by, questions submitted for,
    327–33, 343–51
recusal of Sessions, 168, 176, 213,
    216
Sessions and, 327
specific matters being investigated,
    172–73

Mueller investigation (*cont.*)
  Trump and Dowd practicing
    testimony before, 327–33, 345–46
  Trump finances, investigation of,
    199–201
Muir, David, 33, 34
Mulvaney, Mick, 290, 292
Murdoch, Rupert, 20
Murkowski, Lisa, 206
Muslim ban, 100
MV-22 Osprey, loss of, 73

NAFTA (North American Free Trade
  Agreement), 135, 142, 155–58,
  160, 233, 264, 274
National Economic Council (NEC),
  59–60, 112, 141, 143, 189, 278
National Guard troops, as border
  security, 342
National ICE Council, 283
national security, steel and aluminum
  imports as threat to, 160, 337
National Security Agency (NSA), 27,
  70, 180
National Security Council (NSC)
  Afghanistan War, meetings
    and strategizing on, 117–21,
    124–26, 254
  foreign policy presentations, lack of
    organizing principle for, 195–96
  Iran nuclear deal and, 130
  KORUS, Trump's desire to
    terminate, 265, 305–8
  Middle East, Harvey as director
    for, 108–14
  nuclear North Korea, McMaster
    on Trump and, 280
  process for, 228–29, 310
  Russian meddling in election and, 28
  Syria, chemical attack in, 149–50
  Tillerson accused by McMaster of
    failing to consult with, 211
  Trump insulting McMaster in
    front of, 307
National Security Strategy, 297

National Trade Council, 134, 140
NATO (North Atlantic Treaty
  Organization), 76–79, 124, 132,
  305, 307, 310
Navarro, Peter, 134–35, 140–41,
  142–43, 155, 156, 157, 265,
  266, 274, 275, 277–78, 334,
  335, 336–37
Nazis and neo-Nazis, 238, 239, 240,
  243, 246, 250, 251
NBC, 2, 29–30, 32, 38, 164
NEC (National Economic Council),
  59–60, 112, 141, 143, 189, 278
Neller, Robert B., 246
neo-Nazis, 238, 239, 240, 243, 246,
  250, 251
Netanyahu, Benjamin, 110
The New Republic, 25
New York *Daily News,* 20
New York Times
  on Afghanistan, 254
  on agricultural trade with China, 159
  on Comey firing, 164
  on Dowd resignation, 356
  on immigration, 318
  interviews with Trump, 65, 280
  on Mueller investigation, 172, 197,
    198
  on Porter domestic abuse
    allegations, 336
  on presidential campaign, 8–9, 10,
    11, 14, 24
  on Russian contacts with Trump
    associates, 83–85, 145
  on Russian election interference, 65
  Sessions attacked by Trump in, 213
  on tax reform, 287
  Trump's views on, 14
  on Ukrainian funds paid to
    Manafort, 21–22
  World Economic Forum, on Trump
    speech at (January 2018), 298–99
New York Times v. Sullivan, 318–19
Nicholson, John, 221–22, 311–12, 313
Nielsen, Kirstjen, 284

9/11 terrorist attacks, 51, 52, 108, 116, 119, 121–22, 127, 128, 177, 254–56, 314

Nixon, Richard, 13, 164, 166, 173, 216, 352, 360

Nobel Prize, 95, 233

North American Free Trade Agreement (NAFTA), 135, 142, 155–58, 160, 233, 264, 274

North Atlantic Treaty Organization (NATO), 76–79, 124, 132, 305, 307, 310

North Carolina, presidential election campaign in, 43, 45

North Korea, nuclear proliferation in assassination/replacement of Kim Jong Un, proposals regarding, 181–84, 282

backchannel diplomacy between U.S. and North Korea, 95–97

Bannon on, 259

Bolton on regime change in North Korea, 87

cyber attacks and, 92, 93, 97–98, 280

Graham on, 99–105, 281–82, 302

KORUS and, xvii–xxii, xxiii, 105–7, 142, 264, 304–8

McCain on, 99–105

missile delivery capabilities, CIA conclusions on, 308

Obama administration concerns about, 91–98, 103, 105, 177, 301

PIE (Peninsula Intelligence Estimate), 183

planning contingent U.S. responses to, 181–85

preemptive military strike, study of effectiveness of, 92–93, 94–95

pressure campaign and deterrence/containment strategies, 279–80

"Rocket Man"/"Little Rocket Man" comments, 280, 281, 282

secretiveness of intelligence community about, 177–81

testing, 178–81

Tillerson on, 179, 180, 229, 282

Trump threatening regime over, 282–83

Trump's public statements about, 95, 280–81, 282–83, 300–302

Trump's U.N. General Assembly address (September 2017), 280–81

U.N. Security Council sanctions, 232

U.S., North Korean view of, 96

U.S. citizens imprisoned in North Korea, 96

U.S. travel restrictions and, 180

NSA (National Security Agency), 27, 70, 180

NSC. *See* National Security Council

nuclear weapons. *See also* North Korea, nuclear proliferation in

Air Force research and design tests, 308

Hiroshima, 181

Iran, nuclear deal with, 111, 129–33

Iraq, WMD allegations against, 64

nuclear button, Trump's Tweet about, 300–301

Obama's fears about, 308

in Pakistan, 94

promise to modernize U.S. capabilities, 65

Russia and, 60–61, 132

Obama, Barack
Afghanistan War under, 116, 117–18, 120, 122, 127, 128, 222, 255, 260, 316

Brennan and, 183

Charlottesville and, 239, 243

Hillary Clinton and, 45–46

on election night, 45–46

Graham on mess left by, 316

immigration under, 185, 207, 318

Iran nuclear deal and, 129, 131

Nobel Peace Prize acceptance speech (2009), 95

Obama, Barack (*cont.*)
  North Korea and, 91–98, 103, 105,
    177, 301
  nuclear weapon fears of, 308
  Paris Climate Accord and, 189
  presidential election campaign
    and, 2, 23, 27–28, 44
  Russian campaign meddling/
    collusion and, 60, 61, 62, 64,
    68, 80, 81, 83, 330
  Syria and, 146, 147, 149, 152, 153
  tax reform and, 293
  trade/trade deficit/trade
    agreements and, 139
  transgender troops and, 201
  in transition period, 49, 53, 54, 60,
    61, 62, 64, 68
  wiretapping Trump Tower,
    accusations of, 103–4
  Yemen operation considered by, 72
Obama, Michelle, 64, 68
Obamacare, 101, 206, 234
obstruction of justice, 169, 173, 345,
  350, 357
Old Naval Observatory, 82–83
Olympics (Winter, 2018), South
  Korea, 308
100th day in office, 155
O'Neill, Rob, 243
Operation Desert Storm, 117
OPLAN 5015, 184
OPLAN 5027, 183
oppositional defiance syndrome, 66
Osama bin Laden, 108, 116
Oval Office meetings
  on Afghanistan's mineral wealth,
    310
  Bossert on trade with China, 339
  Cohn disquiet over Charlottesville,
    249
  Cohn resignation, 338
  with Chris Crane, 283
  disorder and disruption in,
    263–64
  on firing of Comey, 162

  with Graham, 101
  on immigration, 320
  on Iran nuclear deal, 131
  Kelly in, 265–66, 283, 284
  KORUS, Trump's desire to
    terminate, xvii, xx, xxi, 105
  on Libya, 230
  on NAFTA, 155–58
  on North Korea, xvii, xx
  on Paris Climate Accord, 191, 193
  PDB briefs, 27, 110, 300
  privacy in, 265–66
  with Sessions, 216
  on Syria, between Bannon and
    Trump, 149
  on tariffs, 160, 334
  on tax reform, 290
  Tillerson belittling Stephen Miller
    in, 133
Owens, Bill, 73–74
Owens, Carryn, 74–75
Owens, William "Ryan," 73, 74, 75

Pakistan
  Afghanistan War and, 116, 118,
    119, 123–27, 312–13, 314
  Haqqani Network in, 258
  India as counterweight to, 146
  nuclear weapons, 94
  Trump on, 300
Panetta, Leon, 53
Papadopoulos, George, 348
Paris Climate Accord, 189–94
pass-throughs, 292, 295
PDB (President's Daily Brief), 27, 110,
  300
Pence, Mike
  Access Hollywood tape and, 31, 33
  on Afghanistan, 122, 123–24
  on Charlottesville, 240, 250, 251,
    253–54
  Flynn lying to, 82, 329
  job numbers and, 175
  on NAFTA, 155, 156
  in presidential campaign, 31, 33, 44

Russian campaign interference/
collusion/Mueller investigation,
81
Saudi Arabia and, 114
on tariffs, 277
on tax reform, 295
Peninsula Intelligence Estimate (PIE),
183
Pentagon
on Afghanistan, 117, 119, 257,
312, 313
foreign policy, Bannon's efforts to
coordinate, 196
foreign policy, lunch and Tank
meeting on, 218–26
on North Korea, 94, 106, 177–78,
183–84, 280, 302
permanent government
institutions, power of, 162
on Russian nuclear capabilities, 60
Saudis and, 113
on Syria, 146, 149, 154
the Tank/Gold Room, 218, 219, 227
transgender troops, 201–3
Perdue, Sonny, 157, 158
perjury traps, in Mueller
investigation, 348, 350, 357
Perry, Rick, 112
Petraeus, David, 87
PIE (Peninsula Intelligence Estimate),
183
Podesta, John, 30, 36
political correctness, 242
Politico, 253
polls, in presidential campaign
KEY2ACT meeting, straw poll at,
42–43
Trump's standing in, 17, 22,
42–43, 45
views on state of country in, 15
polygraphs, 64
Pompeo, Mike, 110, 123, 132, 179,
180, 254, 255, 257–58, 323
populism and populist movement, 2,
4, 5, 13, 25, 237, 298

Porter, Rob
Afghanistan and, 314, 315
on Charlottesville, 240–44, 247,
252
on coordination failure in White
House, 261–63, 265, 266, 271
foreign wars strategy and, 229–30
hiring of, 138–39
Kelly and, 261–63, 268–69, 284,
285, 286–87
KORUS, Trump's desire to terminate,
xix–xxii, 233, 264, 265
McMaster and, 210, 211, 229, 230
on NAFTA, 155–58
on Navarro, 277, 278
North Korea and, 300
on Paris Climate Accord, 190–91, 193
presidential schedule and, 230–31
resignation after domestic abuse
allegations, 336
on "Rocket Man" comment, 281
Russian election interference/
collusion/Mueller investigation
and, 165, 166, 174, 268–69,
270, 271
on Sessions recusal, 176, 216
on tariffs, 159, 160–61, 175, 206,
266–67, 273, 334–36
Tillerson and, 211, 212
on trade/trade agreements/trade
deficit, 140, 141–42, 143, 276
Trump's relationship with, 138–39,
204–5, 271
Porter, Roger, 138
U.S.S *Porter,* 150
Portman, Rob, 293
Powell, Dina, 150, 210
presidential election campaign.
See also polls, in presidential
campaign; Russian election
interference
acceptance of Republican
nomination, 8
Access Hollywood tape, 29–37,
39, 43

presidential election campaign (*cont.*)
   Bannon takeover of, 8–16, 19–24
   Conway as campaign manager,
      16–18, 24–25
   debate preparation, 13
   debate strategy, 26
   debates, 35, 37, 38–40, 41
   election night, 45–47
   final ten days, 43–45
   financing of, 40–42
   headquarters of, 19–20
   "the hidden Trump voter," 24–25
   Kushner's role in, 40
   meeting between Manafort and
      Bannon, 20–22
   preliminary inquiries about (2010),
      1–7
   public track record of Trump and,
      2–5
   rallies during, 9, 11, 17, 31, 33, 35,
      43, 45, 100, 213
   speech announcing candidacy
      (2015), 11
   strategy for, 25–26, 43–45
Presidential Records Act, 262
President's Daily Brief (PDB), 27,
   110, 300
press. *See* media
Priebus, Reince
   on Afghanistan, 120, 126
   Bannon and, 48, 144, 145, 236–37
   as chief of staff, 48, 144, 211
   on disorder and disruption in
      White House, 261
   firing of Comey and, 162, 163–64,
      165
   foreign policy, Pentagon lunch and
      Tank meeting on, 218–26
   on Iran nuclear deal, 129–30, 131,
      132–33
   Kushner and Ivanka Trump,
      problems with, 144–45, 186,
      189–90, 194–95, 217–18, 237
   on Mattis, 227–28
   McMaster and, 145–46

   on NATO, 76, 77, 78
   on North Korea, 100, 101, 102–3,
      186
   on Paris Climate Accord, 189–90,
      192
   in presidential election campaign,
      10–12, 22–23, 25, 31–33, 36, 46
   resignation of, 234–37
   on Russian election interference,
      collusion, and Mueller
      investigation, 80–82, 83–85,
      198, 329, 330, 352
   on Saudi Arabia, 114
   Scaramucci on, 234
   Sessions, Trump attack on,
      213–14, 216
   on Syrian air strike, 144–46, 150
   Tillerson and, 211–12, 227–28,
      287–88
   on trade/trade agreements/trade
      deficit, 138, 141–42, 143
   on transgender troops, 201–2
   in transition period, 55, 60, 68
   Trump's opinion of, 204–5
   Trump's relationship with,
      235–36, 287–88
   Twitter, efforts to control Trump's
      use of, 204–6
   on White House staff, 236–37
Prince, Erik, 122
Pruitt, Scott, 190–91, 192
pushing back/fighting, Trump's belief
   in, 166, 174, 175, 176
Putin, Vladimir, 29, 47, 54, 60–61,
   67, 77, 81, 147, 174, 325, 330

al Qaeda, 51, 72–75, 108, 112, 116,
   256, 257
Qatar, 114, 210
Quarles, James "Jim," 171, 199–200,
   325, 327, 330, 333, 343, 347, 349

racial divide, Trump presidency
   viewed as rekindling, 252, 253.
   See also Charlottesville

Raddatz, Martha, 40, 342
Rajaratnam, Raj, 355
rallies
  at Charlottesville, 240, 245 (*See also* Charlottesville)
  in presidential election campaign, 9, 11, 17, 31, 33, 35, 43, 45, 100, 213
  during Trump presidency, 134, 271, 355
  Trump's fondness for, 271
  White House operations compared to, 231
RAND Corporation, 201
rare earth, 309
Reagan, Ronald, 181, 243, 267, 291, 352
Red Room (White House residence), 76
Renaissance Technologies, 10
Republican National Committee (RNC), 9, 10–11, 23–25, 31, 46–47, 218
Republican National Convention, 60
Republicans. *See also individual Republicans by name*
  Bannon on, 298
  on Charlottesville, 239, 248, 253
  in Gang of Eight, 29, 62
  Graham on bipartisanship, 103
  Graham on state of Congressional majority, 101
  immigration and, 267
  momentum in 2010, 1
  New York Times Republican sources on Trump, 8–9
  presidential primaries, how to win, 2–6
  Priebus and, 234
  Sessions defended by, 215–16
  tariffs and, 233
  tax reform and, 267, 287, 290, 291, 292, 294
  on Trump Tweets, 206
  Trump winning presidential nomination for, 8, 9, 17

Trump's relationship to, 17, 22, 24, 25, 26, 33, 41, 103, 298
residences, presidential
  Camp David, 146, 254
  Mar-a-Lago, 86, 88, 150, 151, 205, 299
  White House, 20, 31, 76, 148, 195, 201, 230, 242, 243, 266, 272, 328, 345
Resolute Desk, Oval Office, xvii, xviii, 101, 160, 165, 208, 262, 338
Reuters, 95, 106, 325
Ri Chun-hee, 91–92
Ri Su-yong, 301
Rice, Condoleezza (Condi), 31, 185
Rice, Susan, 122
Richardson, John, 246
RNC (Republican National Committee), 9, 10–11, 23–25, 31, 46–47, 218
"Rocket Man"/"Little Rocket Man," 280, 281, 282
ROCKSTARS, 182
Roe v. Wade, 25
Rogers, Mike, 62, 180
Romney, Mitt, 17, 42, 239–40, 293
Roosevelt Room meetings, 124, 142, 156, 285
Rose, Pete, 168
Rose Garden (White House), 194
Rosenstein, Rod, 163, 164, 165, 166, 168, 169, 174, 215, 349, 350
Ross, Wilbur, 140, 141, 143, 155–57, 159–61, 233, 265, 266, 274, 310–11, 334, 336–37
U.S.S. *Ross,* 150
Rubin, Robert, 59
Rubio, Marco, 17, 239, 294
Russia
  cyber wars with, 339
  economy of, compared to U.S. and China, 298
  Flynn interview with Woodward on, 60–61
  FSB, 28, 64

Russia (*cont.*)
  Iran and, 132
  North Korean nuclear proliferation
    and, 179, 180
  nuclear weapons and, 60–61, 132
  prostitutes/"golden showers"
    accusation, 64–65, 68–71
  Syria and, 28, 147, 149, 150–51,
    153, 154
  Trump's first briefing on, 62–71
  Ukrainian Trump campaign
    sabotage, propaganda about, 230
  U.S. in Afghanistan and, 313
  on war in Baltics, 132
Russia, collusion with. *See also*
    Mueller investigation
  Dowd on lack of evidence for,
    344–45, 357
  as "fake news," 164
  FBI investigation of, 63
  FBI refusal to deny *Times* story
    about, 83–85
  Flynn's denial of, 82
  initial intelligence report not
    suggesting, 67
  presidential campaign, meetings
    with Russians during, 197–98,
    345, 349
  specific instances suggesting, 172–73
Russian election interference. *See
    also* Mueller investigation
  Access Hollywood tape eclipsing, 30
  Clinton emails, 63, 67, 172–73
  Congress briefed about, 29
  first public release of information
    about, 28–29
  Flynn's discussion of sanctions
    for, with Russian ambassador,
    80–82
  initial evidence of, 27–29
  intelligence report on, 62–71
  Putin's passive response to
    sanctions for, 81–82
  sanctions imposed by Obama for,
    80, 81, 83, 330

Trump addressing missing Clinton
    emails and, 172–73
  Trump's view of, 65, 174, 330
  as "witch hunt," 65, 174, 330
Ryan, Paul, 31, 44, 130, 159, 239,
    248, 286, 291, 292, 294, 356

Salman (Saudi king), 114
Sanders, Sarah Huckabee, 202–3, 241
SAP (Special Access Programs), xviii,
    83, 92, 180, 224, 305, 306
sarin gas attack in Syria, air strike
    in retaliation for (April 2017),
    146–54
Sater, Felix, 199
Saturday Night Massacre (1973), 216
Saudi Arabia, 110–14, 183, 196, 298,
    303, 307
Scaramucci, Anthony, 233–34
Scarborough, Joe, 153, 205
Scavino, Dan, 206, 234, 235
Schmidt, Michael, 164
Schumer, Chuck, 286, 318
SCIF (Sensitive Compartmented
    Information Facility), 83, 150,
    207, 261
Scott, Tim, 293
SEALs, 51, 72–75, 243
Secret Service, 35–36, 175
Sekulow, Jay, 328, 333, 343, 345–46,
    349, 351, 354
Senate Armed Services Committee,
    65, 99, 105, 255
Sensitive Compartmented
    Information Facility (SCIF), 83,
    150, 207, 261
service economy versus industrial/
    manufacturing jobs, 136–38
Sessions, Jeff
  on Afghanistan, 120, 126, 255, 257
  Bannon on, 299
  on immigration, 188, 267
  in presidential campaign, 46
  recusal of, 168, 176, 213, 216
  resignation called for, 213–16

Russian election interference/
collusion/Mueller investigation,
164, 166, 168, 174, 327, 347, 349
Trump's attacks on, 174, 176,
213–16, 299, 347
sexual scandals
Access Hollywood tape, 29–37,
39, 43
of Clintons, 36, 38–39, 165, 352
Russian prostitutes/"golden
showers" accusation, 64–65,
68–71
#TimesUp and #MeToo
movements, Bannon on Trump
as perfect foil for, 299–300
Trump on handling, 175
Shelton, Kathy, 38, 39
"shithole countries" remark, 320–21
Singapore, 220
el-Sisi, Abdel Fattah, 324
Situation Room meetings, 81, 83,
124, 158, 179, 182, 191, 227,
305, 311
60 Minutes (TV show), 32, 311
Slaughter, Anne-Marie, 153
Sony Pictures Entertainment, North
Korean cyber attack on, 97–98
South Africa, Hezbollah in, 109
South Korea. *See also* North Korea,
nuclear proliferation in
Afghanistan compared, 313
case for free trade with, 220
economy of, 305
importance of U.S. alliance with,
219, 305–8
KORUS, Trump's desire to
terminate, xvii–xxii, xxiii,
105–7, 142, 224, 233, 264–65,
300, 304–8
THAAD missile defense system in,
xxi–xxii, 106, 224, 285, 304
troops in, Trump's desire to pull
out, 230
U.S. dependents, consideration of
withdrawing, 178, 302–3

U.S. troops in, Trump's desire to
withdraw, xvii–xviii, 224, 230,
263, 264, 285, 305
Winter Olympics (2018), 308
South Lawn (White House), 323
soybeans, 158, 341
Special Access Programs (SAP), xviii,
83, 92, 180, 224, 305, 306
Spicer, Sean, 133, 191
Starbucks, 136
steel tariffs, 135, 142, 160–61, 233,
266–67, 273–74, 277, 335, 336–37
Steele, Christopher, and Steele
dossier, 63–64, 327
Sterling, VA, Trump National Golf
Club, 166
Stiglitz, Joseph, 233
stock market, 194, 232, 242, 302,
334, 339
Stone, Roger, 172
Strategic & Policy Forum, 247–48
strength/weakness, Trump's concern
about, xxii, 12, 34, 37, 66, 149,
152, 169, 175, 176, 214, 223,
242, 244, 247, 268, 281
Strike Option Five, 53
Submarine Launched Ballistic
Missiles, 60
Surabian, Andy, 19–20
Sweeney, Kevin, 196
Syria
air strike in retaliation for sarin
gas attack (April 2017), 146–54
brutality of Assad regime in, 131
Hezbollah in, 109
ISIS in, 51
jihadists migrating to Afghanistan
from, 312
Russia and, 28, 147, 149, 150–51,
153, 154
Saudi Arabia funding operations
in, 303, 307
Tillerson on, 229
Trump's desire to pull out of, 229,
298

Taiwan, 305

Taliban, 116, 118–19, 121–23, 125–27, 255, 258, 260, 311–13

Tank meeting on foreign policy (Pentagon), 218–26

Tapper, Jake, 36

tariffs, 135, 142, 158–61, 174, 175, 207–9, 232–33, 266–67, 273–74, 277, 334–37, 339–42

tax on American consumers, tariffs as, 334

Tax Policy Center, 295

tax reform, 289–95
    Bannon on, 298
    Cohn on, 57, 249–50, 251, 267, 289–95
    Congress and, 267, 291–93, 294, 295
    corporate tax rate, 57, 289–90, 294, 295, 298
    increased economic growth as means of paying for, 291
    individual personal income tax rates, 290–91, 295, 296
    inversion, problem of, 57–58, 289
    job creation and wage growth, 292, 296
    middle-income families, relief for, 292, 295
    names for bill, 294
    pass-throughs, 292, 295
    percentage of Americans not paying tax, 293–94
    planning for, 291–93
    in presidential campaign, 18
    Priebus consulted by Trump on, 287
    simplification of code, 292
    tax credits and, 293–94

tax returns, Trump's refusal to release, 356

Tea Party movement, 1, 2, 4, 5, 43

TEAK, 303

television watching, obsessive, of Trump, 158, 165, 195, 231, 270, 299, 339

Tenet, George, 64, 182, 183

Terminal High Altitude Area Defense (THAAD) missile defense system in South Korea, xxi–xxii, 106, 224, 285, 304

This Week (TV show), 340

threat to national security, steel and aluminum imports as, 160, 337

301 investigation into Chinese intellectual property violations, 272–73, 336, 337

3M, 248

Thune, John, 293, 295

Tiberius Gracchus, Trump compared to, 25

Tillerson, Rex
    on Afghanistan, 125, 260
    decision memos, on not being consulted about, 287
    on disorder in White House, 211–12
    foreign policy, Pentagon lunch and Tank meeting on, 218–26
    on Iran nuclear deal, 129–33
    KORUS, Trump's desire to terminate, 264, 305, 307
    Mattis and, 132, 210–11
    McMaster and, 154, 210–12, 228–29, 303–4
    moron, describing Trump as, 225, 227, 228
    on North Korea, 179, 180, 229, 282
    NSC process and, 228–29
    on Paris Climate Accord, 192
    Priebus and, 211–12, 227–28, 287–88
    recruitment as secretary of state, 54
    removal as secretary of state, 323
    resignation considered by, 227
    on Saudi Arabia, 110, 112, 114, 303–4, 307
    state department personnel disputes, 132–33
    on Syrian air strike, 150, 154
    Trump, relationship with, 227–28, 287–88, 323

Time magazine, 26
Time-Phased Force Deployment
    (TIPFID), 184
#TimesUp, 299–300
TIPFID (Time-Phased Force
    Deployment), 184
Tomahawk missiles, 148, 150, 151,
    152, 178
Toomey, Pat, 293
TPP (Trans-Pacific Partnership),
    withdrawal from, 139–40, 157
Trade Act of 1974, 272
trade/trade deficits/trade agreements
    agricultural products, 158–61, 220,
        341
    antibiotics produced by China, 275
    arms deals, 220
    Bossert on trade with China, 339–42
    coordination problems, 140–43
    economy and trade deficit,
        relationship between, 137, 159,
        275
    foreign policy, Pentagon lunch and
        Tank meeting on, 218–26
    free trade, Trump's dislike of, 134,
        218, 220
    imports posing threat to national
        security, 160–61
    intellectual property violations by
        China, 272–73, 336, 337
    job losses and, 134, 135, 137
    KORUS, Trump's desire to
        terminate, xvii–xxii, xxiii,
        105–7, 142, 224, 233, 264–65,
        300, 304–8
    NAFTA, 135, 142, 155–58, 160,
        233, 264, 274
    service versus industrial/
        manufacturing economy, 136–38
    tariffs, 135, 142, 158–61, 174,
        175, 207–9, 232–33, 266–67,
        273–74, 277, 334–37, 339–42
    TPP, withdrawal from, 139–40, 157
    "Trade is Bad" note, 208
    U.S. as trade-based economy, 56

    White House staff and Trump's
        views on, 134–43
    WTO, 264, 276
transgender persons in the military,
    201–3
transition period, 47–71
    Priebus and election night, 47
    resistance of Trump to planning/
        financing for, 42
    Russia, Trump's first briefing on,
        62–71
    White House staffing during,
        47–54, 58–60, 66
Trans-Pacific Partnership (TPP),
    withdrawal from, 139–40, 157
treason
    Flynn's denial of, 82
    Trump accusing Cohn of, 249
Trump, Barron, 175, 299, 328
Trump, Donald. *See also* presidential
    election campaign; transition
    period; Twitter, Trump's use of;
    specific issues, e.g. North Korea,
    nuclear proliferation in
    abortion, views on, 3, 6
    anger issues of, 253
    apologies, difficulties with
        making, 34, 242, 244, 249
    as "baby," 14
    bankruptcies of, 274–75
    Bannon, breakdown in relationship
        with, 190, 297–301
    called "dotard" by Kim Jong Un,
        281
    as change agent, 15, 297
    crowdsourcing by, 231
    diet of, 14
    on election night, 45–47
    erratic nature of, 226, 232, 252
    "Executive Time" for, 266
    failure to listen to advisers, 232
    on fear, as real power, xiii, 175,
        275, 300
    fighting/pushing back, belief in,
        12, 166, 174, 175, 243–44

Trump, Donald (*cont.*)
  finances, Mueller investigation of,
    199–201
  Graham, relationship with, 99–105
  grievance, sense of, 299
  impeachment discussed, 164–65,
    355–56
  impulsivity of, xix–xx, 89, 100,
    231, 282
  on lawyers, 268, 271, 354
  leveraging abilities of, 288
  as liar, 208–9, 235, 320, 338, 353, 357
  loneliness of, 169
  loyalty, importance of, 66, 138–39,
    176, 268, 317
  Mattis on, 83
  media, influence of, 195, 231, 291
  media, views on, 14, 86, 195, 356
  military families and, 73–75
  "moving in both directions"
    comment, 280
  100th day in office, 155
  permanent governmental
    institutions, understanding of
    power of, 162
  persona of, 3, 25
  personal appearance of, 66–67
  presidency, definition of job of,
    xxii
  rallies, fondness for, 271
  refusals to pay, 16, 275
  "Rocket Man"/"Little Rocket
    Man" comments, 280, 281, 282
  signing, fondness for, 263
  staff, relationship with, 235–36
  staff chaos and churn, enjoyment
    of, 287
  stress experienced by, 266
  tax returns, refusal to release, 356
  television watching, obsessive, 158,
    165, 195, 231, 270, 299, 339
  as throwback to 1950s America,
    136, 299
  U.N. General Assembly address
    (September 2017), 280–81
  voting record of, 3–4
  weakness/strength, concern about,
    xxii, 12, 34, 37, 66, 149, 152,
    169, 175, 176, 214, 223, 242,
    244, 247, 268, 281
  World Economic Forum, speech at
    (January 2018), 298–99
Trump, Donald, Jr. (Don), 32, 35,
    197, 198, 345, 349
Trump, Ivanka
  Bannon and Priebus, problems
    with, 144–45, 189–90, 237
  Charlottesville and, 245, 249
  Comey, firing of, 163
  on FBI seeking Kushner's financial
    records, 163
  as "first daughter," 145
  foreign wars, Trump's desire to
    pull out of, 229–30
  on immigration, 186, 187, 188
  marriage to Jared Kushner, xx
  on Paris Climate Accord, 189–90
  in presidential campaign, 20, 32
  Priebus resignation and, 236, 237
  Syrian air strike and, 148
  tax reform and, 292, 294
  Yemen, death of Ryan Owens in,
    73, 74
Trump, Melania, 32, 34, 69, 174–75,
    195, 299, 318
Trump International Golf Club, West
    Palm Beach, 316
Trump National Golf Clubs
  Bedminster, 12, 51, 229, 238, 240,
    248, 261
  Sterling, VA, 166
Trump Organization
  business credit score of, 58
  Goldman Sachs not doing business
    with, 275
  tax reform, effects of, 295
Trump Tower, 2, 12, 19, 20, 31, 35,
    42, 46, 49, 55, 66, 67, 103, 136,
    197, 199, 245–47, 345, 349
Trump voters. *See also* rallies

farmers and agricultural producers as, 220

"the hidden Trump voter," 24–25

Tuchman, Barbara, *The Guns of August,* 280

Turnbull, Malcolm, 207–9

Twitter, Trump's use of
on Afghanistan, 115–16
centrality to Trump presidency, 206–7
on CEOs resigning from American Manufacturing Council and Strategy & Policy Forum over Trump's Charlottesville comments, 247–48
Charlottesville, Pence retweeting Trump remarks on, 253–54
on Hillary Clinton missing emails, 173
doubling of number of characters in a single Tweet, 207
Graham on, 103–4
Manafort influenced by, 20–21
on Jill McCabe campaign donations, 84
on *Morning Joe* hosts, 205, 206
on North Korea, 300–302
during presidential campaign, 20, 39
on Priebus's resignation and replacement by Kelly, 234–35
on Putin, 82
on Russia dossier with prostitute allegations, 71
on Russian election interference, 65, 330
Sessions attacked, 214, 215
staff efforts to control, 195, 205–7
Tillerson, removal of, 323
on transgender troops, 202

Tyson, Laura, 233

Ukraine
Manafort, funds paid to, 21–22
Trump campaign sabotage, Russian propaganda about, 230

Under Armour, 247

United Auto Workers, 335

United Kingdom
Bannon on Kushner leak to *Daily Mail,* 145
Brexit referendum, 78
libel laws in, 318–19
MI6, 63

United Nations General Assembly, Trump addressing (September 2017), 280–81

United Nations Security Council, 179–80, 232, 272

United States–[South] Korea Free Trade Agreement (KORUS), Trump's desire to terminate, xvii–xxii, xxiii, 105–7, 142, 224, 233, 264–65, 300, 304–8

U.S.S *Gerald R. Ford* (CVN 78), 213

U.S.S *Porter,* 150

U.S.S *Ross,* 150

Venezuela, Hezbollah in, 109

Veterans Administration reform plan, 18

The Victory Sessions (radio show), 2

Vietnam War, 76–77, 93, 96, 117

Virginia Democratic Party, 84

voting record of Trump, 3–4

Wall Street Journal, 43, 122, 214, 339, 361

Wallace, Chris, 44–45, 107

Walsh, Katie, 22–23, 25

Washington, George, 246, 253

Washington Memorial, 328

Washington Post
on *Access Hollywood* tape, 29–30
on Afghanistan, 254
on Cohn resignation, 339
on Dowd resignation, 356
on Flynn/Russian ambassador discussions, 80–81
on immigration, 318
on Kushner finances, 194

Washington Post (cont.)
  on Mueller investigation, 172, 198
  on nuclear weapons, 301
  on Porter domestic abuse
    allegations, 336
Watergate, 165, 171, 173, 215, 352,
  360
weakness/strength, Trump's concern
  about, xxii, 12, 34, 37, 66, 149,
  152, 169, 175, 176, 214, 223,
  242, 244, 247, 268, 281
West Palm Beach, Trump
  International Golf Club at, 316
Westerhout, Madeleine, 157, 218,
  265–66, 286
White House
  Blue Room, 104
  Cabinet Room, 251, 317, 337
  Diplomatic Reception Room, 242
  Green Room, 317
  Lincoln Bedroom, 328
  Red Room (White House
    residence), 76
  residence, presidential, 20, 31, 76,
    148, 195, 201, 230, 242, 243,
    266, 272, 328, 345
  Rose Garden, 194
  South Lawn, 323
White House staff
  concerns about Trump's erratic
    nature, 226, 232, 252
  disorder and disruption among, 144,
    190, 210–12, 231, 235, 236–37,
    261–66, 268–69, 270–71, 287
  Kelly's senior staff meetings, 285–86
  management of Trump by, xvii–
    xxii, 140–42, 158, 191, 195,
    233, 264, 265, 268–69, 270–71
  national security advisor,
    replacement of Flynn as, 86–90
  Porter's appointment as staff
    secretary, 138–39
  relationship of Trump with, 235–36
  on trade/trade deficits/trade
    agreements, 134–43

transition period, staffing in,
  47–54, 58–60, 66
white supremacist march in
  Charlottesville, VA, 238–44
Whitewater, 352
WikiLeaks, 28, 30, 36
Willey, Kathleen, 38
Winter Olympics (2018), South
  Korea, 308
wiretaps
  Mueller investigation, Trump's
    concern about, 174
  Obama accused of wiretapping
    Trump Tower, 103–4
"witch hunt," Russian election
  interference reports/
  investigation referred to as, 65,
  174, 330
Wolff, Michael, 297
Woodward, Bob, xxii, 42–43,
  44–45, 60–61, 69, 70, 71, 92,
  177–78, 308
World Economic Forum, Trump
  speech at (January 2018),
  298–99
World Trade Organization (WTO),
  264, 276
World War I, 280
WTO (World Trade Organization),
  264, 276

Xi Jinping, 47, 151, 232, 340, 341,
  342

Yates, Sally, 80, 329, 345
Yemen
  Hezbollah in, 109
  SEAL Team Six operation against
    al Qaeda collaborator in,
    72–75, 76
Young, Don, 170

Zinni, Anthony, 82
Zuckerberg, Mark, 190

About the Author

BOB WOODWARD is an associate editor at *The Washington Post*, where he has worked for 47 years. He has shared in two Pulitzer Prizes, first for the *Post*'s coverage of the Watergate scandal with Carl Bernstein, and second in 2003 as the lead reporter for coverage of the 9/11 terrorist attacks. He has authored or coauthored 18 books, all of which have been national nonfiction bestsellers. Twelve of those have been #1 national bestsellers.